THE COMPLETE YOUTH MANUAL

Volume 1

The Complete Youth Manual

VOLUME I

STEVE CHALKE

KINGSWAY PUBLICATIONS
EASTBOURNE

Front cover design by Vic Mitchell

**To
Emily, Daniel and Abigail
the teenagers of a future
generation**

Printed in Great Britain for
KINGSWAY PUBLICATIONS LTD
Lottbridge Drove, Eastbourne, E. Sussex BN23 6NT by
Richard Clay Ltd, Bungay, Suffolk.
Typeset by CST, Eastbourne, E. Sussex.

Contents

Preface

I'm told that C. S. Lewis once claimed that almost 90% of the ideas for his writing were not original but borrowed from elsewhere. I take great comfort in such an idea! Although this book was actually finally written over a period of about six months, it is the result of the experience and understanding that I've been able to gain as an individual over the years and from many different people and sources too numerous to remember.

I would especially like to thank the churches that I have been involved with through the years, for their trust and support as they have allowed me to learn and develop a ministry among young people.

These include Holmesdale Baptist Church in South London where I grew up and became a 'youth'. South Ashford Baptist Church where I had the privilege of first leading a youth group under the wing of my friend the Rev. Steve Flashman. Gravesend Baptist Church where I worked for a year before entering theological college, and where I first met the Rev. David Beer whose friendship and guidance have been a great influence on me. And finally Tonbridge Baptist Church where I again worked with David Beer during my four years as their assistant minister and have since remained a church member. The freedom to develop my work among youth both locally and nationally has been of enormous value to me.

I would like to thank all the tutors at Spurgeon's College where I trained for the Baptist ministry. The principles that I learnt at Spurgeons are the backbone of the work I am involved in today.

Julia Honey, Philip Warland, Andy Simmonds and Will Matheson, the Trustees of Oasis, the Trust which now supports and guides me in my wider youth ministry, are a constant encouragement.

I am very grateful to Nikky Mungeam, my secretary, who has carried a huge responsibility in the preparation of this book. Not only has she had the patience to master the use of our new word processor but also the commitment and enthusiasm to work very long hours to see the task completed. Without her invaluable help this would have been impossible.

Lastly, I want to thank my wife, Cornelia, for her love and support and for the sacrifice of our time together which is the price of this kind of project. Her commitment to Jesus is outstanding and without her help and unending understanding it would be impossible for me to exercise my youth ministry.

STEVE CHALKE

SECTION ONE

1

TEENAGERS – THE MISSING LINK

Understanding teenage culture

> The world is passing through troublesome times. The young people of today think of nothing but themselves. They have no reverence for parents or old age. They are impatient of all restraint. They talk as if they know everything, and what passes for wisdom with us is foolishness to them. As for the girls, they are immodest and un-womanly in speech, behaviour and dress.[1]

Just the kind of sentiment that is expressed countless times each week by everyone from parents to school teachers, magistrates to shopkeepers. It is typical of the kind of complaint heard from many people in the church today.

In fact, this remark was made by Peter the monk, in the year 1274! But he was not the first to notice the downward trend in the behaviour of young people.

> When I look at the younger generation, I despair of the future of civilisation.[2]

That was Aristotle in the year 300 B.C.

It is no new thing for those who are older to sit round and bemoan the behaviour of the young. All that is said in many Parochial Church Councils, deacons' and elders' meetings, or muttered by a group of ladies trying to tidy up the mess left in the church kitchen by the youth club the night before, is merely an echo of what has been said by many other voices in times past.

Young people are frequently exhorted to 'act their age', but this is often nothing other than a thinly disguised demand that

11

they behave like mature adults. This, of course, is an impossibility for an adolescent who by definition is not an adult, but is still in the process of maturing. Mentally, physically, emotionally, socially and spiritually he is not yet fully mature.

What is an adolescent?

The Oxford English Dictionary defines an adolescent as someone who is between the states of childhood and adulthood. James Dobson describes the adolescent years as a 'turbulent voyage'[3] which involves leaving behind the protection of the harbour of childhood and heading for the open sea of adulthood.

It's not easy to be an adolescent; the comforts of childhood are in the process of disappearing but the rewards of adulthood are slow to make themselves available. Adolescents are caught between two ages; they are in transition between two worlds. When they were children they trusted their parents to make decisions about money, food and accommodation. But now they are beginning to move into the world of the 'grown-up' taking their first faltering steps to adulthood; making their own decisions; earning their own living and gradually becoming independent.

An inborn desire

It is not just that society expects all this of the adolescent, but, much more than this, there is a natural inborn desire to 'leave the nest'. Girls of this age used to be called 'flappers', a very descriptive term for those 'trying out their own wings'! This process varies with each individual. Some are over-confident and want to launch out too far and too soon, but others tend to be more than cautious and require a gentle push. The desire for privacy and independence is natural and just as strong in the young human as it is in the young bird who desperately wants to leave the nest. God created this desire and we struggle against him if we try to hold it back. Anne Townsend points out in 'Families Without Pretending' that adolescence is a time of letting go and she adds that from now on the parents are 'watching and supporting the first tentative steps of a new adult, and . . . must learn to make a relationship with them on new terms'.[4]

An explosive mixture

James Dobson asks, 'How would you like to be thirteen years old again by the wave of a magic wand?' Then he gives the answer 'No thanks! . . . Everyone in our culture wants to remain young, but not that young! And why not? Because we grown-ups remember our adolescent years as the most stressful and threatening time of life.'[5]

Doctors and sociologists tell us that life contains several crisis points for the adult, such as marriage, having children, moving, changing job, mid-life, retirement and bereavement. But if we take a careful look at the questions and uncertainties faced at these points we soon become aware that most of the same underlying insecurities and doubts occur together during the adolescent years, when there is not as much experience to call on for support. There are the bewildering physical changes, as well as the sexual anxiety and guilt that develop along with the adolescent's new desires. There is self-doubt and feelings of inferiority, the worries about appearance and acceptance by others, and fears about failure and rejection. Then there is the lack of ability to express oneself as clearly as one wishes. All this within the context of the emotional vulnerability these years bring. The adolescent is an explosive mixture of insecurities and self-questioning. But though this has been human experience for centuries, the modern adolescent faces still greater problems.

The generation gap is created

F. Musgrove, a British sociologist, states that the adolescent was invented at the same time as the industrial revolution took place:

Having invented the adolescent, society has been faced with two major problems: how and where to accommodate him in the social structure, and how to make his behaviour accord with the specifications.[6]

What he is saying is simply that the industrial revolution reconstructed society in such a way as to allow much more room for adolescents as a separate group than had ever been the case before.

In many cultures the young person moved much more easily between childhood and adulthood than he does in the West today. The transition took place at puberty, when the boy or girl was initiated into adulthood, leaving childhood behind for ever. In some so-called 'primitive' societies these initiation rites involved the infliction of pain which the boy had to endure with courage and determination. For instance, a boy would go off into the jungle to hunt alone for several days; if he returned alive he was a man, if not, well it didn't matter anyway!

In Roman times, we are told, the transition from childhood to manhood was signalled by the wearing of the toga, whereas in this country, in medieval times, at the age of fourteen a boy might become a squire, his responsibility being to serve a knight by accompanying him into battle and bearing his arms.

In Jewish society, at the age of thirteen a boy would have his Barmitzvah and pass into full manhood. In rural societies this was the point when the boy joined his father in working the land or going fishing, and so on. As a child he had learnt by watching his father, but now, as he reached the age when he was beginning to want to assert his sense of responsibility, he was given ample opportunity. He became involved in the real responsibilities of life, entering the world of work.

It was not that the youth was pushed without experience into the full responsibility of mature adulthood. At this stage he was still given time and freedom to slowly develop and grow; for example, the medieval boy was a squire, not a knight, or he joined his father on the land in a kind of apprenticeship. Though much is made of the fact that at thirteen a Jewish boy became a man, closer study of the Old Testament reveals that even within this there was some distinction between an adolescent aged thirteen to twenty years and a male of over that age (see Lev 27). A period of adolescence definitely existed, but it came complete with much greater responsibility. It comes as no surprise, then, that some anthropologists say that the adolescents of primitive communities did not suffer the same neurotic 'difficulties' as those of modern industrial societies.

In modern western society the transfer of responsibility is a much more gradual process. As you grow older you slowly collect more of the rights and responsibilities of adulthood. This starts at the age of ten and continues up to twenty-one years. At ten, young people can be considered responsible for criminal offences. At thirteen they may do light work within certain hours and conditions, if local bye-laws permit it. At fourteen they can be allowed to see a criminal trial or go to a PG film alone. They can also go into a pub but must not buy or drink alcohol. At fifteen they can open a Giro account. At the age of sixteen they can leave school and work a forty-eight hour week. They can hold a licence to drive a motorcycle, buy tobacco and drink wine or beer with a meal on licensed premises. They can consent to medical or surgical treatment. They may get married with parental consent, although this is not necessary in Scotland. Girls can legally consent to sexual intercourse. At seventeen they can go into a betting shop but must not bet; they can become a street trader and hold an ordinary driving licence. At eighteen teenagers have reached the age of majority: their parents no longer legally control them. They may get married without parental consent. They may drink alcohol in a pub, watch adult films, place bets and make legal contracts, for example, enter hire purchase agreements. They can be sent to an ordinary prison in England, be tattooed and can vote. At the age of twenty-one they may stand as a candidate in an election and become an MP, adopt a child, or be sent to an ordinary prison in Scotland.

In this way the process of entering adult life is spread out over no less than eleven years!

In the goldfish bowl

Even until quite recently within our own culture, a boy could leave school at fourteen and move straight into an apprenticeship, working alongside, for example, a carpenter, a plumber, an electrician, or a butcher, and there learn his trade 'on the job'. But as our society has developed and become more complex, the educational requirements needed for many jobs have multiplied, so that the adolescent is expected to remain longer within the educational system and today the minimum school leaving age is sixteen. This has led to the assumption that a fairly high level of general education is required for almost all jobs in our society. Today the aspiring electrician will probably stay on longer at school, and be pushed to take GCSE. From school he may well go on to college or university or at least take some kind of sandwich course before being given any real responsibility.

Adolescents have been contained in a gigantic 'educational goldfish bowl', removed against their natural inclinations from responsibility and involvement in what they feel is real life. Society has turned them into a race apart, segregating them from the serious activities of adulthood. They have energy, drive and enthusiasm, but are not given opportunities for responsibility. They are mentally alert and questioning but are kept from decision-making within society. This has exacerbated the adolescent's natural sense of frustration and inadequacy. The message from society is that adolescents are spare parts, unworthy of responsibility; they have ample time on their hands to brood on their plight.

This gap between the child and the adult, which the modern industrial society has created, has been filled by a cultural explosion: the emergence of the 'teenager'.

Rock 'n' roll and the teenage explosion

1953 was an important year. The word 'teenager' was only a few years old, and certainly wasn't the household term it is today. But what happened in 1953? Bill Haley recorded *Crazy Man Crazy*, the first white rock 'n' roll record ever to enter the charts.

If it is true that adolescents are an explosive mixture of emotions and that modern society's segregation of youth is largely responsible for this then it is also true that the emergence of pop music supplied the spark which finally caused that long-threatened explosion to take place. Its arrival also provided the gust of fresh air that fanned the flames of the fire that resulted.

You've never had it so good

In the years that followed the second world war, the standard of living in the West slowly rose. By the mid-fifties a time of plenty had arrived in North America, and this spread to Great Britain towards the end of the decade. Harold Macmillan's slogan was 'You've never had it so good'. Yet there was an undercurrent of unrest amongst the young, a desire for change and action, which the 'luxury' of their segregation from the 'serious' activities of life allowed to develop and spread.

Malcolm Doney, tracing the developments of rock music and culture, explains that in the years which immediately followed the end of World War II, young people were bored and frustrated with the white popular music of the day. It was

'the music of a bygone era . . . dreamy and escapist . . . fine for the Mums and Dads. It was the kind of armchair comfort that had helped them through the war.'[7]

He is referring, of course, to the big band sound which came with singers such as the young Frank Sinatra. The music was smooth and sophisticated, neat and tidy, with professional polished performances but no sense of reality.

'Seen now through the permanent soft focus of nostalgia it seems pleasant and easy. But for the kids of the fifties it was deadly . . . they wanted raw excitement—life'.[8]

Rock—the voice of rebellion

Into this situation stepped tubby Bill Haley and the Comets. The quality of their music was hardly exceptional; what was so riveting was that they had begun to play their own versions of the old rhythm and blues songs which were so popular amongst the blacks of America. *Crazy Man Crazy* was the first of a string of hits for Haley on both sides of the Atlantic, as was the film 'Rock around the Clock'. From then on rock 'n' roll became the teenage music. It was exciting, raw and powerful; it had drive and energy. In place of the well-groomed sophisticated looks of Frank Sinatra came the rock 'n' roll singer, tough, sinister, aggressive and streetwise. Just as rhythm and blues was a musical expression of the frustration, pain and alienation of black people, so now rock 'n' roll was becoming the voice of the young in America and Great Britain, the voice of their rebellion. In 1969 a rock journalist could write,

'Rock music was born of a revolt against the sham of Western culture; it was direct and gutsy and spoke to the senses. As such it was profoundly subversive.'[9]

Your mother doesn't like it

Rock music had one other supreme quality which no doubt contributed greatly to its ability to capture the imagination and commitment of so many teenagers. Put simply, parents hated it; they despised it and all those who were responsible for it. To parents it seemed that rock 'n' roll was the music of depravity. It was well-known that its origins were negroid and it was a development of primitive jungle rhythms and therefore linked with voodoo. It was nothing less than satanic, an instrument of the forces of darkness. This was great news for the young because it meant it was theirs, exclusively. Nothing could be better!

Help save the youth of America. Don't buy negro records . . . the screaming and idiotic words and savage music of these records are undermining the morals of our white youth in America. Don't let your children buy or listen to these negro records.[10]

Of course, in some church circles this attitude still persists. Rock music is unchristian. In Solid Rock, a magazine edited by Tom Morton and produced in 1980, there is an excerpt from a Christian tract entitled Spellbound where the comment is made,

One of the greatest victories in the Occult world was to penetrate the Christian music with their satanic beat. I know of Christian kids who destroyed their rock records, but after listening to Christian rock, the druid beat soon pulled them back into worldly rock music again . . . then the desire to study the bible cools off![11]

The fire spreads

All of this wasn't really Bill Haley's fault and in fact, had it been left to him, rock 'n' roll would probably not have survived. But he was just the forerunner, behind him came other much stronger, far more aggressive and appealing characters. First, there was Elvis Presley, dark and handsome with a growling voice, the idol of thousands of teenagers in Britain and America. The girls dreamt of being his, and the boys admired his macho image. He was a hero to look up to and imitate. He was, in the words of Malcolm Doney, 'the personification of the mothers' nightmares and the daughters' loves'.[12]

At this stage rock 'n' roll was still almost purely American. There were, of course, our very own British Elvis look-and-sound alikes—Tommy Steele, Adam Faith, Billy Fury, Marty Wilde and, most successfully, Cliff Richard, but it was all a carbon copy of the American situation. It was 1963 before the change came with the arrival of the Beatles who were soon to take over and hold high the torch which Elvis had grown weary, or incapable, of carrying. Shortly after them came the Rolling Stones, the Animals and the others. Now rock 'n' roll was truly British, and increasingly became the focus for many young people in their struggle to express themselves. Geoffrey Cannon talks of 'the magic peculiar to rock music of making you think your own thoughts harder and faster and at the same time, making you feel reasons to be connected with your kin.'[13]

Rock 'n' roll became a kind of glue holding the growing youth culture together.

Youth culture arrives

In the post war industrial boom, young people were enjoying their share of the increased wealth. They had greater spending power than ever before and very few responsibilities. They were, in fact, the only age group in society with money to spend on impulse. Manufacturers were presented with a new and untapped market, one that was ripe for exploitation. It has been said that the term 'teenager' was itself invented by advertising men towards the end of the war to give the adolescent market an identity. Adolescents needed their own identity, and for different reasons big business wanted to supply it. John Allan says, 'The advertisers set about prising the money from the kids. The strategy was to make them feel important, special, unique.'[14] What had been missing had been an image around which to build this new identity. Bill Haley and rock 'n' roll arrived on the scene at just the right time and commercial enterprise put all its weight behind both him and his music. Around the music they were to build a whole industry. In the wake of rock 'n' roll came the distinctive clothes, the hair styles, the record players, musical instruments, badges, magazines and books, and even language, all designed exclusively for young people. The youth revolution was on. 'Pop culture' as well as pop music had arrived.

Clifford Hill states: 'The rise of the pop culture in the mid-1950's is generally regarded as the beginning of the social revolution that has been shaking Britain to its foundations . . . ever since.'[15]

The emergence of the pop industry is one of the most significant developments of this century. It has played a massive part in shaping our whole culture, a part that has only been equalled by the new technology more recently made available with the silicon chip.

The 'missing link' is found

Modern society had widened the generation gap to an extent unthought of previously, and into that gap had dropped 'the teenager'. Teenagers dressed differently, thought differently and were generally accepted as having their own separate place in society. The 'missing link' between childhood and adult life had been well and truly found!

The whole situation is summed up in an experience I had whilst visiting a church in the Midlands. 'When I was fifteen, all

I wanted to be was like my dad,' the minister explained to me, 'to have a suit like his.' This particular minister had been a young man in the forties with aspirations typical of the youth of his generation. I have travelled widely through this country meeting young people in many situations but have never found one who would still say, 'All I want is a suit like my dad's.' Nothing could be further from the aspirations and hopes of any teenager alive! My dad is a great bloke; I get on very well with him, especially since leaving home! But never in a million years would I want to wear trousers or a jacket that look anything like his. Today adolescents no longer look to their parents for this kind of role model; instead they look to one another, to their own leaders, the pop stars, and others within their own culture.

When I was young it was different

Many older Christians have explained to me that in their youth, though they may have found church services boring, uninspiring or irrelevant, there was absolutely no thought in their minds that there could be any other pattern. One elderly lady recently told me, 'We knew we had to grin and bear it.' There was never any hint of rebellion. But things are different now. Adolescents have received an enormous boost of confidence, they demand a voice, they have opinions and views and want to be heard; the teenage movement has seen to that.

Often I have heard leaders and others within the church expressing a sentiment which runs something like: 'When we were young we didn't expect all this. Why should we even think about rearranging the services for the young people? We don't do it for other groups. What about elderly folk or middle aged mums? We don't design things just to suit them, and neither will we for teenagers. The church is a family, they must just fit in and take their place.'

It's true that the church is a family but, as well we know, the family unit too struggles with the problems of the teenager. To bring an adolescent through those difficult years requires wisdom and sensitivity. They have a will of their own; no longer can the law be laid down to them. Teenagers do not want orders but advice, and every parent knows that many times that advice is ignored. The social habits of teenagers are different from those of the adult and some working relationship needs to be found which gives them freedom and yet supplies much needed boundaries. It's no good the church saying, 'fifty years ago we didn't have all this fuss with teenagers and so we're not going to stand for it today.' For fifty years ago the teenager did not exist!

Food for thought

We must sit down and attempt to understand the cultural situation in which our young people find themselves. This task is never easy; it requires our best thinking, our greatest sensitivity, and a good dose of the love of God which will allow us to accept a person as he is.

The problem is that youth culture is changing rapidly. For those of us in our twenties, thirties or forties it's no good saying that we know what it's like. We cannot simply regard today's youth culture as nothing more than a reflection of our own teenage years. Just watch a film on television made ten years ago which reflects life then . . . it's almost archaic now, not just because of dress, music and language but also, and perhaps most importantly, because of its attitudes and outlook on life.

In the late fifties young people faced a generally optimistic future. Despite the cold war threats of a nuclear catastrophe, most young people applied themselves to school work, honestly believing that an educated person would be a more fulfilled person. They had questions about the future but saw hope.

In the sixties the mood changed as the anti-establishment feeling became much more widespread. There were marches on the streets with slogans and banners. This was the age of flower power. An alternative society was planned where all you needed was love.

In the seventies, the idealism of the sixties was smashed and disillusionment spread. 'The Beatles said all you need is love and then they broke up,' was Larry Norman's comment.[16] A new slogan emerged: 'If it feels good, do it', and the young became known as the 'me generation'. They were inward looking and unconcerned with the outside world.

But in the eighties things are different again. We no longer live in the 'me generation'. Today's young people face a very uncertain future with immense pressures unknown to previous generations. We have widespread unemployment, and worldwide pollution, hunger and over-population. There is the fear of energy shortages and the global uncertainty caused by the nuclear arms race. There is increased violence and crime and broken homes, which lead to confusion, disillusionment, frustration and depression. Observers have already dubbed the youth of the eighties the 'anxious generation'.

Anxious they may be, but not idle. Increasingly, the young people of the eighties are involved in the big issues, reaching out to help others both individually and through various charitable organizations. Bob Geldof and Band Aid, Live Aid, Sport Aid, School Aid, etc, provide a glorious example of this. Teenagers are also involved with organizations like CND and anti-vivisection. There is a desire to face the problems of late twentieth century life, and find workable solutions.

This summary is, of course, simply a generalization. Each young person is born an individual and grows up with a unique combination of influences caused by family, school friends, geographical location and so on. Bromley is geographically very near to Brixton, though culturally young people growing up in the two towns may be influenced very differently, perhaps resulting in somewhat contrasting views of life, themselves, others and authority. Young people may not have the biblical framework that we would wish, nor a specifically Christian moral code, but we are blind if we write them off as superficial, aggressive, uncaring, concerned solely with their own pleasure.

Teenagers are exploring the world in which they live. This is a difficult task in which they need and are searching for (though it sometimes seems quite the opposite!) advice and guidance. But perhaps more than all this they seek acceptance by adults who will take them seriously and grant them responsibility. Is the church prepared to answer the call?

2

IT'S NO FUN BEING A TEENAGER
Understanding adolescents

The exact age spectrum covered by the term 'adolescence' is a matter of some dispute. J. A. Hadfield in his book *Childhood and Adolescence* states that the term is usually taken to cover the ages from twelve to eighteen.[1] Pete Gilbert writing in Youth For Christ's *This Generation Youth Evangelism File* places the boundaries wider at eleven and twenty-one years[2] and Trevor Partridge of Crusade for World Revival says, 'The age span of adolescence is approximately 11 to 22!'[3] Of course, if we are going to identify adolescence with the teenage years, then it runs officially from thirteen to nineteen. But wherever we place the exact limits of adolescence, it is clear that the needs, aspirations and questions of an eleven, twelve or thirteen year old are quite different from those of an eighteen to twenty-two year old.

Adolescence or adolescents

One of the greatest dangers when dealing with adolescents is to lump them all together as one, believing that their needs are all the same. As we saw earlier, this cannot be done. Teenagers are individuals and cannot be compartmentalized. There are no golden rules that will apply universally to them. It has been pointed out that theory deals with adolescence with a 'ce' whereas the youth leader deals with adolescents with a 'ts' and that makes all the difference! But, while recognizing this, it can

24

be helpful to realize that the period of adolescence consists of various phases which differ fundamentally from one another. The three stages outlined below give the development of an 'average' adolescent. Understanding these stages will help us to have a greater understanding of the young people with whom we work, providing we always remember that the stages are generalizations and generalizations about teenagers are always dangerous unless handled carefully.

Three stages of adolescence

(1) Eleven-to-fourteen year-olds

This period of adolescence has been labelled 'the homosexual stage' though this term is easily misunderstood. The point is simply that during this phase a young person tends to relate far better to his or her own sex than to members of the opposite one. These years usually mark the onset of puberty (which we will deal with later) and also are characterized by 'gang activity'.

Gang formation is a natural impulse although much stronger within boys than girls. They tend to be single sex. Boys of this age-group still regard girls as 'silly', kissing as 'sloppy', and dancing as equally stupid. Girls (publically at least!) consider the boys to be rough, bad mannered and immature. Gangs are held together by a common interest in such things as football, cricket, BMX bikes, a particular group of girls or kind of music.

Some gangs will exist just for the sake of existing, the common interest being nothing more than the sense of belonging to one another. You will often see a gang wandering the streets on a Saturday afternoon or at some time doing absolutely nothing except belonging. In Tonbridge where I used to work, a gang of youths congregated outside the church building almost every night, and would just sit on the fence for hours doing nothing, except being together. They were never really interested in joining in organized activities but would very much appreciate it if time was taken to chat with them and get to know them. On the occasional evening when I am back at the church building, they are still sitting there although they do seem to have moved about ten yards up the road to a new piece of fence, and new faces have joined the gang whilst other older ones have disappeared!

There is usually a tremendous loyalty to the gang which extends to each member, quite irrespective of their personal qualities, simply because they are members. The greatest sin is to sneak, to squeal or split on another gang member.

It is too easy for us to dismiss this gang spirit as 'just a childish phase'. In fact sociologists tell us it is a very important part of the development of any young person. Our churches, political parties, clubs, etc, are all developments of the gang spirit. The concept of loyalty acquired during this time is of immense importance later in life.

Most gangs have a leader. He is a very important figure, to whom the other members will often give almost unquestioning obedience. Since a teenager of this age will also tend to hero worship those that he admires, a boy may model his whole personality around that of the gang leader, taking on his characteristics, both good and bad. At the same time he may completely abandon his old identification with his father, whose authority he will now not accept and whose character, which he had previously tried to imitate, he now rejects. The heroes whom he had previously tried to imitate, he now rejects. The heroes whom he admires need not be his own age; they may be adults, pop stars, sports men and women, a particular teacher or youth leader. We will talk more about the problems and challenges that this creates in the chapter on youth leadership.

(2) Fifteen-to-sixteen year-olds

This period is often known as 'the transition stage' because it marks the phase of adolescence between the homosexual stage, where the teenager spends his time with those of the same sex, and the heterosexual stage when the teenager's attention is on the opposite sex. In fact, this stage usually occurs earlier in girls, often around the age of thirteen or fourteen. As the adolescent grows he discovers that the gang does not satisfy his need for an intimate friend, someone of the same sex with whom he can exchange confidences and share problems. He begins to form close relationships which as a rule are totally asexual in nature although of course sex is one of the main topics of conversation because the adolescent's biggest problem is learning to cope with his new and very powerful sexual desires.

About this time many adolescents tend to become very moody. They will often go off by themselves, disappearing for hours, refusing to take part in programmed activities even of the most exciting kind. They may not even show the slightest interest in the gang which used to be so important to them. An adult will often try to chivvy the youth up with a 'Whatever has come over you? Why don't you go out with your friends or at least take an interest in something or other?'

The reply is simply, 'I don't want to. I don't feel like it.'

The desire for a close friend to confide in as well as the brooding and moodiness are both symptoms of the same thing: the fact that at this age the teenager becomes interested in the opposite sex in a much deeper way than before. As the young person begins to discover his desires and emotions in this area one 'crush' follows another. At this stage he will be attracted to older people of the opposite sex, such as the church youth leader! Beware: what seems to be an innocent counselling session is often anything but, as far as the counsellee is concerned!

(3) Sixteen-to-twenty-one years-old

By this age young people have emerged from the transition phase and are now in what is described as the 'heterosexual stage' of adolescence, where the attraction to the opposite sex realy surfaces.

This stage actually consists of two different phases because at first young people of both sexes find themselves attached to a number of young people of the opposite sex of the same age. At this time sexual curiosity and the simple desire to attract others are very important driving forces. As well as all this, the adolescent is also experimenting and slowly discovering the qualities which he is looking for in a partner of the opposite sex. As a result young people at this stage will often appear to be rather flirtatious.

By the age of seventeen or eighteen the teenager is generally beginning to move on to the second phase, where he is looking for a steady one-to-one relationship. He is beginning to think about marriage and other life decisions, but because the young person does not have the perspective of experience he thinks about these issues in a rather idealistic, or as Aristotle described it, 'high minded'[4] fashion. Idealism is a strong feature of this stage of adolescence.

What makes a teenager?

As we have seen, the teenager is an 'inbetween' person. He is travelling on a perilous journey into adult life away from the shelter and security of childhood. This journey has several stages which test him to his limits but through which he slowly and painfully grows and develops. This growth takes place in every area of teenager life; it involves the whole person: physical, intellectual, social, spiritual, moral and emotional. If we are to understand young people we must carefully look at the effects that this process has on their still-developing personality.

Some will ask 'why bother with trying to understand teenagers? It's impossible; they don't even understand themselves!' The second part of this statement may well be true. It therefore becomes all the more vital that instead of expressing the attitude displayed in the first part of the sentence, we attempt to get alongside young people and exhibit care and concern as we grapple with the problem of understanding them. This is a difficult task, for the areas of development mentioned above are all inter-related, and bring many pressures to bear on one another. Together they form a bewildering, constantly changing kaleidoscope.

(1) Physical growth

Anybody involved in work with teenagers is aware of the rapid physical changes that take place in the early stages of adolescence. Puberty begins with a sudden period of growth in height, so that adults will often remark, 'Haven't you shot up!' It is straight after this 'spurt' of growth that sexual development begins to take place. Puberty begins earlier in females than in males, which generally accounts for girls' smaller stature (they have grown less before their growth 'spurt' starts). In girls puberty starts around the age of eleven whereas in boys it is at about thirteen. However, it can occur earlier, as early as nine or ten in girls, or as late as sixteen, seventeen or eighteen.

For girls this is the time when they experience the start of menstruation (the average age for the first period is twelve and a half), breast development and growth of body hair under arms, on legs and in the pubic region. Many members of both sexes will experience the problem of spots, blackheads and acne.

For boys this is a time of equally rapid change. Their voice breaks, they grow at a dramatically fast rate, their muscles develop and they become much stronger. They also experience the growth of body, facial and pubic hair and sexual organs mature and become larger. Boys will also begin to experience the occasional 'wet dream' or 'nocturnal emission'.

It is also the time when sexual awareness begins, which again is usually earlier in girls than boys. Boys become very interested in girls' bodies, whereas girls are usually more fascinated by the boy himself—his walk, the way he talks and his personality. It is the age of crushes which usually last only a few weeks or so before the next one starts. The teenager falls in and out of love regularly!

These physical changes can be terrifying for young teenagers. Their bodies are doing all sorts of frightening things which nobody has fully prepared them for. They are not sure what is happening, they wonder whether there is something wrong with them and whether, perhaps, they have some kind of disease. For instance, as breasts develop they often become sore and painful. Many a girl secretly wrestles with the fear that she has contracted cancer.

For the girl there is the worry of menstruation: will she bleed to death? Some girls dread their first period. A boy worries about what's happening to him when he has his first 'wet dream', and he is acutely embarrassed when his voice starts cracking and screeching.

For those of both sexes who develop late there is the terrifying question, 'Will I ever mature?' The boy worries because he has not started shaving and has grown no pubic hair. Will he ever be capable of sexual intercourse? And his voice is so high that he sounds more like a girl than a man. The same kind of fears surround the girl who listens to her friends talking about their periods but has not had one herself: 'Is there something wrong with me?' Her friends all look like women, but she doesn't even wear a bra. She thinks, 'Perhaps I'm going to be stuck like this forever?' For those who develop unusually early there are similar problems, as again they ask the question, 'What's wrong with me? Am I ill?'

Sexual thoughts are uppermost in the adolescent's mind, which as we are often reminded, is the teenager's primary sex organ! It is estimated that the adolescent's thoughts will turn to this subject on average approximately once every fourteen minutes! Will God punish him for his sexual thoughts?

Fantasy plays a significant role in their life, with about 95% of all single males and 40% of all females being involved in masturbation at some time during adolescence. There are some very worrying rumours about this habit: it will make you weak and ill, drive you mad or cause blindness. Very many young people are torn by the agony of guilt over masturbation. They wish they could stop but they can't. What would their parents or friends say if they knew?

Physical appearance is very important to teenagers but it is estimated that over 80% of them are unhappy with their looks. For some reason they feel ugly and unattractive. They are too short, for example, or too tall, or they have spots. As a result they feel that they will never be attractive to the opposite sex. A teenager's feeling of sexual or physical failure is aggravated by the media, which present stereotyped ideas of 'success'. For instance, what is prettiness? Answer, 34-24-34!

If we begin to analyse the feelings that result from the process of physical development, we would have to list such things as anxiety, fear, depression, insecurity, lack of self-esteem, inferiority, inadequacy, shyness, self-doubt and over-sensitivity. All these feelings vie with the excitement and challenge of growing up. The teenager will often compensate for feelings of insecurity with a show of bravado and aggression.

(2) Intellectual growth

It is during our teenage years that we really begin fully to develop our ability to think in abstract terms and to tackle philosophical questions. Therefore the teenager will start asking
life's difficult questions: 'Who am I?' 'What is the meaning of
life?' 'What do I believe, and why?' In his search for answers
his thinking will be shaped by the big institutions of our society:
the family, education, law and government, and the church,
and also by television, radio, pop culture, magazines and peer
groups.

Today, we live in a very competitive world which puts enormous pressure on the teenager to succeed academically. Where
academic success does not come, a deep sense of inadequacy
and failure often sets in. It is also true that one of the greatest
causes of failure is the fear of failure. The teenager, looking at
all that is demanded of him academically, is very often intimidated, and automatically feels a sense of deep failure.

Many teenagers have a sense of intellectual frustration. They
just don't feel clever enough. Their brain will not work fast
enough and added to this problem they do not feel able to
express themselves clearly. Their command of language is not
strong enough and when they try to explain themselves they
simply get tied up in knots. Adults tend to walk all over their
arguments in minutes, dismissing them as worthless and naive.

(3) Social development

Every one of us has a need, to some degree or other, to conform to those around us but during the teenage years this desire
is much stronger, heightened by the insecurities which accompany development towards adulthood. The adolescent hates to
be different whether in dress, habits, speech, pocket money, or
the things he is allowed to do. It is very important that youth
leaders and parents take into account this need to conform. To
be different can bring humiliation and unpopularity, and the
young person will come to despise people who he can see have
so little understanding of his needs that they don't see this.

The desire to conform will often push the teenager into actions which his better judgement tells him are wrong; for example, involvement with drugs, glue, drink, sex and the occult. I very much enjoy reggae music nowadays and, in concert, even go as far as performing one or two songs in this style. But as a teenager I belonged to a particular peer group which did not allow such freedom of choice. I hated reggae! We discover a strange paradox within the teenager who, while struggling for independence, individuality and self-expression, will at the same time dress almost identically with his friends and develop an exclusive allegiance to a particular brand of pop music—all in the cause of conformity.

(4) Spiritual/moral development

When he asks, 'Who am I?' and, 'What is life's meaning?' the young person is exploring spiritual and moral matters. In my work in schools and colleges up and down the country, I have discovered first hand that there are comparitively few atheists amongst teenagers. The vast majority of teenagers in the UK believe in God, although they are usually very unclear about what this God is like. Most of those teenagers who do not have a clear belief in God have an open mind on the subject.

Because in adolescence it is natural to examine the beliefs you have been taught as a child, many teenagers will question a belief in God or Christianity which up until this point has been based on parental teaching and example. When the adolescent begins to question it is important that he be taken seriously and given satisfactory answers, rather than being continually fobbed off with the simple reply, 'Have faith!'

As teenagers face these questions they will tend to be very idealistic. This should not be despised by adults. As Hadfield tells us, idealism 'is necessary for the full development of a man as a human being'.[5]

In Athens in classical times, at the age of eighteen the youth was taken to the Grove of Agroulos where he took his oath: 'I will never bring discredit in these arms, nor desert the man next to me in the ranks, but will fight for the sanctities of the common good, both alone and with others.'[6]

Idealism also held a high place during the age of chivalry. When a boy came to the age of fourteen, he might be made a squire and, as we have already pointed out, be appointed to serve a knight. In doing so he was expected to show courage, obedience, helpfulness and self-sacrifice. Then when he reached the age of twenty-one he too became a knight. After spending a night in prayer and confession he took vows: 'To be a brave, loyal, generous, just, and genteel knight, a champion of the Church, a redresser of the wrongs of widows and orphans, and a protector of women.'[7]

Hadfield makes a most important statement when he says:

> Idealism in youth comes at a very significant time . . . strong sexual desires on the one hand, and idealism on the other . . . appear to spring from the same common source, namely, the need for someone or something outside of the adolescent to fulfil and complete himself.[8]

The teenager begins to find this fulfilment physically and emotionally through a boy or girlfriend and later husband or wife, without whom he feels incomplete. But fulfilment also comes through idealism, for without aims and purpose the teenager will be left with a feeling of incompleteness. Unfortunately, teenage idealism often leads ultimately to a deep sense of dissatisfaction, self-questioning, inadequacy, inferiority and insecurity, for young people are very conscious of the discrepancy between what they are and what they would like to be.

(5) Emotional development

The adolescent faces great emotional strains in coping with the four areas of development that we have already outlined. But as well as, and as a result of all this comes the emotional trauma of working out new relationships within the family unit.

The young person striving for independence very often feels as though his parents still regard him as a child. In reality, teenagers need and, in fact, want less independence than they think, whilst parents generally need to give more independence in the right kind of areas than they imagine to be possible. This tension is a normal part of growing up.

During the teenage years all emotions are more intensely felt. As James Dobson states:

> Fears will be more frightening . . . pleasures will be more exciting . . . irritations will be more distressing, and . . . frustrations will be more intolerable. Every experience will appear king-sized. Their emotions move quickly up and down . . . they are . . . human yo-yo's.[9]

Adolescents are easily swayed by the emotion of the moment and because they experience their feelings so deeply they tend to be explosive, often regretting their behaviour soon after the event.

It is also important to mention that a major factor in the lives of many young teenagers is the emotional stress and insecurity which is caused by the broken home. It is common knowledge that one in three marriages ends in divorce, whilst it is estimated that over 50% of those which continue are actually very unhappy, unsatisfying, and often only kept together for financial reasons or through the lack of courage to do anything else about the situation. Because the teenager is getting such a bumpy ride he needs a point of stability. Traditionally this has been provided by the home but where that fails him he urgently needs to find security elsewhere.

External pressures

We have outlined the five areas of growth within the teenager and the problems they bring. But, as we have already seen, there are externals that further complicate the situation. The teenager, like us all, will feel pressure from outside. Peer groups, family life, education and the media, all squeeze the teenager by putting enormous pressure on internal insecurities.

If we are to understand the young people with whom we work, then we must give them the compassion, love and understanding which they deserve. It is vitally important that we grasp the complexity of the situation in which they find themselves. Life, it seems, is a hurdle course which they are told they must bravely face and run.

The teenager and the Bible

In his very helpful book, *Christian Youth Work*, Mark Ashton is concerned with what he describes as 'theory and theology'. At one point he states that 'The most serious weakness in the Christian outreach to teenagers today is not a failure to under- stand our culture, it is a failure to take the Bible sufficiently seriously'.[10]

Too often Christians have approached youth work in a totally secular manner, listening very hard to all that the sociologists and psychologists have to tell them about the make-up of young people, but totally ignoring the biblical doctrine of man and his fallenness. It is nothing less than diabolical when the church is conned by the secular voices which surround it into believing that the world of the Old and New Testaments has no relevance to the problems we face in society today. Just as the Bible has very much to tell us about marriage and divorce, so it has much to say about young people. Nor are we to research the subject of 'understanding youth' with purely secular tools and then apply a veneer of biblical thoughts to what has been a sociologi- cal study. The basis from which we start as Christians is quite distinct from that which others may regard as foundational to their thinking. Christian youth work is not a secular cake with biblical icing; instead the basic recipe is filled with biblical ingredients.

The Bible and the newspaper

Secular understanding tells us that through sociological insight we can discover the pressures and problems faced by teenagers and then, by seeking to be sensitive, can help them to discover their own path into maturity and fulfilment. But in fact what God says through his word, as revealed in Scripture and ulti- mately through Jesus Christ, is that real fulfilment can never be achieved in this way. Fulfilment is not just a matter of being right within ourselves but comes as we are also right with those around us, and with God. Human nature is flawed; we are all tainted with original sin. The Bible is clear that each one of us has free will, and has used that freedom to reject God's law. Each one of us has broken the first commandment, which is to 'love the Lord your God with all your heart and soul and mind', and thus we have rebelled against his authority. Each one of us needs to repent of our rebellion against, and apathy towards God our Creator. True fulfilment and freedom is not the result of achieving everything we want and obtaining all that brings outward success but in fact is the opposite, coming through the surrender of our will and personality to God's will. As the old hymn says, 'Force me to render up my sword and then shall I be free.'

We must not end up in the situation where we come to believe that a teenager's attitudes and behaviour are simply the result of his internal struggles and environmental surroundings. We have been talking about some of the pressures which are brought to bear on any teenager through our culture but the question of exactly how the individual deals with these and develops his behaviour patterns is ultimately one of personal responsibility. It is not good enough to say, 'I am as I am because I was hit on the head with a hammer at the age of three and a half, and fell down a manhole when I was ten!' We are all sinful by nature and choice.

Institutions and other external pressures influence us because they appeal to our own sinful inclinations and internal crises and traumas simply aid and abet our selfish desires. The Christian youth worker's task is to take eternal biblical truth and apply it to the changing influences of twentieth century life, to hold the Bible in one hand and the newspaper in the other.

Abundant life

The Christian also needs to state the biblical teaching that the teenager, like everybody else, is not to be valued on the basis of what he has achieved or possesses. This is especially important in these days of such high unemployment amongst the young. Conversation at social gatherings is very often built around a discussion of the roles which the participants play within society. To the question, 'Who are you?' the answer very often comes back, 'Oh, I'm training to be a doctor', or 'a lawyer', or, 'I'm a teacher', etc. But what of those who have no employment? What of those who feel depersonalized by their daily task, or those who feel they cannot succeed in the eyes of the world for one reason or the other? What of those who live with the failure of unfulfilled ambition? What happens to the person who makes such proud boasts when, through retirement or illness or redundancy, he is robbed of his role and therefore, it would seem, his reason for existence! As Christians our job is to state clearly that a man or woman's value is not dependent upon the salary and professional position that they manage to command. Our value is quite independent of all of this and is derived from the fact that out of his love God created us as individuals to live for him. It is for this reason that we have real purpose. Even though we have all turned our backs on our Creator, he still offers us true fulfilment through Jesus Christ who claimed, 'I have come in order that you might have life—life in all its fullness' (Jn 10:10, GNB).

3

TO BE OR NOT TO BE

The place of youth work in the life of the church

Mark Ashton, Secretary of the Church Youth Fellowships Association, commented on a recent survey about the attitudes of teenagers towards the church: 'If the survey's statistics of decline in Church going during adolescence are anything to go by, there is a drastic failure by the Church to communicate to young people.'[2] But why should the church work with teenagers anyway?

God's agenda

On the day of Pentecost Peter stood up and preached to the adults who had gathered together in Jerusalem, with the result that many of them were converted. There's no mention of a fringe meeting for teenagers led by one of the other apostles! Paul on his missionary journeys preached to all sorts of groups in many situations as he took his message into different cultural settings, but never, so far as we know, to adolescents; with the possible exception of Timothy, his work was focussed on adults.

It seems to be clear that the early church did not embark on a programme of organized youth work. There no first century youth pastors! Jesus took children on his knee and showed a special affection for them but no mention is made of his dealings with youth. It is true that once he had a conversation with a 'rich young man', but we cannot be at all sure what that term implies, and one conversation does not give us grounds for surmising that he was actively involved with work among this age group.

As a result of this 'biblical evidence' it is possible to relegate youth work to a very secondary place in church life, or even to reject altogether any kind of emphasis on evangelism and work amongst this age group. The claim is sometimes made that this is clearly in line with the teaching and practice of the early church. Youth work, it is said, is just not on God's agenda!

In fairness, this view is perhaps a reaction to the situation that has arisen in many churches where the word 'evangelism' has become almost completely synonymous with children's work and nothing more. Some churches have opted out of responsibility to adults. In fact, some of the church's critics have long accused it of indoctrinating children, because they are immature and cannot argue back, yet of not daring to challenge adults who could easily demolish its arguments.

Although the danger of using an emphasis on children or youth to avoid adult evangelism needs to be recognized, the thinking that attempts to dismiss youth work on biblical grounds is misguided, stemming from a shallow understanding of the New Testament and its cultural background. As we discovered in chapter one, it was only recently that the concept of 'the teenager' arose, so that in New Testament times there was no such thing as an adolescent as we now know it. The early church could not evangelize teenagers or adolescents as a separate group because they did not exist! This does not mean they did not evangelize people of this age, but simply that they were regarded as part of the adult world. In Jewish thinking only two states existed, child and adulthood. Perhaps Paul's comment to the Corinthians suggests this. He states, 'When I was a child, my speech, feelings and thinking were all those of a child; now that I am a man, I have no more use for childish ways' (1 Cor 13:11, GNB) He talks of childhood and then manhood with no mention of adolescence.

When Jesus was twelve years old his parents left him behind in Jerusalem where they had been attending the feast of the Passover. They did not actually miss him until they were well into the journey home; in fact a whole day had elapsed before they began searching for him (Lk 2:41–44). If we are honest we struggle today with what we feel is the irresponsible attitude displayed by Mary and Joseph that could allow them to leave their twelve year old in the city of Jerusalem while they set out on the road back to Nazareth! What we fail to understand is not only the solidarity and sense of corporate responsibility of the community who had all travelled to Jerusalem together but also that at the age of twelve, Jesus was on the very brink of adult life, with his barmitzvah only months away. We have already seen that this did not mean he would be pushed out into the adult world and expected to behave with the full maturity of manhood from the day he was thirteen, but none the less Jesus was afforded a much higher degree of personal responsibility than we would give to a child of the same age.

The church's mission to youth

Today we are in a completely different cultural setting. The teenager has arrived, and represents a very important and influential element in our society. Because the church has been commissioned by Christ to bring the good news of the gospel to the whole world it has a responsibility to this element of society. There are many who desperately struggle to capture the teenager's attention, time and money. There is a multitude of voices which offer direction and purpose. It is therefore of the greatest importance that as the teenager is bombarded by advice, views and information he be given a good, clear and accurate understanding of what God has to say about his life as revealed through Jesus Christ. In fact, even before the 'teenage awakening' there were those who recognized this need. Hudson Taylor, the founder of the China Inland Mission (now the Overseas Missionary Fellowship), once wrote with great insight,

> If we think that boys and girls in their teens are too young for soul experiences we are indeed mistaken. At no time in life is there greater capacity for devotion if the heart's deepest strings are open to the love of Christ.[3]

Trevor Partridge of Crusade For World Revival states,

These are the spiritually sensitive years of life, it is during these years that important life changing decisions are made and if the challenge of the gospel is clearly presented, decisions can be reached for Christ. What a tremendous opportunity and challenge we have to present Christ to the youth of our nation.[4]

The granting of responsibility ·

In 1985, Paul Hardcastle had a number one hit single with *Nineteen* commemorating the tenth anniversary of the end of the Vietnam War: 'The average age of a combat soldier was nineteen . . . they saw active service every day for one year . . . they came under fire on every day of that year.'[5]

In wartime the American nation turned to its youth, thrusting them into the firing line, pushing them into responsibility in this awful unwanted task; Great Britain did the same in the Falklands crisis. But for the most part modern society has segregated its teenagers in the giant educational goldfish bowl we have already talked about, depriving them of responsibility and involvement in 'real' life. It is important that the church responds to them on a different basis, giving to them the opportunity to get their teeth into what they consider a real challenge. Christians are often tempted to complain about the difficulties that modern society presents them with, but here is an opportunity handed to the church as a result of the insensitivity of the secular world. Does the church have the courage and enough understanding of young people to accept it?

Too often the church has judged young people in their late teens—young people who are of the same age as those called upon to fight for their countries—to be more or less totally irresponsible for anything but the most menial tasks. Recently I spoke with a non-Christian professor who was involved in research into some of the religious cults active in our country today. He said that he had come across many young people involved in such movements as the Unification Church (Moonies) and the Church of Jesus Christ of Latter Day Saints (Mormons) who had explained to him that they had been brought up within the traditional Christian church, but had never been given real responsibility or a sense of challenge.

Now they had found a cause not only to believe in, but to live for, where they were respected by others and where their involvement was regarded as vitally important. He claimed that it was time that the church once more began to capture the imagination of young people, who, he said, had so much to offer, who were capable of incredible devotion and the possessors of vast resources of energy, drive, vision and enthusiasm.

The place of youth work in the church

In a recent survey carried out by the British Council of Churches it was discovered that six out of every ten Christians in this country made their commitment to Christ during their teenage years. When over half of those of us who are Christians made that decision during adolescence, we are foolish not to give very careful thought to the place of youth work within the overall stategy of the local church. Here are people of massive need and also enormous potential! Never could Jesus' statement have been more true: 'I tell you, open your eyes and look at the fields! They are ripe for harvest' (Jn 4:35). If the church fails the young there are many waiting in the wings with very different gospels to proclaim and sell!

Attitudes to youth work

We have established that youth work is a valid area of ministry in which the local church should be involved, and we have looked briefly at some of the barriers to communication with young people. But there is more than one motive for work amongst young people, and not all are good:

(1) A way to the adults

During the early part of this century many churches saw children and young people simply as a means to an end, that being to draw adults 'under the sound of the gospel'! It is still a quite commonly held principle that the way to 'reach' adults is firstly to 'win' their children. So, a Sunday school and/or youth fellowship are started on a housing estate with the prayer that one day these activities will give birth to an adult church. Through the young it is hoped to gain access to the homes from which they come and so eventually to win their parents.

Two things need to be said about this policy. Firstly, it does not work. Experience shows that very rarely do adults respond to the gospel because of their children. Roy Joslin in his fascinating book *Urban Harvest*[6] gives many examples of London churches which pursued this policy earlier in the century and are now, humanly speaking, on their last legs.

Secondly, it is devious. Even if this policy did produce results, it would still amount to the exploitation of young people. It is dishonest and degrading because it sees them as nothing more than bait used to hook those for whom we are really fishing.

The church should be involved with the young for their own sake, because it is recognized that they have needs themselves which Jesus Christ wants to meet, and not use them as pawns in a spiritual chess game. The world exploits and uses teenagers to its own end. Let's make sure the church does not adopt this same policy.

(2) Pew fodder

Sometimes youth work is undertaken to satisfy the local church's desire to see a 'nice group of young people' out on the Sunday evening. It brings a sense of security to feel that the church is reaching youth. If this motive is analysed it often amounts to little more than the desire to feel 'that all is well in the garden' and to have the church building full Sunday by Sunday. Thus, young people are seen as 'pew fillers' or 'fodder', acceptable to the rest of the congregation as long as they do not step out of line, or make any demands. All they are required to do is sit in neat rows and keep coming. They are again only wanted as a means to an end and not for their own sake.

(3) The church of tomorrow

There is yet another common motive for youth work which can be summed up in the statement, 'the young people of today are the church of tomorrow'. Often this statement betrays the fact that young people are simply seen as a means of perpetuating the institution, or, even worse, that they are not actually a real part of the church today.

The church consists of all those who belong to Christ; Christian young people are already part of the church and older church members need to appreciate this fact. Young people are not 'the church of tomorrow', they are very much part of the church family today! Together Christians both young and old should be working to build the church of tomorrow.

The local church and youth leadership

Responsibility for youth work has often been conveniently pushed on to the shoulders of anyone willing to accept the challenge. It is time that the 'burden' was put back where it really belongs; with the whole church. But this has tremendous implications for the way in which youth leaders are found and supported.

(1) Who appoints the youth leaders?

Very often, though the decision is eventually rubber-stamped by the church, youth leaders are more or less self-appointed and then left to get on with their demanding work without real support from the church. This should never be the case. Youth leaders should be regarded in the same light as anybody else with a responsible teaching role within the church. They should be set apart and commissioned by the church under the direction of the Holy Spirit (see Acts 13:2) in just the same way as Paul and Barnabas were sent off.

If the church has appointed leaders to the task of evangelism and teaching amongst teenagers it also carries the ultimate responsibility for this work. Responsibility and authority have been delegated to the youth leader who is accountable not only to the Lord but to the local church. This will also mean that he or she should not be carrying the full responsibility for finding co-workers or the headache of financing the group's ongoing life!

It is particularly important that the local church should take upon itself the responsibility prayerfully to set apart and then support its youth leaders in the light of what has already been said in chapter two about how youth workers so often become the heroes of teenagers. The youth leader is not only in a very influential position but also a very vulnerable one.

When the church takes this responsibility it will be forced to face such practical questions as:

'Do we want to work with youth?'

'What is our aim?'

'Where does youth work fit into the strategic outreach of the church?'

'Is it accomplishing its task within the church and the neighbourhood?'

'Are we helping to hammer out a theology that's true to the Bible and relates to today's teenagers?'

'Are our youth leaders properly pastored and encouraged?'

'Do we send our leaders away for training at the fellowship's expense?'

'Do we ask too much of them by expecting them to be actively committed to other areas of the church's work as well?'

Too often lonely youth leaders have laboured on against great odds, with insufficient manpower, few resources, little training and no real support or understanding from their local church, who only seem to show any interest when things go wrong.

(2) Training for youth leaders

Just as those called to work in what we recognize as 'foreign mission fields' need to be properly trained for their task, so do the church's youth leaders. Some friends of mine are now working with the Bible and Medical Missionary Fellowship in India for which they had the opportunity of training at All Nations Bible College. Nobody would have expected them to take up their task without the benefit of this training; it was obviously necessary both theologically and practically and their friends generously supported them throughout this time. Yet often when we turn to work in our own country we adopt a completely different set of principles, wanting to see good results, in double quick time, without any real investment in any kind of training. Of course it is not usually possible for a local church youth leader to be given the opportunity of 'full time' training, or of being employed on this basis, but it is possible to provide the finance and support to enable him to attend week-end conferences and seminars and to purchase resource books and other materials that are helpful. Many youth leaders would never dare even to suggest that their local church finance their attendance at a conference of particular interest and yet for the church to do just this would be a forward looking investment. The best results are usually achieved when those with responsibility have the tools and the know-how to achieve the task.

(3) Who finances the youth work?

Many churches channel a great deal of finance into their Sunday schools which cater, in the main, for younger children, but very often this is nowhere near matched when it comes to a commitment to youth work. If work amongst youth is seen as an important emphasis within the life of the church then the financial commitment to it must be real.

(4) Who prays for the youth leaders?

Youth leaders, just as much as the missionary in a foreign land, are working across cultural frontiers and need the active sacrificial and effective prayer support of their fellowship. If the church were sending missionaries to Zaïre they would pray regularly for them and expect to receive regular prayer sheets. The same should be true of the church's relationship with its youth workers. In return for the prayer support, these leaders have a responsibility to keep the local church fully informed about developments amongst the young people. In this way the church as a whole can stand alongside the youth worker in his joys as well as his disappointments and heartaches and can begin to understand the tensions between their culture and that of the young people.

The youth leader's attitude

It is vitally important that when the youth leader speaks about his young people to other church members he should not be apologetic but speak in order to bring about the same constructive approach to young people that he himself has.

On the other hand, it is just as important to present the best possible image of the church to the young people! Many a youth leader has fallen into the trap of giving voice to his own frustrations in front of the youth group and stirring up within them an unhealthy resentment of the church of which he and they are a part. It is an act of great discipline and maturity to avoid this trap, especially when a clash has occurred and the youth leader feels that his opinion and/or the position of the young people have not been sensitively taken into account.

Even if you have a sense of achievement or relief because you realize your local church has not fallen into the kind of traps outlined here, it is still wise to look carefully at your church and see how the youth ministry within your fellowship can be improved. It is good to make a periodic assessment of our work. There is a time for changing what we are doing, as well as a time for reaffirming our conviction that some things in which we are involved should remain unchanged. Whether we decide to keep things as they are or to make alterations, the important thing is that we know why we have come to these conclusions.

Having set out these principles which are not only biblical, but lift youth work to the place it rightfully deserves within the church, perhaps it is important to comment briefly on an opposite danger which arises for the local fellowship that takes youth work seriously.

Young, free and beautiful

Today we live in what is without doubt a youth-dominated society. Our magazines, television adverts and the world of entertainment are filled with images of the young. A current television advert for the *Sun* newspaper contains the line, 'The *Sun* is for you because you're young and beautiful.' Youth is the god that our culture worships.

It was recently said that to be old is 'the greatest sin it is possible to commit today.'

But the Bible does not see young people as a more important group than any other in society. Through the Bible we see God's care lovingly expressed for all age groups and learn that he uses all kinds of people to achieve his purposes. For instance, we read that Jeremiah was known to God whilst he was still in his mother's womb. Later, when he protested at being called by God to be a prophet, his excuse was that he was a mere youth! But the Lord dismissed this objection, making it clear that he was well able to use a youth to do his work. On the other hand, Moses was eighty years of age when God called him, and Abram was seventy-five! Joel's prophecy which was quoted by Peter on the day of Pentecost states, 'In the last days, God says, I will pour out my Spirit on all people. Your sons and daughters will prophesy, your young men will see visions, your old men will dream dreams. Even on my servants, both men and women, I will pour out my Spirit in those days' (Acts 2:17-18). The Bible is full of stories where God chooses to use both young and old alike. Young people are not more exalted in his sight than any other age group. Therefore, whilst the place of youth work within the church is important, it should never be allowed to become the one dominating factor in the life of the local fellowship. The church is commissioned to reach adults as well, and to bring both young and old into the family.

4

BUILDING BRIDGES

Communicating with young people

Over two-thirds of teenagers read their horoscopes at least once a week. More than half are no longer virgins by the time they are sixteen years of age, and more than a quarter believe in reincarnation. So states Clive Calver, the General Secretary of the Evangelical Alliance, in a paper on Youth and the Church. There are also the growing problems of teenage drug addiction, glue sniffing, homosexuality, violence, occult involvement, racism, suicide, pregnancy, abortion and unemployment, and so on. In our major cities girls of thirteen, fourteen, fifteen, and upwards are involved in prostitution. Calver goes on to claim that if these things had 'been predicted ten years ago as part of our children's cultural background in the mid nineteen-eighties we would have dismissed them as wild scaremongering'[1]. This is the background against which the church now works here in Great Britain, but how did this situation come about?

Christian morality abandoned

Since shortly after the turn of the century the church in Great Britain has known a pattern of decline. Though we have now reached the stage where many parents of teenagers have themselves no concept of biblical moral absolutes, the teenager is still told by his or her parents that to sleep with their boy or girlfriend, for instance, is morally wrong. But when they enquire, 'Why?' the answer comes back, 'Because I say it is.' There is no longer any absolute authority beyond that of the parent; it is simply a matter of what society feels is right. Therefore the teenager quite rightly asks (or thinks), 'Why should I behave in a way that you claim is right when there is no ultimate reasoning behind it?' He then pushes ahead with his own course of action, rejecting what he sees as parental hypocrisy, and abandoning any moral boundaries not pleasing to his desires. But though teenagers reject Christian morality, they desperately need a code of moral absolutes within which to operate. Like all of us, they actually need boundaries and limits if they are to reach personal fulfilment. What is the church doing to provide this much-needed framework for life?

Boring . . . boring!

In the course of the school's work in which I am involved around the country, I often say to teenagers: 'Think about church, now can you give me one descriptive word to sum up your thoughts?' Without doubt or hesitation the reply is always, 'Boring'! Even variations on this—such as dull, drab, irrelevant and old-fashioned—are rarely mentioned. There is no doubt that young people could use all of these words to describe the church but 'boring' is the word which it seems is always on the tip of their tongues. Among today's teenagers there is without doubt a new openness to the spiritual dimension of life. There is even an interest in Jesus as an historical figure and spiritual leader, but sadly there is no interest whatsoever in the church.

If we are to do anything constructive about this we need to understand why adolescents in general have reached this devastating conclusion!

A teenage creed

Every group in society holds a wide range of opinions, ideas, prejudices, suspicions and beliefs. These are built on information received from the institutions and influences which surround them. In chapter two we looked at those which have the greatest influence on the lives of teenagers: pop culture, peer group pressure, family beliefs, education and the church itself. All these have worked together to convince the young that the church is quite irrelevant to them.

The basic problem which the church faces when dealing with young people is not hostility but sheer apathy and indifference. 'You don't need to go to church to be a Christian', is probably the nearest thing that the average teenager has to a creed. What goes on in church is seen as out of date, dull and lifeless. The liturgy is confusing, the buildings are cold, hymns are old-fashioned, prayers are long and boring, surpassed in tedium only by the sermons which are all too often totally unintelligible and seen as unrelated to life in the real world.

Have faith, young man

It's too easy for the church to blame the present situation on the young themselves. During the course of this century, there has been a massive failure to relate our beliefs to contemporary culture and the issues that confront us in the twentieth century so that the Christian faith has become something which is held in a vacuum. As a child and later a young adolescent Christian, I was for ever being told by the church to 'have faith' and, by implication, to 'stop asking such awkward questions!' This approach to the young will just not do. Our Christian faith is rational, and has real answers for and insights into our world situation. If young people regard the church as irrelevant it is not primarily the fault of the media, nor of the Bishop of Durham and his supporters. In fact, however way out some of David Jenkins' statements may be, and at odds with what the Bible clearly states, it is probably true that he has attracted more attention to Jesus as a person than the evangelical church has for years!

Those people who do go to church are commonly regarded by teenagers as hypocrites because in the minds of most people the statement, 'I'm a church-going Christian' means, 'I'm a very good person . . . and I think a lot of myself.' Attendance is also associated with being snobbish and intellectual. As Tony Dann of British Youth for Christ points out, 'The gap between most young people and the Church is vast.'[2]

In our schools, religious education no longer consists solely of biblical study; today, the phenomenology of religion and the study of ethics take up most of the syllabus. Assemblies are no longer a daily occurrence and when they do take place they often have little or no Christian content. Another problem is that in cases where there is 'Christian' content, it is often presented out of a sense of duty. In many cases those taking part have no faith themselves and therefore the content is bound to be dull and dry, if not totally misleading!

Added to this developing picture, parents no longer send their children to Sunday school. In fact there are many young people in our country today who have never been inside a church building, and have never received any Christian teaching in their home. The result of all this is that very few young people have any real understanding of Christian teaching.

Jesus Christ and Peter Pan

While most young people have an inborn belief in God and the supernatural and are inquisitive about the spiritual side of life, they believe in Jesus only at the level of the fairy story. The common understanding is that he probably never really lived and that if he did there is now very little we can know about him. The Bible is seen as unreliable and inaccurate, written long after the events described. On top of all this, it has been changed and distorted through the centuries, and is corrupted with each new translation. Teenagers banish Christ to the realms of Peter Pan, Father Christmas or Alice in Wonderland. In fact, the only contact many young people have with Christianity is as it is portrayed on the television in the Sunday service, Songs of Praise or more often, the half hour situation comedy where the vicar is always portrayed as a lovable but rather forgetful old fool who has been caught in a sort of time warp and really belongs somewhere back in the 1950's. (Having said all this, it needs to be recognized that once the historical facts have been presented to teenagers, then an openness to Jesus often appears.)

No real answers

Teenage idealism often leads young people to begin to think out the great issues of life such as race, ecology, the nuclear debate, politics, the peace movement and religion itself. As they work through these questions their idealistic principles tend to push them to rather black and white answers. In 1984 Leslie Francis published a report called *Teenagers and the Church* in which a number of issues were listed that young people wanted the opportunity to talk about in church but had not been able so to do. Over half of the sixteen to twenty year olds interviewed wanted to hear about personal relationships, sex, marriage, homosexuality, racism, law and order, the third world, work, the environment, unemployment and pop music. Just under half wanted to talk about the occult, cults, prayer, the Bible, television and politics.[3] These findings indicate just how big the gap is within the churches between what many young people want to explore and what the adults are prepared to talk through with them. So the little contact that most teenagers have with Christianity and the church convinces them that it is muddled and has nothing real to say to today's world. It seems to exist within a vacuum, with a lot more to say about our heritage and tradition than the difficult business of twentieth century life.

The non-book culture

There is a further problem. The experts tell us that we now live in a non-literary society. It is not that we are illiterate but that most of us just do not read, except when we have to. This situation is in great measure due to the influence of television. (It seems that every few months we hear a new set of alarming figures concerning the huge number of hours of television watched by the average man, woman, girl, boy or family pet!) A survey which was carried out recently amongst lawyers discovered that even in this 'intellectual' group in our society there were few who read anything beyond that which their profession demanded. Teenagers are used to the fast moving images and rapidly changing pictures that television brings. Even radio is no longer listened to seriously, but has become what is often referred to as 'wallpaper', simply a type of background noise which blocks out the silence! This situation presents a serious problem for the church which has traditionally communicated mainly through the book and the lecture (better known as the sermon!). Even when a young person is interested in the message of Christianity, unless he knows someone on the inside, he may be unable to decipher it and will finally give up in frustration.

Bridging the gap and communication with youth

Rob White, the National Director of British Youth For Christ, states that there are three areas where the gap with the youth of our country must be bridged by the church if we are going to communicate effectively with them.

(1) Bridging the generation gap

The late US senator, Robert Kennedy, once said, 'The gap between generations will never be closed, it must be spanned.'[4] If the generation gap is to be spanned by the church it is imperative that we begin to understand how today's youth feel, for it is not age which separates adults from teenagers, but misunderstanding.

As we have seen, teenagers tend to have a deep sense of insecurity, inadequacy and a lack of self-esteem. They feel that they are unimportant to adults and that their ideas and opinions do not matter. It is the task of the church to overcome this problem.

If the feelings of young people about themselves could be summed up in a word it would have to be 'insecurity'. What is needed most in our churches is not so much sophisticated and hi-tech youth programmes (though they can have their place) but love, care, understanding and, most of all, acceptance. We must never totally segregate youth from other age groups within the church. Though it is important to provide special programmes for the various age groups, it is unbiblical to section off young people altogether. The Bible states that the church is a family, and Rob White reminds us that, 'For the Church to survive it needs to learn to relate to young people and find ways of developing as an all aged family.'[5]

The church should be giving young people a sense of security and importance by showing that it places great value on them, and the only way in which it can ultimately do this is by giving them real responsibility. In my experience most church leadership teams are very slow to give responsibility to young people. The excuse is made that 'they will make mistakes', and that 'they lack experience'! Of course, both of these statements are true, but they are also true of most existing church leaders themselves! It is far too easy to be fooled by our own propaganda into not seeing ourselves for what we are, or, to be more accurate, are not!

In family life children are given responsibility, and through the teenage years this privilege grows, so that by the time the child reaches the age of eighteen he is accepted as a fully fledged adult. Our churches on the other hand often treat eighteen year olds as almost totally unreliable and untrustworthy. We are told they are treated in this fashion because they are irresponsible, but what comes first, the chicken or the egg?

When I was in my teens, I played bass guitar in a band called *Manna* which was led by Steve Flashman. At the time I was fifteen, sixteen and seventeen and Steve was already training at Spurgeons College in South London to be a Baptist Minister. He was a gifted communicator with a call from God to preach, yet very often he would give me the privilege and responsibility of preaching. It was not that Steve did not want to do the job, for it was his motivation and vision that had created the group and had given us so many evangelistic opportunities in the first place. I knew that he was really trusting me, when so many budding ministers would have held tightly on to the reins and the opportunity to preach for themselves. Today I believe I owe much of my call and vision to that trust and responsibility.

We must also make sure that the responsibility we give is genuine responsibility. Teenagers soon know when what they are told is 'real responsibility sharing' and 'giving them an opportunity' is, in reality, nothing more than using them to do the jobs that nobody else wants!

(2) Bridging the credibility gap

We have seen that most young people have little or no real knowledge of the gospel and the church, and are not about to come to us and beg to have their ignorance and prejudice dispelled. The Nationwide Initiative For Evangelism Assembly at Nottingham University in 1981 produced a report on Pop Culture in which they commented that 'young people do not consider the Christian Church possesses relevance to their deep needs'.[6] The report continues:

> We recognised that in relation to young people in a pop culture:
>
> (a) we ourselves and the Churches have failed to communicate and share because of our negative attitudes, even to the extent of seeing youth as a problem, finding their music loud and offensive
>
> (b) we have not been accepting, nor have we listened to their questions or heard their cries
>
> (c) the churches have failed to understand that the 'pop' culture is a valid expression of life and cannot simply be explained away as youth's escape from life
>
> (d) we have not provided an atmosphere or place which can receive the respect of young people and does not cause them to 'lose face' with their peers
>
> (e) we have not within the Christian Church made young people feel they are a valuable and intrinsic part of the Family.

The church has got to go out into the world and begin to share its faith in God where the people are. This is no new idea—far from it; it is simply a working out of the New Testament principle of incarnation. 'The Word became flesh and lived for a while among us' (Jn 1:14). In New Testament times evangelism was something that tended to happen on the outside of the church rather than inside it. When the church met together it was basically for worship, teaching and fellowship.

Today we like evangelism to happen within the church in a neat and tidy fashion. The evangelist stands up to speak at the gospel rally, concert or service whilst the audience sits in well-ordered rows and submissively listens to his message, at the end of which they make their response to the 'appeal' and become tame Christians. This is what we call 'outreach'.

I have discovered that I am acutely embarrassed when an audience is disruptive and refuses to be polite. In fact, when we meet this kind of response we tend to feel a sense of failure and react by getting very uptight and angry with our audiences. We quickly become insecure about what we are doing, and in an attempt to avoid this feeling we complain about their lack of manners and openness to Christ and spiritual things. But Paul was used to being barracked, and taunted by hecklers. He was used to debate and open, often aggressive, questioning. It is only when we allow people to respond and ask genuine questions, and when we are prepared to accept their honest response to us, that we can begin to appreciate the thinking of the secular world around us and build credibility bridges with our society. This kind of evangelism is not neat and tidy; it is very costly in terms of time and pride. It also requires genuine love for non-Christian young people, for what they are, rather than what we want them to be.

The Greek verb meaning 'to preach' (*kerussein*) also means 'to proclaim', or 'to announce' and, as David Watson points out, 'The basic idea behind these words is that of a herald who delivers a message that has been given to him by the King.'[7] The herald's job was simply to stand on the street corners and make sure that everybody heard the message which he had been entrusted to bring by the king. How both he and the message were received was not his concern; his duty was over once he had made the king's mind clear and understandable to all. If he carried out this duty faithfully but then found the message was not obeyed he was not held responsible. But if he failed in his duty to stand in the public places and make the message clear, then the people's disobedience was his responsibility. We are called to 'herald' the gospel—to proclaim it openly. It is our job to make sure that our listeners understand the message, and this means we must give opportunity for questioning, debate and open disagreement. We must step out from our ivory towers.

Our churches need to become more involved in the local

community in schools and colleges. Perhaps one thing that should be especially mentioned here is the subject of local church involvement in school Christian Unions. This subject is covered in a more practical way in chapter 5 of this book, but for now the important concept to grasp is that the church fails itself if it does not recognize its responsibility to see that young teenage Christians are supported in their working environment throughout the week. It is very short-sighted when a local church congratulates itself on the size of its Sunday evening youth fellowship while making no real attempt to support its young people throughout the week in their school environment. Many young Christians live double lives, boldly proclaiming Jesus at the weekends but petrified of making a public stand at school during the week.

I well remember the occasion when a stranger straight off the street came to me for counselling one day in Tonbridge. As I sat and talked with him I discovered the school he attended, where he was in the upper sixth year. One of the Christians from our youth group went to the same school and so I mentioned that I knew him.

'How do you know him?' was the surprised reaction. I explained that he was a Christian and came to the church.

'Oh no, you must have got the wrong one . . . no not him.'

That was an interesting comment because until that time I had regarded the individual concerned as a very consistent Christian! I am still sure he was very sincere but simply lacked confidence and became overwhelmed whilst at school, unable to apply his faith in a lonely non-Christian environment.

The best evangelists amongst young people are young people themselves. Therefore, the church can most effectively bridge the credibility gap with the young by enabling and equipping the existing young Christians to be heralds. Time and money invested by a local church in the support of a school Christian Union is time and money very well spent.

Again, as teenagers are converted through local schools' missions and other evangelistic activities it will become clear that the discipling of young people who already have a Christian friend, who has previously been witnessing to them, is a very much simpler task than working with people who have no natural Christian link. In fact, in my experience most teenagers who become Christians and then stick are those who already have a Christian friend.

(3) Bridging the culture gap

I have been involved in many missions amongst young people up and down the country. Never has one which has been well organized and prayed over been unsuccessful in terms of seeing multitudes of teenagers becoming Christians. The problem that we face in this country is not making Christians but making disciples. Young people are spiritually hungry and readily respond to the gospel when we present it to them in clear and down-to-earth terms. The breakdown occurs when we try to integrate the new converts into the church, for it is this which they see as irrelevant.

Many young people who are totally committed to Christ have explained to me that they would never bring their friends to a church service. They may even feel that when one of their friends is very interested in Christianity and Jesus he must be protected from the church! Though it is difficult to generalize concerning either youth culture or church culture, the fact is that there is little point of contact between the two. Our job is to bridge that gap.

During the World Cup in 1986, France played a tense quarter final with Brazil. Unfortunately, I was unable to watch the match on television as I was driving home at the time. I decided to listen to the game on Radio Two only to find out, to my horror, that it was not being broadcast by them or by any English speaking station. As I flicked through the medium wave in desperation I at last found a station that was carrying a commentary on the match, the only problem being that it was broadcasting in French! Try as I might I could not understand a word of what was being said nor even, to my total frustration, pick up the gist of what was happening from the noise of the crowd or the level of excitement of the commentators. Occasionally I heard the name of the French hero Platinée mentioned but in what context it was impossible to tell. By the time

I reached my home in Tonbridge half time had been reached and I was pretty sure that the score was at least two all. You can understand my surprise when on eagerly switching on the television set I discoverd that no goals had been scored at all during the first half. In fact, the best that had happened was that Brazil had missed a penalty!

The point is clear. Although I had a burning interest in the subject of the commentary and was listening very hard, I could not gather the tiniest morsel of useful information except the name that I already recognized (at least I knew Platinée was playing!). Consequently the conclusion I reached about the game was far different from the message that the commentators were attempting to put across. Many teenagers find themselves in exactly this position. They have a deep interest in Christianity and a desire to understand its truths. But the language that we use is as foreign to them as the football commentator's French was to me. Occasionally they hear the name of the hero, Jesus Christ, but are quite unable to discover the content of the message.

Perhaps there are those who feel that this kind of analogy is going too far and that I am being too negative about the church; it is very difficult for us to understand exactly how confusing and alien we can sound to the outsider. The religious terminology which we often fondly call 'the language of Zion', along with our styles of music, dress and preaching are all exceptionally difficult for young people to cope with. On top of this there is our very confusing attitude to things like discos, the pub, pop music, smoking, dress and hairstyles. We need to think hard and build carefully bridges that will cross this cultural gap. It is a long leap from youth culture to church culture but there are very many stepping stones which we can make use of.

In the second section of this book we will be dealing with the subject of discipleship groups. These are a must for any new Christian. We ask too much if we require a young person to go peacefully in one week from an evangelistic event which is carefully aimed to communicate to him to a seat in a church pew.

5

IS IT A BIRD? . . . IS IT A PLANE? . . . NO, IT'S A YOUTH LEADER

The principles of Christian youth leadership

Outstanding athletic ability, endless energy, good looks, a wardrobe full of the latest fashions, a body like an Olympic athlete's, street credibility, an answer for every question, a dictionary knowledge of pop music and an outgoing and charismatic personality that draws young people like honey attracts bees . . . and that's by no means the end of what is expected of an effective youth leader. As a result, most of us, recognizing only too well our shortcomings, turn away feeling totally inadequate for such a task. We just don't measure up to this picture of a Christian Superman and even those who do get involved often struggle with a sense of, 'I'm not really cut out for all this; but nobody else will do it.'

The basic mistake

Dr John Mott once said, 'A leader is a man who knows the road, who can keep ahead, and who can pull others after him.'[1] To a large extent the qualities which allow a man or woman to do this are ones that can be learnt and practised. People assume you've either got 'leadership ability' or you've not got it! But this is just not true. Youth leadership, like most things in life, needs to be worked at—it's often a case of '90% perspiration and 10% inspiration'. God grants the basic gifts and abilities but it's our responsibility to work at them. It's also important to remember that no one person will ever possess all the attributes that would make the ideal leader (if such a things exists anyway!). There are very few 'superstar' youth leaders, and even where they do exist they are not always altogether good for the ongoing pattern of youth ministry within a local framework. Without good forward planning, when an attractive leader leaves the town or moves on into some other job the youth group often simply collapses.

When is a leader not a leader?

In this chapter we will explore the qualities and disciplines that can, with hard work and thought, be developed within the youth leader. We can begin to do this by examining four things that a leader is not:

The leader is not a dictator who gives orders that others carry out. Jesus taught that the leader should be the servant and that he who wants to be greatest should be the least. This was not just his teaching but also his practice (see Jn 13:12–17). From Jesus we learn two fundamental lessons: leadership is about servanthood and it is also about example, as we put into practice the qualities we are teaching others. Therefore, it would not be right to take a discussion of Christian leadership further without briefly mentioning the subject of personal faith and commitment to Jesus himself. It is so easy for us to end up serving an institution, rather than a person. It is too easy for us to be devoted to the church rather than to Jesus. Young people quickly detect the pseudo Christian and we have a responsibility to examine ourselves continually concerning this issue.

The leader is not a 'yes man' who simply listens to the opinion of others and acts upon their ideas and initiative. It has been said that 'a committee is an animal with four back legs'. All committees and working groups need leadership. The leader has to achieve a good balance between under- and over-involvement, if the work is really going to benefit.

The leader is not a one man band who does absolutely everything by himself, making all the decisions and single-handedly carrying out the task. If the leader is doing his job properly he will be very important to the work but never indispensable.

Where the leader does become a one man band it always leads to three problems: firstly, the feeling that he is indispensable, which will bloat his ego; secondly, a group of co-workers and leaders who do not really feel part of a team; thirdly, the inevitable collapse of all his work when he leaves.

Part of any leader's responsibility is to train others to carry on the task when he leaves. The 'lively' youth work that crumbles because its leader leaves or has to spend time away has in fact always been weak. The superstar who holds everything together himself is actually no real leader at all. It is vitally important that leaders build a good support structure which enables responsibility to be shared.

The leader is not simply a figurehead who remains at a distance from the group. It is his job to become involved. In Philippians 2:5-11 we read how Jesus did not cling to his equality with God but emptied himself taking the form of a servant. He was 'found among us'. 'The Word became flesh and . . . we have seen his glory' (Jn 1:14). Jesus did not stand at a distance but was totally involved; we do well to follow his example.

Effective leadership

Good leadership in any area of life depends upon our ability to make the best use of the resources available to us. The most important as well as the most difficult area in which to do this is that of human resources. This is what sometimes gets called 'man management' but it's really just about getting the best out of people. A man is often made a foreman because he's a good craftsman, or a manager because he's a good salesman. Of course, a manager must have the technical competence necessary to achieve the results which are required, but more than this he must also have the understanding and skill needed to get others to work with him. That is what leadership is all about.

There are several methods of getting people to do what you want and so of achieving your goal, but not all are good.

(1) Coercion

When I was young I went to a club where I was told that if I became a Christian I could write my name in the leader's leather-bound book. That seemed like a good enough reason for becoming almost anything, and so I made my commitment. It is easy to try and tempt people into following you by offering them what seems to glitter. Many youth groups run on the principle of always being one step ahead of those in the same town, of importing the latest technology and the newest ideas, all designed as incentives to keep the teenagers coming. This policy will never work in the long-term for rather than producing disciples of Jesus it tends to produce 'Christian groupies'.

(2) Fear

A second means of motivation has often been fear. Many a youth leader has resorted to putting down those he or she cannot cope with, or to humiliating the teenager who will not toe the line. Obviously this approach is wrong under any circumstances but it is especially harmful with teenagers who already feel insecure and self-conscious without finding themselves a laughing stock in front of their friends. This kind of treatment will only cause deep resentment.

(3) Inspiration

It is often said that there are two ways to get a donkey moving: to whip its backside and to dangle a carrot in front of its nose. The inference is that the second method is more commendable than the first. Although this may well be the case, both methods are highly dubious when applied to leadership of young people rather than donkeys! Rather than constantly threatening the youth group and other leaders, or dangling incentives in front of them to prompt them into action, the leader should aim to inspire the rest of the group with his vision and, by involving them in the task, draw out their best energy and efforts because they want to give them.

Three aspects of youth leadership

Good leadership is the result of the leader constantly and carefully considering three fundamental aspects of his or her task. We will now look at these in turn:

(1) Achieving the goal

To achieve your set goals is not only important for its own sake but also because the whole leadership team and/or youth group can share in the sense of achievement which results. For instance, a couple of years ago I took a group of young people from our youth fellowship to an inner-city church for a week of mission. This church had twelve members, ten of whom were over sixty. There were no teenagers whatsoever and only three children in the Sunday school. Our goal was to see God bring new life to that church and through our hard work and planning to present him with a vehicle he could use for this purpose. During the mission (and afterwards too) many young people and adults became Christians and the church has seen God's Spirit at work in many ways. Within six months there was a Sunday school of fifty and a youth group of eighty, complete with several youth leaders! My whole youth group were able to share in the sense of achievement which resulted; we were living out the things that they had so often sung about and been taught about for years. Therefore they were ready to give themselves to new goals and targets which we went on to set.

(2) Developing individuals

Each individual member of the youth group (including the co-leaders) has a need for personal development, achievement and growth and the youth leader must always recognize this fact. It is his job to help increase the self-esteem of the teenagers with whom he is working. This consideration is especially important in the light of all we have said in previous chapters about the way in which teenagers often secretly feel about themselves. The youth leader should continually be asking such questions as:

'Does this person have the maximum responsibility and

authority I can give to him?'

'Are his achievements acknowledged by me and by the group?'

'Is his creativity encouraged and fostered?'

'Does he know what I think of him?'

'Do I really know him as a person?'

'Do I understand his aspirations and limitations?'

'How much time do I actually spend talking and listening to him?'

In this way, as each individual is cared for and made to feel secure and important, he will give of his best.

(3) Building a team

If it is important to achieve your goals and to encourage the development of each individual member, it is also vital that attention be given to producing a good team spirit within the youth group. Only then will it be really healthy. If this need is not recognized and given time and energy, cliques and even hostile competition may begin to develop. Individuals will then be harmed and the goals of the group will become impossible to achieve. The youth leader should therefore be on the look-out for possible causes of disruption as well as asking himself questions such as:

'Do I welcome and encourage new ideas from my co-leaders and from the young people?'

'Do I listen to what others feel about the youth group?'

'Am I sure that my co-leaders and the group members understand our objectives and aims?'

A balanced approach

These three considerations are very important for every youth leader. He cannot afford to ignore any one of them as they are clearly all interdependent, so that if insufficient consideration (or too much consideration) is given to one area it is bound to have an adverse effect on the other two. For instance, failure to have clear goals and to achieve them will produce low morale amongst individual co-leaders and eventually amongst the youth group as a whole. This in turn will destroy the sense of team unity and belonging. In the same way, a failure to allow individuals to grow and develop will inevitably lead to jealousy and resentment which will detract from the ability of the group to work together as a real team. As a result they will not achieve their goals.

(1) Goal-centred approach

The kind of youth leader who is most likely to fall into this trap is the real 'go-getter', the visionary, the ball of fire, always armed with new ideas and lots of talk. He runs a full programme of events for the young people who, in reality, are simply asked to attend, smile, watch his latest idea and keep the numbers at the meetings up. But the only real need being met is that of the leader who needs to feel that he is being 'successful' and is 'full of bright ideas'. Actually, morale in the group is probably at a very low ebb, because the members do not feel important. Some are probably continuing to attend simply out of a sense of duty or because their parents force them to. This can apply to co-leaders as well as group members.

(2) Individual-centred approach

The kind of leader who runs the greatest risk of falling into this trap is the 'pastor' or 'encourager', for it is possible to become so wrapped up with those you are counselling and caring for that you lose all perspective on the overall situation and you and your group no longer have a sense of direction. All that matters is that the group exists, that the individual young people come and that their pastoral needs are met. The tasks of evangelism, growth and mission are no longer real considerations. Eventually this situation will lead to the youth group meeting simply because they enjoy the company and have a good time; there may be no known reason for its existence beyond this!

(3) Team-centred approach

It is possible for the leader to become so involved with developing a sense of teamwork and unity within the youth group that it becomes a clique where everybody is expected to think and do the same. There is no longer any room for real freedom of expression and even the opportunity for honestly and openly talking about needs, doubts and questions disappears. Opinions cannot be voiced if they in any way conflict with those of the 'team'. This situation is bound to have an adverse effect on the ongoing life of the youth group.

The qualities of a youth leader

We will now examine the qualities and duties which are important to the youth leader as he works in the three spheres of youth leadership outlined above.

(1) The leader must plan

I once heard of a leader of whom it was said that if he was locked in a room for three hours with a pen and a blank piece of paper and instructions to write down his thoughts on where his group was headed and why it was going there, he would at the end of the time still have a blank sheet! Often Christian youth work is undertaken without ever facing up to these questions. The leader must think ahead, asking such questions as:

Where is the youth group going?
Why is it going there?
What are we trying to achieve through it?
How are we going to do this?
What is my role?
Why am I involved?
How do I relate to the youth and other leaders?

It is very important that the leader should know what the group's objectives or goals are and that he should communicate these, firstly to his colleagues and then to the young people as a whole within the group. He may find himself confessing 'We have a youth group because all churches have youth groups!' Or, only slightly better, 'We have a youth group to win people to Christ!' Though this second answer sounds very spiritual it is often nothing more than an excuse not to think through the real issues and to evade questions like, how? Where? Who and why? Of course, organization can go too far if we come to believe that through it we can ensure God's blessing. Instead, our attitude should be that we want to allow God to work as freely and easily as possible and therefore we plan for this, creating openings and opportunities which he can use in the lives of people both inside and outside the group. (We will deal further with this whole subject in chapter five.)

(2) The leader must be imaginative and enterprising

In this way he or she wins the confidence of those around him. This is not as difficult as one might at first think. As a preacher, I know well the saying, 'All original thought and no plagiarism makes a very dull sermon.'

In other words, be alert, the world is full of good ideas. Look around for them and when you find a good one take it and use it, adapting it to your situation. Also, listen to the ideas and suggestions of your group and co-leaders, carefully think them through and if something seems right, take it on board and use it.

(3) The leader must delegate

Very recently I listened to a vicar bemoaning the lack of response on his 'patch' and the impossibility of the task which faced the church. Minutes later he was talking about the problem of working with a curate. In his opinion, curates created far more problems then they ever solved: 'By the time you've told them what to do you may as well have done it yourself.' As far as he was concerned, training them was an intolerable burden! It's too easy for the youth leader to end up with the same attitude. We must take the risk of giving away responsibility and in doing so give space to others to develop.

We have already stated that the one man band style of leadership will ultimately produce very poor results. To achieve the task it is vital that the leader should delegate— delegation releases him for different work and keeps the other leaders as well as the whole group involved. Thus he gets the best out of himself and out of everyone else. But it should be recognized that there is a difference between delegation and abdication! The leader still has to accept final responsibility whilst realizing that those to whom he delegates will probably never do the job exactly as he wants and sometimes not at all. He must give clear details of the job and check up in good time on the progress that is being made. This course of action will bring with it many disappointments. Often the teenager he relies on will let him down so that he will be tempted to say, 'It's easier to do it myself!' It's been said that the youth leader should always 'treat teenagers as adults, expect them to behave like children but continue treating them as adults'.

(4) The leader must communicate and motivate others

It is his job to inspire the other leaders and the young people with his vision. It is no good delegating responsibility unless they can see a good reason for the job being done. The leader therefore needs to motivate them. It is important to say things like, 'I need your help', rather than, 'You do it, not me'. The leader should also enthuse and challenge those around him by a combination of dedication, optimism, imagination and commitment to Christ. His job is to make other people *want* to work and to grow in their faith, rather than feel they should work because he ordered them to, and if they don't they will feel guilty.

(5) The leader must give support

He must encourage and give backing to his co-workers and young people as they take on responsibilities. It is important to remember again how insecure teenagers are; they need a constant supply of encouragement. Encouragement is especially important when things go wrong and the group or an individual faces failure. The leader must then show that he still believes in their ability. This is just as true in the case of disciplinary action.

(6) The leader must co-ordinate

It is his job to get the other leaders and the whole group working harmoniously together and build the sense of team unity. He will be able to do this best by his own example. It is obviously no good the leader trying to call the tune if others see him as always doing his own thing with no reference to, or respect for, their views.

(7) The leader must continually re-evaluate the situation

How is everything going? Are we still accomplishing our goals? Whenever we stop just to sit and think or plan we are tempted to feel that we are wasting time! We need to learn that time spent planning and re-evaluating the situation is time very well spent, for it saves hours, if not days, weeks and months of otherwise wasted time at a later date.

(8) The leader must make decisions

Though it is important that he listens to individuals and to the group as a whole as well as to his assistant leaders, in many situations the leader has to make the final decisions. Perhaps he has to decide between differing opinions put forward by the group, sort out a difficult problem or deal with discouragement and failure. No problems are ever solved by running away from them; they need to be faced squarely. He should not try to avoid this. He must take the initiative and deal with difficult situations in a positive way. Sometimes it is better to make a decision and later to learn you have made a mistake than not to decide anything at all!

(9) The leader must identify with young people

This does not mean that he must wear all the latest fashions and listen to every new album that enters the charts. Nor does it mean that he must dye his hair, wear an earring and continually hide his real age. Young people do not want a leader who attempts to copy them and tries to be exactly like them. They need to feel independent and different in some respects—to be some degree removed from their leader. He is not one of the boys; everyone else knows it and no one will respect him if he doesn't recognize it too. In fact, if the leader could become just like one of the young people, he would no longer be able to lead them effectively. But, having stated this, the leader must not stand aloof and apart from his young people. It is important that he should take seriously their points of view and attempt to understand them, that he should spend time familiarizing himself with their culture and the influences that bear on their lives.

(10) The leader must be available

This is probably the most important quality of the leader. Jesus made himself available to his disciples, sometimes shutting out everything else to be with them. His disciples saw him in action. During his three year ministry they had the opportunity of getting close to him, asking him questions, enjoying his company, and feeling his acceptance of them. In the same way it is important that the youth leader give quality time to his young people, and that he be honest, caring and trustworthy. It does not matter that he does not have the answer to every theological question that is thrown at him—rather than trying to invent an answer quickly, an honest response is much more helpful. Young people will learn much more from watching him and being able to trust him than listening carefully to his official replies to difficult questions.

Jesus had time for people, and this made them feel important and valued. We will never convince anyone that they can trust us if we are not prepared to give time sacrificially to them, and do it without making them feel that we find it frustrating. Through Jesus, God's word 'became flesh', and through each one of us it should become flesh again! We are not called simply to preach the good news but to be the good news. It's no good talking about good news when you are bad news. Today our daily programme is often so busy that we do not have time to spend on people. We can easily reach the point where we see them as an intrusion, robbing us of our valuable time. The youth leader must be available.

6

SETTING SAIL

How to plan your church's youth programme

Of all the teenagers who go to church in Great Britain at the age of fourteen, 71% have stopped by the time they reach their twentieth birthday. That is the claim made by Dr Leslie Francis as the result of a survey made across the denominations by the British Council of Churches.[1]

But such findings can come as no real shock to those actively involved in ongoing youth work. Recently I spoke to a Baptist minister who commented on the fact that of the twenty young people who professed Christianity and were baptized by him three years ago, only two now remained in the youth group, and one of these had just married a non-Christian!

So why can't we keep our young people? Or, to put the question more creatively, how can we build into our church life an effective strategy for youth work that will not only see young people won for Christ but also bring about their development into Christian maturity?

The road to nowhere

Many youth groups never achieve much because they are not sure what it is they are trying to do. It is just not good enough for us to hold out the vague hope that teenagers will be converted and then grow to be 'good church members'. If we have an aim it must be carefully looked at and a plan of action drawn up. If you set out on a journey not knowing how you are going to travel, or exactly where your destination is, you'll probably never arrive! In the same way there is a need for careful planning of every aspect of the life of your group together with the development of an overall strategy for its growth and witness.

First things first

From the most forward-looking churches with all the latest ideas and facilities at their disposal, through to those where youth work consists of a strict diet of Bible Study supplemented only by rather sparse helpings of table tennis; from the small fellowship struggling to cope with a handful of difficult teenagers, without adequate leadership; through to the biggest churches with several full-time workers, the first and foremost principle in Christian youth work is one that's as old as the church itself! It has nothing to do with the trappings of modern high-tech evangelism, sophisticated structures of youth leadership and grand youth programmes. It can be summed up in one word: *example*.

It is example, love and genuine Christian commitment evident in the lives of the leaders that makes the difference between a group in which new Christians are regularly born and nurtured into maturity and those which only seem to produce a superficial attachment which melts away with the passing of years (in some cases even months!). This is not to say that love always produces the desired result. It would be naive to believe this. Jesus spoke about this problem in the parable of the sower, pointing out that sometimes God's word is not allowed to grow into maturity within a person's life (Mk 4:19). He warned that many would fall away, unable ultimately to take up their cross and follow him. Love can be rejected. By its very nature it has to give that freedom to those it cares for.

Christians or church 'groupies'?

This emphasis on example is not in any way to downgrade detailed planning (which the rest of this chapter looks at closely) or the use of all the resources available. It simply means that without the leader's depth of commitment to Christ (rather than to the church), such things will not produce strong Christians, only church 'groupies' who hang on because they are fascinated by one new idea or gimmick after the other. If we are not careful we simply build a youth group hungry for sensation, for a visit of the latest Christian rock group or most popular Christian speaker. Large numbers can sometimes hide a constantly changing clientele. In these groups, though the size of the overall group is maintained, youngsters simply come in excited for a month or two and then drift away again, only to be replaced by somebody else. When the gimmicks run out, so do the people. Paul said, 'Follow my example, as I follow the example of Christ' (1 Cor 11:1)—and that must be the goal of each youth worker. To quote Lawrence Richards, 'The youth leader is not primarily a talker or organiser. He is a model, a person who by the power of his Christian example motivates dedication to Jesus Christ.'[2]

Mark Ashton states:

> The key to effective Christian youth work is people—people in whose lives Christ is alive, and who will open themselves to young people, not to talk down to them, nor to dominate them with attractive and charismatic personalities, but to show them how to love one another as Christ commanded us. 'Personal work' is fundamental to youth work. We have to build personal relationships. We have to maximize opportunities for life-to-life discipling, where we can live alongside young people and they can absorb the Christian faith from the atmosphere around them.[3]

Working together—the Youth Council

In many smaller churches the youth leader is working entirely alone—if this is the case with you, skip on to the next section and save this one for the future!

A church's youth work will flourish best when there is an overall co-ordinating group of leaders who represent the whole spectrum of what's going on within the fellowship, right through from the Bible study to the uniformed organizations, from the young people's fellowship to the Saturday Night Club, the drama group and the football team. This group should meet for discussion and prayer once every month, avoiding the temptation to do so less frequently. It is probably good to have a church leader such as an elder or a deacon sitting on the Youth 'Council' or 'Committee' to ensure that there is good understanding and liaison with the rest of the church. Too many youth groups have suffered from a breakdown of communication between themselves and the rest of the church or at least its leadership. This leader may act as chairman of the group.

The Youth Council's task is to:

(1) Develop an overall strategy for the work, ensuring that the different youth activities in the church complement one another and are working towards the same goals without producing conflict in the lives of the young people themselves. In this way practical acknowledgement is given to the fact that the individual young person is not the property of any one of the youth movements within the church.

(2) Ensure that individual young people do not slip between groups without proper pastoral care and backup.

(3) Keep a diary into which all special youth events must be entered at a monthly meeting before they become a fixed part of the programme. Conflicts may otherwise arise with regard to use of time, too many commitments on too many nights of the week, as well as direct clashes in dates requiring young people to be in two places at once! In my experience of youth work around the country, this practical step would save a lot of unnecessary tension and bad feeling between leaders of different aspects of the church's youth work.

(4) Build a sense of trust and fellowship between the various youth activities of the church. You cannot really work harmoniously with someone you don't know well and don't spend time with. The meeting gives the leaders an opportunity to get to know one another and develop the relationships on which all effective work must be based.

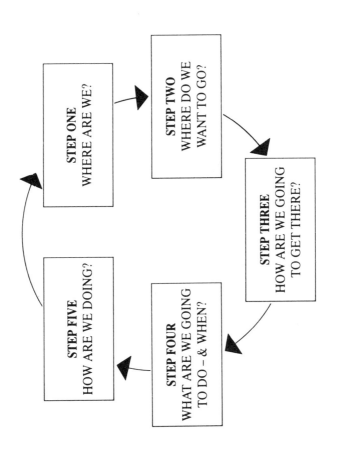

Five steps to developing an effective youth programme

At least once a year the Youth Council (and, on a separate occasion, the leaders of each youth activity) should set aside some time, preferably a whole day, when they can retreat together to pray and think over the work for which they are responsible. The group should spend its time looking at the following steps:

Step one: Where are we?—a diagnostic examination

Take a good hard look at the strengths, weaknesses and needs of your youth work. Do you have any basic aims? Are they being met? In this way a realistic picture is built up of the present state of your group.

Step two: Where do we want to go? Setting long-term goals

In the light of the evidence you have collated, discuss your priorities, setting some long-term goals. Such goals could for instance be to see:

(a) more conversions;

(b) new members added to the group (perhaps—more specifically—doubled in size);

(c) more intergration between the different youth groups in the church;

(d) more integration with other age groups within the church;

(e) more development of leadership gifts and qualities amongst the young people;

(f) a greater depth of commitment to mission and evangelism.

It is possible to tackle too much all at once and, therefore, achieve nothing, so write your goals down in order of priority and concentrate on the top three.

Step three: How are we going to get there? Setting short-term objectives

Having set your overall goals and put them in order of priority, you should set about establishing short-term objectives which are designed to answer the question, 'How do we get from where we are to where we want to be?' Objectives are the practical steps that can be taken towards progressively achieving your long-term goals.

For instance, if one of your goals was the development of leadership gifts and qualities amongst the young people, you could write down a set of objectives such as:

(a) identify those young people with leadership qualities;

(b) select from this list a small group who would most benefit from leadership training at the moment;

(c) make these young people aware of their leadership potential;

(d) set up a relevant youth leadership training course for those concerned;

(e) encourage these young people by beginning to hand over authority to them. This involves allowing them to make mistakes without heavily criticizing them as a result;

(f) set up a mechanism whereby progress can be monitored, lessons learned, and gifts encouraged further rather than be squashed by negative comment.

Step four: What are we going to do—and when? Implementing decisions

Your short-term objectives should now be timetabled and acted upon. For example:

(a) *Within a month* we will draw up a list of those young people that we believe have leadership gifts.

(b) *At next month's* Youth Council meeting we will discuss this list and select a small group to be approached for a training course.

(c) *In two months' time* we aim to have spoken to all of these about the potential we believe they have, and have called them together for an initial meeting.

(d) *In three months' time* we aim to have set up and started a twelve week leadership development course.

(e) *Within four months* we aim to be giving those on the course practical opportunities for expressing their gifts, for example by handing over the leadership of worship or of some teaching. We will include a 'talk back' feature in subsequent meetings to look at the lessons being learned by course members.

(f) *By this time next year* we aim to have moved beyond the training stage to a situation where some of these we now recognize as having leadership potential are actually fulfilling that role within the life of our church.

FIG 6:2

Time Scale	Goals
1 Month	Draw up up list of potential leaders
2 Months	Hold initial meeting to explain your aim
3 Months	Have leadership course running
4 Months	Create practical opportunities for gaining experience
1 Year	See members of course in leadership roles

Step five: How are we doing? Assessing progress

This important step is often ignored. You should continually evaluate the effectiveness of the methods you have been using and the goals that you have been pursuing.

Because short-term objectives have been set it is easier to monitor your progress towards the overall goal as well as recognize weaknesses and compensate for them. If you acknowledge that you have not achieved some of your short-term objectives or have fallen behind on them, you can reassess the situation and draw up a revised timetable or strategy. This will lead right back into step one, and so round the circle.

The value of our goals and objectives

When these five steps are followed your youth work is given clear direction, enabling you to chart where you are going and the steps you need to take to get there.

Setting goals and objectives helps us to escape the verbal fog of phrases such as 'our purpose is to give glory to God' or 'to have an effective youth work' or 'to win our town for Christ'! These sound spiritual but they are actually meaningless. They are too vague to give clear direction and simply enable us to evade the real questions we should be answering. Before they mean anything they must be unpacked: 'What do we really mean?' 'What specific objectives can we set down which will result in their being achieved?' 'What practical things can we do and plan over the next year/years which will help us to realize this goal?'

There are two main reasons why people tend to back away from setting goals and objectives in their area of work:

(1) Fear of failure

You may be afraid that you will not be able to achieve your goals and so be left with a massive sense of failure. For instance, it's easy to talk about 'winning the town for Christ' but less comfortable to translate that into real terms and set a target of doubling the size of the church in two years! But having clear objectives is not a case of setting cruel task masters but simply of putting down helpful pointers that will assist you in achieving your task. They are there to guide you, not to dictate to you. If an objective is not reached, sit down and reassess the situation by asking the question, 'Why have we failed to reach our target?' Once the cause or causes (there may well be a combination of them) have been identified, set new targets in the light of your findings. Don't feel that you have failed, for if the objective had not been set in the first place you would not now be in this positive position.

(2) The feeling that planning is not spiritual

Another reason why some Christians find it difficult to set short-term objectives is the feeling that it's rather unspiritual because such methods are borrowed from the secular world of management! Surely it's not right for God's people to rely on 'worldly' methods when his Spirit should be our real guide and strength? We should be putting our confidence and trust in God rather than twentieth century management techniques.

To take this view is to misunderstand the real situation, for several reasons:

(a) Perhaps the terminology is new but modern management techniques are simply a way of restating good old common sense principles.

(b) Are we to distrust everything that is not explicitly Christian? Are we not to make use of television, radio, video, telephone, banking and accounting techniques? It is naive to reject all thinking because it is not specifically Christian. We appreciate art that was not created by Christians and in the same way we should appreciate good, clear thinking which enables us to be effective in God's service.

(c) It is not a case of either/or. Our confidence should be firmly placed in God, recognizing that we are totally reliant on him. Good planning simply enables us to provide him with the best that we can offer as a vehicle which he can use. God had a very definite plan and purpose in bringing Jesus into the world. He came as the Word made flesh (John 1:14) to die so that 'whoever believes in him shall not perish but have eternal life' (John 3:16). In Ephesians 1, Paul tells us about God's plan for his people which was established 'before the creation of the world' (v 4). Jesus himself was aware of God's timing and plan within his ministry. On several occasions in John's Gospel he states that his 'time has not yet come' (2:4, see also 7:6, 7:8, 8:20 etc) but in 17:1 he prays, 'Father, the time has come. Glorify your Son.' In the same way we know that Paul had a very definite plan for the evangelization of the Gentiles and that his ultimate goal was to preach the gospel in Rome (see Rom 1:13).

Far from destroying our faith, setting goals and objectives should actually help it to flourish. It may be difficult to believe that your whole town is going to be won to Christ, but if a target is set of increasing youth group membership by 50% over the next two years, and this happens, it then provides a visible illustration that God is at work. As a result, the group is enthused to believe and pray for more success. Objectives are simply statements of faith (see Philippians 3:13-14). We believe that this is what God wants us to do and we trust him to achieve his will through us.

Setting clear goals and objectives also helps you to give your time to those things which are important rather than simply urgent. The way you spend your time should be dictated by the important not the immediate, and this will only happen when, through the process described above, you have determined your priorities.

Having well-defined goals and objectives also helps to build a strong team sense. Without targets to reach it is impossible for there to be a real sense of oneness and belonging. I have spoken to many a minister who feels that the church in which he serves is not giving enough financially or shows little commitment in terms of human resources such as time and talent. Almost without exception, this is simply because the members do not feel a sense of oneness and purpose. They are either unaware of or uninspired by the set of objectives and goals that have been decided upon by the leadership.

Planning a weekly programme

Many youth leaders suffer from the 'Help! . . . What can I do this week?' syndrome so that instead of enjoying their work it is full of stress, strain and the kind of anxious feeling that develops in the pit of the stomach when you know you're up against a deadline and you don't have any ideas! Actually there is absolutely no reason why any youth leader should ever be in this position because as a result of working through steps one to five, a programme can be planned well in advance.

Your group's weekly programme should be planned at least one school term ahead to enable you (or someone else) to book visiting speakers, relevant videos etc. Each element of the programme should be chosen because it contributes to the objectives that have been set and therefore fits the term's overall theme, rather than just because it sounds exciting! The impact of such elements is halved if your programme is simply a collection of individual evenings with no direction.

There is no shortage of resources available to help you in planning and for use in your programme. Make yourself aware of these by writing to Scripture Union, Scripture Press and other such groups (addresses are given at the back of this book) and have a long chat to your local Christian Book Centre manager.

Teaching about the Christian life and discipleship will never produce a mature Christian unless it includes the opportunity of involvement. If you are teaching about evangelism your youth group must be allowed to evangelize. If they have talked about sharing their faith with others you should provide the setting which enables them to do just that, perhaps for the first time. Remember your programme must never be sterile, divorced from practice. Biblical teaching must incorporate a healthy emphasis on doing. The second section of this book deals with practical ways in which this can be done.

SECTION

TWO

7

TAKING AIM

General rules for planning a project

Take one

'We're really sorry that more people didn't come; we certainly tried our best . . . I personally wrote to over thirty churches . . . but it was a wonderful evening and I'm sure it has proved most beneficial in the lives of those that were present.'

How many times each week is this kind of comment heard on the lips of the organizer of one type of Christian event or the other?

Take two

The visiting group and evangelist arrive for a week's schools mission only to find that very little has been organized for them to do. In the case of the few opportunities that do materialize, teachers are badly informed about who they are and what is going to happen. At the end of the week the organizers can only afford to give them 'a little something towards' their expenses, though they wish it could have been more.

Take three

A disillusioned youth leader wearily makes his way up to the speaker or singer at the end of a 'disappointing' evangelistic evening with a washed-out look all over his face which says more than mere words ever could. Though the hall was full, there was little or no response to the appeal.

Stop and think

In each of these cases what was lacking was good planning and clear thinking. The result is that either the organizer, or those taking part, or both are left disillusioned and dejected. For instance in 'Take Three' what the leader had not realized was that the performer was well known to at least 95% of the audience who had travelled from churches throughout the district to be present because the event had been advertised in the Christian press. (You may have Billy Graham on your stage with support from Luis Palau, having specially flown them both in from America, but if you don't have any 'fish in the pond', even the world's greatest fishermen will be unsuccessful in their attempts to fill the nets!) After the event many an organizer is left asking the question, 'Was it really worth it all?' and some even ultimately end up blaming God for his apparent failure to honour the hard work that has been done in his name. On the other hand, there are performers and speakers who have grown embittered because of the sense of being let down, used, and abused time after time. I have known several organizers and performers who have grown so negative in their attitude that they have finally withdrawn from any real involvement of this kind altogether. However, with thought and good preparation things can be very different.

Setting your sights

Below are several questions which should be answered when you first set out to plan any kind of event or project. They are outlined here, but should be regarded as an integral part of each of the following chapters. At first they may appear to be in a rather strange order, for they ask that you decide both your aim and target group before deciding what the actual event should be. So often things tend to happen the other way round: we decide to have a concert and only then try and come up with a reason for it. No project should ever be undertaken for the sake of it, or simply because it's a good idea. Strong Christian youth work is the result of having a good clear strategy that uses its resources carefully and therefore powerfully. Each project you run should contribute towards achieving the goals and aims that your youth group has set itself. Therefore the projects outlined here, in section two of this book, will always have the greatest impact when they are planned as the result of developing the kind of strategy that is explained in section one. Remember, activity is not the same thing as direction.

(1) What is your aim?

Whether organizing a youth service or town wide mission, it is essential to be able to state your aim clearly and simply. It is a good exercise to get out a piece of paper and then jot down ideas until you reach the point where in one phrase or sentence you can sum up what the proposed project is designed to achieve. Sometimes organizers will say, 'Our project is far too complex to be described in this superficial kind of way,' but actually however broad the aim it should be possible to focus and summarize it in a few words. If we are not careful we can simply end up making excuses for muddled and woolly thinking. So first decide whether your project is designed for:

(a) Evangelism

(b) Pre-evangelism

(c) Ministry to Christians

(d) Worship

(e) Entertainment/fellowship

(f) Other

In fact often the proposed project will cover a combination of any or even all of these areas but will still have a particular emphasis in one direction or the other.

(2) What is your target group?

Firstly, what age group are you aiming at?

(a) Younger teens

(b) Older teens

(c) A combination of (a) and (b)

(d) Older teens and twenties

(e) An event run by youth but aimed at an older age group

Secondly, what is the spiritual status of your target group?

(a) All Christians

(b) All non-Christians (are they churched or non-churched?)

(c) A mixed audience (what percentages?)

Thirdly, where will your target group be drawn from?

(a) One school

(b) Several schools

(c) One area of the town, townwide, further afield

(d) A local church or churches

(e) Some other contact point

Finally are there any other distinctive characteristics about the target group?

You may feel that some of these details are laborious and unnecessary. In fact, they are very important because they help you pinpoint your purpose and therefore plan the most effective project possible from every point of view. For instance, the effect of your publicity will be maximized if prepared carefully in the light of these questions.

(3) What kind of project do you need?

Only after the first two questions have been answered are you in the best position to deal with this one. As stated earlier, someone may have the bright idea of running a huge concert starring one of the better known Christian bands or of inviting their favourite speaker into the town for one night or even a whole week. Or the church may suddenly decide it is about time they had a mission and did some evangelism. The problem in each of these cases is that the motivation may well be nothing more than the desire to run an event. If we are honest, one of the chief reasons for a lot of Christian activity is that it makes us feel good. So first decide on your aim and target.

In reality, this whole process may take place in the mind of a good youth leader almost at a subconscious level. He spends a lot of time thinking over issues relating to the group and then suddenly has the idea of running a particular project. In these cases it is still necessary to go back and answer questions one and two at a conscious level, checking that you really have faced all the important issues.

Having made these three fundamental decisions, you are now in a position to move on to the detailed planning of your event. The specific issues that you will need to deal with are outlined in the following chapters, but here we will briefly look at one last universal problem . . . money.

Finance—working out a budget

As soon as you have decided what you want to do, it is essential that you sit down and answer these two questions:

(1) How much money do you have to spend and where will it be generated from?

(2) What are the costs that you face?

To answer these effectively it is important to draw up a projected budget. This should include all expenses, under such headings as:

(a) Administration

(b) Publicity

(c) The hire of a venue

(d) Artist's and speaker's expenses, fees and gifts

(e) Hire of equipment

(f) Follow up material

(g) Hospitality for visitors

(h) Refreshments

Then your income should be projected under the headings:

(a) Ticket or programme money

(b) Sale of refreshments, books, records etc

(c) Church and other support

(d) Gifts and donations

(e) Other income

So many projects fail simply because this kind of planning is never done. 'We'll just muddle through', is an attitude which is not only dishonouring to God, but also to all others involved, especially those who are financially reliant on you (professional groups or speakers etc). Make sure your project is different!

How long does it take to organize an event?

Any event worth putting on will take a significant amount of time to organize. It has been said that the minimum amount of time for something which is located in your church building should be three months, that something in an independent venue within your community should be six months and anything bigger, for instance town wide, should be at least one year. Though this is a good general rule, in my experience some of the events and projects that have been most valuable have only taken place at short notice, but of course, in these cases the need for effective planning is even more necessary.

Each of the following chapters represents a project that I have personally been involved in planning and organizing at a local level. They also reflect experience that I have been able to build up as I have travelled around the country working with other churches at 'the performing end' of things. Each chapter will examine the particular questions that need to be faced when organizing the kind of project outlined as well as presenting (where relevant) a step by step check list for you to work through.

8

THE YOUTH SERVICE

After three hours we remember 70% of what we hear but after three days only 10%; and we remember 72% of what we see after three hours but only 20% after three days. On the other hand, we remember 85% of what we hear and see after three hours, still retaining 65% of it after three days. But best of all, if we *do* something we remember 95% of it after three hours and 85% after three days.

Sadly, much Christian teaching takes place at a hearing level only and, therefore, it is not surprising that it often seems so ineffective. It is clear that we ought to be concentrating our teaching efforts not only on *hearing* but also on *seeing* and most importantly on *doing* to achieve the best long-term results. This is exactly what Jesus did, for besides the fact that he was often visual in his teaching methods, the disciples also had the opportunity of seeing the gospel at work and of taking on the responsibility of doing as they were sent out by him. They were actively involved in the work, which meant that Jesus' message became deeply rooted into their lives. Jesus did not ask Peter whether he could intellectually grasp the principle that he was the world's Messiah, but instead challenged him to follow him and become a fisher of men. This was action rather than talk. In the New Testament, being a Christian was something that you did.

I remember 'very tactfully' telling the minister of my home church, when I was about sixteen, what an absolutely awful job he was doing and how, in my opinion, the worship services were about as exciting as 'getting a string vest as a Christmas present'. Part of a teenager's make-up is to be idealistic and outspoken. Not only is this character trait quite natural but it is also a necessary part of growing up. Teenagers will therefore often be critical of the Sunday service. The most positive way to cope with this situation is from time to time to allow them to take part in leading and planning worship, thus giving them the opportunity to learn by doing. As they begin to understand the thinking behind public worship, they will begin to see why it is conducted in the way it is. The repeated experience of leading worship will also gradually change teenagers' understanding and concept of the role of the congregation in worship. It will help them to understand that the 'church service' is not like a double decker bus where two men, the driver and conductor, seem to do everything while everybody else sits watching, but that the congregation's preparation for worship and participation in it is very important.

How do you run a youth service?

First things first

You should first go to the minister, vicar, elder or other church leader(s) to explain your idea and the thinking behind it. You should ask whether it would be possible for the young people to lead a service, perhaps on a regular basis every two or three months, so that they can begin to understand a little more of what worship is about.

Brainstorming

Having obtained the permission of the church leaders to lead a youth service, sit down with the young people themselves and explain the privilege that has been given to them. Then ask for their ideas on what the content of the service should be. This will often result in a great deal of discussion. Already issues relating to worship are being unearthed and examined. Make sure you record all the ideas and suggestions that are made.

Group planning

Now appoint a small group (or committee) to do the detailed planning and to look at the suggestions that the other young people have made. They must decide whether the service is to be of an evangelistic or teaching nature and if it is to be aimed especially at young people, children or the whole family of the church. (If it is to be evangelistic, it is a good idea to think about the possibility of linking it with another event such as a concert the night before.) Then a theme for the service must be chosen. Having made these decisions, look together at the elements that make up a worship service, taking into account all the suggestions of the larger group. Explain to the planning group exactly why public worship has these elements, making sure you are open to their suggestions rather than just forcing your will on the group and decide on what elements you are going to put into the service. You will probably want to include:

Hymns
Worship songs
Songs (performed)
Prayers (open or led)
Interviews (testimonies)
Drama/Mime/Dance
Offering
Sermon
Communion
Other elements

Explain that the material for the service needs to be chosen with two principles in mind: (See Rom 14 and 1 Cor 8).

(a) Is this honouring to God?

(b) Does this help or hinder the faith of others? Certain elements may be honouring to God but, because of existing prejudices or fear, may not be conducive to harmonious relationships within your fellowship.

Sharing responsibility

Now appoint group members to be responsible for the different elements which will make up the service. Firstly you need somebody to co-ordinate the whole thing and lead the worship. A good idea is to draw together a worship band for the youth group if this is possible, and appoint a co-ordinator/ leader. The same can be done with drama, mime and dance.

You may feel that it is right to invite an outside speaker to come in to preach. Many good youth speakers are booked well in advance, so plan well ahead. If you are having an outside speaker, who will pay his expenses? Will it be the youth group, or does the church see this as their responsibility?

Music and drama

If a music or drama group are taking part in leading worship they must be thoroughly rehearsed and of a good standard. Worship is not a performance but this is no reason for lack of preparation.

If you are forming a worship band for the occasion make sure they are not too loud! It is particularly important that the members of the band understand that they are not there to 'do' the worship but rather to lead others into worship (which is impossible if their volume distracts and even deafens the congregation!).

Drama is often rehearsed in the church hall but it needs to be run through in the main auditorium. Is there a balcony? If there is, can what is being performed down at the front be seen? Perhaps the balcony could be closed for the service?

A dress rehearsal

On the day of the service it's good to call together all those taking part in leading the service for a last minute run. This will help them feel more relaxed later on. There are those who labour the point that worship should be Spirit led and not 'engineered' in this kind of way, but to see careful preparation as necessarily blocking God's Spirit from working is misguided.

9

YOUTH CAMPS, CONFERENCES AND HOUSEPARTIES

Fruit picking on the Saturday afternoon, an evening barbeque and learning what the Bible had to say about boy/girlfriend relationships (which was very exciting though unfortunately rather theoretical because Mary Hooper had just refused to go out with me!). Those are some of the memories of my first ever youth weekend spent at Ashburnham Place, near Bexhill in Sussex, at the age of thirteen.

In this chapter we will look specifically at a weekend conference, although the principles discussed can also easily be applied to longer camps and houseparties.

The value of the youth weekend/conference

A youth weekend provides a great opportunity for working with teenagers because:

(1) Within this context there may be up to six teaching sessions as well as numerous other workshops and discussion groups, besides all the informal chat that such circumstances allow. This amount of input is probably more than you would get from several months of Sunday meetings and services.

(2) The teaching can be made far more relevant to the teenagers' particular needs than it ever could be in the context of a Sunday service. Rather than having to relate generally

to all age groups it can be directly geared to their view of home, school and the world. It can also deal with questions which would be totally inappropriate in the presence of older church members.

(3) It enables the leaders of a group to get to know their young people at a much deeper level as they see them at close quarters, thus developing a deeper understanding of their personalities and relationship to God.

(4) Within the atmosphere of a weekend spent together, friendships can be more closely developed both amongst the teenagers themselves and with the leaders. Somehow the leaders seem to be more human and approachable than before! It is often in the informal chat over coffee or last thing at night that some of the most valuable work of developing relationships is done.

(5) Often, an honesty develops that is not found in other settings. As the weekend progresses and the group gradually begins to feel relaxed and secure, barriers fall, real questions are asked and a degree of participation that is not normally possible results. I have been on weekends where even those who have appeared the hardest and most insular at the beginning of our time together have opened up by the end of the conference and wanted to talk—often more than others.

At home or away

The first decision you have to make is whether this weekend conference is going to be at home (held within the buildings of your local church) or a getaway weekend, at a conference centre or other venue.

The main advantages of staying at home are:

(1) The budget price. It's much cheaper because you don't have to pay for a centre or for travel. The youth group simply turn up at the church building on Friday evening with their camp beds and sleeping bags and you are in

business!

(2) Those young people with Saturday jobs or other commitments can still benefit from at least some of the teaching and activity of the weekend rather than feeling excluded and left behind altogether.

On the other hand the advantages of going away are:

(1) Going away for a weekend often serves to knit the group together in a much more powerful way.

(2) Because you are away from home there are not so many distractions. If you stay at home your young people are given the opportunity to attend the sessions during the day but find excuses to opt out during the evening to go to a friend's party etc. (Warning, such toing and froing can also occur when a weekend is held at a conference centre only a few miles from home.)

Staying at home

(1) Sleeping accommodation

Is there adequate room for sleeping the number of young people that you are expecting? The dormitory accommodation for the two sexes should be well separated. This is important not only from the point of view of standards amongst the young people themselves, but because of exaggerated stories that are otherwise bound to get back to parents and others in the community.

(2) Cooking facilities

Are the cooking facilities good enough and, of course, who will do the cooking? Perhaps some of the ladies within the church can be persuaded to help out in this way?

Going away

If you are going away, decisions must be made as to where you will stay:

(1) A church building

Many churches allow their buildings to be used from time to time for youth conferences. This is especially true of churches with larger premises and those that are situated on the coast or in other picturesque parts of the country. Again, questions regarding cooking and sleeping arrangements need to be carefully looked at. The chief benefit of this option is that whilst getting the young people away from home it is much cheaper than going to a conference centre. Many of the churches that are used more regularly in this way will have a standard charge for the use of their premises but if not, the question of finance needs to be dealt with early.

(2) A conference centre

This is moving slightly up market and therefore is going to cost that bit more, although there is a considerable variation in price and facilities offered. Certain major factors should be immediately considered:

(a) How much will the weekend cost per head? Remember to add on your travelling costs.

(b) How many people does the centre take?

(c) What kind of sleeping accommodation is available? This may be dormitory, bunk beds or single and double rooms. Do you have to take sleeping bags or is bedding available?

(d) Is the weekend self-catering or are meals included in the price?

Conference centre names and addresses can be obtained through the Christian press or from Dovetail Trust.

(3) Camping

During the summer months a camping weekend under canvas is a possibility. Some conference centres run camp sites which are set up permanently throughout the summer months. Another option is to use a farmer's field and set up your own camp, with the young people taking along their own two or three sleeper tents and using a barn or marquee for meals and teaching sessions and for the main meetings.

If you camp on a site which offers no facilities you will need to provide:

(a) Tents
(b) Toilets
(c) A marquee for meetings and eating
(d) A cooking area and equipment
(e) Lighting equipment
(f) Tables and chairs
(g) A team to erect this equipment!

Two questions

It is important to work carefully through the questions raised in the first chapter of this section, by which time you should know the answers to the following two questions:

(1) Is the weekend basically for Christians or non-Christians?

Are you working with young people on the fringe of the church or perhaps from a school Christian Union or other setting who either know very little about Christianity, or who have some understanding of the faith but have never made any real commitment to Christ themselves? On the other hand, is the weekend basically of a teaching nature, aiming to encourage and challenge those who are already Christians? It may be that the weekend is a combination of these two aims.

(2) Is there a particular age range (within the youth group) that you are aiming at?

If you are aiming at a specific age group, how are you going to ensure that they are the ones that have the first opportunity of taking up the invitation to be present? (Many centres only take thirty or forty young people and if you fill your places up on a first come first served basis, you may discover that you've missed out almost altogether on the people that the event was originally planned for.)

Theme

A youth weekend presents you with the opportunity to examine how Christian faith relates to the world in which teenagers live and work with a frankness and honesty that could not be expressed quite as openly in the context of a church service or even perhaps a weekly youth meeting. To make the most of this, it is important to choose the right theme carefully. There are a number of ways of approaching a subject:

(1) To study a book of the Bible.

(2) To look at a particular biblical personality.

(3) To take a contemporary subject such as 'Understanding culture', 'Relationships' or 'Communicating your faith in today's world' etc.

The important thing is that the teaching given is made practical and relevant as it is continually applied by the speaker or speakers to everyday life.

You may feel that you want to approach a speaker first and then talk with him about his choice of subject for the weekend and the use of time. On the other hand, you may feel that you want to choose a subject that is especially pertinent to your youth group and ask him to address it.

Personnel

To make life easier for yourself, build up a team with whom you can share the workload. This team should meet together several times during the planning stage of your weekend, the first occasion being as soon as possible after the idea is initially agreed upon.

You need to appoint:

(1) An administrator—to hold the various elements of the planning together.

(2) A treasurer—to sign the cheques!

(3) A programme organiser—to work out the timetable for the

weekend (see below.)

(4) A speaker—it is obviously most important to choose the right speaker(s). If you do not personally know of people who can help you it is best to contact an organization such as British Youth For Christ or Scripture Union who have many workers and associates especially gifted in this kind of work amongst teenagers. The Christian press is also a good resource for spotting the names of potential speakers. The well trained youth leader is always on the look out for possible speakers as well as other resources for future use. A good idea is to keep a notebook in which ideas, names of speakers, addresses etc can be recorded.

(5) A cook—who will probably want to appoint several assistants. (Only applicable if self-catering.)

(6) A front man—the figurehead for the weekend, who is seen to hold the whole thing together, make announcements, lead worship etc (although others may be involved in these responsibilities).

Timetable

Below is outlined a typical timetable for a getaway weekend. This, of course, can be adapted in any way that is desired.

Friday Evening
    8.00 – arrive
    8.15 – evening meal
    9.00 – introductory session (consisting of worship, meet the speaker, introduction to the theme of the weekend)
  11.00 – bed

Saturday Morning
    8.00 – rise
    8.30 – breakfast
    9.15 – a time of quiet (giving the opportunity to spend time alone if they choose to!)

    10.00 – session one (consisting of worship, teaching, activity
         groups)
    11.00 – coffee
    11.30 – session two
    12.30 – discussion groups
    1.00 – lunch

Afternoon—free for sporting activities, ramble, outing to local
ten pin bowling centre, etc.

    5.30 – evening meal
    6.30 – session three
    8.00 – concert/talent show/barbeque etc
    10.00 – late night extra (a chance to put questions to the
         speaker? A late night ramble?)
    11.00 – bed

Sunday

    8.00 – rise
    8.30 – breakfast
    9.15 – time of quiet
    10.00 – session four
    12.00 – free time
    1.00 – lunch
    2.30 – session five (and communion?)
    4.30 – tea
    5.30 – depart for home—(sometimes the group will travel
         back for the evening service in their own home
         church where the visiting preacher will speak. This
         will form the last official session of the weekend.)

If the weekend getaway is planned over a bank holiday then,
obviously, an extra day is available!

If this timetable is expanded out into a week long programme
the teaching sessions will probably take place in the morning
and evening with afternoons left free each day.

Travelling

In the case of a getaway weekend the decision has to be made whether to travel by:

(1) Coach

(2) A fleet of cars belonging to older members of the youth group, youth leaders and perhaps one or two kindly church members or the dads of young people. In many situations (depending on how far away from home you are going) this works out to be a far cheaper method of travel (especially if the driver's don't claim for their petrol!) and also has the advantage of leaving some transport with those on the youth weekend for use in emergency or for any visits off the site.

Finance

The finances need to be dealt with at an early stage, as outlined in the first chapter of this section of the book. In this particular case the major items that need to be budgeted for are:

(1) The cost of the centre or other accommodation

(2) Speaker's fee and travelling expenses

(3) Food (if the weekend is to be self-catering)

(4) Transport costs

(5) Any outing that may take place on the Saturday afternoon or other times (such as bowling or ice skating)

(6) Publicity—brochures and programmes

The cost of the centre will obviously account for a large part of the budget and needs to be looked at carefully. Many centres issue a contract which quite fairly states that if you pull out of the weekend within a given time period you are liable to pay a percentage of the booking fee. Many of these schemes work on a sliding scale so that as the proposed date comes nearer the cancellation fee you are liable to pay rises. With some larger centres (accommodating more than one group at a time) you book a certain number of beds and are under obligation to pay for them all, even if in the event you do not use them all. Obviously, such factors considerably affect whether or not you break even on your weekend, so clear and careful thought is necessary.

To set a realistic cost for each teenager attending you should simply add up your total expenditure, calculate the number of young people you are expecting, take 75% of that figure and divide your overall budget by the result. You then have the real cost of a place on your weekend. If more than 75% of those you are optimistically expecting to attend actually come, you will have an operating surplus which can be ploughed back into your work for another project. Alternatively, you may have the backing and support of your church who will either subsidize each place or agree to underwrite the whole weekend so that you are able to budget on 100% attendance of the number you estimate and, therefore, keep the cost of the weekend for each young person down to an absolute minimum.

Booking forms

Between six and four months before the event you should produce a booking form which gives some information about the weekend for your young people to take home to their parents. Such a form should include a few details about the accommodation, the theme, the speaker and other activities. It must carry the dates, the cost and a tear-off booking slip to be returned by a given date. This should ask the young person to fill in his name, address and age. It must also be signed by one of the parents of those under the age of eighteen (this not only ensures that the parents have been informed, but that they have seen the leaflet and have given their consent to their teenager spending a weekend away under your care—big responsibility!). It is a good idea to ask for a deposit with each completed booking form. This helps prevent a situation where a weekend is a 'sell out' at the stage when the booking forms are returned, only to have a lot of people drop out, so that few of the provisional bookings eventually result in attendance. All this does is block up the system and stop others going who would like to go.

Brochure

Once you know who is going to be on the weekend, prepare a brochure that will be issued to each young person about a month before the weekend takes place. This should give more details of the venue, who the speaker is, and what the programme contains, including all the leisure time activities available. It should also explain what the young people need to bring, for instance, waterproof shoes and coat, and at least two pairs of jeans (in case one gets soaked!). It should list everything that the young people are likely to leave at home if not reminded, including a Bible, note book and pen, guitars, other instruments and bedding (if necessary). Forms should also be available for parents to sign giving their young people permission for swimming, boating, rock climbing or other activities that include an element of danger.

A lock-in

A lock-in is actually a variation on the theme of a youth weekend. The young people arrive on the church premises at about 7.30 or 8.00 pm on a Friday evening prepared to stay for the night. After everybody has arrived the doors are locked, hence the expression 'lock-in'. The programme of activities is arranged to run right through the night, the event ending with breakfast the next morning, after which everybody creeps home to bed for the rest of the day! The lock-in should have a varied programme consisting of films on video (anything from *Superman* to *Born Again*), short teaching sessions, worship sessions and occasional drinks and light snacks. A feature that proved very successful in Tonbridge was roller skating. So was born the 'Roller Lock-In'. It's possible to hire sets of roller skates from secular companies at reasonable rates (so long as you discover the size of your young people's feet beforehand).

That particular programme ran something like this:-

    7.30 – arrive and register
    8.00 – first roller skate session
    9.00 – first teaching and worship session
    9.45 – supper
    10.30 – second roller skating session
    11.00 – second teaching session
    12.00 – film: *Superman*
    2.00 – roller skating session
    2.45 – short teaching session with singing
    3.15 – roller skating session
    4.00 – film: *Born Again*
    5.00 – a snack
    5.15 – roller skating session
    6.15 – cartoon time
    7.15 – final roller skating session
    8.00 – worship session and breakfast
    9.00 – home to bed!

I know that to most youth leaders this must sound an absolutely horrendous way to spend an evening. To put their minds at rest, I can assure them it is! But it's also great fun if you are young and can spend the next day in bed, and it increases the sense of unity and belonging that young people have.

A lock-out

A variation on the theme of a lock-in is a lock-out. Again, the young people arrive at the church building to be picked up by coach and travel, for instance, down to the coast. This kind of activity can only be undertaken during the warmer months of the year, perhaps in the summer holidays. The coach drops the young people who spend a night on a ramble together along by the seashore, stopping for the occasional snack or drink (making sure that they are well out of earshot of any local housing!). Finally they arrive on a deserted beach in the early morning for a cooked breakfast and time of worship around a bonfire, which has previously been prepared by some of your very dedicated co-workers or one or two of the church leaders (perhaps including the minister or vicar!). After this the coach returns everybody back to the church building where once again all the young people go home and spend the rest of the day in bed!

10

A CONCERT

The hall is packed and the music is great! The audience, many of whom are not Christians, are thoroughly enjoying an exciting set from a terrific band. A number of counsellors have been trained and are standing by and a more than ample supply of follow up literature has been purchased from the local Christian bookshop. A small group of older people are praying throughout the concert. All that remains is for the band to 'deliver the goods', present the gospel and act as the human agents who will bring the sheep into the fold!

Unfortunately, this is where everything goes sadly wrong! From the organizers' point of view, the group do nothing more than make a few subjective remarks about the situations which led to the writing of their songs and the way in which they felt God was speaking to them at the time. As for the band, they wish that a preacher had been booked to speak after their set because they don't feel able to live up to what they know is expected of them. By anybody's account there is no cohesive presentation of the gospel and all concerned are left with a sense of failure and disappointment!

This is a far too common situation but one which you can easily avoid if your concert is carefully planned. For the purpose of this chapter we will concentrate on how to organize a specifically evangelistic concert although most of the principles outlined will have reference to any context.

Choosing a band

Before finally booking a band for a concert you should always ask them the following questions:

(1) How do they see their role?

Not every Christian musician considers himself to be an evangelist and the non-evangelist will feel uncomfortable in a situation where he is required to preach or, still worse, give an appeal! Many bands will always choose to work with an evangelist if given the opportunity. There are also those who see the first purpose of their work as being to encourage and build up Christians rather than working in directly evangelistic situations which their songs are not really suited to. Others would say that they are not in the business of directly confronting people and appealing to them to become Christians because their work is primarily art. They consider their work to be a creative expression of the gift God has given them and only evangelistic in the sense that because they are Christians their music reflects Christian thinking.

(2) What age group do they prefer working with?

Some artists are obviously better suited to a university or college type audience whilst others are much more at home with the local kids straight off the council estate. Check to make sure the band you are booking are happy with the situation you have planned and that their musical style is appropriate to your audience. It is important that they are doing more than looking for work and you are doing more than looking for a big name to make your event a success!

Local or national artists

The names of 'famous' Christian groups and solo performers will not mean anything to non-churched teenagers (unless you've booked Cliff Richard!). Therefore finance can often be saved by using good local bands rather than national ones. However, it may be felt that using nationally known artists will inspire the confidence of the young Christians who will therefore feel more able to bring along their non-Christian friends, or that the ministry of a particular band would be best suited to the particular situation.

Visiting artists and finance

View seriously your financial responsibilities towards those coming in to take part: 'The labourer is worthy of his hire'! Even if you are using amateur or part-time artists and speakers you should see that their travelling expenses are fully met (around twenty to twenty-five pence per mile, depending on the size of their vehicle, is currently (1986) a realistic level) and provide them with a gift in recognition of their ministry and its future development. Expenses for meals and other incidentals should also be met.

If you are employing professional Christian workers it is your responsibility not only to meet all their expenses but also to pay them generously, recognizing that they are often totally dependent on the income they receive for the work they do. Failure to act responsibly in this way can inflict great hardship on them and their families and cause considerable unhappiness and bitterness. Often a travelling worker has found himself in the unenviable position of actually subsidising Christian youth work across the country with his time and talents at the rate of perhaps hundreds of pounds per month because of their irresponsibility and/or bad budgeting!

Many artists or travelling speakers will now advise you about the realistic cost of their work per night or week. If you don't feel that you can meet this figure it is important to talk to them about the situation before they come. There are very few workers who would not be involved in a project that is well planned with a clear aim and meeting a genuine need even though there is a lack of finance to cover all their costs. It is a different situation when they feel that they have been taken for granted, not consulted and forced to subsidize badly planned events.

Things to check with the band:

(1) General

Make sure they know:

(a) Date of event
(b) Their contact's name and address
(c) The organizer's name, address, home and work telephone numbers
(d) The starting time, how long you want them to play for and the finishing time
(e) The numbers and the age group that you expect
(f) Your aim
(g) Map of venue and directions to it
(h) The nearest parking place to the stage door

(2) Equipment

Ask:

(i) Have you agreed a time of access for unloading and setting up their equiment?
(j) Are they supplying their own PA system?
(k) Are they supplying their own lighting, equipment, piano etc?
(l) Do they supply their own sound and lighting engineers?
(m) How many power sockets do they need?
(n) How big a stage area do they need?

(3) Publicity and Sales

(o) Do they have any particular publicity that you can make use of?
(p) Do they want to sell LP's, tapes, T-shirts, badges etc?

(4) Fees

(q) Do they charge a fee and can they indicate how much their expenses will be?
(r) Do they want to be paid in cash or by cheque, on the night or by post?

(5) Hospitality

(s) How many people will they be bringing with them?

(t) Do they need a meal on arrival or after the performance?
(u) How many dressing rooms will they need?
(v) Do they need overnight accommodation?
(w) How many are single, how many are married couples?

(6) Helpers

(x) How many humpers and helpers do they need?

(7) Counselling

(y) Do they know about the counselling arrangements you have made for the evening and how they fit into these?

Many bands will send you their own booking form (normally two copies—one to return and one to keep yourself) which will include many (or all) of these details, though you should never take any of them for granted. Always work through this list, checking it against their booking form in case there are additional things that you need to clarify with them. If the group or artist does not supply a booking form make sure to write to them setting out all the relevant information and asking for a confirmation of their booking in writing for your files.

Planning the evening

(1) Choosing a date

Concert dates have an uncanny knack of clashing with one another. I cannot remember the number of times that I have been to give a concert only to be warned that the audience will be much smaller than originally planned because the date clashes with another Christian event in the town. Clashing dates can only be avoided if concerts are planned well ahead and diaries checked with the surrounding churches. This, of course, is only necessary if the event is designed to cater for a townwide audience. Often a concert will be set up just for the young people from one school, college or particular area of the town, so that the fact that there is another event organized at another location in the town is of no real importance.

Remember that if the name of a well-known singer or band is

advertised around the local churches or in the Christian press
the concert hall is bound to be crammed full with Christians
who have turned out to see their heroes in action. This leaves
any non-Christians who attend and who will probably arrive a
little later with poor seats or worse still, no seats! What was
designed as an evangelistic event becomes little more than an
evening of Christian entertainment.

(2) The venue

It is often said that evangelistic concerts should always take
place on neutral territory away from church buildings. But
though it may be easier for non-churched young people to
attend a concert if it is held in their school, the local town hall
or some other familiar venue, this does not in any way remove
the problem of how to get them over the doormat of your own
buildings next time. Often a young person makes a decision to
follow Christ at a concert in a school hall but is never able to
make the transition from that environment to the local church
building or indeed even to an informal house group. It is often
right to hold a particular evangelistic event in a secular venue,
but in that case questions as to how those converted are to
make the transition to the geography of normal church life
must be carefully answered beforehand. (See chapter fourteen
on follow up.)

Check that the proposed venue is suitable for the concert:

(a) Does it have enough electrical power points? (I remember
    doing a concert not so long ago with one round pin, five
    amp socket available!)
(b) Stage area—is it big enough for the band and any drama
    that may take place?
(c) Is the hall big enough to accommodate the number of
    people expected?
(d) Does the venue provide a dressing room, counselling room,
    kitchen area and room for record and book displays?

(3) Booking a secular venue

When booking a secular venue it is very important to plan well
ahead as many concert and community halls are booked as far

as a year in advance. Besides the questions that have already been raised, the following points should be covered:

(a) Ask for a sheet explaining the terms of hire, and read them carefully. You may be required to take out a public liability insurance to comply with the regulations.

(b) Make sure you understand exactly how much the hire of the hall will cost and that you are aware of any extra costs for the use of dressing rooms etc.

(c) Check on what time it will be possible to have access before the event and until what time afterwards.

(d) Check on whether you are allowed to sell refreshments and other items (in some centres the right to sell such items is held by the management only).

(e) Make your official booking in writing, listing all your requirements and stating how much you believe this will cost. Ask for written confirmation of the booking and these other details with a statement of the hire charge.

(4) Personnel

Now find those from your church or within the youth group itself who are willing and able to carry the responsibilities listed below:

(a) Administrator
(b) Stage manager
(c) Prayer secretary
(d) Publicity man
(e) Press officer
(f) Counsellors (including a chief counsellor who may double as follow up officer)
(g) Humpers and helpers
(h) Box officer manager
(i) Lighting and PA [public address] men
(j) Stewards
(k) Hosts for overnight hospitality and accommodation (comfortable beds please!)
(l) Piano tuner

(5) Equipment

Check that you have arranged for the following list of equipment to be available:

(a) Adequate public address system—check on the group's specifications—they may well provide their own system. If you have two bands playing, will they use the same system? Who will provide this?

(b) Lighting system—as for PA—is it possible to black out the hall?

(c) Chairs

(d) Bookstall—it's possible to arrange a sale or return arrangement with most Christian bookshops.

(e) Refreshments

(f) Tables for bookstall and PA equipment

(g) Counselling cards, pens and other literature (you may find it useful to issue counsellors with badges)

Publicity

'Money spent on publicity is money well spent.' True? Well almost, so long as it's money spent on the right kind of publicity. Depending on the kind of project you are organizing, publicity will be of greater or lesser importance. Obviously, if it is an event to which you are inviting outsiders it is important to spend considerably more time and finance in this area than if you are running an internal event where the best publicity will be word of mouth. Estimates of the percentage of an overall budget that should be spent on publicity for an 'outreach' event range from 15 to 25%. What is obvious is the importance which should be attached to good publicity.

Listed below are some of the more common publicity methods that you may choose to use (though not all are applicable to every kind of event). For more information see chapter twenty-two.

Posters*	Programmes
Handbills*	Press release*
Advertisements*	Local press
Mailshots*	Local radio
Tickets*	Television

* including details of ticket sources and a telephone number for information.

Tickets

Often an entrance fee is charged to give the event 'value'. This fee may not bear any realistic relationship to the overall cost of staging an event which is subsidized through direct giving from other sources. There can be no doubt that certain audiences will show far greater respect for an event which has cost them something to get into.

If you decide to sell tickets on a realistic financial basis aiming to cover the cost of the event through their sale, the way in which their price should be calculated is as follows. Make as accurate as possible an estimate of the audience that you are expecting and work out what 60% of that figure is. Divide the projected cost of the event by that number and you have the price of your tickets. You will now break even on 60% of the audience numbers you expect. If more attend you will make a profit which can then either be ploughed back into further work or given away.

Who will attend?

In my experience one of the biggest problems is the many evangelistic concerts that are planned where, in spite of the organizers' best efforts, few or no non-Christians actually attend. In some way or other your advance preparation needs to ensure that they will be there. Often a youth group has attracted a number of non-Christians into its life and its leaders now want to use an evangelistic concert as a means of helping the newcomers make a decision about Christ. But non-Christians cannot be expected just to turn up out of the blue at a concert, so if previous contacts have not been made, the concert must be planned in conjunction with schools work or some other means of outreach. Unless a youth group are very highly motivated, few of them will bring non-Christian friends along to an evangelistic concert but when there is schools work during the week or few days leading up to a concert the result is very different, with many non-churched non-Christians being present.

Follow-up

It is essential to have good counselling on the evening and then well organized follow-up. Many concerts will produce large numbers of converts but if follow up is not well planned and thought through, the majority of those who make decisions to follow Christ will be lost. (See chapter 14 on this subject.)

11

SCHOOLS WORK

'A modern day Jekyll and Hyde', that's what one was called recently by a friend of mine. The alarming thing is that they are everywhere. Who exactly are they? Well, let's take a look at one of them.

Roger has been a Christian for about a year and has recently been learning a lot about the Bible. Last month he went on his church's youth weekend which helped him a great deal and he's now beginning to take real responsibility within the group. In fact, he took part in planning and leading a youth service just last week. The church is very pleased with his obvious spirituality and growing maturity and his mum and dad, who are both Christians, are grateful that their son has 'turned out so well'. The only problem is that outside his church and family nobody really knows that Roger is a Christian at all; in fact, quite frankly some of his school friends would be amazed. What Roger has not yet learnt to do is connect what he knows about God with the way in which he lives. He leads a double life. He is a real Doctor Jekyll and Mr Hyde.

Why do we need to do 'schools work'?

As we have already seen, many churches take pride in what they regard as a healthy youth group, without paying much attention, if any at all, to the way in which its members live beyond it. But the young people in your youth group spend so much of their time in school that school obviously plays a very important role in their lives and the development of their Christian witness. It is also true that during adolescent years the young person is formulating the basic ideas and opinions that will determine the course of the rest of his life. Recently I was told by a church leader that working with schools was not really the responsibility of their minister, who should be doing 'more important' things with his time. But whilst it may well have been true that their pastor was not the right person for the job, it was short-sighted to regard such work as unimportant.

There are three main reasons for local church involvement in schools:

(1) To support and encourage young Christians in their everyday working environment. The church has a responsibility to help young Christians 'go public' about their faith amongst their non-Christian friends. If we do not teach young people to be bold in their teenage years, we may very well be permitting a timidity to put down roots within them that will last a lifetime.

(2) The best evangelists amongst teenagers are young people themselves. If we are to make an impact on the schools in our community, the most effective way of doing this is to enable existing Christians in the local schools to feel confident in their witness. Visiting speakers are abusing their position if they seek to evangelize, and teachers also have to be very careful not to fall into the trap where they too would be accused of indoctrinating the pupils, but it is quite natural for the students themselves to share with their friends what they have discovered about Jesus Christ.

(3) If it is not easy to be a Christian student in school, neither is it easy to be a committed Christian teacher. Christian teachers, especially those running Christian Unions or with responsibility for assemblies, need the support of the local churches. They often feel themselves to be in a very responsible, yet at the same time vulnerable position, out on a limb, beyond the church's attention and prayers.

It can be seen that it is very important that whenever possible local churches work with the schools in their area. The best way of doing this is to support the work of the Christian Union where one exists, or to help establish one where it does not. The school Christian Union is often a lifeline for Christian pupils, providing them with the support, fellowship, teaching and confidence necessary to maintain a healthy personal witness. Christian Unions are also a good base for planned evangelism. Most churches pray for and financially support missionary work in countries far distant, but as somebody recently wrote, our schools are 'the forgotten mission field'. If our churches can be helped to grasp the difficult, often very hostile and spiritually ignorant, cross-cultural environment in which many school Christian Unions operate they should be more ready to support this missionary work.

In chapter thirteen there is also a discussion of intensive schools work in relation to a special mission which includes assemblies, concerts and lessons.

Ways in which the local church can help an existing Christian Union

(1) By taking up or creating opportunities to speak in local schools

From time to time Christian teachers may invite local ministers and other Christians into their school to take assemblies or Religious Studies lessons, or to speak at the Christian Union. When such opportunities arise it is important that they are accepted, both to provide the help that the member of staff is calling for, and to encourage the development of an ongoing relationship with the Christian Union. If those invited cannot attend or for some reason do not feel that it is right for them personally to become involved, rather than just turning down the opportunity they should always phone or write to the school, suggesting names of others who would be suitable to help, or offering other dates on which they are available. Local churches should also be prepared sensitively to take the initiative if necessary. When I arrived in Tonbridge, one of the first things that I did was to ring all the local schools and ask for an appointment to see the Head of Religious Studies or, in some cases, the Head Teacher. At that meeting I simply introduced myself as the new Baptist minister and asked if there were any ways in which I could be of service to the school. I made it clear that I would always be available to help with assemblies, the Christian Union or lessons if needed. Several times the offer was snapped up there and then.

(2) By offering ongoing help to those responsible

Often young Christians will make the complaint, 'I don't go near the Christian Union because it's so boring.' Though sometimes this is just an excuse for not having the courage to attend, it may well have some truth in it. Often one solitary Christian member of staff battles on with the task of trying to run the Christian Union without any external support or encouragement. It is the local churches' responsibility to help the teacher(s) involved by sensitively offering practical help and advice—which may also include spending time and money on implementing these ideas. For instance, there may be something the church or youth group could buy, such as audio visual equipment or books, or it may be right for you to sit down and talk about the possibility of a school mission, jointly sponsored and organized by the church and the Christian Union.

(3) By encouraging your young people to attend

Often in a school where there is a Christian Union many of the young Christians do not have the courage to attend it, and therefore cannot link themselves into the support that can be received through its activities and teaching. So it is the task of your youth group to provide encouragement. The popular comment that the Christian Union is boring and that those who do go are 'wallies', should be carefully listened to but met with the positive response that Jesus constantly identified with those who were weak. By the power of his personality and involvement he was able to change individual lives and ultimately the face of history. To be Christlike is to get involved. If those with energy and enthusiasm do not do so, the Christian Union will remain weak and boring which, it should be pointed out, reflects on all Christians not just the CU members!

(4) By talking about school in your youth group

Sit down and talk to your young people about school. Through casual and informal conversations with individuals it is possible to learn all sorts of things about attitudes and feelings regarding this part of their lives. You can help a great deal by relating your weekly Bible teaching, as far as possible, to the school situation. Get the kids to talk about what is happening in their schools and in their CU. It will encourage those who are involved and challenge the others. You should often include a time of prayer with the specific opportunity for those who wish to pray for their schools, for Christian teachers and for the life of the Christian Union.

(5) Keep your church informed about school

A good idea is to arrange a special 'Schools Sunday' for your church. In the afternoon the youth group may put on a tea for the whole church after which each of the local CU's can report on what is happening in their school and give their prayer needs. Then those present can form small groups to pray about what they have heard. Later some of the young people may take part in the evening service. The effect of this is that the adults in the church have their eyes opened to what is actually going on in the schools and, therefore, begin to pray with a new enthusiasm.

Starting or re-launching a Christian Union

Where a Christian Union does not exist at all, how can a local church or youth group help start one? There are three lines of approach which we will list in order of preference.

(1) Always work through known Christian teachers if possible. Never undertake schools work without first consulting them. It is important that you understand the atmosphere within the school and the views of the staff before plunging in too deeply.

If you do not do this, they will probably feel that the ground is being cut from under their feet, and may also consider that you are being insensitive to the situation that exists within the school. (What's worse, they will almost certainly be right!) If you work with teachers in the school and win their confidence they will be able to advise and help you so that you don't tread on any toes. Of course, if the Head Teacher or Deputy is a Christian this is the place to start.

(2) If you do not have natural 'opening' into the school through a Christian teacher, make contact with the Religious Studies Department. In some cases you may have doubts about whether the head of RS is a Christian, but it is still important that you do not seek to work behind his back, or to undermine any of the work that he has been doing. Failure on your part within these guidelines can result in exclusion from the school, not only for yourself and any that you might seek to bring in but for all other churches and Christian speakers.

(3) Lastly, if you cannot make contact with any other sympathetic helpful members of staff, you should contact the Head Teacher. Your initial contact with him is vitally important: your task is to dispel any doubts and suspicions he may have about who you are and what you want to do, thus putting his mind at rest. The minister of your church is probably the best person to make this first contact on your behalf.

The aims of a Christian Union

Often CUs are started for no better reason than it seems good to get the Christians in a school together, though nobody is very sure why. To prevent it from generating into nothing more than a 'holy huddle', a Christian Union should have two very clear aims:

(1) To provide its members with the support and help they need to live as Christians in the school environment. It's easier to be a Christian if you are one in a group.

(2) To act as a base for evangelistic outreach in the school.

Each CU should see the school in which it is set as a mission field.

The role of the Inter-School Christian Fellowship

The ISCF exists to encourage work in schools. It is a part of Scripture Union and has a team of regional and local staff, together with a large number of voluntary workers who are able to advise and encourage Christians in schools all over the country. Through their literature and other resources they can help you with organizing a CU and establishing a programme. A representative would not only be willing to visit local schools to talk with interested staff and pupils, but also to come along to your youth group and talk about setting up and running a Christian Union (a good idea, even if the schools in your area already have CUs). The addresses for ISCF are given at the back of this book.

12

OPEN AIRS AND STREETWORK

It was a bank holiday Monday in an English village to which I had been invited by one of the local churches to take part in their outreach. Traditionally this day had been given over to open air work. Even the younger members of the congregation, by which I mean people in their thirties, told me what a wonderful experience the annual open air was. I had been given a great privilege, for I was to be the preacher! The plan was that we all should meet at the church building just after lunch and from there proceed on our mission.

It was a boiling hot day with the sun blazing down from the sky. There was no breeze, the streets were deserted and the village was absolutely silent because everybody who could move had gone out for the day. On arrival at the church the person who was obviously in charge led us in a prayer and then gave us the running order for the afternoon. Basically we had a half hour service which we would do three times at three different locations around the village. After several hymns and a reading I would be asked to step forward and preach 'the word'. After the afternoon's outreach we would all return to the church building for a tea, which was already laid out on the trestle tables and consisted of cucumber sandwiches, fish paste and some of the other traditional church delicacies! The organ, which was portable, was to be played by an old lady who was somewhere between eighty and ninety years of age. Despite the fact that we were in the middle of a heat wave, she found it necessary to be wrapped in a winter coat with a scarf, and to protect her delicate hands as she played the keyboard, she wore a pair of fingerless woolly hand knitted gloves.

We proceeded to the first venue which happened to be the middle of a deserted village green. We set up the rather antiquated looking organ, which the poor lady had to pump hard with both feet whilst attempting to play at the same time (a difficult task for anybody even at the prime of life), and passed round a set of *Golden Bells* hymn books. The first hymn was announced and we began to sing; an interesting feature of the afternoon proved to be that the lady playing the organ found it impossible to read the words at the same time as reading the music and so, instead of singing along with us she lahed and hummed the tune with the organ, obviously feeling that she must give it a hand with its job. As there were only about ten of us anyway the considerable power of the bellowing organ, aided and abetted by its player, completely drowned the singers.

A reading, a prayer and another two hymns later it was announced that 'our brother from London will now bring God's word to us' at which point I was nudged forward by the group and told to preach. I dared not ask exactly who I was supposed to be bringing God's word to. Actually, even if somebody had been evading my gaze by hiding behind a car or lamp post, I was separated from him by at least fifty yards and it would therefore have proved quite impossible for him to hear what I was about to say. Being the obedient young man that I was at that stage I stood and for the next ten minutes preached my heart out in one of the most evangelistic sermons this planet has probably ever heard. (I knew it was good because at the end they all patted me on the back and somebody even suggested that I may well be chosen as the preacher for next year as well!)

We repeated this little scenario twice more that afternoon before returning in triumphant mood to the chapel for tea. The church was ecstatic, things had gone so well. I was told it was just like the old days; the gospel had been powerfully preached and, as I was reminded, God's word would not return to him void. So ended one of the funniest and yet most tragic afternoons in my life. But what happened in that small village that afternoon was typical of what goes on year in year out in open air meetings all over our country.

It is a fantastic privilege to live in a country that gives us freedom to stand on the street and openly proclaim the truth about Jesus Christ, but the sad thing is that it is often abused or simply wasted. Enthusiasm, commitment and drive have not always been matched by common sense and as a result many Christians have a low opinion of outdoor work, regarding it as embarrassing and a thing of the past, something which they would never be involved in. In fact, open air work can be a very powerful tool in the hands of those who know what they are doing, and is especially powerful when used amongst young people.

The witness of the congregation mentioned above on that bank holiday Monday was not just ineffectual but also counter-productive. The one person we did meet that afternoon happened to be mending his car as we came along the road. We planned to hold our third service opposite his Ford Cortina but as soon as he saw us he hurriedly put down the bonnet and rushed indoors. Half an hour later, as we retreated back up the same street, I glanced back to see him returning from the shelter of his council house to get on with fixing his car. It was not just that we had failed to communicate but, rather more seriously, that we had communicated almost the exact opposite of what had been planned. Our witness left this amateur car mechanic more suspicious and cautious of the local church than he had been in the first place.

The do's and don'ts of an open air meeting

For purposes of clarity let us make a distinction between 'an open air' and 'streetwork'. By 'an open air' we will refer to an organized meeting with a programme designed to attract an audience. 'Streetwork' refers to the broader task of meeting, entering into conversation with, and presenting Christ to, the public on the streets. Firstly, let's look at the open air meeting.

(1) Choosing a site

Running a successful open air is not simply a case of finding somewhere to stand and preach or sing and hoping for the best. A lot of thought must go into choosing the correct kind of site. Below are some of the criteria that should govern your choice of site:

(a) Do use a place where people gather or congregate and constantly move by. This may be the middle of a shopping centre or some swings in the middle of a housing estate, or a piece of green opposite a row of shops etc. It's no good performing in the middle of a village green, you won't be heard and you'll look somewhat strange huddled together a great distance from anybody else. The green will act as a barrier between you and others and people will not cross it to see what you're doing even if they're interested because it looks 'nosey' and they will draw too much attention to themselves.

(b) Do not block the pavement. Make sure that in choosing your site it is possible to leave plenty of room for shoppers and others to pass by.

(c) Do not block shop doorways or window space. This is most inconsiderate and is likely to lead to bad feeling, arguments and even official complaints.

(d) Do not use loud amplification. The invention of the public address system has been seen by some as the foolproof way of forcing people to hear the gospel: 'If people won't stop and listen we'll get them anyway!' This is insensitive and uncaring. Think of yourself in the local park on a sunny summer's afternoon relaxing in the quietness, when all of a sudden a fourteen year old lad with a ghetto blaster mounted on his shoulders strides by and stops a few yards away with it playing at full volume. To him the music is simply wonderful, he cannot understand why everybody does not want to listen. To you it is a pounding noise that is destroying your peace and you take offence at this invasion of your privacy. We mut be careful not to inflict ourselves on people during our open air work. If a public address system is used at all, it should clarify speech for those standing around, not penetrate the plate glass of the surrounding shops. We wish to draw attention to ourselves by the colour and attractiveness of our presentation, so that the public wants to stop and listen and watch. We must not force our views upon them.

(e) Do not stop passers-by. This follows on from the last point. I myself have been stopped almost forcibly on several occasions whilst innocently wandering past an open air meeting. I remember well an experience that I had as a teenager in my home town of Croydon, when not only was I stopped and preached at but when I protested that I was already a Christian, was given a knowing look that said, 'So you think you'll get off the hook that way do you, sonny?' I was then subjected to another ten minute dose of the gospel. I finally managed to break into the conversation to explain that I really did have to go, and managed to make a getaway, but a handful of tracts were still shoved into my hand and several Bible verses hurled in my direction as I hurried away.

Open airs and the law:

Do we need a licence?

It is our legal right in Great Britain to hold open air religious meetings in any public thoroughfare and also to make use of means other than speaking—for example, music or drama—as long as they pertain to the religious message. But though you do not need a licence or permission, it is courteous and in the interests of good relationships to:

(1) Inform the legal department of the local council

The best way of doing this is to make an appointment and then go along and explain exactly what you are intending to do, or, if you don't have much time, to phone and talk to somebody responsible. The benefit of an appointment or of phoning rather than writing is that as you explain what you are going to do they have the opportunity of asking questions that immediately arise which you can answer there and then. This saves an exchange of letters which could take some weeks. A letter on its own is not only rather cold and impersonal but, of course, may not be dealt with for weeks.

(2) Inform your local police

Let them know the date, time and venue of the event as well as your intentions, making it especially clear that you do not plan to sell anything or collect money. In the event of any complaints from other people, the fact that you have consulted them will help you considerably! The police have the job of maintaining law and order so they will wish to ensure that:

(a) You do not cause a disturbance. Legally it is the job of the police force to see that any public event is peaceful and, therefore, they are also bound to investigate any complaints made against you. The third time they have to move you on, they are empowered to arrest you.

(b) You do not cause an obstruction. Though, as we have said, you are free to hold an open air meeting, the law states that technically obstruction results when the same air space is held by a person for more than sixty seconds. Therefore the police are empowered to arrest you under this law if complaints are received.

(3) Inform nearby shopkeepers

Again, this helps build a good relationship, which will make it easier for you to return.

The programme

(1) Forming a crowd

The picture we all have of the traditional open air consists of a speaker on a small wooden box with a ring of Christians tightly packed round him or, even worse than this, a row of Christians lined up behind the speaker glaring at passers-by. It is important to support those taking part in the presentation but it is a big mistake to follow either of the patterns outlined above.

The ring of Christians around the speaker creates a barrier which, instead of welcoming others in, barricades them out. A row of Christians lined up behind the speaker can resemble an American football team waiting to pounce. Any audience become the opposition side!

It is vital that for open air work you have a small crowd (a team of fifteen to twenty people is excellent) who simply stand around and watch the performance, so helping to give anonymity to others who gather round and watch. This will help to prevent the crowd that gathers from feeling threatened or exposed and will probably result in their staying longer.

(2) Only performers at the front

Some of the Christians standing round in the crowd have the work of just being there, maybe praying for some of the time whilst others are appointed to chat to those who seem interested and give them any relevant literature. Those who form part of the crowd are as important to the success of the programme as those who 'perform', and those who are responsible for handing out literature and getting into conversation with the public should receive training on exactly how to carry out their task. The team involved should be well briefed on where to meet, what is going to happen, when it's going to happen and their particular role. They should not be asked to fulfil roles for which they have not been prepared.

(3) Presentation

This can consist of drama, music, preaching, mime, conjuring, sketch board work, and so on. There are one or two principles to be remembered.

(a) *Be colourful* Music should be loud and rhythmic, drama should be filled with action and costumes should be good. The general principle is plenty of movement, action and colour.

(b) *Be brief* Short talks and short sketches are far more telling than long ones. A short programme has a greater impact than a long one. A typical programme should last between ten and fifteen minutes only and, after a break (when the cast can chat with the crowd) should be repeated. Normally people will not stand around for longer than this and will not pick up the main message of your presentation if it goes on longer. Keep it short and sharp!

(c) *Be relevant* The programme needs to be put together well in advance so that each element fits the theme and adds to what has already been said. This is especially true of chat and testimonies which must be to the point. It is sometimes good to vet items beforehand. For instance, get those who are presenting their testimony to sit down with somebody else whom they can trust to edit it, thus producing a tool which is short and punchy.

(d) *Be prepared* Open air work is front line evangelism. Because it is not within the confines of a church building where, generally speaking, the audience is conditioned to sit and keep quiet even if they are bored, you will sometimes get very lively responses from the audience! Be prepared for this to happen. Do not become angry with those who are negative and do not take their comments as a personal insult. Remember that in the New Testament the apostles were quite used to open debate and abuse!

(4) Using literature

Street work is probably best when linked with some other evangelistic event, perhaps a coffee bar or a concert. Colourful publicity can be handed out to those who are interested in knowing more. Gospels and other evangelistic literature such as *Journey into Life* should also be on hand. It is also useful to have something about your local church and what goes on there, along with a map of how to find it.

How to organize 'streetwork'

Handing out literature

This may simply consist of pairs of young people going out on a busy Saturday morning or afternoon and standing chatting to other teenagers whilst handing out invitations or tickets to an evangelistic concert that evening. Though much more informal than the Open Air, to be effective it still requires planning and a great deal of preparation.

A street questionnaire

Another approach is to produce a street questionnaire which the young people in your group can be trained to use. This provides them with an easy way into conversation and creates the opportunity to present Christ to those interested. The questionnaire needs to be designed for your particular situation, but should start with general questions and then move specifically to Christian belief. The last question should make it easy for the interviewer either to end the conversation without embarrassment, or talk more about Christianity.

Sample Questionnaire

1. How long have you lived in Tonbridge?

2. Are you at school, work or unemployed?

3. In your opinion, is Tonbridge a good place to live?

4. Are there enough facilities for young people in the town?

5. If not, what more could be provided?

6. Do you think the church can help young people? How?

7. Do you go to church? Never? Seldom? Often?

8. Do you believe in God?

9. If you could get to know him personally would you be interested?

If the answer to question 9 is 'Yes' the interviewer can then go on to ask, 'Would you like me to explain how I think you can do that?' In this way an open door has been created for the presentation of the gospel. If the answer is 'No' he can simply say, 'Thank you for your help, that's the end of the survey.'

13

AN EVANGELISTIC MISSION

The early Christians had a burning desire to tell others of Jesus; they could do nothing other than share their faith. We, on the other hand, have to be continually coaxed into outreach with neat pre-packaged formulae which we are assured will bring success!

Taking a closer look

The early church's enthusiasm for evangelism was overwhelming. The way in which eleven men set out to take the world by storm, and within three hundred years had 'turned it upside down' (Acts 17:6, AV) to the point where the Roman Empire itself had a Christian emperor is remarkable! But the claim that evangelism in the New Testament was simply spontaneous rather than organized is somewhat misleading. In Acts we read of how Paul had to argue the case for evangelizing the Gentiles and allowing them access to the church. There was a great deal of heated discussion over exactly how Gentile converts should be treated and what should be expected of them. We also have the story of how the apostles appointed seven deacons to take care of the practical needs of the widows in Jerusalem so that they could be released to get on with the work of preaching and teaching. All of this has much more of the flavour of debate, decision making, planning, organization and method to it than it is popular to recognize. Though it's heart stirring stuff to hear about how the early church got on with the job of evangelism almost without thinking about it, such teaching not only fails to represent the facts fully but also guarantees those who grow up on it a continuous sense of guilt and failure. Though it is true that we need to rediscover the sense of compulsion that drove the early church to share its faith, it should also be remembered that, like us, they found it necessary to plan and organize their outreach and mission.

Planning a mission

(1) If you are thinking of planning a local youth mission the first thing to do is to sit down and ask yourself the questions outlined in chapter seven.

(2) Now talk the whole idea through with the leadership of your local church. There is no point at all in proceeding against their wishes or without their full knowledge, backing and support; in fact, such a course of action might prove to be very counter-productive. The aim of any mission must be eventually to integrate converts into the body of the church, which means that evangelism undertaken outside this context will ultimately prove to be of little or no lasting value.

(3) Having got the go ahead from your church or group of churches (see chapter nineteen) you are now ready to do the detailed planning for the mission. Many of the elements that make up a youth mission, such as schools work, street-work, coffee bars, concerts, are dealt with in detail in other chapters, but below are some additional guidelines which you may find useful.

Artists and speakers

There are several professional bands, drama companies, solo singers, dance groups and speakers who spend a lot of their time working on church based missions around the country. Details of some of those who are available can be obtained from organizations such as British Youth For Christ and Scripture Union (both addresses are given at the back of this book), but you will probably have seen some in action and will already know which ones you have confidence in. You will normally need to book between six and twelve months in advance (in some cases much more). Make sure that those you are proposing to book know exactly what is being asked of them and that they feel happy working within this context; also look carefully at your financial responsibility towards them (see chapter ten).

Besides inviting in professionals, it is often good to give local talent the opportunity to participate. Many local Christian bands and drama companies have good material, but give them plenty of warning and don't stretch them beyond their resources and ability.

Timetable

It is mentally, spiritually and physically demanding to be involved in frontline evangelism, so do remember that those you are bringing into your town to work on the mission need to rest and sleep and that it is counter-productive to drive them so hard that they end up looking like the living dead! Of course, you want to make the most of their time with you but this must allow them to relax and think. A good principle to work on is the two-thirds day. For instance, if a visiting band are working morning and evening they should be given the afternoon to relax and prepare. It is important that you talk this through with those involved in your particular mission.

Schools work

Getting it right

If you are planning for schools work to be a major part of your mission you must do a lot more than simply approach Head Teachers of senior schools asking for the opportunity to take assemblies and lessons. I have been involved in several schools missions where we have been aiming at the fourteen plus age group but where I have spent most of my time taking assemblies and lessons for second or even first years (eleven and twelve year olds)! For details of how to build contacts in a local school see chapter eleven.

A typical mission of this kind consists of work throughout the week in local senior schools with one or more evening evangelistic events towards the end of the week. Those taking part in full-time work on a mission would normally go into schools for assemblies, lessons and lunch-time concerts in which their job would be to:

(a) Present facts about Christianity
(b) Dispel distorted and misleading images of what a Christian is
(c) Advertise evening evangelistic events
(d) Help build an ongoing relationship with the staff, thus creating the opportunity for future visits

Assemblies

These are of great value because they present the opportunity of speaking to a large number of young people at one time. Many schools no longer have an assembly for the whole school but, instead, each pupil attends one or two assemblies a week with their year or house group. However, such gatherings still offer the opportunity of speaking to several hundred young people at one time.

Lunch-time Concerts

Personally I not only enjoy performing at lunch-time concerts but also feel that they are of enormous value. I believe that a good package is to take an assembly or series of assemblies which, besides standing on their own, advertise the lunch-time concert. Word will soon get around and even those who were not at the assembly will be there at lunch-time. This concert should build on the message of the morning assembly and give an opportunity for pupils to meet the band, drama group etc. A renewed invitation can also be given to the evening event(s) taking place that night and/or later that week. Organizers should talk to the band or singer booked to discover their attitude towards talking individually to people.

Lessons

Often it is possible to take Religious Studies or other lessons. This gives the opportunity of spending a considerable period of time with a smaller number of young people; often a class of thirty or several classes together. Once again, it is good if the teaching content of these lessons can build on the theme developed in the assembly, although of course sometimes those you meet in the classroom will not have had the opportunity to attend.

Intensive or extensive

You may choose to work intensively, concentrating on one or two schools throughout the mission, or extensively, visiting as many as possible for a 'one off' package ideally consisting of an assembly and lunch-time concert together with some lessons.

Time planning

If you are using a group who need to set up public address equipment for assemblies or concerts, time needs to be given to this and access needs to be gained to the school hall perhaps an hour to an hour and a half before morning assembly or a lunch-time concert. Time must also be allowed for packing away equipment and this will affect the number of lessons the group are able to take. It is very useful to have a couple of local 'humpers' who are free to travel with the group throughout the mission and help them with setting up and packing up equipment. These helpers can double up as guides to make sure the group get to the right place at the right time.

Education or indoctrination

It should also be remembered that school is a place of education not indoctrination and that therefore the content of all Christian work there should be truly educational. Sometimes there will be teachers who are not particularly well disposed towards Christians coming into the school to teach. If they have reason to believe that the pupils are coming under pressure to accept the Christian faith and 'give their lives to Jesus' they will be antagonized still further. Such a situation makes life very difficult for Christian staff members and has, unfortunately, also been the cause of many schools being permanently closed to Christian work. The place for direct evangelism is not in the classroom but at an evening evangelistic event which young people have attended of their own free will knowing exactly what it is they are coming to.

Streetwork

If you are aiming for older teens then it may be right to think beyond schools work. What about the sixteen and eighteen plus age group who have left school? Perhaps an important factor in your mission should be streetwork, when you can make contacts and advertise evening evangelistic events (see chapter twelve).

Evening evangelistic events

How many events?

Concerts may take place at different venues throughout the week(s) or at one central location at the end of the mission. You could plan a 'Video Show' and put on a series of three, four, five or even six different presentations on consecutive evenings (see chapter sixteen). The value of this is that young people are given the opportunity to come along several nights running and then to go away and talk through what they have heard with their friends before returning to hear more the following night. The more opportunity teenagers have to think about and assess the gospel, the more equipped they are to make a reasoned decision about becoming a Christian. If we are not careful we ask young people to make the most life-changing decision that they could ever contemplate on the basis of no more than a ten or fifteen minute chat at the end of a concert.

Venues for evening events

A venue for the evening event(s) may be a secular one or one that is owned by the church (see the discussion of this question in chapter ten). The important factor to consider is ease of access to the venue by public transport. I have known missions where I have spent most of the week working in an area which is five or six miles from the venue for evening events. The public transport service is often non-existent or inconvenient and the last bus runs before the end of the event that you have advertised. You cannot rely on parents being willing to run their teenagers in and out of your event in the family car so the venue must be easily accessible to the audience you want to reach.

Honesty

Organizers should always be honest about the purpose of an evening event. In assemblies, lessons and lunch-time concerts it is right to mention that, besides the music, drama, videos, etc, the evening will explain more about Jesus Christ and what a Christian is. You may feel that this is bound to put teenagers off coming altogether, but I've found it makes little difference to the numbers attending and, on the positive side, you know that the audience is open to hearing about Jesus Christ and how he relates to them.

Head hunting

A common danger that arises in the context of 'event' evangelism is the danger of being too numbers orientated. If the appeal produces a certain number of conversions it is regarded as a great success; if not, it is seen as a failure. Though I believe it is the evangelist's responsibility to make an appeal and so offer those who have heard the gospel the opportunity to respond to it publicly, this response will only ever be a rough indication of what God has been doing on any particular night. There will be those who stand or come forward who perhaps shouldn't and those who should have but didn't, added to which there will be some who God speaks to in a very real way but who then need to go away and think before making any decision. It has been said that those who make a first time commitment at such events should only really be counted as converts after one year of sticking to their decision.

About a year ago I was involved in a mission that was written about in the national Christian press. Over the course of four nights some one hundred and thirty young people made decisions for Christ. This disclosure greatly improved my reputation but gave entirely the wrong impression, because today only about thirty, or forty at the most, of those converts continue with their faith. The church that enters into an evangelistic mission of any kind, especially amongst the young people, without recognizing that there will very often be a high fall off rate is a church that is blinkered. Jesus himself spoke of the seed that fell on stony, shallow and thorny ground, and for those reasons never reached maturity.

Worship

If it is at all possible, build the concept of worship/celebration into a mission. Very often a youth mission will finish with a Sunday evening worship service to which all the young people who attended the evangelistic events, especially those who made some public response, will be invited. In this way not only are new converts introduced to the concept of worship but a start is made towards bridging the gap between frontline evangelism and ongoing teaching and discipleship through the regular ministry of a local church. The presence of the visiting evangelist(s) and others who have been a focal point throughout the mission is always a great help because it provides the continuity which is much needed at this early stage in bridge building.

Counselling and nurture groups

Both of these issues must be carefully considered at an early stage of planning. They are dealt with in detail in the next chapter.

Publicity

This should be handled in the same way as for a concert. Plenty of handbills are necessary not only for street work but also to accompany the school workers as they go into assemblies and lessons. Each young person should be able to have a copy of a handbill, because very often they will think of the handbills as tickets and those who do not possess one will not consider themselves able to attend your event. The handbill should clearly show:

(1) The name of the event

(2) The date(s) of the event

(3) The venue

(4) A map of how to get there

(5) The opening time of the doors and the starting time of the presentation

(6) The finishing time (this is very important in teenage work as parents will often want to know what time their children will be back home)

(7) The cost of admission. If it is free this should be clearly stated (I tend to think that evangelistic presentations should be free but there are arguments both ways)

(8) The age group the presentation is aimed at

Prayer

In 1984, Mission To London and Mission England very successfully used the principle of prayer triplets. In this scheme three people would get together and pray for three other people who were good friends of theirs and whom they hoped to invite along to evangelistic events. In many cases those who were prayed for became Christians long before the missions themselves actually took place. A number of central prayer and information meetings should be held from an early date and prayer sheets, cards and 'up-dates' should be provided. When people feel involved and kept up to date, they will pray more effectively and also give more realistically.

14

FOLLOW-UP

Evangelistic counselling and nurture of new Christians

Laurel and Hardy, Tom and Jerry, Jack and Jill, Rolls and Royce, salt and pepper . . . evangelism and follow-up. This last pair are as inseparable as the others. There is little point in organizing evangelistic events if you are not prepared to care for those who respond to the message. Mass evangelism must always go hand in hand with individual pastoral care and attention because where the former is divorced from the latter disaster will follow. In fact, evangelism without follow-up can even provide the inoculaton against Christianity which later prevents the patient from getting the real thing! Follow-up begins with good clear counselling at conversion and then involves the careful ongoing nurture of each convert. Without this care, new Christians are soon confused and often lost, which in turn may create the kind of negative attitude that says, 'I've heard it all before, but it doesn't work.'

Evangelistic counselling

A few weeks before one evangelistic concert at which I was due to sing, I rang the organizer to enquire, amongst other things, about the number of counsellors who would be available. I was quickly informed that it was not expected that much would happen and so it was 'really not worth' organizing counsellors! I also learnt that there were no plans to have any evangelistic literature available, no nurture groups had been arranged and there was no way of making a record of any young people who responded. I pointed out that it was reasonable to assume that there may be those who would make some response to the gospel, and almost grudgingly the organizer agreed to see what he could do.

On the night of the event I was told that the organizers could probably at a push rustle up between ten and fifteen counsellors if needed, but at the close of the evening about fifty people responded to the gospel in one way or the other and needed counselling. Those in charge were in a state of shock and in the confusion there were at least a few who, though they wanted to talk, did not receive the opportunity. In fact, no one was quite sure about who the counsellors were and who wanted counselling!

If a message is going to be presented at the end of an evangelistic event with the opportunity to respond, the facility must exist for those who do, to sit down and talk through their decision. The need for evangelistic counselling and the role that belongs to the counsellor need to be taken seriously and looked at well in advance of the event itself.

Training

Each local church should have a number of people, both young and old, who have been trained in evangelistic counselling. There is no space within the confines of this book to present such a training course but many are available from good Christian bookshops. It is important, however, to make several general comments that may not be found elsewhere.

(1) Age and experience

Some claim that the role of counsellor does not belong to teenagers themselves but to older Christians with more experience and maturity, in whom those seeking advice will place a greater degree of confidence. Others argue that it is right that Christian teenagers be given the responsibility of counselling, thus providing them with the opportunity to gain experience. The most convincing counsellors, it is claimed, will come from the same age group as those being counselled. In fact there is no black and white answer to this question. It will be different in differing situations because it is dependent upon exactly who the young people are in your group, how old they are, and how mature they are as Christians. Other counsellors at youth events should include youth leaders and others who are 'in tune' with the young. It is not age that drives the gap between the generations but lack of understanding. The important quality of a counsellor is the ability to relate to the world of those with whom he speaks so that they can identify with and understand him.

(2) Sex

Wherever possible, counselling should be male to male and female to female. We all know of the kind of teenage girl who only ever seems to have problems when a particular male youth leader is there to help sort them out! Or the boy who, while being counselled by an older girl, is actually paying a lot more attention to her shape than to what she is saying!

(3) Don't keep those being counselled for too long

It's easy for the counsellor to fall into the trap of believing that he has to pack a whole discipleship course into one initial counselling session in order to ensure the continued spiritual life of a new Christian! This is obviously not true and can actually be quite harmful, for several reasons:

(a) The person who has just become a Christian will not normally be able to grasp very much of what the counsellor has to say, but what he really needs to get hold of is that he has been forgiven for all that is wrong in his life by God because of what Jesus Christ did when he died on the cross and that now he has been given the Spirit to enable him to live a new life. The only other thing that the counsellor needs to explain is when the follow-up classes will actually take place. If that comes across loud and clear, the counsellor has done a good job. If the counsellor tries to say much more it all becomes confusing rather than helpful and the main points will have been lost.

(b) The problem is often not just that the counsellor says a lot which is unnecessary but that he takes far too long to do so. The gospel is harmed when the publicity for the evening gives the finishing time as 10.00 pm but at 10.15 the counsellee is still being kept and his father is still waiting outside in the car with the engine running or his friends are still waiting inside the hall with very worried looks on their faces because they've just missed the last bus home! We must respect those whom we counsel. If we have told them in our publicity that they will be away from the building at 10.00 we must keep our word. The programme should finish at 9.45 so that fifteen minutes can be devoted to counselling. Unfortunately I have witnessed many incidents where a young Christian's first encounter with the non-Christian world is in the shape of his father who storms into the building to drag him away from a bewildered counsellor, whilst swearing and uttering threats to all concerned because he has been kept waiting: 'You're never coming here again . . . I'm not having you mixed up with religious nuts . . . I'm going to sue you lot . . . you wait,' are all expressions that I've heard in such circumstances. Let's be careful not to make a young person's first night of being a Christian a night that he, and we, have to try and forget.

(4) Counselling cards

It is very important that counselling cards should be available so that a record can be made of each young person who responds in any way. You need to have a record of:

(a) Home address

(b) School

(c) Any church connection

(d) Particular response to the appeal

Often I have witnessed a situation where somebody stands up at the end of an evangelistic evening to hand out sheets of blank paper and pens, and shout orders across a crowded coun selling room to those who are actually doing the counselling. This is a policy guaranteed to make those who are being counselled feel as though they are being processed. Apart from the embarrassment of such a situation, it rarely works anyway because the counsellors will invariably forget to take down one of the most important details, so making effective follow up difficult. It is essential that the counselling card be ready well before the event and that the training course include the opportunity for the counsellors to become familiar with it. It must also be made clear that completed cards should be handed back to the organizer at the end of the evening, and under no circumstances be taken home by the counsellor, which is another common problem—one that is as unhelpful as forgetting to fill it in to start with!

Young people should never be asked to fill in the counselling card themselves. This can happen when, for instance, the counsellor asks the counsellee's name but fails to hear it properly or feels unable to spell it. Because he is embarrassed to ask for clarification he decides that the easiest way out of the situation is to ask the young person to fill in the form. The problem arises when the teenager goes straight home and enthusiastically reports to his parents that he has just become a Christian and signed a form to that effect down at the church. This is guaranteed to ring alarm bells with the unsympathetic parent: 'What has my son signed up for?' 'What has he been forced into?' 'What kind of pressure has been used?' To most non-Christian parents this has the taste of 'one of those cults', the kind they have read about in the Sunday press. Make sure that your counsellors explain exactly what the card is for— that it is simply to give you a record of their decision so that you can help them as they grow in their Christian faith. The counsellor should not demand the information but should ask the young person if he minds giving details of his name and address, etc, and should allow the opportunity to refuse. Only then should the form be filled in. As many of the details as possible concerning the nature of the commitment should be completed after the counsellee has left. Finally the form should be handed in. Counsellors should also, or course, have a good working knowledge of any literature that is being used and given away.

(5) The term 'counsellor'

Though we have used the term 'counsellor' many times in this chapter, it is not the best description for general use. The term sounds very professional and in everyday life 'counsellors' are people to be avoided except in dire circumstances. They are people you go to when you're in trouble, experts who tend to see right through you and know your every thought. At the end of an evangelistic event I simply say, 'There are some Christians here who would like to chat briefly about the decision you've just made to follow Jesus.'

(6) Listening and asking

It is important that the counsellor be trained to listen carefully to exactly what the counsellee has to say about why he came forward, rather than jumping to the conclusion that he necessarily wants to become a Christian. It is just as important that the counsellor should also have the ability to assess when and how to ask questions which will enable the counsellee to clarify why he has responded to the invitation. This saves you the embarrassing situation where somebody is pushed by a counsellor into 'becoming a Christian' only to have the job of sheepishly explaining at the end of the session, 'But I made a commitment to Christ three years ago . . . it's just that I find it so difficult to pray!'

Don't expect everybody to know why they have come forward; some come simply because they need help in explaining to others why they are Christians, some may not even be sure whether they are Christians or not. Counsellors need to be patient and should be trained never to try and force the conversation in a particular direction or to push somebody into God's kingdom. I once heard Floyd McClung say, 'Don't try to do the Holy Spirit's work for him . . . you haven't got what it takes!' Give each young person room to manoeuvre. If they are not totally sure that they want to become Christians they should be given the opportunity to go away and think it over, rather than being pushed into something that they are not ready for.

(7) Chief counsellor

It is good to appoint somebody suitable as chief counsellor with the responsibility of working out the practical arrangements well before the event and communicating these to the other counsellors. Each counsellor should be informed of exactly what is required of him at the end of the evening. He will want to know where the counselling room is; when he should move through to it; by what process he will be paired up with someone wishing to be counselled; where he should leave the counselling card (and pen?) afterwards, and so on. The more practical planning that is done, the more efficient the process, which not only leaves more time for counselling but also helps make everybody feel more relaxed.

(8) Literature

Counsellors should understand that there are three strands of follow-up for those who become Christians at evangelistic events:

(a) Local church (through nurture groups etc)

(b) School (through the Christian Union)

(c) The counsellor himself. A counsellor's responsibility to those whom he counsels does not end as he prays a prayer of commitment with them and sends them on their way with a handful of literature. At this stage he may well be the only Christian that these young people know. It is the counsellor's responsibility to pray for them and to stay in touch, at least until other relationships have been formed. The counsellor can do this quite easily by saying something like, 'And I'll meet you outside here next week for the first of the "following Jesus" meetings.'

Nurture of new Christians

The question of exactly how prospective converts are to be nurtured should be part of the main agenda when the planning of a mission or other evangelistic event is decided on.

I once visited a mission committee which was made up of members of several churches in a particular area. They had booked me to present an evangelistic concert on a Friday evening at which, I had been informed by letter, four hundred non-Christian teenagers would be present. At the meeting I asked them two questions:

(a) How could they be so sure so many non-Christians would be present?

(b) What plans and preparations were being made for the care and nurture of any converts afterwards?

A silence fell across the room which said much louder than words ever could that absolutely no thought had been given to either issue.

There are many excellent follow-up or nurture courses for new converts published by a number of different organizations and available through any good local Christian bookshop. Once again, it is far beyond the scope of this book to provide an alternative to these, nor is it necessary! A list of some of these publications can be found at the back of this book. All I will do here is outline a few basic principles which apply universally to follow-up work with teenagers but which are often not included as part of a training package.

(1) Planning ahead

Nurture or discipleship meetings need to be planned well before any evangelistic event takes place. This means that the venue, date and time can be announced at the event itself and that each counsellor can personally invite those he counsels: 'I'll meet you back here at 7.30 pm next Friday for the first of a series of meetings for all those who want to know more about being a Christian . . . Can you come?' This meeting can also be announced from the stage at the end of the evening because there may be those who would like to attend but did not make any public response to the appeal.

Why is it so important to work in this way? Simply because in the case of teenage work, especially among the unchurched, it is practically impossible to plan effective follow-up after the event. Let's examine the alternative.

Often the plan has been to collect together the counselling cards after the event, then sit down to analyse them and set up home nurture groups on the basis of geography (where the convert lives in the town) or existing church contact. Then a letter is written inviting the convert along to the meeting or a visit is made to his home. Unfortunately, this plan of action does not normally work, for several reasons.

In the summer of 1984 I was sent a considerable number of follow-up cards relating to teenagers who were counselled for conversion at Mission To London. I was asked to visit their home, to establish a link and invite them to a nurture group. The problem was that I had no natural reason to call on any of these young people. I would pluck up courage and knock at their front door only to be greeted in every case by one of their parents (teenagers tend to leave the door bell to their parents, unless they are expecting a friend). I would then have to ask to see their son or daughter, at which point they would, understandably, want to know why (that's when I'd really begin to wish I wasn't there!). I would try to explain as simply as I could that their child had become a Christian or expressed interest in the Christian faith at Mission To London. None of the parents I ever spoke to were Christians and I could tell from the look on their faces that they found this news rather disturbing; either they knew nothing about it, or did know but were not sympathetic. One father flew into a rage there and then, calling down his son from the bedroom to inform him that this was the last time he would ever set foot inside a church: 'We don't want anyone in our family mixed up with this sort of thing,' he yelled. This attitude was understandable because, of course, most people in our country believe that they probably are Christians and that 'Christian' equals 'good person' (which accounts for the popularity of the statement, 'You don't need to go to church to be a Christian'). A 'born again' Christian is 'a religious maniac'. Of all the teenage contacts who came from non-Christian homes whom I visited from Mission To London there was not one that resulted in any continued contact with the church. Home visiting is not a realistic means of follow-up for a teenager under the age of eighteen.

Letters posted through the door are just as unhelpful—few teenagers normally receive neatly typed envelopes through the door. But whether it is typed or hand written, when the letter arrives they are at school and their mother, who picks it up from the front door mat, spends the whole day wondering what it contains. When the teenager arrives home the letter is presented to him, maybe even with some excitement and they are required to report on its contents after opening it, which draws the same kind of response as the call at the door.

The chief problem that must be overcome is the deep suspicion of non-Christian parents concerning what has happened to their child. They are understandably worried as they often have a distorted and misleading idea of what the church is.

The best way of coping with this difficult situation is, therefore, to simply tell the teenager about the nurture group on the night of his conversion. For a teenager to come home and say, 'I went down the church with my friends tonight, it was good and we're going to go again next Friday,' will probably only arouse the response, 'It's a passing phase, he'll soon grow out of it.' The parents can see that this is something their child wants to do. They probably believe that it's 'taking religion too seriously' but since he's going with his friends, and is not being forced they probably shrug and say, 'It's his choice.' In time, of course, the parents will learn that their teenager has become a Christian and that he has made many new Christian friends. But all this will happen as a gradual process while the parents have the chance to discover that being a Christian (whatever that really means) has not taken their child away from the family and brainwashed him, but has, if anything, made him a better son!

(2) One central group

As the result of any evangelistic event or mission, whether organized by one church or townwide, there will be those who are converted who are friends of existing Christians. These young people will quite naturally become involved in the church to which their friends already belong. The problem arises over those who are contacted through schools work or by some other means who have no natural friendship with an existing Christian. For these, one central group should be set up. This is preferable to trying to divide them—whether it be geographically, into different house groups or denominationally, by sending them to a church to which their counselling card indicates they have some affiliation.

As we have recognized in section one of this book, the gang spirit is particularly important during teenage years. Daniel and Andy are best friends and respond to the gospel together at a concert. Daniel happens to live at one end of the town whilst Andy lives at the other. If you work on a geographical basis you will ask them to go to two different home groups or centres, but the chances are that neither will go anywhere! There is another difference between them. Daniel was christened at St Agnes whereas Peter used to go to the Baptist Sunday School which he left six years ago. When asked by their counsellors if they have any church contact both thought it was important to put these down. However, an attempt to send them to the church they claim to have contact with is not only unrealistic but will again split their friendship.

In relation to a townwide event, the establishing of one central nurture group for those who do not have a natural connection with one particular church creates a problem because it means that the churches involved have to acknowledge the fact that everybody in this category will end up with the one fellowship who are chosen to run the group. This obviously demands a great deal of commitment and maturity from all the participating churches.

(3) Running a nurture group

Several points need to be made about the functioning of a nurture group.

(a) Rather than referring to the meeting as the 'Discipleship' or 'Nurture' group, both of which sound somewhat technical, come up with another name which you think will be suitable in your situation. Names that I have come across include 'Talking Shop', 'Just Looking' and 'Master Class'.

(b) The group should meet once a week on a convenient night with a programme that lasts about one and a half hours (for example, 7.30–9.00 pm). This leaves time for coffee and chat afterwards but means that those present can still be away by 9.30 (especially important if your group is to be held mid-week). Its life should be about ten weeks, though again this will vary, depending on the literature you are using.

(c) Existing Christians and especially the counsellors should attend the group on a regular basis, taking every opportunity to befriend those who have so recently made a commitment.

(d) There should be a number of leaders who can share the responsibility of running the group. This will prevent it turning into a one man show.

(e) The programme should include worship and prayer as well as teaching and discussion. It's good to use a worship band if possible. Teaching should be varied: from the front, in small groups, and through drama, videos, etc. The group should present the new convert with lively, relevant worship and teaching and thus create a natural bridge into the life of the adult church.

15

PLANNING A COFFEE BAR
AND USING VACANT PREMISES

'Innpacked' was the name given to the evangelistic coffee bar held back in 1970 where I became a Christian. Since then I have been involved in all sorts of Christian coffee bars in venues ranging from a disused pub to an old canal barge, and an empty supermarket to a double decker bus. But it's not just unusual venues that can be used in this way. With a bit of flair and imagination even the dustiest old church hall can be transformed into a great coffee bar.

One of the first projects that we ran in Tonbridge was a coffee bar called 'Streetbeat' which took place in July 1982 when premises formerly occupied by a supermarket became vacant in Tonbridge High Street. It was an ideal setting for an evangelistic coffee bar—right in the middle of the town and next to the River Medway. We negotiated with the owners who eventually gave us their permission to use it, though this was only obtained six days before the event was due to start! Publicity, sound and lighting equipment, tables, chairs, decorations, refreshments, counsellors, bouncers, stewards, electricity and water supplies, had to be arranged with great speed, not to mention the programme! 'Streetbeat' was a great success, although it did test our organizational abilities to the full.

The basic principles behind the organization of a coffee bar are dealt with in the next chapter, 'The Video Show,' and also in chapter ten, 'The Concert'. Here we will look at a subject which has already been raised in this chapter and which we will be raising again in several of those following.

The short-term use of vacant commercial premises

How do you go about acquiring the use of empty premises?

This seems such a daunting prospect that many simply never attempt it. Actually like most other tasks it is simply a matter of knowing what to do and when:

(1) Take a walk through your local high street with a pen and note pad, taking down the names of any suitable empty shops and their street numbers, and note down from the boards outside the particulars of the estate agents who are handling the sales.

(2) First try to contact the shop owner (rather than the estate agent). Your enthusiasm and your personal contact will very often sell an idea to the owner, whereas the same idea may fail when put forward by the non-commital estate agent.

   At this stage always make phone calls rather than trusting to letters. A friendly phone call briefly explaining why you require the use of the premises and explaining that it is only for a short period of time, will often go a lot further towards winning support than a formal-sounding letter. Besides this, you can wait weeks for a reply to a letter, whereas the telephone is immediate and, if the property is not available, you know at once. Always ask to speak to the boss if possible. You can waste a lot of time talking with those who have no real authority and who will probably only pass on a rather inaccurate and brief message to those responsible. If the boss is out, rather than leave a message, courteously ask when he will be available to speak to you and say that you will phone back.

(3) If you are unable to make direct contact with the owner, negotiate through the estate agent handling the sale.

(4) Shop premises are obviously a great financial asset and also

a costly liability if they stand empty. Therefore, though it may appear to the public that for months on end a certain shop stands empty, in fact, there is almost certainly a great deal of activity going on behind the scenes. The present owner is probably doing his best to sell as quickly as possible in order to release the capital that he has tied up in the premises. Because he hopes to sell, it is usually not until two or three weeks before the proposed dates that a shop owner will definitely promise you the use of his property (and then it is likely to be for not more than a month at a time!). In spite of this, it is good to make an initial enquiry some months beforehand. Though it is very unlikely that you will be promised anything at this stage, the owner or agent may well ask you to contact them again nearer the dates you require. By establishing contact in this way, you avoid springing your project on them at the last moment. This gives those concerned plenty of time to think through your case and, therefore, increases your chances of gaining a positive response if the property is still available when you need it. There may also be other groups in the town looking for the same kind of arrangement, so it helps to introduce your name as early as possible. Basically the owner needs to know that your use of his premises will not interfere with his plans. With tact and diplomacy, it is often possible to arrange for the free or nominal hire of shops for a coffee bar or other events such as those outlined in other chapters in this book.

(5) When, and if, permission is granted for use of particular premises you need to immediately get in touch with:
   (a) The Electricity Board to arrange to have power supplied.
   (b) The Gas Board (if necessary).
   (c) The Water Board (you need working toilet facilities if nothing else).
   (d) The local police station, to advise them when you are using the building and to inform them of the purpose. Don't be afraid that they will ban your project. As long

as you have the owner's permission and you do not cause a disturbance or have any official complaints filed against you by the public, you are in the clear.

(e) The fire service. They will make a visit to the premises and as a result will ask you to comply with certain regulations. They will want to know exactly what use the building is being put to, and will then advise you as to the maximum seating capacity, the required width of gangways leading to fire exits, the way in which such exits should be lit and marked, the number and type of fire extinguishers needed and the correct level of stewarding etc.

(f) The department of health and hygiene. If you are going to be cooking and serving food as part of the project it is important to make sure your facilities are adequate and meet the required standards. (This does not apply if you are simply selling pre-packed sweets and drinks.)

(g) Insurance. Have you got the necessary cover—for premises, equipment, customers and staff?

Though all this may sound daunting, you will find that most people are pleased that something imaginative is being done in the community and will give you all the help and advice that they possibly can. After the event, make sure to write and thank all those who have given you help, giving them a short report of how the project went. If you run a similar project at a future date you will need the good will of these same people. Coverage in the paper and on local radio also ensures that the community becomes aware of what you are doing. Again, this helps with future planning.

16

THE VIDEO SHOW

What have Top of the Pops, The Tube, Breakfast TV and
Wogan all got in common? . . . Give up? They, like all other
television programmes, make use of fast-changing images to
hold the viewer's attention. If television holds the same camera
shot for thirty seconds, that is considered a very long time! Also
on each of the programmes we have just mentioned no one
item would normally last for more than a few minutes. Surely
there is a lesson here for the church to learn about evangelism
and communication in the television age?

Early in 1984, the old bus garage in Tonbridge became disused. I enquired about its availability for short-term use for a
nightly youth event and though at first I was turned away,
finally (some nine months of consistent campaigning later) permission was given for this purpose. At about the same time I
had an interesting lunch with Steve Goddard and Tony
Cummings of *Buzz* magazine where, over their egg and chips,
they explained an idea for using videos on a large screen as an
evangelistic tool amongst teenagers. Later as I drove home
along the M25 I suddenly realized that the bus garage was a
perfect venue for using videos in an evangelistic presentation
and would give me an ideal opportunity to try out my ideas
about communication. I felt that by using pre-recorded videos
of Christian bands on a large screen, as well as live music,
interviews and drama it should be possible to present an audience with the same kind of fast-moving menu that television

offers. So was born the idea of the *Bus Company Video Show*.

The content of the show

The show eventually ran each night for a week from 7.30 to 10.00 pm. A typical show began with the venue in darkness and then as the lights came up there was a welcome from the presenter who introduced the first music video on the big screen. The lights blacked out and the video played until, during the last frames, it faded and the lights came up again. Then the presenter announced the guest band for the evening who performed two songs with lyrics and chat that fitted into the evening's theme. Two video camera operators picked out shots of the band which were beamed up onto the screen. As the band left the stage it was instantly blacked out and once more a video was projected. At the end of this, lights came up on a second stage where a drama sketch was performed. The presenter briefly chatted about the sketch, reinforcing its message. Next came the opportunity for the audience to participate as three teenagers came up on stage for 'Video Box' (their chance to comment on video clips from current chart songs and contemporary Christian material). This was followed by a couple of songs from the resident band, *Tony Clay and the Ambassadors*, who had spent the previous week working in the local schools advertising the show. Tony chatted and introduced the audience to a local Christian policeman (known to many of the teenagers present) and talked with him about his faith. This was followed by another video which played into a fifteen minute break (for people to get drinks, look at books and LP's and to visit the loo).

The second half of the programme followed in the same kind of style as the first, slowly expanding and explaining the message already introduced. Finally, at the end of the evening, the gospel was preached and people invited to respond to Christ.

Each video used in the *Video Show* was carefully chosen to play a part in the clear presentation of the gospel, though this did not mean that all the videos used were made by Christian artists. Secular artists with whom those present would be familiar and could readily relate were featured each evening. For instance, on one evening we showed a video of *Wide Boy*, a song by Nik Kershaw that had recently been in the charts. The song and video depict a young man who becomes a famous pop star but whose life is empty and leads to loneliness and depression. This song related superbly to our theme for that night: 'Is there life before death?' One young person commented, 'It was like getting the news straight from the horse's mouth.'

We decided that we would run our own free bus service to and from the show each evening for teenagers who came from surrounding villages. To this end we managed to obtain the free use of several double deckers, one of which was kindly supplied by the local bus company along with its own driver and conductor! Each evening this bus made a run through several villages in Tonbridge while another single decker did exactly the same on the other side of town. After the show, both did a return journey. We had four other double deckers permanently parked in the garage to form a back drop for the stage, and these doubled up as dressing rooms and a base for a team of people in their early twenties whose job it was to provide security each night by living on the premises.

The show had a great impact on the town and by the end of the week we were running lunch-time presentations as well as the evening ones. By the end of the week lunch-time audiences were numbering about three to four hundred, with evening attendances as high as nine hundred. In fact, on the last evening we gave admission to nine hundred and turned away about two hundred people! We estimate that about half of each evening's audience were already on the periphery of church youth groups whilst the other half had no Christian connection whatsoever and had been attracted by publicity in schools during the previous week and the free bus service! Several hundred teenagers were counselled during the course of the week, of whom about a hundred and twenty were actual conversions. About 50% were known to be still in the local churches after one year.

We produced a press release which was distributed to the Christian and secular market. As a result of becoming front page headlines in the local paper plus one or two phone calls, we were able to get good television coverage by TVS on their six o'clock News Show 'Coast to Coast'.

Why use the video show?

Using this Video Show format for evangelism amongst teenagers has several benefits:

(1) The show is fast-moving and so the audience does not get easily bored. Even if they don't like a particular element in the programme, they know that this image will soon pass and the next element of the programme will be different and exciting.

(2) There are many amateur local Chrisitan bands, singers and drama groups who whilst being able to perform perhaps three or four items very well during the course of an evening, are overstretched when asked to present a whole concert. The video show format offers them the opportunity of performing and learning without pushing them beyond their capabilities.

(3) It gives the opportunity to develop a particular theme and to make sure that all the items reinforce the same message. Through the evening a foundation can be laid and slowly built on, block by block, to the point where, after a 'preach' which ties all the ends together, a response can be called for on the basis of more than the emotion of a particular moment.

(4) Whereas a traditional schools mission may include one or two evening concerts at the end of the week, through the use of the Video Show a whole series of evangelistic presentations can be put on. Because teenagers have the opportunity to come back night after night they are able to hear, go away, think, chat with friends, ask questions and return again and again before finally making a well thought through decision to follow Christ.

How to plan your own Video Show

Since the Bus Company Video Show I have been involved in similar presentations at Greenbelt and Spring Harvest, and also in the development of a travelling version as part of my work in schools, colleges and churches around the country. As well as this, a number of youth leaders and ministers in this country and abroad have enquired about setting up similar shows as part of their outreach. One or two churches have been in a position to purchase the necessary equipment but many others have been able to hire and borrow it to make their own local video show a possibility. Below is a check list that should enable you to do the same.

(1) Resources needed

(a) Venue
(b) PA system
(c) Lighting
(d) Video projector, screen and mixer
(e) Video recorder
(f) 2 cameras
(g) Supply of videos
(h) Staging
(i) Seating
(j) Publicity

(2) Personnel

(a) Drama groups
(b) Bands/solo performers
(c) Interviewees
(d) Presenters
(e) Administrator
(f) Publicity agent
(g) Prayer secretary
(h) Stage manager
(i) Stewards
(j) Counsellors
(k) Sound man
(l) Lighting operator
(m) Video operator
(n) Two camera men

(3) Follow-up

Planning for follow-up must be done well in advance of the event itself and firm plans laid that can swing into action from the time the first convert is won. (This subject is dealt with in chapter 14.)

17

BEGGARS BANQUET
RESTAURANT

'Eat less . . . pay more.' That was our motto as we served lentil soup, very small portions of chicken curry and rice and glasses of water for as much money as the public were willing to part with at the *Beggars Banquet*, a restaurant which served Third World meals at western prices in the centre of Tonbridge High Street. It was open all day six days a week for a month leading up to Christmas in 1983, and was manned by our youth group with help during school and college hours from other church members. All the profits made were then given to Tear Fund for relief work in the Third World.

Getting involved

The *Beggars Banquet* was a very practical way of helping those in great need, but it also served several other functions. Not only did it give our young people a goal to work for but it was of great benefit to the whole town by helping them express their concern for the Third World at Christmas, a time of year when there is a great awareness that the western world has so much while others have very little or nothing. Lastly, it provided us with a way of telling the town that the church was actively involved in the relief of world suffering.

Rather than simply contributing towards Tear Fund's finances we wanted to give specifically to a project which we could take on ourselves. We were told that there was a project in Southern India to drill wells in some of the small villages that had been very badly hit by the severe famine of over five years' standing and that the cost of drilling one well was about £1000. Our youth group thought that we might be able to raise £1000 through the shop, and so we adopted a village and a well drilling project.

Praying for a shop

It was early in October when I originally talked through the idea with our youth group and asked them to pray about the provision of a suitable shop. Eventually, after several disappointments, we homed in on a disused bakers'. Ideally situated in a central position in the town, it was just the kind of thing we were looking for. I phoned the owners (see chapter fifteen) and briefly explained our project to their property manager, only to be informed that unfortunately they couldn't help because they had a long-standing policy not to let their empty shops out on a short-term basis. He explained that they had already turned down five charities who had made similar requests in the last month. While he was talking I began to think about Elijah calling down the fire on the mountain side and Moses parting the Red Sea: they could do all that and I couldn't even get a measly shop! So I knelt down there and then in my office while the man was still speaking on the phone, and silently prayed, 'Lord, you know that we need premises if this project is to go ahead, but that can only happen if you change this man's mind.' At that very moment the voice at the other end of the phone said, 'On the other hand . . .' and before I knew what was happening he was promising to do his best for me. By the following afternoon we had the keys to the shop and its use right up until Christmas Eve.

Besides our rather thin lentil soup, small chicken curry and a glass of water which had a minimum price of £1.80, we served several other more English meals, including potatoes in their jackets, beans on toast and chicken supreme. Many people would pay for a £2 meal with a £5 note and refuse the change. Others bought cups of coffee for £1 or more, while some popped in simply to make a donation before rushing off again. We were overwhelmed by the enthusiastic response. Television South filmed the restaurant and interviewed us about the concept behind it for their regional news programme, while national radio coverage meant that a number of cheques arrived for the project from distant parts. Cliff Richard was contacted, but couldn't come. Instead he sent an autographed photograph which was framed and then auctioned to the highest bidder, finally going for an astonishing £651! (The buyers were another youth group who ran a sponsored event to pay for it.) By the end of the first week we had already raised over £700, so we decided that rather than aim for £1000 and one drilling project, we'd go for £2000 and two wells! The final profit we were able to give Tear Fund totalled over £4000 with which they eventually drilled five wells in five different villages.

How to serve your own 'Beggar's Banquet'

(1) Find your premises and contact the necessary parties (see chapter 15). Remember that, as your shop front is your best publicity, it's no good getting premises in some back-street where no one ever goes.

(2) Contact Tear Fund or some other Christian relief agency and sort out what kind of scheme you are going to support. Remember that people are more likely to give to a specific cause than to the general kitty!

(3) Set a financial target just beyond that which you think is attainable. You now have a challenge on your hands.

(4) When you've got your shop, appoint from your youth group a:

(a) General manager	(e) Waitress team
(b) Chef	(f) Accountant/cashier
(c) Kitchen team	(g) Publicity/press secretary
(d) Head waiter	(h) Maintenance and decoration crew

(5) Now together start work at obtaining the following items:

(a) Paint
(b) Carpet
(c) Lighting
(d) Tables
(e) Chairs
(f) Cutlery
(g) Crockery
(h) Cooking utensils
(i) Cookers (we used old ones run by calor gas and borrowed from the Boys Brigade)
(j) Fridge
(k) Freezer
(l) Microwave oven
(m) Cash desk and accounts book
(n) Heating—we used fan heaters
(o) Washing-up liquid and tea towels
(p) Serviettes and trays

Notes

(a) *Decoration*—people don't like eating in shabby conditions (and in any case you will have to meet health regulations). You may need to paint your premises (it's amazing what a couple of cans of emulsion can do). With some old carpet, a few plants, a bit of lighting you can have the place looking quite inviting! The *Beggars Banquet* took a week to clean and decorate before we could open the doors to the public.

(b) *Cooking equipment*—for quick service you must be well equipped.

(6) Menu—you're not the Ritz! Be practical. Don't offer food that you can't produce quickly. Do you have a local Cash and Carry card?

(7) Publicity—personally visit your local paper. This is a front page story and they want the news as much as you need the publicity. Don't be intimidated by the mystique of the media!

(8) Put a prayer and news sheet out to all the local churches, which will not only inform them but encourage their active support.

Don't be put off by this massive list. Much of the equipment we used was donated or lent free of charge by local businesses. Local traders will want to help and just need to be approached. We had enormous help from so many people and shops in the area. All kinds of things were donated, from cash registers and microwave ovens, to fridges, paint and even dining tables and chairs. When we got permission to use the shop I was given a gift of £50 to help set it up and when we opened I still had £5 left in my pocket!

18

RADIO CHRISTMAS

Health Warning . . . only read the following chapter if you want a really tough challenge. Radio Christmas was the most technically complicated and time consuming project that I have ever been involved with on a local scale! Because of this I have set out two versions of it here, first the project in its original form as we ran it in Tonbridge, and then a much simpler idea for running the same kind of scheme on a smaller scale.

Radio Christmas—version one

In July 1984 I was asked by Invicta Radio (Kent's commercial radio station) to present a weekly Sunday morning show. This helped me to see the opportunities that broadcasting presents to the church, and also gave me some insights into the practical aspects of producing and presenting radio. So was born the idea of Radio Christmas, a radio station which would broadcast for a month leading up to Christmas Eve and focus on the same principles as the *Beggars Banquet* (described in chapter seventeen) had done the year before.

Getting started
We negotiated with the Home Office regarding the possibility of obtaining a 'Community Radio' licence to broadcast around the town on medium wave or FM, though it soon became clear that any form of broadcasting would be illegal and therefore a

non starter. Not wanting to give up, we hit on the idea of setting up a studio in the town centre which would actually cable a signal up and down both sides of the High Street and into each shop. Because we were not broadcasting we knew that this scheme would not require a licence. Shoppers who heard Radio Christmas as they wandered in and out of the shops in the town centre and as they passed our studio, would have the opportunity to pop in and leave a donation for relief work in the Third World (we had already decided to support a project which had been set up by World Vision to work amongst children at a feeding station in Southern Ethiopia). At the studio they would also be able to make a record request or dedication for a friend or for those working in a particular shop or simply just wish the whole of Tonbridge a happy Christmas.

Cabling the High Street

In effect our plan was to run one huge public address system around the town centre, sending a signal through an ordinary two core cable up one side of the High Street (which is about half a mile long) across the road and then down the other. We planned to run the cable along the shop faces, just above their name boards, and then when a particular shop wanted to be fed our signal we would tap into the line, run a cable through a window or other opening and down into the store. By fitting a five pin DIN plug or a phono socket to the end and connecting it up to their hi-fi or other sound gear the shop could then receive our programming through their ordinary equipment. This meant we didn't have to provide speakers and that we only had to supply the signal at line level. Our signal was then amplified by each individual shop. This gave the shop complete control not only of the volume but also of the on/off switch.

The big problem was getting hold of enough cable and then installing it. In all we needed about one and a half miles of cable which I estimated could cost as much as £1000 to buy. We prayed about this little problem and then approached several national cable making companies, whose names I found in the *Yellow Pages*, with the result that eventually one agreed to supply all we needed completely free of charge. A local store agreed to provide all the DIN plugs and phono sockets we required on the same basis. We employed a team of three young men who had previously been involved with running the radio station for 'Greenbelt' to work in Tonbridge for a week installing the cable, tapping off points down into the individual shops, and connecting the stereos. In the end, as well as cabling the entire High Street we were able, with the help of British Telecom (who gave us free use of several land lines under the town's river and railways), to 'wire up' the local leisure centre and the two biggest supermarkets in the town which were situated elsewhere.

Running repairs

A major problem we faced was that because we were running one huge public/address system which linked the whole of Tonbridge High Street, any break or short in the cable had a rather drastic effect on the reception in many of the shops. On one day almost half of the shops were unable to receive any signal at all for almost three hours, during which time we frantically searched almost every inch of the cable up and down the High Street, only to discover eventually that the broken cable was in the studio where the girl serving coffee to the DJs had trodden on it with her stiletto heel! There was one other difficult day when again reception totally disappeared all down one side of the High Street. A search eventually revealed that where our cable ran along the front of a building site (a new shopping arcade was in the process of being erected) an unknowing construction worker had authorized the pouring of about three tons of concrete on top of it. It was completely severed! We found that we always needed to have at least one engineer on duty.

Building up a record library

Another local store sponsored the project by donating the top thirty each week, along with a generous supply of other Christmas records. We also wrote to the big record companies informing them about what we were doing with the result that we obtained from some of them free copies of LPs and singles which they were promoting. In this way we built up an adequate record library which was supplemented with 'Golden Oldies' given by members of the youth group and records that those who worked as DJs brought in with them for their own shows. We contacted the Performing Rights Society who gave us an exemption certificate on the payment of royalties for the records we played.

Wiring up the shops

We now had to obtain the support of the local shop owners as well as their willingness to participate in the scheme. To do this we first visited a meeting of the local Chamber of Trade and obtained their backing, which gave us credibility as we approached individual shopkeepers. The Chamber circulated a letter to all their members and we then visited every shop in the High Street to introduce further the concept of Radio Christmas. We spent a lot of time explaining to owners and managers how they could be involved by allowing it to play on their premises. Whether or not a shop wished to take our signal it was important that we gain permission from the owner to run our main cable along the front of his premises. In the end well over half of the shops in Tonbridge High Street who were able to receive our signal participated in the scheme whilst a fair percentage of those who did not were only left out because they did not possess the necessary stereo equipment to be wired in! Throughout the project we had a waiting list of shops wanting to come on to our network.

We negotiated with the town council regarding the cable which we were proposing running against the shops up each side of the High Street and which also had to run across many side streets. They gave us permission to do this but stipulated that where we crossed a street we must provide adequate clearance (twenty feet) for articulated lorries and buses.

Manning the studio

We set up our studio in the front of the local United Reformed Church which, besides being ideally placed right in the centre of the High Street, is also a very attractive modern building with a glass front. This meant that the studio was very visible to the whole community and that the station was brought into the heart of the shopping area.

Our DJs were all members of the youth group at Tonbridge Baptist Church or ministers of local churches. I gave them all a crash course in how to operate the studio desk, although some presenters preferred to have an assistant to do this for them rather than 'self-op'. We also arranged for local celebrities to visit the studio, to be interviewed and record a Christmas greeting for the town which we could then play as a kind of 'jingle' from time to time. Through our contact with a local hospital radio station we also obtained a set of Christmas jingles.

As the DJs introduced records or talked about discs they would, from time to time, chat about the meaning of Christmas or their own Christian commitment. We also advertised all that was going on in the churches over the Christmas period and had in the studio a good supply of free leaflets which gave details of events and explained what Christmas was really about and how to become a Christian.

The Radio Christmas Schools Cassette

We visited all of the local primary and junior schools as well as a few senior schools and recorded their choirs singing Christmas carols. Besides playing these on the air, we produced a tape for £2.50, of which we sold several hundred copies. The cost of production was just under £1 so that £1.50 went to the Ethiopian famine relief fund. For this it was necessary to contact the Performing Rights Society, supply them with the names of the authors and arrangers of the pieces of music we used.

Because we had already been granted exemption from royalties on the project we did not have to make any payment to them with regard to the production of the cassette.

Jesus on the air waves

We negotiated with Radio Kent (the BBC station, Invicta's rivals!) who agreed to do a three hour 'outside broadcast' from Tonbridge to launch the project. This got us off to a promising start and gave us some great publicity. The station was on the air for four complete weeks leading up to Christmas Eve. We broadcast from Monday to Saturday and from 9 am to 8 pm each evening (because several of the larger shops were open until that time). We obtained the interest of local newspapers and radio as well as regional television. TVS gave us considerable air time on their six o'clock show 'Coast To Coast' which follows the national news.

The four weeks spent operating Radio Christmas was very hard work indeed, but the impact on the town and surrounding towns was quite tremendous. By Christmas Eve we had raised almost £7000 for relief work in Ethiopia and successfully united the whole town in an effort to give to others. We had also shown the whole community that the church was alive and actively involved in meeting the needs of the Third World. On top of all this, Radio Christmas gave us the opportunity to present the gospel to all sorts of people who would never otherwise hear it. Several who are now mature Christians were converted during the project or as a direct result of it.

Radio Christmas—version two

Radio Christmas was a technically complicated and time-consuming project both to set up and run. There will be those who are drawn to the idea of running their own radio station who are intimidated by the work load involved in setting up and maintaining such a project. An exciting and simpler alternative (one that I would like to try some time) is to negotiate with a large department store in your town and then set up a station inside it. All the management need to do is give you a few feet of floor space in a corner somewhere to run your studio, and allow you to tap into their existing public address system from your mixing desk. This will then carry your signal around the store providing good Christmas music, instead of the usual muzak. Because of local press publicity, much attention and custom will be attracted to the store (two commodities which more than compensate the management for the inconvenience of having the studio on their floor space!).

Obviously, this scheme is far easier to organize than a townwide project. The only cable needed is that which connects with the shop's internal public address system; there are no negotiations with Council, British Telecom or the Chamber of Trade; nor do you have to find an empty shop or conveniently placed church building. So try Version Two this Christmas and Version One next year!

Resources needed

Personnel
(a) DJs (we operated a system with two and three hour shows)
(b) Tea makers (we served tea and coffee to those who popped into the studio)
(c) Receptionists (to take requests, sort out records and handle the donations)
(d) Technical staff (essential that at least one is always on duty!)

Equipment
(a) Studio
(b) Mixing desk (at least six channels)
(c) Microphones and microphone stands (two or three)
(d) Two record decks
(e) One cassette deck
(f) One reel to reel machine (helpful but not essential)
(g) Compressor (this stops too much variation in the sound level output)
(h) One accurate clock with second hand
(i) Records and tapes
(j) Jingles (again not essential)
(k) One and a half miles of cable!* (you will have to do your own measurements)
(l) Ample supply of DIN and phono sockets/plugs*
(m) Cable joining blocks* (used for running off the cable into each shop)
(n) Amplifier to act as line driver*
(o) Small amplifier and speaker to act as a studio monitor

system and run a couple of speakers outside for passers-by.

*These items are only applicable to Radio Christmas Version One.

19

INTER-CHURCH ACTIVITY

'Streetbeat', 'The Bus Company Video Show' and 'Radio Christmas' were all projects which were originally undertaken on a townwide basis in Tonbridge and involved a group of seven churches working together. All of the other projects mentioned in this book were planned and organized by Tonbridge Baptist Church. Working on an inter-denominational basis is more difficult than working alone, so why do it?

Reasons for inter-church activity

It's good to get involved with the churches in your town for a number of reasons:

(1) Involvement of this kind demonstrates that the church is one. We spend a lot of time painstakingly attempting to teach this principle to young people, whereas it is often very obvious that there is little real evidence to suggest it is true. To spend time working together, learning together and getting to know each other is of the greatest value to all involved. It also becomes a visible expression to the community that the churches are one. One of the greatest of the stumbling blocks which prevent people of all ages becoming Christians is undoubtedly the problem of which denomination is the true church. Only by working together can we convince others that we are one.

(2) Working together with other denominations and groups will open the eyes of your own young people to new ideas and increase their vision and concept of the church as a whole. It is too easy for them to grow up within one denominational structure, unaware that God is at work beyond their local fellowship and even their denomination. It is obviously good for our teenagers to see how other Christians work and think.

(3) By giving our young people the opportunity of meeting other Christians from across the town we help them to understand that they belong to something big, which is a very practical way of encouraging them to live for Christ at school. It is great for them to see that there are teenagers from each of the schools right across the town who share a common faith with them.

(4) Inter-denominational activity enables teenage boys to meet teenage girls and vice versa! This may sound rather unspiritual but, in reality, one of the biggest problems for many young people in our churches is that they do not have the opportunity to meet Christians of the opposite sex—or at least, suitable members of it! Many eventually become romantically involved with non-Christians and as a result often drift away from a living walk with Christ.

(5) By working together you can often plan projects on a larger scale, because you will obviously have greater resources at your disposal and be in a position to call on more support. When it comes to evangelism this means that it is possible to make a bigger impact on your town or area.

How to go about it

If you want to work together with other youth groups in your town, here are some practical steps to take:

(1) Write a letter to the other church youth leaders in your town explaining to them what you want to do and why. A week later, phone round them all and find out how they

feel about this. If they are in favour, you are in business.

(2) Arrange a meeting. This is easiest to achieve by phone, though even then it can prove quite difficult. The best way of approaching it is to suggest a number of dates to each person you ring, asking them to indicate which ones would be most convenient. You will probably be able to draw together at least one date when the majority, if not all, of those involved can be present.

(3) At this first meeting your task is to consider carefully and then clarify the group's aims. You may think such matters are so obvious that it is not worth spending time discussing them. In Tonbridge an inter-church youth association had existed for many years and once a year they arranged a barn dance and a sports day. Nobody quite knew why these particular events were organized or why nothing else ever happened, but as I became involved with the group the answer was actually quite clear—it was simply not the stated aim to do anything else. The group had no clear, written purpose to guide their thinking and so down through the years they had become nothing more than a barn dance committee.

(4) Contact the council of churches or the ministers' fraternal. It is very important to talk to them at this stage. Explain to them your vision and aims and obtain their advice and support.

(5) Having got this far, some kind of leadership structure must be set up before you move on to the next stage of working out a strategy and planning particular projects. Your group will only ever be as good as its leadership. You need to appoint a chairman, a secretary and a treasurer with the time, energy and vision for the job. It's no good choosing the most gifted Christian person in town if he is already over-committed to other things. Also, remember that although these are the three most important appointments, everyone who serves on the committee needs to be in a position to take on responsibility.

(6) Now get on with the job, remembering to involve as many as possible of the young people themselves in real responsibility. Your planning group should meet on a monthly basis for business, and if possible on a separate occasion for prayer.

(7) You may decide that you want to explore the possibility of becoming a Youth For Christ Centre or of affiliating to some other national youth organization. The great value of this course of action is the invaluable external support and objective advice based on a wealth of experience gained over the years that such an organization can offer. In Tonbridge we chose to become a Youth For Christ Centre because of their great emphasis on, and experience in, evangelism. If you are interested in such a course of action, contact those concerned who would be glad to send a representative to discuss the possibility further. The address of British Youth For Christ is given at the back of this book and more information can be obtained from their headquarters.

20

HOW TO USE THE MEDIA

'The local press are never interested in what we do at all, in fact we think that they are probably biased against the church and Christian events.' Many Christians adopt this view because at one time or the other they informed the press about what they were doing and got little or no response. Now they feel it's just not worth the effort of trying to get coverage for their events. Even when it comes to the Christian press or the Christian Sunday morning slot on the local radio, there is still the feeling, 'They won't be interested . . . we're just not big enough news.' Having worked as a presenter for a local radio station and also been involved with other media, I've discovered that nothing could be much further from the truth!

Below are three principles that it is important to grasp concerning the media:

(1) All media are continually searching for good news material; it is their life-blood. Added to this, at a local level there are several interesting developments. Generally speaking the readership of local newspapers is falling and in an attempt to halt this slide most publishers are increasingly aware that their papers must develop good public relations. When it comes to local radio, again the management are very keen to reflect what is happening throughout the community. If you are running something newsworthy, they are missing out on an opportunity if they do not report it. They

need your news as much as you need their interest! This is especially true in the many areas of the country where there are now two local stations, one BBC and the other IBA (Independent Broadcasting Authority), where a rivalry develops in the attempt to attract the bigger audience. As a result they are very keen to know and report on what is going on in the community. The Christian press are also keen to know what you are doing. When we ran 'Streetbeat' in Tonbridge (described in chapter fifteen) we did not bother to issue a press release because of the hurried nature of the project. Some months later the editor of a weekly Christian newspaper gave me a telling off, pointing out that I had a responsibility to him and others in his position to keep them informed! I have since had this message reinforced by several others.

(2) All 'media people' are very busy with tight schedules and deadlines so the time and effort they can give to this quest is limited. We often imagine that local papers and radio stations and the Christian press operate with a huge staff waiting to pounce on each and every relevant story that breaks. This is not true! Every local paper, local radio station, Christian magazine or denominational newspaper that I know of is run by a small, highly committed staff who work as hard and fast as they possibly can to meet their deadlines and simply do not have the time to hunt for material. Whilst presenting a Sunday morning show for local radio, I was forever longing that local Christians would write in informing me of what they are doing but this very rarely happened, although I sometimes got complaints that I should be giving more coverage to what they were doing! It was somehow expected that I would miraculously know what was going on across the country and approach them. Unfortunately, I had no means of knowing this at all, except what I could read in the local papers or the Christian press or stumble upon during my travels! As I was also working as assistant pastor of a church with a congregation of over four hundred, a time-consuming task in itself! I did

not have the time or energy to do much hunting. Although there are about a hundred local radio stations in this country, I only know of two or three that have a full-time religious producer or presenter.

(3) All 'media people' are continually bombarded with badly presented information and publicity for almost every sort of event imaginable, and simply don't have the time to work their way carefully through it all. Therefore, any material that you present must stand out from the crowd.

How to prepare and use a press release

In some situations adverts are well worth taking out but the best coverage always comes free, when a newspaper or magazine writes up your event in its editorial space. So exactly how do you get the local and even national media to cover your event? Though there is no watertight answer to this question, and nothing you do can ever guarantee coverage, a good press release can be a most effective tool.

What is a press release?

A press release should give the facts about your event in a snappy and exciting manner, using short phrases, sentences and paragraphs, and with clear headings for easy scanning. The first paragraph should contain the most significant news (in case someone reads no further!) and should be presented in a way that will capture attention. People will pay attention to something that is humorous, heart-warming or out of the ordinary, so let this be your first sentence.

The press release should be typed with double spacing on one side only of A4 paper, with at least a two inch margin down one side. At the bottom put the day-time telephone number of at least one person from whom further information can be obtained by a reporter.

How to use a press release

(a) Look through the Yellow Pages to obtain the addresses and telephone numbers of local newspapers and radio stations. Any numbers you cannot find can be obtained from Directory Enquiries.

(b) Ring all these contact numbers. Very briefly explain your story to the receptionist and ask who you should contact about it. Make sure to have a pencil and pad ready to write down their name and position. If you don't have the address of some of these contacts, make sure you get that too as personally addressed mail is far more likely to be dealt with.

For those with plenty of money, Pimms of 4 St Johns Place, St Johns Square, London EC1 4AH publish a monthly media directory covering everything from radio and television to the national, local specialist and Christian press. The directory has a listing of every news publication of any sort produced in Great Britain, including the names of sub-editors for the national press (and those responsible for church news). It lists every radio and television programme both nationally and regionally and gives the name of the appropriate producer, as well as the address at which to contact him, along with a telephone number. Those without the money and wishing to look at this directory should try the reference section of their nearest main library.

(c) Two or three weeks before your event, post your press release to the people whose names you've been given. As you continue to put on events you will slowly build up your own contact list. Record names, telephone numbers and addresses in a notebook. These contacts will gradually come to trust and respect you, knowing that if you are involved in an event it is worth covering because it will be well organized.

(d) Very many press releases arrive on the desk of editors and producers so make sure your press release is followed up with a phone call several days later.

(e) Don't give up. None of this will guarantee success, and

even if you do get a story in a local paper or the national press, you may sometimes be disappointed with the finished product. While I worked with the youth group in Tonbridge, though we had many stories which had good coverage locally and some which were covered nationally by newspapers as well as radio and television, we also had more failures at this level than I can remember! In fact, there may be no apparent objective reason why one story is taken and another ignored. Just keep on going.

21

WALKING ON WATER

Learning to take risks

'One of the greatest failures of all time.' That's the way Peter's attempt to walk on water is most generally remembered. At Spring Harvest in 1986 Peter Meadows preached a sermon at the closing Communion in Prestatyn which I remember very clearly. He spoke about the time when Peter saw Jesus walking on the water and at once climbed out of the fishing boat he was in and took a few steps across the choppy lake towards his Master. As soon as he took his eyes off Jesus and looked at the wind and waves he rapidly began to sink. It was only the hand of Jesus that saved him from certain death. The other much wiser disciples decided sensibly to leave Jesus to do any walking on the water that had to be done whilst they kept their feet firmly inside the boat.

But how many people do you know who have walked on water? Besides Jesus himself, Peter is the only man in the history of the world ever to achieve such a great accomplishment. It was truly *Guinness Book Of Records* material! Peter's few steps across the water, far from being one of the greatest defeats or failures of all time, was one of history's most outstanding achievements.

I remember being told some years ago that if you came up with a really good idea and presented it to an Englishman, by the time you had finished telling him about it he would have thought of three reasons why it would never work. On the other hand, if you gave the same idea to an American, by the time you had finished explaining it to him he would have thought of three ways in which it could be put into practice.

Get out of the boat

Two years ago I attended a management course where the lecturer stated that he felt all British people tend to be pessimistic in their outlook. If you take this basic outlook on life and mix it with a good dose of Christian teaching about personal responsibility and sin you are often left with people who feel totally inadequate, insignificant and unworthy—people who do not believe in themselves or in God's ability to use them in any significant way at all.

We are told of all sorts of reasons why the church in this country is not growing: it needs to work harder at this or that, it needs to plan more effectively and efficiently, to give more generously, to pray more consistently, to re-appraise its priorities and increase its vision. Whilst I am sure that many of these things are in part true there is a far more fundamental problem than all of this, which these other answers often serve to increase rather than help solve. There is the need to believe in ourselves because God believes in us and has chosen to use us. This is not humanism, in fact it is the very opposite! Our assessment of our worth is not based on human considerations but on God's ability to take hold of us and use us beyond our wildest dreams. The church needs to be positive and optimistic, to follow Peter, and get out of the boat! Yes, there was failure mixed with his great success, but don't forget that Peter took several steps more across the water than any other human being has ever done before or since! He started to sink only when he began to think about the situation he was in and his limitations rather than looking at Jesus who had already told him to come.

Think big . . . plan realistically

In our youth work we need Peter's obedience and enthusiasm, but most of all we need his trust. How often has a really good idea been squashed because of an 'It's impossible, we've tried before, it didn't work then and it won't work now' attitude! As a well-known poster states, 'Most people who say things are impossible are proved wrong by those who do them.' It is said of the people in Dallas, Texas, that they think big and build bigger. God wants Christian youth leaders who will think big, plan realistically and then build! We are to have large vision but also the energy to do the hard work that brings the vision into being. It's easy to talk in grand terms; it's difficult to translate these into reality. But it can be done when people are prepared to stick at a task even when at first it seems impossible.

Several of the projects that I have outlined in the second section of this book have been ones that I have been told outright would never work. For instance, take the Video Show described in chapter sixteen. About three weeks before the first event was due to begin I drove home late from Sevenoaks, where I had been speaking, and I will never forget the sinking feeling that I had when I was in that car. I would have done anything rather than have to go through with the Video Show which I felt sure would be one of the biggest disasters ever; I almost called the whole thing off.

Listening to God

Please don't read this book and feel that if you are to ever be a worthy youth leader you have got to put its projects into practice one after the other, slowly working your way through the chapters. The outlines given here can be used as they stand, adapted, or even stood on their heads. The aim of this book is to provide guidelines and principles that can be used on projects similar to the ones mentioned or translated into totally different settings, to form the basis for all sorts of new and exciting ideas. Don't just copy what I or others have done but take hold of the opportunities that you are given. I ran the 'Bus Company Video Show' because we happened to live in a town that had an empty bus station, and I happened to have a conversation with Steve Goddard of *Buzz* magazine about the use of video. I'm sure God provided these two resources and my job was simply to bring them together and work hard to make the idea happen. Listen to what God is saying to you— there are many openings and opportunities for those who have ears and eyes that are open.

I am now developing other projects which are not outlined here. Recently we have set up a Trust and are working on a housing project for homeless teenagers, a telephone counselling project and an advice centre as well as a scheme to give young people full-time training in evangelism. These are all opportunities which God has provided and the amazing thing is that beyond them there are many more which he will introduce to us at the right time. William Carey, the man who founded the Baptist Missionary Society, once said, 'Expect great things from God, attempt great things for God.' When we expect great things from God we must be prepared to be the answer to our own prayers by attempting great things in his name. My hope is that this book will inspire many who read it to attempt great things in God's name.

CHECKLISTS

FOR CHAPTERS 8 TO 18

CHECKLIST TO CHAPTER 8

Youth Service

		Allocated to	Done
6 months	Decide aim and target group (see chapter 7). Talk idea through with minister/church leaders. Book date or series of dates. Discuss finance of possible outside speakers etc with church leaders. Book speaker (confirm in writing).		
4 months	Inform youth group. Brainstorming session. Decide theme. Appoint planning group.		
3 months	Hold planning group meeting. Allocate jobs. Book publicity/invitation cards.		
2 months	Rehearse drama/music etc.		
1 month	Fix date and time of dress rehearsal. Contact speaker, inform him of arrangements. Ask for readings, songs, hymns etc. Encourage youth to invite friends. Arrange hospitality for speaker.		
2 weeks	Remind participants of date and time for dress rehearsals. Clear music arrangements with church organist!		

		Allocated to	Done
1 week	Remind participants of date and time of dress rehearsal! Check last minute details with speaker.		
On the day	Meet speaker. Dress rehearsal. All participants to arrive by stated time. Prayer meeting. Pay speaker.		
After the event	De-briefing meeting. Encourage those who took part. Start planning for next date. Letter of thanks to speaker.		

Youth Houseparties, Conferences and Camps

		Allocated to	Done
1 year – 6 months	Decide on aim and target group (see chapter 1).		
	Check idea and proposed date with church leaders.		
	Appoint planning group.		
	Book speaker(s) and confirm in writing.		
	Decide whether to stay at home or go away.		
	How many places do you need?		
	Within what radius must the venue be?		
	Decide on 3 possible venues.		
	Option 1 2 3 Decide theme, consult with the speaker.		
	Plan timetable (consult with speaker).		
	Book films and other resources (confirm in writing).		
	Set departure and return times.		
	Book coach for transport and confirm in writing.		
	Prepare budget.		
	Will the camp be subsidized by central funds?		
	Prepare and distribute publicity sheet/ booking form.		
	Book all necessary equipment.		
3 months	Book Saturday afternoon outing/bowling centre etc and confirm in writing.		
	Prepare menu (if self-catering).		

		Allocated to	Done
2 months	Check with centre for rules and regulations concerning meals and curfews etc. Prepare brochure for those attending. If planning to attend a local church on the Sunday morning, write and inform them.		
1 month	Distribute brochure. How many volunteer drivers do you need for transport to and from the church? Ask for volunteer drivers.		
2 weeks – *1 week*	Buy food. Check with coach for last minute details. Check with speaker for last minute details. Check with venue. Check all other participants. Hold briefing/prayer meeting for leaders.		
At event	Pay speaker. Pay centre.		
After *event*	De-briefing meeting. Pay coach company etc. Write thank yous to speaker, centre and any other participants.		

Concert

		Allocated to	Done
1 year – *6 months*	Decide on aim and target group of concert (see chapter 7). Check idea with church leaders. Appoint planning group. Contact artists, speakers etc. Decide on mutually convenient date. Book artist and confirm in writing. Book hall and confirm in writing. Check details. Prepare budget. Fix ticket price. Circulate information around local organizations, churches and supporters.		
4 – 3 *months*	Book schools visits. Appoint required personnel. Order publicity (is this obtainable from the artist?). Order tickets. Book sound and lighting equipment (if necessary). Book piano tuner (?). Confirm all bookings in writing.		
8 weeks	Prepare counselling cards. Plan counselling arrangements. Plan counselling training. Order counselling literature. Brief bookstall manager/local Christian bookshop.		

		Allocated to	Done
	Distribute tickets to sales outlets. Fix accommodation for guests (if needed).		
6 – 4 weeks	Prepare press release. Put tickets on sale. Distribute posters etc.		
4 – 3 weeks	Distribute press release (see chapter 20). Work out final programme and timing of evening.		
2 weeks	Hold production meeting (see personnel list). Check through all details of bookings with band, hall, equipment etc.		
1 week	Contact band. Check on counselling arrangements. Hold prayer/briefing meetings. Buy refreshments.		
On the day	Meet band at hall with humpers. Brief refreshment and bookstall helpers and stewards. Meal for band. Prayer meeting. Counsellors' meeting. Pay artists. Introduce guests to overnight hosts.		
After the event	De-briefing meeting. Follow-up (see chapter 14). Letters of thanks.		

Open Air

		Allocated to	Done
3 months	Decide on aim and target group (see chapter 7). Appoint planning group.		
2 months	Choose site. Arrange amplification (if appropriate). How will this be powered? Battery, generator or supply from nearby shop? Inform local council. Plan programme. Inform youth group and church.		
1 month	Prepare or obtain literature to be distributed. Prepare questionnaire. Commence rehearsals for drama/music etc.		
2 – 1 week	Inform police. Inform local shopkeepers. Check availability of material with all performers. Prayer/briefing meeting. Publish programme. Confirm meeting time for open air.		
On the day	Prayer meeting. Briefing.		

Evangelistic Mission

		Allocated to	Done

1 year –
6 months
	Decide aim and target group (see chapter 7).
	Discuss idea with church leadership.
	Discuss with other local churches if appropriate (see chapter 19).
	Appoint steering group:
	  (a) Administrator
	  (b) Treasurer
	  (c) Prayer secretary
	  (d) Press/publicity officer
	  (e) Chief counsellor
	  (f) Representatives of all youth groups in the area or of the different activities within the local church.
	Book visiting evangelist(s), bands etc.
	Arrange initial planning meeting with them.
	Plan counselling and nurture arrangements.
	Plan training sessions for counsellors and nurture group leaders (see chapter 14 and checklist).
	Prepare budget.
	Inform other local churches.
	Initiate planning for separate concerts etc (see separate checklists).		

4 months	Produce prayer, news and information sheet for churches. Approach possible local participants. Meet with visiting participants (discuss their ideas). Draw up provisional programme.		

		Allocated to	Done
3 months	Order publicity. Order tickets. Prayer and news up-date to churches. Approach schools (booking schools work). Start prayer groups. Order evangelistic literature.		
2 months	Up-date churches. Arrange hospitality for visiting bands, speakers (comfortable beds, doubles for married couples, singles for singles!). Prepare press release (see chapter 20). Check programme with participants. Prepare counselling cards. Start counselling and nurture training sessions.		
1 month	Distribute publicity posters etc. Up-date churches.		
2 weeks	Check all bookings for last minute details.		
1 week	Up-date churches. Final briefing/prayer meeting for counsellors.		
After the event	De-briefing meeting. Letter of thanks.		

CHECKLIST TO CHAPTER 14

Follow-up

		Allocated to	Done
1 year – 6 months	Plan follow-up classes. Appoint chief counsellor. Decide on follow-up/nurture materials. Plan venue or venues for nurture groups, dates, times, duration of course. Order materials. Decide on evangelistic literature. Order material. Plan training course for counsellors (training day). Plan training course of nurture group leaders (training day). Appoint nurture group leaders. Approach possible counsellors.		
4 – 3 months	Get samples of nurture literature for group leaders. Run nurture group training course. Prepare counselling card.		
2 – 1 month	Run counsellors' training course or day. Collect evangelistic literature. Collect nurture group material.		
1 week	Briefing/prayer meeting for counsellors. Briefing/prayer meeting for nurture group leaders.		
On the day	Final briefing for counsellors. Issue badges etc.		

		Allocated to	Done
	Announce central nurture group meetings at event. Collect completed counselling forms.		

After event	Process counselling cards.
	 Issue copies to:
	    (a) local churches
	    (b) schools
	    (c) nurture group leaders.
	 Check on progress of nurture groups after 1 week.
	 Check on progress after 1 month.		

Using Vacant Shops and Premises on a Temporary Basis

		Allocated to	Done
1 year – 6 months	Decide on idea, aim and target group (see chapter 7). Talk through idea with church leadership.		
4 – 3 months	Make list of suitable vacant shops etc in locality. Contact owners (by phone if possible) registering interest in the temporary use of their premises. If favourable, ask for date when confirmation could be given. If it is not possible to contact owner, contact estate agent handling sale. Keep a look out for new empty shops coming on to the market.		

1 month	Contact the list of owners again.
	If the use of a particular shop is agreed, confirm booking in writing.
	Now immediately:
	Appoint planning group.
	Contact relevant authorities:
	   (a) electricity board
	   (b) gas board
	   (c) water authorities
	   (d) local police
	   (e) health and hygiene
	   (f) fire services
	Check on insurance cover.
	Prepare and order publicity etc.		

		Allocated to	Done
	Book schools work (?). Book bands (?). Book speaker (?). Others (?). Arrange renovation and decoration of premises. Issue prayer/information sheet to churches. Prepare press release. Distribute press release. Arrange tables/chairs and all other necessary equipment.		
1 week	Prayer meeting/briefing session for all involved.		
After the event	Leave premises clean and tidy. Write letter of thanks to owner and others involved.		

COFFEE BARS

For coffee bars, work through relevant checklists:

1 Evangelistic mission
2 Planning a concert
3 Temporary use of vacant premises.

Video Show

		Allocated to	Done
1 year – *6 months*	Decide on idea, aim and target group (see chapter 7). Discuss and agree the idea with church leaders. *If you're looking for an equivalent of your local bus station, work through chapter 15 and checklist.* Appoint planning group. *Now work through checklists for* *'Evangelistic Mission' and 'Concert'.*		
4 – 3 *months*	Book video projector, screen and mixer. Video recorder. 2 cameras. Supply a video. Book personnel. Local drama, mime, interviews etc.		

CHECKLIST TO CHAPTER 17

Beggars Banquet

		Allocated to	Done
1 year – 6 months	Decide on aim and target group (see chapter 7). Discuss idea with church leaders. *Work through 'Using Vacant Shops' checklist.*		
4 months	Contact relief agency. Decide on relevant project to support.		
1 month	When you've got your shop, appoint personnel. Obtain equipment. Order and obtain publicity/ prayer sheet. Prepare press release. Prepare menu.		
2 – 1 week	Order food. Decorate shop.		

Radio Christmas

Version One		Allocated to	Done

1 year –
6 months
	Decide on idea and aim (see chapter 7).
	Do you want to work with Radio Christmas Version One or Version Two? (if Two, see next checklist).
	Discuss idea with church leaders.
	Appoint planning group:
	  (a) administrator
	  (b) treasurer
	  (c) technical manager
	  (d) press and publicity officer.
	If planning on an inter-church basis, see chapter 19.
	If planning to use a vacant premises as a studio, see chapter 15 and relevant checklist.
	Decide on the exact area which you wish to cable (High Street, shopping centre, shopping mall etc).
	Measure this area, calculate where you will cross roads etc.
	Contact large national cable manufacturers and ask for their help, tell them about your project and its aim, obtain required length of cheap or free 2-core cable (if this proves impossible you may then consider Version Two).
	Approach British Telecom if needed.
	Contact relief agency and decide on relevant project to support.		

4 months	Approach the local branch of the Chamber of		

		Allocated to	Done

Trade, ask for their support and backing of your project.

Contact highways department of local council (obtain permission to cross side streets with cable etc).

Write to Performing Rights Society asking for exemption from royalties on charitable basis.

3 months Send a letter to all the shops in the High Street (if possible this should be done jointly in the name of the church and the chamber of trade). This letter should:

    (a) Inform them about Radio Christmas

    (b) Ask for their permission to cable above their shop face.

    (c) Ask for their involvement, playing the station on their premises.

Include a tear-off slip for their reply on which they can also request a personal visit to talk through further details.

Appoint a team of shop visitors. Familiarize them with the overall concept and then visit each shop giving more details, offering Radio Christmas and explaining how it would work and be fitted.

Check that each shop has suitable equipment for receiving your signal.

Send out a prayer and information letter to all the local churches. In this, ask for volunteers to act as receptionists, tea makers and members of a crew for laying cables.

Appoint a team of engineers under technical manager.

Approach local shops for supplies of sockets and plugs, records etc.

Get technical team working on the setting up and operation of a studio. For this, they will need the list of equipment printed on page 177.

Write to record companies telling them of your project and asking for singles and LPs which may be available.

Write to local celebrities asking for their involvement.

Negotiate with local radio station for outside broadcast coverage of your project.

	Allocated to	Done
Write to schools about taking part in the production of a cassette for sale. Up-date to churches (asking for golden oldy records and any others to add to your record library). Write to local churches for information concerning Christmas services to be included in your publicity. Write to the relief agency you are working with asking for publicity concerning the project you are supporting.		
2 months Appoint team for the installation of cables. Decide on hours of broadcasting. Work out timetable for shows. Appoint DJs, studio receptionists, tea makers. Install cable (this job will probably have to be done slowly over the course of the next 2 months on Saturdays and other convenient times). You will need several good sets of ladders. Design and print dedication forms.		
1 month Design and print leaflet including information of what is on and happening over the Christmas period in the churches. Finalize station timetable.		
6 weeks Record cassette in schools. Have it copied by a recording company such as ICC or Springtide (addresses given at the back of this book). Inform the Performing Rights Society of this. Print cover and inserts.		
2 weeks Prayer and information up-date to churches.		
1 week Install studio. Hold prayer/briefing meeting for all involved.		
After the event Thank you letters to all involved. Disconnect shops. Take down cable and all other apparatus.		
Version Two		
1 year – Decide on idea and aim.		

		Allocated to	Done
6 months	Discuss idea with local church leaders. Appoint planning group as Version One. If inter-church, see chapter 19. Approach local department store with your idea. If they are interested, proceed with arrangements as for Version One although, of course, cables and permission from local council is not necessary.		

Index of Resource Agencies

This list is by no means exhaustive but simply a collection of some of the organizations and agencies that I have found valuable.

General

British Youth For Christ
Cleobury Place, Cleobury Mortimer, Kidderminster, Worcestershire DY14 8JG. Tel: 0299 270260
Church Youth Fellowships Association (CYFA)
Falcon Court, 32 Fleet Street, London EC4Y 1DB. Tel: 01-353 0751
Frontier Youth Trust
130 City Road, London EC1V 2NJ. Tel: 01-250 1966
Pathfinders (Specialize in 11-14 age group)
Falcon Court, 32 Fleet Street, London EC4Y 1DB. Tel: 01-353 0751
Scripture Union
130 City Road, London EC1V 2NJ. Tel: 01-250 1966

Schools and Colleges

Inter-Schools Christian Fellowship (Schools work of Scripture Union)
130 City Road, London EC1V 2NJ. Tel: 01-250 1966

Universities and Colleges Christian Fellowship
38 De Montfort Street, Leicester LE1 7GP. Tel: 0533 551700

Relief Organizations

Tear Fund
100 Church Road, Teddington, Middx TW11 8QE. Tel: 01-977 9144
World Vision
Dychurch House, 8 Abington Street, Northampton NN1 2A3. Tel: 0604 22964

Street Work

Open Air Campaigners
London – 102 Duke's Avenue, Muswell Hill, London N10 2QA. Tel: 01-444 5254
Birmingham – 32 Norfolk Road, Erdington, Birmingham B23 6NA. Tel: 021-350 6151
Tell A Tourist
24 Elm Grove, London N8 9AL. Tel: 01-348 1908

Video Sale and Hire

Bagster Video
Westbrooke House, 76 High Street, Alton, Hants GU34 1EN. Tel: 0420 89141
CTVC
Beesons Yard, Bury Lane, Rickmansworth, Herts WD3 1DS. Tel: 0923 777933
International Films
235 Shaftesbury Avenue, London WC2. Tel: 01-836 2255
Scripture Union Sound and Vision Unit
130 City Road, London EC1V 2NJ. Tel: 01-250 1966
Word UK
9 Holdom Avenue, Bletchley, Milton Keynes MK1 1QU. Tel: 0908 648440

Cassette Copying

ICC Studios
Silverdale Road, Eastbourne, E. Sussex. Tel: 0323 26134
Springtide Sounds
11 Wilmot Road, Tottenham, London N17. Tel: 01-801 2629

Denominational Organizations

Assemblies of God
106-114 Talbot Street, Nottingham NG1 5GH. Tel:0602 474525
Baptist Union of Great Britain and Ireland
Baptist Church House, 4 Southampton Row, London WC1B 4AB.
Tel: 01-405 9803
British Council of Churches
2 Eaton Gate, London SW1W 9BL. Tel: 01-730 9611
General Synod Board of Education (Church of England)
Church House, Dean's Yard, London SW1P 3NZ. Tel: 01-222 9011
Methodist Association of Youth Clubs
2 Chester House, Pages Lane, Muswell Hill, London N10 1PR.
Tel: 01-444 9845
United Reformed Church
86 Tavistock Place, London WC1H 9RT. Tel: 01-837 7661

For Further Reading

Overview Of Christian Youth Work

Mark Ashton, *Christian Youth Work* (Kingsway Publications, 1986).
Understanding Adolescence
James Dobson, *Preparing For Adolescence* (Kingsway Publications, 1982).

Ideas

Bob Moffett, *Crowdbreakers* (Pickering and Inglis, 1983).

Nurture Courses For New Christians

Ralph W. Neighbour, *Survival Kit* (Youth Edition)
(Convention Press)
Ralph W. Neighbour, *New Life With Jesus Christ* (Christian Publicity Organisation).

Youth Evangelism

This Generation Youth Evangelism File (British Youth For Christ).

Notes

Chapter one

1. Quoted in *Jesus is Alive* (Falcon, 1972), p. 15.
2. *ibid.*
3. James Dobson, *Preparing For Adolescence*, (Kingsway Publications, 1982), p. 9.
4. Anne Townsend, *Families Without Pretending* (Scripture Union, 1976), p. 103-4.
5. James Dobson, *op. cit.* p. 9.
6. F. Musgrove, *Youth and the Social Order* (Bloomington, 1965) p. 33.
7. Malcolm Doney, *Summer in the City* (Lion Publishing, 1978), p. 2.
8. *ibid*, p. 1.
9. Quoted by Graham Cray, 'Rock: power and illusion', in T. Morton (ed.), *Solid Rock* (Pickering and Inglis, 1980), p. 4.
10. Quoted by Malcolm Doney, *op. cit*, p. 3.
11. Quoted by John Allan, 'Christian Rock Today', *op. cit*, p. 6.
12. Malcolm Doney, *op. cit*, p. 4.
13. Quoted by Graham Cray, *op. cit*, p. 4.
14. John Allan, *Youth Workers Manual* Vol 1:1 (The National Youth Council of Assemblies of God in Great Britain and Ireland, 1984) p. 1.

15. Clifford Hill, *Towards the Dawn* (Fount, 1980), p. 52.
16. Larry Norman, 'Why don't you look into Jesus' from the album *Only Visiting This Planet* (Word, 1972).

Chapter two

1. J. A. Hadfield, *Childhood and Adolscence* (Penguin, 1962), p. 185.
2. Pete Gilbert, *This Generation Youth Evangelism File 4:4* (British Youth For Christ, 1985), p. 2.
3. Trevor Partridge, *Youth Workers Manual*, Vol 1:3 (The National Youth Council of Assemblies of God in Great Britain and Ireland, 1984), p. 1.
4. Quoted by J. A. Hadfield, *op. cit*, p. 24.
5. *ibid*, p. 240.
6. *ibid*.
7. *ibid*, p. 241.
8. *ibid*.
9. James Dobson, *Preparing For Adolescence* (Kingsway Publications, 1982), p. 105.
10. Mark Ashton, *Christian Youth Work* (Kingsway Publications, 1986), p. 55.

Chapter three

1. Quoted by William Barclay, *By What Authority* (Darton, Longman and Todd, 1974), p. 205.
2. Quoted by Clive Calver, *Youth Workers Manual*, Vol 2:1 (The National Youth Council of Assemblies of God in Great Britain and Ireland, 1985), p. 2.
3. Quoted by Trevor Partridge, *Youth Workers Manual*, Vol 1:3 (The National Youth Council of Assemblies of God in Great Britain and Ireland, 1984), p. 4.
4. *ibid*, p. 4.
5. Paul Hardcastle, *Nineteen* (Chrysalis, 1985).
6. Roy Joslin, *Urban Harvest* (Evangelical Press, 1982), p. 129-138.

Chapter four

1. Clive Calver, *Youth Workers Manual*, Vol 2:1 (The National Youth Council of Assemblies of God in Great Britain and Ireland, 1985), p. 1.
2. Tony Dann, *This Generation Youth Evangelism File 4:5* (British Youth For Christ, 1985), p. 1.
3. Leslie J. Francis, *Teenagers and the Church* (Collins, 1984), p. 49.
4. Quoted by Trevor Partridge, *Youth Workers Manual*, Vol 1:3 (The National Youth Council of Assemblies of God in Great Britain and Ireland, 1984) p. 1.
5. Rob White, *Youth Workers Manual*, Vol 1:10 (The National Youth Council of Assemblies of God in Great Britain and Ireland, 1984), p. 2.
6. Nationwide Initiative For Evangelism, Special Interest Group E Report, *Young People In Pop Culture* (1981).
7. David Watson, *I Believe in Evangelism* (Hodder and Stoughton, 1976), p. 35.

Chapter five

1. John Mott, quoted in *Guidelines B2* (British Youth For Christ, 1978), p. 1.

Chapter six

1. Leslie J. Francis, *Teenagers and the Church* (Collins, 1984), p. 29.
2. Lawrence O. Richards, *Youth Ministry* (Zondervan, 1972), p. 128.
3. Mark Ashton, *Christian Youth Work* (Kingsway Publications, 1986), p. 114.

PRAISE FOR ROBERT DEVEREAUX AND *SANTA STEPS OUT*!

"The book could qualify as the single most
outrageous novel you'll ever read."
—*Cemetery Dance*

"*Santa Steps Out* is a novel so refreshing and inspiring to read
that it breaks down the walls of genres and sits comfortably
outside of everything. A highly recommended novel.
Christmas will never be the same again."
—*Masters of Terror*

"There are scenes that will haunt me forever.
Reading this book made me want to bitch-slap Robert
Devereaux. So icky, yet so magnificently rendered."
—Elizabeth Engstrom, author of *Lizard Wine*

"Robert Devereaux impregnates sacred childhood figures with
the irrepressible stream of his imagination and is responsible
for the spectacular and unashamed rebirth of the old myths."
—Ramsey Campbell, author of *The Last Voice They Hear*

"Prepare for a strange and stimulating ride
when you hop in the sleigh with Santa."
—Amazon.com

"This is strange, strange stuff and, thanks to Devereaux's
splattery talents, not one bodily fluid goes undescribed.
Truly disturbing."
—*Fangoria*

"*Santa Steps Out* gives us a glimpse behind the placid scenery
we *thought* we knew as children . . . and what a glimpse it is!
One warning should accompany this book, however: *Keep this
and all other dangerous objects out of the reach of children!*"
—P. D. Cacek, author of *Night Prayers*

CALIBAN'S SPELL

As the transformation began, Trinculo gazed up goggle-eyed at me, his young dumb face a-brim with unadulterated trust.

My skin pulled in smooth and taut, my broken bald pate shifting into soft curves and sprouting thickets of greasy red hair. Carbuncles shrank to tiny gems, then vanished.

Even as these shifts seized me, I saw Trinculo's hair untwist and wriggle back inside his skin. His complexion darkened, then claimed that darkness. The skull beneath his scalp pocked and crimped. All over, the brawny man collapsed in upon himself, his back hunching up, the gauzy closed-fan green of fins emerging from his sleeves and the bottoms of his breeches.

ROBERT DEVEREAUX

CALIBAN
And Other Tales

LEISURE BOOKS   NEW YORK CITY

A LEISURE BOOK®

March 2002

Published by

Dorchester Publishing Co., Inc.
276 Fifth Avenue
New York, NY 10001

ISBN 0-8439-4977-5

For Victoria
heart, spirit, soul
and just the right amount of spice

ACKNOWLEDGMENTS

My first appreciation goes to Miriam Gilbert, mentor, director, and friend during my eight-year graduate stint at the University of Iowa. Professor Gilbert is equally at home in the worlds of academia and the stage, and her love of Shakespeare is utterly contagious. Enjoy, Miriam!

Thanks unbounded also to Don D'Auria, my editor at Leisure Books, for allowing me to stretch the definition of horror in unusual directions. Don's eclectic taste in fiction, his support for fresh, new voices as well as for worthy, weathered ones, and his willingness to take risks outside the often illusory box of genre expectation are a godsend to readers everywhere.

For putting their faith, funds, and energies behind these stories the first time around, I offer an auctorial wave, wink, nod, twitch, and thank you to Dennis Etchison, Poppy Z. Brite, Norman Partridge, Bryan Cholfin, and the editorial triumvirate at *Weird Tales*.

Finally, my gratitude to the amazing Victoria Peters, for her wholehearted support of my creative efforts, for her unerring instincts as a Personal Coach, and for the rich, rare, and loving life with which Dame Fortune has blessed us.

TABLE OF CONTENTS

CALIBAN
And Other Tales

Bucky Goes to Church

His real name was Vernon Stevens, but folks called him Bucky on account of his teeth and his beaverish waddle and, well, just because it was such a cute name and he was such a cute little fat boy, all cuddles in infancy, a ball of impish pudge in childhood, primed to take on the role of blubbery punching bag in adolescence.

Kids caught on quick, called him names, taunted him, treated him about even with dirt. Bucky smiled back big and broad and stupid, as if he fed on abuse. The worst of them he tagged after, huffing and puffing, arms swinging wildly like gawky chicken wings, fat little legs jubbing and juddering beneath the overhang of his butt to keep up with them. "Wait up, you guys," he'd whinny, "no fair; hey, wait for me!" They'd jeer and call him Blubberbutt and Porky Orca and Barf Brain, and Bucky just seemed to lap up

their torment like it was manna from heaven.

But, hey, wuncha know it, gang, somewheres in Bucky's head he was storing away all that hurt: the whippings at home from his old man's genuine cow-leather belt, a storm of verbal abuse stinging his ears worse than the smack of leather on his naked ass; the glares and snippery from his frowzy mama, she of the pinched stare, the worn, tattered faceflesh, the tipple snuck down her throat at every odd moment; the bark of currish neighbors yowling after him to keep his sneaks off their precious lawns; teachers turning tight smiles on him to show they didn't mind his obtuse ways, Bucky'd get by okay if he did his best, but they'd be triple goddamned if they were going to go out of their way to help him; and the kids, not one of them daring to be his friend (Arnie Rexroth got yanked out of first grade and shuffled off to Phoenix, so he didn't count), all of them coming around quick enough to consensus, getting off on taking the fatboy's head for a spin on the carousel of cruelty, good for a laugh, a good way to get on with the guys, a great way to forget your problems by dumping them in the usual place—on Bucky Stevens's fat sweaty crewcut of a head.

Well, one day, about the time Bucky turned fifteen, he woke to the mutterings of a diamond-edged voice inside his left frontal lobe. "Kill, Bucky, kill!" it told him, and, argue with it as he might, the voice at last grew stronger and more persuasive, until there was nothing to do but act on its urgings. So Bucky gathered all that hurt he'd been storing away and pedaled off to church one Sunday morning on his three-speed

with his dad's big backpack tugging at his shoulders like a pair of dead man's hands. The weight of the hardware inside punched at his spine as he pedaled, though it was lighter by the bullets lodged in the bodies of his parents, who lay now, at peace and in each other's arms, propped up against the hot-water heater in the basement. He couldn't recall seeing such contentment on their faces, such a "bastard!"-less, "bitch!"-free silence settling over the house.

He pumped, did Bucky, pumped like a sweathog, endured the TEC-9 digging at his backbone, kept the churchful of tormentors propped up behind his forehead like a prayer. His fat head gidded and spun with the bloodrush of killing his folks: his dad, dense as a Neanderthal, the ex-marine in him trying to threaten Bucky out of it, arms flailing backward as his forehead swirled open like a poinsettia in sudden bloom, his beefy body slamming like a sledge into the dryer, spilling what looked like borscht vomit all over its white enamel top; his mom down on her knees in uncharacteristic whimper, then, realizing she was done for, snarling her usual shit at him until he told her to shut her ugly trap and jabbed the barrel into her left breast and, with one sharp squeeze of his finger, buckled her up like a midget actress taking a bloody bow, pouring out her heart for an audience of one.

Bucky crested the half-mile hill at Main and Summit. The steeple thrust up into the impossible cerulean of the sky like a virgin boy's New England–white erection humping the heavens. Bucky braked, easing by Washington, Madison,

Jefferson. The First Methodist Church loomed up like a perfect dream as he neared it. It was a lovely white box resting on a close-clipped lawn, a simple beautiful spired construction that hid all sorts of ugliness inside.

Coasting onto the sidewalk, Bucky wide-arced into the parking lot and propped his bike against a sapling. Off came the backpack, clanking to the ground. A car cruised by, a police car. Bucky waved at the cops inside, saw the driver un-smiling return a fake wave, false town cohesion, poor sap paid to suspect everyone, even some pudgy little scamp parking his bike in the church lot, tugging at the straps of a big bulky backpack. Grim flatfaced flatfoot, hair all black and shiny—stranded separately like the teeth at the thick end of an Ace comb—was going to wish he'd been one or two seconds later cruising Main Street, was going to wish like hell he'd seen the TEC-9 shrug out of its canvas confinement and come to cradle in Bucky's arms, yes, indeed.

Not wanting to spoil the surprise, Bucky pulled his Ninja T-shirt out of the front of his jeans, pressed the cool metal of the weapon against his sweaty belly, and redraped his shirt over it.

He could hear muffled organ music as he climbed the wide white steps. The front doors, crowding about like blind giants, were off-white and tall. And good God if the music mumbling behind them wasn't "Onward, Christian Soldiers," as wheezed and worried by a bloodless band of bedraggled grunts too far gone on the shell shock and homesickness of everyday life to get it up for the Lord.

18

Bucky tried the handle. The door resisted at first, then yielded outward.

The narthex was empty. Through the simulated pearls of Sarah Janeway's burbling organ music, Bucky could see an elaborate fan of church bulletins on the polished table stretched between the inner doors. Programs, the little kids called them. Through the window in the right inner door to the sanctuary, the back of a deacon's bald head hung like some fringed moon. Coach Hezel, that's who it was; Bucky's coach the year before in ninth grade, all those extra laps for no good reason, push-ups without end, and the constant yammer of humiliation: how Bucky had no need for a jockstrap when a rubber band and a peanut shell would do the trick; how he had two lockermates, skinny Jim Simpson and his own blubber; how the school should charge Mr. Lardass Stevens extra for soap, given the terrain he had to cover come showertime.

Bucky unshirted the gun, strode to the door, and set its barrel on the window's lower edge, sighting square against the back of Hezel's head. A clink as it touched glass. Hezel turned at the noise, and Bucky squeezed the trigger. He glimpsed the burly sinner's blunt brow, his cauliflower nose, the onyx bead of one eye; and then the glass shattered and Hezel's mean black glint turned red, spread outward like burnt film, and Miss Sarah Janeway's noodling trickled to a halt at the tail end of "with the cross of Jeeeee-zus."

Bucky kicked open the door and leaped over Hezel's still-quivering body. "Freeze, Christian vermin!" he shouted, ready to open up the hot

shower of metal tensed in the weapon, but it sounded like somebody else and not quite as committed as Eastwood or Stallone. Besides, his eyes swept the shocked, hymnal-fisted crowd and found young kids, boys of not more than five whose eyes were already lidded with mischief and young girls innocent and whimpery in their pinafores and crinolines, and he knew he had to be selective.

Then the voice slammed in louder and harsher—(KILL THE FUCKERS, BUCKY, KILL THEM SONS O' BITCHES!)—like a new gear ratio kicking in. Bucky used its energy to fight the impulse to relent, dredging up an image of his dead folks fountaining blood like Bucky's Revenge, using that image to sight through as he picked off the Atwoods, four generations of hardware greed on the corner of Main and Garvey: old Grandpappy Andrew, a sneer and a "Shitwad!" on his withered lips as Bucky stitched a bloody bandolier of slugs slantwise across his chest; Theodore and Gracia Atwood, turning to protect their young, mowed down by the rude slap of hot metal digging divots of flesh from their faces; their eldest boy, Alan, over-bearing son of an Atwood who'd shortchanged Bucky on fishhooks last July and whose head and heart exploded as he gestured to his lovely wife Anne, who danced now for them all as her mist-green frock grew red with polkadots; and four-year-old Missy, who ran in terror from her bleeding family, ran toward Bucky with a scream curling from her porcelain mouth, her tiny fists raised, staggering into a blast of bullets that lifted her body up with the press of its re-

gard and slammed her back against a splintering pew.

A woman's voice rose through the screams. "Stop him, someone!" she yelled from the front. Bucky pointed toward her voice and let the bullets fly, bloodfucking whole rows of worshippers at one squeeze. Most lay low, cowering out of sight. The suicidal made escape attempts, some running for the doors behind Bucky, others for those up front that led into the pastor's study or back where the choir warmed up. These jackrabbits Bucky picked off, making profane messes out of dark-suited bodies that showed no sense of decorum in their dying, but bled on hard-to-clean church property everywhere he looked.

He eased off the trigger and let the blasts of gun-thunder vanish, though they rang like a sheen of deafness in his ears. "Keep away from the doors!" he shouted, not sure if he could be heard by anyone. It was like talking into fog. "Stay where you are and no one will get hurt," he lied, stepping over dead folk to make his way forward. The crying came to him then, thin and distant, and he saw bodies huddled together as he passed, the wounded and the not-yet-wounded. Call them all what they were, the soon-to-be-deceased.

"Shame on you, Vernon Stevens," came a quavery voice. Bucky looked up. There in the pulpit stood the whey-faced Simon P. Stone, sanctimonious pastor who'd done nothing—his piety deaf to cruelty—to keep Bucky from being the butt of his confirmation class two years before. The knuckles of his thin right hand were white

with terror as he clutched, unconscious, a fistful of gilt-edged Bible pages. His surplice hung like a shroud from his taut gaunt shoulders, a tasteful Pontiac gray, sheen and all. A lime-green tippet trailed like an untied tie down the sides of his chest.

"Come down, Satan," said Bucky, hearing sirens in the distance through the bloodpulse of his anger, "come down to the altar and call your flock of demons to you."

"No, Vernon, I won't do that." Pastor Stone's eyes were teary with fear—he of little faith not ready, no, not after decades of preaching, to meet his Maker.

Bucky looked around through the sobbing, saw crazed eyes turn away from him, saw between pews the sculpted humps of suited shoulders like blue serge whales stuck in waves, saw—yes! saw Mrs. Irma Wilkins, her red velvet hat a half-shell, really, with black lace crap on it, her gloved hand dabbing a crumpled hanky to one eye. "Mrs. Wilkins," Bucky said, and her head jerked up like a startled filly, "come here!" Her lids lowered in that snippy way, but she rose, a thin frail stick of a woman, and sidled out of her pew. And as she neared, Bucky was back at the church camp five summers before, out in the woods, holding one end of the crossbranch from which depended the iron kettle, its sole support him and another kid and two badly made and badly sunk Y-shaped branches, and the wind shifted and the smoke of the fire blew like a mask of no-breath into his face and clawed at his eyes no matter how hard he tried to blink past it, and he turned away and let go of the

branch, saying, "My eyes!" and the rude blur that was Irma Wilkins rushed in to catch the branch and to sting him with her condemnation, even now as she approached in this church he could hear her say it, *"Your eyes? OUR STEW!"* as if the fucking food was more important than Bucky's vision, and to her it *was*, and that voice of hers, that whole put-down attitude reduced Bucky to nothing; but Bucky knew he was something all right, and he saw her pinched little lipless mouth as she came closer, by God it looked like a dotted line and by God he'd oblige her by tearing across it now with his widdle gun, better that than live his whole life hearing this nasty woman's voice reduce him to nothing; and he opened up his rage upon her, rippling across her face with a rain of bullets until her head tore back at the mouth like the top of a Pez dispenser thumbed open, shooting out a stream of crimson coffins, spilling gore down the front of her black dress like cherry liqueur over dark chocolate, and mean Irma Wilkins went down like the worthless sack of shit she was, and Bucky felt damned proud of himself, yes he did, happy campers.

Bucky swung back to Pastor Stone. "Bring 'em all to the front of the church and I won't harm a one of 'em," he said. "But if you refuse, I'll pick 'em off one at a time just like I did Mrs. Wilkins here."

Rest of them had ears. They needed no coaxing, but coaxed instead their whimpering kids out of hiding, out into the aisles and up the red runners to the altar, where Pastor Stone, trembling like unvarnished truth, raised his robed

23

arms as if in benediction, as if he were posing for a picture, Pastor Simon P. Stone and his bleating sheep.

The muffled squawk of a bullhorn turned Bucky's head to a tall unstained window at his left. A squat man in blue stood on the grass at the near edge of the parking lot, legs planted firmly apart, elbows bent, face and hands obliterated by a black circle. "Vernon Stevens," came his humorless voice, "lay down your weapon and come out with your hands raised. We will not harm you if you do as I say. We have the church surrounded. Repeat. The church. Is. Surrounded." The bullhorn squawked off and the black circle came down, so that Bucky could see clearly the ain't-I-a-big-boy-now, pretend courage painted on the man's face. Glancing back, Bucky saw bobbing blue heads through the two small squares of window that let onto the narthex, a scared rookie or two, the long stems of assault rifles jostling like shafts of wheat in a summer breeze.

Doubt crept into him. And fear. His finger eased off the trigger. Tension began to drain from his arms.

FINISH THE JOB! came the voice, like a balloon fist suddenly inflating inside his skull, pressing outward as if to burst bone. *LOOK AT THEM. BUCKY! LOOK, AND REMEMBER WHAT THEY'VE DONE TO YOU!*

And Bucky looked. And Bucky saw. There was Bad Sam in his Sunday best, frog-faced pouting young tough, a lick of light brown hair laid across his brow, freckles sprayed on his bloated cheeks, Bad Sam who'd grabbed Bucky off his

bike when Bucky was nine, slammed him to the cement of the sidewalk by Mr. Murphy's house and slapped his face again and again until his cheeks bruised and bled. And through his tears, he could see Mr. Murphy at his front window, withdrawing in haste at being discovered; Mr. Murphy who'd always seemed so kind, tending his tulip beds as Bucky biked by, and now here he was in church along with his tiny wife and their daughter Patricia in a white dress and a round-brimmed hat that haloed her head. And next to her stood Alex Menche, a gas jockey at the Exxon station, corner of First and Main, whose look turned to hot ice whenever Bucky walked by, who never blinked at him, never talked to him, but just stared, oily rag in hand, jaw moving, snapping a wad of gum. And back behind Alex he caught a glimpse of Mr. Green the janitor, who'd yelled at the lunchbox crowd in second grade to "Shutup!" even when their mouths were busy with peanut butter. And odd Elvira Freeborn, New Falls's weirdo-lady, who laid claim in good weather to a corner of the city park across from the town hall and had conversation with anyone who chanced by and lingered there—even weirdo Elvira had come up to him one day when he'd been desperate enough for company to go seek her out, had come up all smiles, her hair wispy gray and twisting free of its bun, and said, "My, my, Vernon, you are one fat ugly thing, yes you are, and if you were mine, I'd sew your mouth shut, I would; by God I'd starve that flab right off your bones and I'd see about getting you a nose job for that fat knob of a honker you got on your face and—" on and on

and on, and now her eyes were on him here in church, off-yellow glaring cat's eyes like a reformed witch having second thoughts. And beside her was Sarah Janeway the organist, who'd laughed and then tried to hide it when Bucky auditioned for the children's choir at the age of eight, a no-talent bitch with her wide vacant eyes encircled in wide glasses rimmed in thin red and her hair cropped short as her musical gifts and her absurd flowered dress poking out of the shimmering green choir robe down below, and she was standing there white-faced and whiny, and then the bullhorn bullshit started up again, and Bucky brought his one true friend up to his chest and let the surge of righteous wrath seize him.

He made them dance, every last one of them.

He played the tune. They tripped and swayed to the rhythm of his song. Wounds opened like whole notes in them. Sweeping glissandi of gore rose up like prayers of intercession.

Behind him he felt a flood of cops rush in to pick up the beat and join him, to judder and jolt the music out of *him* with music of their own. Bucky, tripped out on giving back in spades what New Falls had so unstintingly bestowed upon him over the years, turned about to spray death into the boys in blue at his back. But there were too many of them, and a goodly number were already in position, rifles beaded on him.

Then pain seized his right knee and danced up his leg in small sharp steps, like invisible wasps landing on him, fury out. Needles of fire Watusied across his belly. Two zigzags of lead staggered up the ladders of his ribs and leaped

for Bucky's head. Something impossible to swallow punched through his teeth, filling his mouth with meat and blood.

And then his brain lit up like a second sun and all the pain winked out. The terrible thunder of weaponry put to use went away, only to be replaced by organ music so sweet it made Bucky want to wet his pants and not give a good goddamn about the consequences.

He felt himself drift apart like a dreamer becoming someone else. The cops froze, caught in mid-fire. About him, the church walls roiled and wowed like plaster turned to smoke. But it wasn't smoke. It was mist, fog, clouds. They billowed down into the church, rolling and shifting and swirling among the corpses. Bucky glanced back at the altar, saw the bodies of his victims posed in attitudes of death, saw Pastor Simon P. Stone, his robed arms out in crucifixion, veed at the waist as if he'd just caught the devil's medicine ball in his belly.

But right behind Bucky, close enough to startle him, was his own body, bits of flesh being torn out like tufts of grass at a driving range, shoots of blood looking like hopeful red plants just coming into sunlight. He circled, by willing it, about his body, feeling the cumulus clouds cotton under his feet, soothing his soles, as he gazed in astonishment at his head, pate cracked open all around like the top of an eggshell, hovering a foot above the rest of it in a spray of blood and brain. He reached out, touched the stray piece of skull, tried to force it back in place, but it was as if it were made of stone and cemented for all eternity to the air. Likewise the

27

freshets of gore issuing like bloody thoughts from his brain, which, though not cold, were as stiff as icicles.

The music swelled, recaptured his attention. Looking about for its source, he saw emerge from each tiny cloud a creature, all in white, all of white and gold, delicate of hand, beatific of face, and every one of them held a thing of curves in its hands. Their angel mouths *O*'d like moon craters. Thin fingers swept in blizzards of beauty across iridescent harps. And yet their music was neither plucked nor sung, but a pain-pure hymn rolling out in tones richer than any man-made organ.

They made the bloody scene beautiful, sanctifying it with their psalm. And now their bodies swerved as though hinged and they raised their eyes to the dioramic massacre before the altar and up past the huge golden cross even to the white plaster ceiling above it, beyond which the spire lofted heavenward. With a great groan, as if angelic eyes could move mountains with a look, the top of the building eased open, sliding outward on invisible runners to hang there in the open air. And down into the church descended a great blocky bejeweled thing, an oblong Spielbergian UFO, Bucky thought at first. But then he saw the sandals, the feet, the robes, the hands gripping firmly the arms of the throne like Abe Lincoln, the chest bedecked in white, and the great white beard, and he guessed what he was in for.

But when the head came fully into view, Bucky had to laugh. Like Don Rickles trapped in a carpet, the face of an angry black woman

grimaced out from behind the white beard and mustache of God. Her cheeks puffed out like wet sculpted obsidian, her dark eyes glared, and just in front of a Hestonian sweep of white hair, a tight black arch of curls hugged her face like some dark rider's chaps curving about the belly of his steed. The white neck of the deity was stiff and rigid, as if locked in a brace.

"Bucky Stevens," She boomed, Her eyes moving from him to a space of air in front of Her, "you'd best be getting yourself up here this instant, you hear?"

"Yes, Ma'am," he said, drifting around his exploding corpse and sailing up over the bloody crowd at the altar. He could still sense how fat he was, but he felt as light and unplodding as a sylph. "You sending me to hell?" he asked.

She laughed. "Looks to Me like you found your *own* way there." Her eyes surveyed the carnage. "First off, young man, I want to say I 'preciate what you did for Me. I like sinners who listen to My suggestions and have the balls to carry them out."

"That was *You?*"

"Does God lie?"

"No, Ma'am."

"Damn right She don't, and I'm God, so you just shove those doubts aside and listen up."

"Um, scuse me, Ma'am," said Bucky, shuffling his feet in the air, "but how come God's a black woman? I mean, in Sunday School—"

"God ain't a black woman, Mr. Bucky, least-ways no more She ain't. She's been that for a while, oh 'bout three weeks or so." She smiled

suddenly. "But now She gets to be a fat white boy named Bucky Stevens."

Bucky brightened. He didn't doubt for a moment what She'd said. He couldn't. It speared like truth into his heart. "You mean I get to . . . to take over? There's no punishment for killing all these people?"

God chuckled, a high-pitched woo-wee kind of sound. "That ain't what I said a-tall." She did a stiff-necked imitation of a headshake as She spoke.

Bucky was mystified: "I don't get it."

God leaned forward like She had a board strapped to Her back. "I'll be brief," She said, "just so's you can hustle your fat butt up here quicker and let Me come down and do My dying. I killed Me a whole officeload of people three weeks ago, got blown away by a security guard after I hosed those heartless fuckers at Century 21. Same sorta miracle that's happening to you now, happened to Me then. Only God was this unhinged lunatic I'd seen on Dan Rather the week before, some nut who went to O'Hare and picked off ground crew and passengers not lucky enough to be going through one of those tubes. He got blown away too, became God, then talked Me into wiping out my co-workers when they gave Me the axe. So I did it, and coaxed you along same's He did Me, and here we are."

The music was doing beautiful things to Bucky's mind. He grew very excited. "You mean I'm going to be in charge of everything? I can make any changes I feel like making, I can stop all the misery if I want to?" God ummm-

hmmmed. "But why would anyone, why would *You*, want to give that up?"

She looked agitated, like She wanted to laugh and cry and holler all at the same time. Instead She said, "As My momma used to say, young Master Stevens, experience is the best teacher a body can have." She glared at him suddenly, and Bucky felt himself swept forward and up.

He windmilled his arms, struggling to find his center of gravity, but found himself fluttering and turning like an autumn leaf, tumbling spout over teakettle toward the great black face, toward the crazy brown eyes. He headed straight between them, fearing he'd smash on the browbone, but instead doubled and split like a drunkard's vision and fell and swelled into the black pools of God's pupils. In the blink of an eye, he inflated. That's how it felt to him, like his head felt when they stuck his arm and taped it down, knocking him out for an ingrown toenail operation when he was ten, only all over his body this time and he didn't lose consciousness. He unlidded his eyes just in time to see the stocky black woman wink at him before She put Her hands together as if in prayer, sang out, "So long, sucker!" and swan-dived into his shattering body.

Bucky gazed about at the angels on their clouds and felt guy wires coming from their *O*'d mouths as if He were a Macy's Day balloon and they the marching guardians who kept Him from floating free. The throne rose slowly and the angels with it. Bucky took His first God-breath and felt divine. Like Captain Kirk, He was in command now, He sat at the helm, and things

31

by God were going to fly right from here on out.

But then, as He lifted above the church and its roof clicked into place, time unfroze and, with it, the pain of those inside. He felt it all, like a mailed fist slamming into His solar plexus again and again: Simon Stone, small and mean inside like a mole, gasping for one final breath; Sarah Janeway, two months' pregnant, trying in vain to hold back the rope-spill of her intestines; kindhearted Elvira Freeborn, in so many ways the sanest person there, who let her dying fall over her like a new sun dress, a thing of razor and flame. And even the dead—Coach Hezel, the Atwoods, Irma Wilkins, and the rest—even from these, Bucky felt the echoes of their suffering and, transcending time, seeped into their dying a thousand times over.

And then He rose over New Falls, did Bucky Stevens, feeling His holy tendrils reach into everyone that wept and wandered there. He knew at last the torment of His parents and the riches they'd lost inside themselves, and it made His heart throb with pain. Bucky rose, and, in rising, sank into every hurting soul in town, spreading Himself thick everywhere. And all was painful clarity inside Him. It grew and crackled, the misery, and still He rose and sank, moving like Sherwin-Williams paint to engulf the globe, seeping deep down into the earth. Bucky wanted to scream. And scream He did. And His scream was the cause, and the sound, of human misery.

He tried to bring His hands to His face. To puncture His eardrums. To thumb out His eyes. But they clung like mules to the hard arms of

the throne, not budging, and His eyelids would not shut, and His earflaps sucked all of it in like maelstroms of woe. Pockets of starvation flapped open before Him like cover stories blown, and each death-eyed Ethiopian became unique to Him—the clench of empty stomachs, the wutter and wow of dying minds.

Like dental agony, layer beneath layer surprising one at the untold depths of it, Bucky's pain intensified and spread, howling and spiraling off in all directions. And after a while, it didn't exactly dull, nor did He get used to it, but rather He rose to meet it, to yield to it as the storm-tossed seafarer gives up the struggle and moves into the sweep of the sea. He was the pincushion of pain, He was the billions of screaming pins, He was the billions of thumbs pressing them down into flannel. He suffered all of it, and knew Himself to be the cause of it all. Caught in the weave, He *was* the weave.

He almost smiled, it was so perverse; but the smile was ripped from His face by new outrage. There seemed no end to the torment, no end to burgeoning pain. As soon as He thought He'd hit bottom, the bottom fell out. He began to wonder if the black woman had lied to Him, if maybe He was trapped in this nightmare for all eternity. While He watched with eyes that could not close, new births killed young girls, new deaths tore at mourners, new forms of woe were kennel-bred and unleashed. Bucky was fixed in His firmament, and all was hell with the world.

Plunged down the slippery slope of despair, He cast His great eyes about, sought for pustules of resentment, found them. The seeds of His re-

demption they were, these seething souls. The black woman—Miriam Jefferson Jones—had, like Her predecessor, been nursing others along, and now Bucky reached out to them and took up the whisper in their ears, the whisper momentarily stilled at the shift in deity. Heavens yes, Sean Flynn, He assured the young man leaned against the stone wall, huddled with his mates, it's only proper you elbow under their fuckin transport at night, fix old Mother Flammable there, crawl the hell out o' there, give it the quick plunge, watch all them limey bastards kiss the night sky over Belfast with their bones. And yes, Alicia Condon of Lost Nation, Iowa, it's okay to take your secret obsession with the purity of the newborn to its limit, it is indeed true that if you could wipe out a whole nursery of just-delivered infants before they hit that fatal all-corrupting second day of life, the Second Coming of My Own Sweet Son would indeed be swiftly upon the sinning race of mankind. And yes, oh most decidedly yes, Gopal Krishnan and Vachid Dastjerdi and Moshe Naveh, you owe it to your respective righteous causes to massacre whole busloads, whole airports, whole towns full of enemy flesh.

There were oodles of them walking the earth, ticking time bombs, and all of them He tended and swayed that way, giving with a whisper gentle nudges and shoves toward mass annihilation. New ones too, promising buds of bitterness, Bucky began to cultivate. Some one of them was certain to bloom any moment now—oh God, how Bucky prayed to Himself for it to be soon— at least one brave quarterback on this playing

field of sorrow was sure to snatch that ball out of the sky and run for all he was worth, pounding cleat against turf, stiff-arming those who dared try to block him, not stopping till he crossed the forbidden line and slammed that bleeding pigskin down in triumph.

That was the hope, through agonies untold, that kept Bucky going. That was the hope that made things hum.

Ridi Bobo

At first little things niggled at Bobo's mind: the forced quality of Kiki's mimed chuckle when he went into his daily pratfall getting out of bed; the great care she began to take painting in the teardrop below her left eye; the way she idly fingered a pink puffball halfway down her shiny green suit. Then more blatant signals: the creases in her crimson frown, a sign, he knew, of real discontent; the bored arcs her floppy shoes described when she walked the ruff-necked piglets; a wistful shake of the head when he brought out their favorite set of shiny steel rings and invited her, with the artful pleas of his expressive white gloves, to juggle with him.

But Bobo knew it was time to seek professional help when he whipped out his rubber chicken and held it aloft in a stranglehold—its eyes *X*'d shut in fake death, its pitiful head lolled

against the back of his glove—and all Kiki could offer was a soundless yawn, a fatigued cock of her conical nightcap, and the curve of her back, one lazy hand waving bye-bye before collapsing languidly beside her head on the pillow. No honker would be brought forth that evening from her deep hip pocket, though he could discern its outline there beneath the cloth, a coy maddening shape that almost made him hop from toe to toe on his own. But he stopped himself, stared forlornly at the flaccid fowl in his hand, and shoved it back inside his trousers.

He went to check on the twins, their little gloved hands hugging the blankets to their chins, their perfect snowflake-white faces vacant with sleep. People said they looked more like Kiki than him, with their lime-green hair and the markings around their eyes. Beautiful boys, Jojo and Juju. He kissed their warm round red noses and softly closed the door.

In the morning, Bobo, wearing a tangerine apron over his bright blue suit, watched Kiki drive off in their new rattletrap Weezo, thick puffs of exhaust exploding out its tailpipe. Back in the kitchen, he reached for the Buy-Me Pages. Nervously rubbing his pate with his left palm, he slalomed his right index finger down the Snooper listings. Lots of flashy razzmatazz ads, lots of zingers to catch a poor clown's attention. He needed simple. He needed quick. Ah! His finger thocked the entry short and solid as a raindrop on a roof; he noted the address and slammed the book shut.

Bobo hesitated, his fingers on his apron bow. For a moment the energy drained from him and

he saw his beloved Kiki as she'd been when he married her, honker out bold as brass, doing toe hops in tandem with him, the shuff-shuff-shuff of her shiny green pants legs, the ecstatic ripples that passed through his rubber chicken as he moved it in and out of her honker and she bulbed honks around it. He longed to mimic sobbing, but the inspiration drained from him. His shoulders rose and fell once only; his sweep of orange hair canted to one side like a smart hat.

Then he whipped the apron off in a tangerine flurry, checked that the boys were okay playing with the piglets in the backyard, and was out the front door, floppy shoes flapping toward downtown.

Momo the Dick had droopy eyes, baggy pants, a shuffle to his walk, and an office filled to brimming with towers of blank paper, precariously tilted—like gaunt placarded and stilted clowns come to dine—over his splintered desk. Momo wore a battered old derby and mock-sighed a lot, like a bloodhound waiting to die.

He'd been decades in the business and had the dust to prove it. As soon as Bobo walked in, the tramp-wise clown seated behind the desk glanced once at him, peeled off his derby, twirled it, and very slowly, very deliberately moved a stiffened fist in and out of it. Then his hand opened—red nails, white fingers thrust out of burst gloves—as if to say, Am I right?

Bobo just hung his head. His clownish hands drooped like weights at the ends of his arms.

The detective set his hat back on, made sympathetic weepy movements—one hand fisted to

his eye—and motioned Bobo over. An unoiled drawer squealed open, and out of it came a puff of moths and a bulging old scrapbook. As Momo turned its pages, Bobo saw lots of illicit toe hops, lots of swollen honkers, lots of rubber chickens poking where they had no business poking. There were a whole series of pictures for each case, starting with a photo of his mopey client, progressing to the flagrante delicto evidence, and ending, almost without exception, in one of two shots: a judge with a shock of pink hair and a huge gavel thrusting a paper reading DIVORCE toward the adulterated couple, the third party handcuffed to a Kop with a tall blue hat and a big silver star on his chest; or two corpses, their floppy shoes pointing up like warped surf-boards, the triumphant spouse grinning like weak tea and holding up a big pistol with a BANG! flag out its barrel, and Momo, a hand on the spouse's shoulder, looking sad as always and not a little shocked at having closed another case with such finality.

When Bobo broke down and mock-wept, Momo pulled out one end of a checkered hanky and offered it. Bobo cried long and hard, pre-tending to dampen yard upon yard of the unend-ing cloth. When he was done, Momo reached into his desk drawer, took out a sheet with the word CONTRACT at the top and two *X*'d lines for signatures, and dipped a goose-quill pen into a large bottle of ink. Bobo made no move to take it, but the old detective just kept holding it out, the picture of patience, and drops of black ink fell to the desktop between them.

*   *   *

Momo tracked his client's wife to a seedy three-ring motel off the beaten path. She hadn't been easy to tail. A sudden rain had come up and the pennies that pinged off his windshield had reduced visibility by half, which made the eager Weezo hard to keep up with. But Momo managed it. Finally, with a sharp right and a screech of tires, she turned into the motel parking lot. Momo slowed to a stop, eyeing her from behind the brim of his sly bowler. She parked, climbed up out of the tiny car like a soufflé rising, and rapped on the door of Room Five, halfway down from the office.

She jiggled as she waited. It didn't surprise Momo, who'd seen lots of wives jiggle in his time. This one had a pleasingly sexy jiggle to her, as if she were shaking a cocktail with her whole body. He imagined the bulb of her honker slowly expanding, its bell beginning to flare open in anticipation of her little tryst. Momo felt his bird stir in his pants, but a soothing pat or two to his pocket and a few deep sighs put it back to sleep. There was work afoot. No time nor need for the wild flights of his long-departed youth.

After a quick reconnoiter, Momo went back to the van for his equipment. The wooden tripod lay heavy across his shoulder and the black boxy camera swayed like the head of a willing widow as he walked. The rest—unexposed plates, flash powder, squeeze bulb—Momo carried in a carpetbag in his free hand. His down-drawn mouth puffed silently from the exertion, and he cursed the manufacturers for refusing to scale down their product, it made it so hard on him in the inevitable chase.

They had the blinds down but the lights up full. It made sense. Illicit lovers liked to watch themselves act naughty, in Momo's experience, their misdoings fascinated them so. He was in luck. One wayward blind, about chest high, strayed leftward, leaving a rectangle big enough for his lens. Miming stealth, he set up the tripod, put in a plate, and sprinkled huge amounts of glittery black powder along his flashbar. He didn't need the flashbar, he knew that, and it caused all manner of problem for him, but he had his pride in the aesthetics of picture-taking, and he was willing to blow his cover for the sake of that pride. When the flash went off, you knew you'd taken a picture; a quick bulb squeeze in the dark was a cheat and not at all in keeping with his code of ethics.

So the flash flared, and the smoke billowed through the loud report it made, and the peppery sting whipped up into Momo's nostrils on the inhale. Then came the hurried slap of shoes on carpet and a big slatted eyelid opened in the blinds, out of which glared a raging clown face. Momo had time to register that this was one hefty punchinello, with muscle-bound eyes and lime-green hair that hung like a writhe of caterpillars about his face. And he saw the woman, Bobo's wife, honker out, looking like the naughty fornicator she was but with an overlay of uh-oh beginning to sheen her eyes.

The old adrenaline kicked in. The usually poky Momo hugged up his tripod and made a mad dash for the van, his carpetbag shoved under one arm, his free hand pushing the derby down on his head. It was touch and go for a

while, but Momo had the escape down to a science, and the beefy clown he now clouded over with a blanket of exhaust—big lumbering palooka caught off-guard in the act of chicken stuffing—proved no match for the wily Momo.

Bobo took the envelope and motioned Momo to come in, but Momo declined with a hopeless shake of the head. He tipped his bowler and went his way, sorrow slumped like a mantle about his shoulders. With calm deliberation Bobo closed the door, thinking of Jojo and Juju fast asleep in their beds. Precious boys, flesh of his flesh, energetic pranksters, they deserved better than this.

He unzippered the envelope and pulled out the photo. Some clown suited in scarlet was engaged in hugger-mugger toe hops with Kiki. His rubber chicken, unsanctified by papa church, was stiff-necked as a rubber chicken can get and stuffed deep inside the bell of Kiki's honker. Bobo leaned back against the door, his shoes levering off the rug like slapsticks. He'd never seen Kiki's pink rubber bulb swell up so grandly. He'd never seen her hand close so tightly around it nor squeeze with such ardency. He'd never *ever* seen the happiness that danced so brightly in her eyes, turning her painted tear to a tear of joy.

He let the photo flutter to the floor. Blessedly it fell facedown. With his right hand he reached deep into his pocket and pulled out his rubber chicken, sad purple-yellow bird, a male's burden in this world. The sight of it brought back memories of their wedding. They'd had it performed

by Father Beppo in the center ring of the Church of Saint Canio. It had been a beautiful day, balloons so thick the air felt close under the big top. Father Beppo had laid one hand on Bobo's rubber chicken, one on Kiki's honker, inserting hen into honker for the first time as he lifted his long-lashed eyes to the heavens, wrinkle lines appearing on his meringue-white forehead. He'd looked to Kiki, then to Bobo, for their solemn nods toward fidelity.

And now she'd broken that vow, thrown it to the wind, made a mockery of their marriage.

Bobo slid to the floor, put his hands to his face, and wept. Real wet tears this time, and that astonished him, though not enough—no, not nearly enough—to divert his thoughts from Kiki's treachery. His gloves grew soggy with weeping. When the flood subsided, he reached down and turned the photo over once more, scrutinizing the face of his wife's lover. And then the details came together—the ears, the mouth, the chin; oh God no, the hair and the eyes—and he knew Kiki and this bulbous-nosed bastard had been carrying on for a long time, a very long time indeed. Once more he inventoried the photo, frantic with the hope that his fears were playing magic tricks with the truth.

But the bald conclusion held.

At last, mulling things over, growing outwardly calm and composed, Bobo tumbled his eyes down the length of the flamingo-pink carpet, across the spun cotton-candy pattern of the kitchen floor, and up the cabinets to the Jojo-and-Juju-proofed top drawer.

* * *

Bobo sat at his wife's vanity, his face close to the mirror. Perfume atomizers jutted up like minarets, thin rubber tubing hanging down from them and ending in pretty pink squeeze bulbs Bobo did his best to ignore.

He'd strangled the piglets first, squealing the life out of them, his large hands thrust beneath their ruffs. Patty Petunia had pistoned her trotters against his chest more vigorously and for a longer time than had Pepper, to Bobo's surprise; she'd always seemed so much the frailer of the two. When they lay still, he took up his carving knife and sliced open their bellies, fixed on retrieving the archaic instruments of comedy. Just as his tears had shocked him, so too did the deftness of his hands—guided by instincts he'd long supposed atrophied—as they removed the bladders, cleansed them in the water trough, tied them off, inflated them, secured each one to a long thin bendy dowel. He'd left Kiki's dead pets sprawled in the muck of their pen, flies growing ever more interested in them.

Sixty-watt lights puffed out around the perimeter of the mirror like yellow honker bulbs. Bobo opened Kiki's cosmetics box and took out three squat shallow cylinders of color. The paint seemed like miniature seas, choppy and wet, when he unscrewed and removed the lids.

He'd taken a tin of black paint into the boys' room—that and the carving knife. He sat beside Jojo in a sharp jag of moonlight, listening to the card-in-bike-spoke duet of their snores, watching their fat wide lips flutter like stuck bees. Bobo dolloped one white finger with darkness, leaning in to X a cross over Jojo's right eyelid. If

only they'd stayed asleep. But they woke. And Bobo could not help seeing them in a new light. They sat up in mock-stun, living outcroppings of Kiki's cruelty, and Bobo could not stop himself from finger-scooping thick gobs of paint and smearing their faces entirely in black. But even that was not enough for his distracted mind, which spiraled upward into bloody revenge, even though it meant carving his way through innocence. By the time he plunged the blade into the sapphire silk of his first victim's suit, jagging open downward a bloody furrow, he no longer knew which child he murdered. The other one led him a merry chase through the house, but Bobo scruffed him under the cellar stairs, his shoes windmilling helplessly as Bobo hoisted him up and sank the knife into him just below the second puffball. He'd tucked them snug beneath their covers, Kiki's brood; then he'd tied their rubber chickens together at the neck and nailed them smack dab in the center of the heart-shaped headboard.

Bobo dipped a brush into the cobalt blue, outlined a tear under his left eye, filled it in. It wasn't perfect, but it would do.

As horsehair taught paint how to cry, he surveyed in his mind's eye the lay of the living room. Everything was in readiness: the bucket of crimson confetti poised above the front door; the exploding cigar he would light and jam into the gape of her mouth; the tangerine apron he'd throw in her face, the same apron that hung loose now about his neck, its strings snipped off and spilling out of its big frilly kangaroo pouch; the Deluxe Husband-Tamer Slapstick he'd pad-

dle her bottom with, as they did the traditional high-stepping divorce chase around the house; and the twin bladders to buffet her about the ears with, just to show her how serious things were with him. But he knew, nearly for a certainty, that none of these would stanch his blood lust, that it would grow with each antic act, not assuaged by any of them, not peaking until he plunged his hand into the elephant's-foot umbrella stand in the hallway and drew forth the carving knife hidden among the parasols—whose handles shot up like cocktail toothpicks out of a ripple of pink chiffon—drew it out and used it to plumb Kiki's unfathomable depths.

Another tear, a twin of the first, he painted under his right eye. He paused to survey his right cheekbone, planning where precisely to paint the third.

Bobo heard, at the front door, the rattle of Kiki's key in the lock.

Momo watched aghast.

He'd brushed off with a dove-white handkerchief his collapsible stool in the bushes, slumped hopelessly into it, given a mock-sigh, and found the bent slat he needed for a splendid view of the front hallway and much of the living room, given the odd neck swivel. On the off-chance that their spat might end in reconciliation, Momo'd also positioned a tall rickety stepladder beside Bobo's bedroom window. It was perilous to climb and a balancing act and a half not to fall off of, but a more leisurely glimpse of Kiki's lovely honker in action was, he decided, well worth the risk.

What he could see of the confrontation pleased him. These were clowns in their prime, and every swoop, every duck, every tumble, tuck, and turn, was carried out with consummate skill. For all the heartache Momo had to deal with, he liked his work. His clients quite often afforded him a front-row seat at the grandest entertainments ever staged: spills, chills, and thrills, high passion and low comedy, inflated bozos pin-punctured and deflated ones puffed up with triumph. Momo took deep delight—though his forlorn face cracked nary a smile—in the confetti, the exploding cigar, what he could see and hear of their slapstick chase. Even the bladder-buffeting Bobo visited upon his wife strained upward at the down-droop of Momo's mouth, he took such fond joy in the old ways, wishing with deep soundless sighs that more clowns these days would re-embrace them.

His first thought when the carving knife flashed in Bobo's hand was that it was rubber, or retractable. But there was no drawn-out scene played, no mock-death here; the blow came swift, the blood could not be mistaken for ketchup or karo syrup, and Momo learned more about clown anatomy than he cared to know— the gizmos, the coils, the springs that kept them ticking; the organs, more piglike than clownlike, that bled and squirted; the obscure voids glimmering within, filled with giggle power and something deeper. And above it all, Bobo's plunging arm and Kiki's crimped eyes and open arch of a mouth, wide with pain and drawn down at the corners by the weight of her dying.

Momo drew back from the window, shaking his head. He vanned the stool, he vanned the ladder. There would be no honker action tonight. None, anyway, he cared to witness. He reached deep into the darkness of the van, losing his balance and bellyflopping so that his legs flew up in the night air and his white shanks were exposed from ankle to knee. Righting himself, he sniffed at the red carnation in his lapel, took the inevitable faceful of water, and shouldered the push broom he'd retrieved.

The neighborhood was quiet. Rooftops, curved in high hyperbolas, were silvered in moonlight. So too the paved road and the cobbled walkways that led up to the homes on Bobo's side of the street. As Momo made his way without hurry to the front door, his shadow eased back and forth, covering and uncovering the brightly lit house as if it were the dark wing of the Death Clown flapping casually, silently, overhead. He hoped Bobo would not yank open the door, knife still dripping, and fix him in the red swirl of his crazed eyes. Yet maybe that would be for the best. It occurred to Momo that a world that contained horrors like these might happily be left behind. Indeed, from one rare glimpse at rogue-clown behavior in his youth, as well as from gruesome tales mimed by other dicks, Momo thought it likely that Bobo, by now, had had the same idea and had brought his knife-blade home.

This case had turned dark indeed. He'd have lots of shrugging and moping, much groveling and kowtowing to do, before this was over. But that came, Momo knew, with the territory.

Leaning his tired bones into the push broom, he swept a swatch of moonlight off the front stoop onto the grass. It was his duty, as a citizen and especially as a practitioner of the law, to call in the Kops. A few more sweeps and the stoop was moonless; the lawn to either side shone with shattered shards of light. He would finish the walkway, then broom away a spill of light from the road in front of Bobo's house, before firing the obligatory flare into the sky.

Time enough, then, to endure the noises that would tear open the night, the clamorous bell of the mismatch-wheeled pony-drawn firetruck, the screaming whistles in the bright red mouths of the Kops clinging to the Kop Kar as it raced into the neighborhood, hands to their domed blue hats, the bass drums booming as Bobo's friends and neighbors marched out of their houses, spouses and kids, poodles and ponies and piglets highstepping in perfect columns behind.

For now, it was enough to sweep moonlight from Bobo's cobbled walkway, to darken the wayward clown's doorway, to take in the scent of a fall evening and gaze up wistfully at the aching gaping moon.

Clap If You Believe

I understand her parents' wariness. A woman like my Tinkerbell is bound to attract the amorous attentions of the wrong sort now and again. So when they open the door and appraise me like a suspect gem, not smiling, not yet inviting me in, I understand and forbear. "Good evening," I say, and let the silence float like untroubled webs of gossamer between us.

After a time, Mr. Jones turns to his wife and says, "What do you think?"

"The eyes look reasonably sane," she replies, to his nod, "though that's not always an airtight indicator these days, and there *is* a worrisome edge to them."

I look down, stifling the urge to defend myself, and am gratified to hear Mr. Jones say, "Man with his hobbies and profession is bound to have

sharp eyes. I say we give him the benefit and let him in."

She sighs. "Oh, all right. Come in out of the heat, young man. Put your shoes there." A serried rank of them faces the wall like naughty students: practical ones for Mr. and Mrs. Jones, scuffed high-tops for twelve-year-old Melissa, and, looking more like shed leaves than footwear, Tinkerbell's familiar green-felt slippers. I unknot and loosen my buffed black Florsheims and set them beside my beloved's footwear, thinking what a marvel her tiny feet are and how delightful it is—ensconced alone in her cozy apartment after a date—to take her legs, right up to the thighs, into my mouth and lightly tongue those feet, her tiny soles, the barely perceptible curve of her insteps, the sheer white-corn delicacy of her ten tiny toes. How ecstatically my darling pixie writhes and wriggles in my hand, her silver-sheened wings fluttering against my palm!

"Hi, Alex." I look up and there's Melissa standing by an archway that leads to the dining room.

"Hi, Melissa," I say, wiggling my fingers at her like Oliver Hardy fiddling with his tie. The zoo is only four blocks from their house and we've begun, Melissa and Tink and I, to make a regular thing of meeting there Saturday afternoons. Once, over snow cones, Melissa told me that Tink had been miserable for a long time, "but now that you've come into her life, Alex"—this from a twelve-year-old—"she flits about like a host of hummingbirds when she drops in for Sunday dinner and makes loads of

happy words twinkle in my head, in all of our heads." Hearing Melissa say that made me glad, and I told her so.

Melissa giggles at my finger-waggling and says, "Come on in and sit down."

I look a question at the Joneses. Mrs. Jones gives an unreadably flat lip-line to me. Mr. Jones, instead of seconding Melissa's invitation, comes up like an old pal, leans in to me, and says, "You and me, after dinner, over cigars in my study."

I'm not sure what he's getting at, but I feel as if he's somehow taken me into his confidence. I say, "That's fine, sir," and that seems to satisfy him because he steps back like film reversed and stands beside his wife.

A familiar trill rises in my brain. The others turn their heads, as do I, to the stairs, its sweeping mahogany banister soaring into the warm glow upstairs. And down flies my beloved Tinkerbell, trailing behind her a silent burst of stars. Her lovely face hovers before me, the tip of her wand describing figure eights in the air. "Hello, Alex my lovely," she hums into my head. Then she flits to my cheek, the perfect red bow of her lips burning cinnamon kisses there. Recalling the sear of those kisses on other parts of my anatomy, I feel a blush rising.

"Tinkerbell," I say, using her full name, "perhaps we should—"

"Yes, daughter," Mrs. Jones breaks in, clearly not at all amused, "your young man is correct. Dinner's on the table." She glares at me and turns to lead the party into the dining room. Melissa comes and takes my hand, while Tink

flits happily about my right shoulder, singing into my head her gladness at seeing me. When she holds still long enough for me to fix a discerning eye on her, I'm relieved to see that she's not yet showing.

Once dinner is underway, the ice thins considerably, and in fact Tink's mother rushes past her more cautious husband to become my closest ally. Maybe her change of heart is brought on by my praise for her rainbow trout amandine—which praise I genuinely mean. Or maybe it's brought on by the dinner conversation, which focuses on me half the time, on Tink the other half. Mrs. Jones asks surprisingly insightful questions about my practice as a microsurgeon, pleasantly coaxing me into more detail than the average non-medico cares to know about the handling of microsutures and the use of interchangeable oculars on a headborne surgical microscope. I'm happy to oblige as I watch Tinkerbell hover over her dinner, levitating bits of it with her wand—nothing flamboyant, merely functional—and bringing it home to her mouth.

After some perfunctory questions about my butterfly collection (I've sold it since meeting their daughter, as it disquiets her) and my basement full of miniature homes and the precisely detailed furniture that goes with them (I met Tinkerbell at a show for just such items), the talk turns to their daughter. It's a little embarrassing, what with Melissa beaming at me, and Tinkerbell singing into me her bemusement at her mother, and her father looking ever more resigned, and his wife going on and on about her

tiny daughter, giving me a mom's-eye view of her life history as if Tinkerbell herself weren't sitting at the table with us. Mrs. Jones is in the midst of telling how easy it was to give birth to a pixie and how hard to live with the fact thereafter when I suddenly laugh, quickly disguising it as a choke—water went down the wrong way, no problem, really I'm all right. Tink has made me a lewd and lovely proposition, one which has brought to mind the heartaching image of her as last I enjoyed her, looking so vulnerable with her glade-green costume and her slim wand set aside, arching back on her spun-silver wings, her perfect breasts thrust up like twin peaks on a relief map, her ultra-fine fingers kneading the ruddy pucker of her vulva, awaiting the tickle and swirl of my ultra-fine horsehair brush, the hot monstrosity of my tongue tip, and the perfect twin-kiss of my cock-slit, as we began our careful coitus.

I give Tink a quick stare of admonition—a joke and not a joke. She beams, melts me, and goes back to her meal. The entire scene suddenly amuses me greatly, this whole silly ritual of meeting the parents, getting their approval for the inevitable, most of which—in particular the essential proof of the rightness of shared intimacy—has already come to pass. But I contain my laughter. I act the good son-in-law-to-be and show these kind, narrow people, under whose love and tutelage my fiancée grew to maturity, the esteem and good manners they expect.

"Alex, would you please pass the peas?" says Melissa when her mother pauses to inhale. Mrs. Jones has launched into yet another diatribe

against an educational system too unfeeling, too inflexible for special students like her Tinkerbell. Already under fire have come the lack of appropriate gymnastic equipment, the unfeeling cretinism of a certain driver-ed instructor, and Tinkerbell's unmet needs for special testing conditions in all her academic subjects. As I pass the peas, the head drama coach falls into the hopper of Mrs. Jones's tirade for refusing even to consider mounting a production of *Peter Pan* and giving Tink a chance to perform the character they've named her after, a casting inspiration Mrs. Jones is certain would have brought her daughter out of the cocoon of adolescent shyness years earlier than had been the case.

"But the worst of it, Alex," she says, and I thank God that she's spoken my name for the first time (and that dropped so casually into the conversation), "is that no one in all those years has had the slightest clue how to teach Tink— or even how to discover—the uses of her wand, other than as an odd utensil and for occasional cleaning tricks. It might have kept this family solvent—"

"Emma," warns Mr. Jones, defensive.

"—well, more solvent than it was. It might have saved people's lives, cured disease, made world leaders see reason through their cages of insanity, brought all kinds of happiness flowing into people's hearts the world over." She asks me point blank to help her tiny daughter discover the full potential of her wand, and I promise I will. I don't mention, of course, that we've already found one amazing use for it in our lovemaking, a use that makes me feel incredibly

good, incredibly potent, and incredibly loving toward Tinkerbell. It occurs to me at that moment, listening to Mrs. Jones's spirited harangue, that the wand might indeed have other uses and that perhaps one of them, a healing use, might reduce the failures and increase the triumphs I witness every day in the operating room. I get excited by this, nod more, stoke food into my mouth faster than is strictly polite. We're bonding, Mrs. Jones and I. She can feel it, I can feel it, Melissa is grinning like an idiot, and Tink is humming snatches of *Lohengrin* into my head. "I love you, Alex," she wind-chimes, "I love you and the horse you rode in on." Looking aside, I watch her playing with her food, wanding a slow reversed meander of mashed potatoes into her mouth, biting it off in ribbons of white mush. Her unshod feet are planted apart on the damask and her wings, thin curved planes of iridescence, lie still against her back.

After dinner, Mrs. Jones is ready to usher me into the parlor for more bonding. But her husband holds up his hand to cut her off, saying, "It's time, Emma." "Oh," she says. He's got some bit of gristle in his craw, some one thing that's holding back his approval of me.

"Ah, the study," I say. "The cigars."

"Just so," he says in a way that suggests mantalk, and pretty serious man-talk at that. I follow him out of the dining room. Mrs. Jones and Melissa have odd looks on their faces. Even Tink's hum is edged with anxiety.

The study is dark and small, green-tinged and woodsy. There's a rolltop desk, now closed, and the rich smell of rolled tobacco and old ledgers

pervades the air. He fits a green eyeshade around his head, offers me one. I accept but feel foolish in it, as if I'm at Walt Disney World wearing a Donald Duck hat, bright yellow bill as brim.

Mr. Jones sits in a rosewood swivel chair and motions me to a three-legged ebony piano stool in front of him. I have to look up a good six inches to meet his eyes. "You smoke cigars?" he asks.

"Not unless you count one White Owl in my teens."

He chuckles once, then drops it. With a soft clatter of wood slats, he scrolls up the rolltop and opens a huge box of cigars. He lifts out two of them, big long thick cylinders of brown leaf with the smell of sin about them and the crisp feel of currency in their wrappings. I take what he offers and follow his lead in preparing, lighting, and puffing on the damned thing. I'm careful to control my intake, not wanting to lose face in a fit of coughing. The cigar tastes peculiarly pleasant, sweet, not bitter, and the back of my head feels like it's ballooning.

"My wife," he begins, "likes you. I like you. And Tinkerbell likes you; but then, she's liked every last one of her boyfriends, even the slime-sucking shitwads—can we speak man-to-man?—who used Tink for their own degenerate needs and then discarded her."

I don't want to hear this.

"Not that there've been lots of men before you. She may be a pixie, our daughter, but she's got the good sense of the Joneses even so. But you know, Alex my boy, you'd be surprised at the

number of men in this world who look and act perfectly normal, men whose mild exteriors cover sick vistas of muck and sludge, men who make regular guys like you and me ashamed to be called men."

"I assure you, sir, that—"

"—and I'd believe those assurances, I really would, even though I've believed and been fooled in the past. My little girl, Tinkerbell Titania Jones, is special to me as she is; not some freak, not a thing of shame or suspicion, no, but a thing of grace and beauty."

"She is indeed, Mr. Jones."

He fixes me in his glare and exhales a puff of blue smoke. It hangs like a miasma about him, but he doesn't blink. His eyes might be lizard eyes. "I had doubts when she was born, of course. What father wouldn't? No man likes to be deceived by his wife, not even through the irresistible agency of a stray faerie or incubus, if such there be in this world. But there are mannerisms of mine I recognized quite early in my daughter, mannerisms I was sure were neither learned nor trumped up by some phantom lover bent on throwing a cuckolded husband off his trail."

He cranes his neck and stares, about fifteen degrees askew of my face. It's a look I recognize from my first meeting with Tink at the miniaturists' show in Sacramento the previous winter. I'd asked her to dinner and she went all quiet and contemplative, looking just this way, before finally venturing a twinkled yes. I could tell she'd been stung before, and recently.

"She's mine," he says. "Some mutation, if you

want to be cold-bloodedly clinical about it, but all mine. And I love her dearly, as parents of special children often do."

He takes a long puff, exhales it, looks at me. "Now I'm going to ask you three questions, Alex. Only truthful answers are going to win my daughter's hand."

I feel odd about this turn in the conversation, and yet the setting, the cigar smoke, the close proximity of this beast in his lair, make it seem perfectly normal. I nod agreement and flick a squat cylinder of ash into the open glass hand, severed, of a four-fingered man.

"First," Mr. Jones says, not stumbling over any of the words, "have you had sex with my daughter?"

My head is pounding. I take a long pull on my cigar and slowly exhale the smoke. My hand, holding it, seems big and beefy, unworthy of my incisive mind. "She and I have . . . made love, yes. We love each other, you see, and it's only natural for—"

"No extenuation," says Mr. Jones. "Your answer is yes. It's a good answer, it's the truth, and I have no quarrel with it. I would think you some sort of nitwit if you hadn't worked out some mutually agreeable arrangement between you. No, I don't want to know how it's done. I shudder to think about it. When she drops in, she seems none the worse for wear. If she's happy, and you're happy with her—and with the limitations you no doubt face—then that will content her mother and me."

I think of course of vaginal sinkings, that nice feel of being gripped there by a grown woman.

And I think back years to my first girlfriend Rhonda, to her mouth, to the love she was kind enough to focus down below from time to time, though less frequently than I would have preferred.

"That leads, of course, to my second question," says Mr. Jones, putting one hand, the one without the cigar, to his temple. "Will you be faithful to Tinkerbell, neither casting the lures of temptation toward other women nor consenting to be lured by them?"

I pause. "That's a complex question."

"It is indeed," he says, with a rising inflection that asks it all over again.

"I don't think," I tell him, my hands folded, my eyes deeply sincere, "I will ever fail my beloved in this way. Yet knowing the weakness of myself and other men, the incessant clamor of the gonads that I daresay all males are prey to, I hesitate to say yes unequivocally to your question. But Tinkerbell gives me great satisfaction, and, more importantly, I believe I do the same for her. Something about her ways in bed, if you will, seems to silence the voice of lust when I'm around other women. Besides which—and I don't mean this flippantly—I've grown, through loving Tinkerbell, to appreciate smaller women. In fact, on the whole, I've come to find so-called normal-sized women unbearably gross and disgusting."

Mr. Jones looks askance at me. "Alex, you're a most peculiar man. But then, I think that's what my daughter's going to need, a peculiar man, and yet it's so damned hard to know which set of peculiarities are the right ones."

I'm not sure how to take his comment, but then, I'm in no position to debate the issue. "Yes, sir," I say.

"Almost out of the woods," says Mr. Jones, grinning. "The third one is easy." He tosses it off like a spent match: "Do you love Tinkerbell?"

This question throws me. It seems simple enough, but that's the problem: It's too simple. Does he want a one-word response or a dissertation? Is it a trick question of some sort? And is the time I'm taking in deliberating over it actually sinking my chances? What is love, after all? Everybody talks about it, sings about it, yammers on and on endlessly about it. But it's so vague a word, and so loaded. I think of French troubadour poets, of courtly love and its manufacture, of Broadway show tunes and wall-sized faces saying "I love you" on big screens, saying it like some ritual curse or as if it signaled some terrible loss of control akin to vomiting.

And I say, "Yes and no," feeling my way into the open wound of shared camaraderie, ready to provide reasons for my equivocation, a brief discourse that will show him the philosophical depths of my musings and yet come about, in the end, to a grand paean of adoration for his daughter.

But before I can begin, he rises from his chair and reaches for me, and the next thing I know, the furniture hurtles by as if in a silent wind and the doors fly open seemingly without the intervention of human hands and I'm out on the street in front of their home, trying to stop my head from spinning.

It's dark out there but muggy. I ache inside,

ache for my loss. It's not fair, I think. She loves me and I love her, and by God we belong together. I'll call her in the morning when she's back in the city, I'll send roses, I'll surprise her with a knock on her door. We'll elope. This isn't the Dark Ages, after all. Tinkerbell and I don't need her parents' permission to marry.

Doors slam in the house. Downstairs, upstairs. A high-pitched voice, Melissa's, shouts something childish and angry, is answered by falsely calm parental soothings. None of the words can I make out.

The first floor goes dark after a while, then bit by bit the second. From where I'm standing, it looks like a miniature house, one of my basement models. I raise both hands and find I can obliterate it completely.

There is one golden glow of light hovering behind a drawn tan shade upstairs. Her bedroom, the room she grew up in. I want to clap my hands, clap them in defiance of her parents—she'll know what that means, she'll surely understand. But the energy has drained from my arms and they hang useless at my sides.

Behind the shade, my lost love's light moves slowly back and forth, back and forth, growing dimmer, casting forth ever smaller circles of gold with each beat of my heart.

The Slobbering Tongue That Ate the Frightfully Huge Woman

Sally Holmes was married to a swell guy. She liked working in the lab. Holding clipboards and making notes for Dr. Baxter while hiding her beauty behind glasses and a tight bun was her idea of fun. She did it well.

And she gave her husband John a nice home. Soon, if they could figure out where children came from, there'd be pattering feet to feed. John was a good man. They'd been childhood sweethearts. Now John was a police lieutenant. She didn't understand his work. Heck, truth be told, she barely understood her own. But all Sally had to do was to poise her fountain pen smartly above her clipboard and act as if she

were saying clever things, and Dr. Baxter was more than pleased to keep her around.

The one thing Sally liked about Dr. Baxter, other than her paycheck, was his way with words. He was a blob in pretty much every respect, balding, sags of flesh stuck on his face like sneezed boogers on a mirror. But when he spoke, his labials, his fricatives, his palatals, his urps of intelligence, the way his moist pink tongue oystered in his mouth—all of those oral sorts of things made Sally go all soft and squoozy inside.

For months he'd been working on something top secret, putting in so many hours he might as well have camped out at the institute. He let no one into his inner lab. But the notes he dictated tantalized her. He overworked his staff, but Sally didn't mind (she knew that *John* did). It just meant more toward their nest egg, more smart repartee over the clipboard, and more of that clever tongue.

When Dr. Baxter invited her that evening into his inner lab, just him and her around, Sally had no inkling that anything more than science was on his mind. He held the unsealed door for her, and she stepped in, sniffing a barnyard stench she'd caught wind of before.

John lay there in his pajamas, wanting his wife next to him. It felt so great to hug her, pajamas to pajamas, and give her a pristine little kiss good night. And every so often—once every few months if he was lucky—she'd be open to cuddling in the dark, to undoing certain strategic snaps and letting him shoot an icky mess inside

her while she lay there so calm and sweet and receptive. He'd give his standard, "Sorry," in her ear, then roll off her, shame in him, yes, but feeling glad too that she hid her disgust so well.

It proved she loved him.

Still, he sensed there was something missing in their marriage. As Sally flitted about the kitchen or Hoovered the rugs or knelt to dust the baseboards, John felt as if there were a crack in her smile—almost as if, God forbid, a first wrinkle were appearing in that smooth peach-infant face of hers.

His wife needed reassurance.

Oh, heck. He'd drop in at the lab. Yes, yes. He'd dare to be different. Flinging the covers back, he leaped out of bed. Would he put on the clothing he'd tossed into the hamper? No. New ones. He wouldn't sweat too much in them and he could wear them again tomorrow.

Sally'd be thrilled to see him. A sweet surprise.

Baxter anticipated her amazement.

"Oh, my!" she ejaculated, her fetching shoulder blades flexing like coy airplane struts under that white coat she plumped out so well in front.

"You've never seen a ten-foot cock before?" The bird was indeed awesome there in its cage, its magnificent head turned in quirk, one squint-eye wide as a saucer. Too bad he hadn't chosen a hen for his experiments. She would've made one heck of a meal, and there were other interesting avenues (so to speak) that might have been explored. He was tired of cleaning up after Giganto here, and tired of feeding him. Damn rooster was due for death.

"Goodness, Dr. Baxter," Sally exclaimed. "What've you been up to?"

"See that?" he said, pointing to the bell jar on the table, with its throbbing pink crystal. "I concocted that substance. I call it gargantuum. It makes organic matter grow. Don't ever disturb that glass container or there's no telling what will happen."

"I won't." She shook her pretty little head so that her radiant tresses primped and fluffed like in a shampoo commercial; no, wait, he was imagining that. Her bun held her hair tight, severe, puckered like a clenched rectum.

Baxter stepped in front of her. "But that's not why I invited you into my inner lab."

"It isn't?"

"No." He eased the carving knife from his cavernous coat pocket. "I'd like you to undress for me, Sally—nice and slow, nice and sexy, one button, one snap at a time."

Sally blanched fetchingly. "I can't do that."

He placed the blade against her neck. "You can," he insisted, "and you will. But first, undo that God-awful, fershlugginer bun. Let your Prellity down, sweetcakes."

Tears welled up as she reached to free her hair. Her breasts rose with the motion. Dr. Baxter fixed on them with those ugly eyes of his. He was a loathsome lunk of a man. Except for his tongue. Poor thing seemed shanghaied into saying awful things, but somehow that didn't diminish its beauty.

The magnitude of her anger startled her.

Sally'd never been angry about anything in her life, not one blessed thing.

But, even as her fingers worked the buttons and tears gathered in her eyes, she was angry about this. Her anger was hot and solid, coming deep from her insides but hiding itself as it grew. He couldn't detect it. But she could surely feel it. And soon, but she feared not soon enough, it would lash out at the scientist Sally had trusted to be good but who was very bad indeed.

"Not fast enough," he said. His free hand shot forth and yanked her lapel to one side, so that her white satin slip showed from her right shoulder strap down to where it cupped in lacy fullness her huge right breast. Where his brutish paw touched her, her flesh ached.

She looked at the knife in his hand, the sharp blade, the brown rippled wood of its handle. She wanted so badly to wrest it away from him, to use it on him.

"Faster!" he said, drool dripping from his lips. You never knew about people. You just never knew.

John adored being a police lieutenant. All the boys in blue, nice decent Christian fellas, loved and respected you. You got to wear stylish suits with paper-cut creases ironed into the legs. They snugged your badge into a real nice soft-leather case that felt as cozy as suede when you whipped it from your inside coat pocket and held it up for a citizen's eyes.

He maneuvered the Plymouth along the quiet streets, a bouquet of long-stemmed roses lying beside him.

A lanky young man was walking an Airedale. John hit his horn lightly, waved, took the return wave. The dog's no-nonsense yap filled the air with glee. Life was good. Life was very good. Life was very very very good.

But it could be better.

He could assure Sally that he loved her, that there'd never be for him any woman in the world but her. That was what a wife wanted to hear. For John, there'd only always been Sally. No one else. And there never *would* be anyone else. Never never never.

He hummed a sprightly tune.

There was Baxter Enterprises ahead. The guard at the gate grinned at him. He lifted the flowers, said, "For my sweet honey," and the mustachioed geezer in uniform nodded and waved him through. "Say hello to the missus for me," the guard shouted, shrinking in the rear-view mirror.

"I will," yelled John. He rolled up the window, the corners of his mouth hurting from his smiles, and pressed on toward the main building.

Baxter had his way with her. Though smart and snappy as always, Mrs. Holmes was passive like a good dolly ought to be. On the floor, upon the air mattress he forced her into blowing up, he felt all her secret places, he tasted her, he lay his bulky frame on her and forced his manhood inside her. The air was thick with bird smell, tainted by hints of formaldehyde from the embryos jarred on the table above them.

So enthralled did he become and so passive

and almost not-there was his victim that he lost track of his carving knife. And suddenly there was a tugging at his hand, and an emptiness there. Then his shoulder caught fire, a jag of outrage sinking thickly inside. His secretary wiggled like a ba-zillion panicked eels out from under him as the pain erupted, a swift deep cramp in his upper torso.

He screamed, not continuous but blips—sharp, barked, like a wounded mutt. Her face flared and bloomed. Shrew, he thought. Termagant. That's what she had turned into. She gripped the knife handle and yanked it out. He felt somehow as if his lungs followed it, and yet it was a hurt he needed from her. She had repented. She would help him to a hospital, stanch his blood, bandage him, make him all better, hold him, kiss him, dump her dorky boy in blue.

Then she docked him. She fisted his shaft, razored a chill below, pressed it in, cutting through no-resistance, through sponge cake, burrowing and spreading a volcano of agony. Her first thrust had enervated him. He could only make faint shows of protest as she unmanned him. Suddenly he could no longer feel the squeeze, although he saw the purple flesh blanch in her fingers, saw her pry his member away, felt his groin skin peel up, a gigantic splinter of pain, toward his navel.

His thing thwapped on the floor where she tossed it.

He rocked and screamed, energy draining from between his legs. His attacker—*he'd* been the attacker; now *she* was—bounded up, clat-

tered in his tools above, came back with a bone
saw.

And then, oh my God, she severed his hands.

Rage drove her on. This monster had touched
her in all her secret places. Now she was dis-
mantling him, all his offending parts off and
away. That's the way it had to be, Sally's crazed
mind told her.

His resistance was all in his voice. The bone
saw snagged on the air mattress, which burbled
its air away through washes of blood. But the
vile hand snapped off, cracking and tearing like
an uncooked lobster claw. The other, as his
stump feebly brushed her back with sticky protest, proved even easier.

Time for his tongue.

She'd brought back a bull castrator—why he
had one, she didn't stop to ask. But her bloody
hands tore at his jaws and jammed the instrument deep down into his throat, watching the
tongue slither in snug where a pizzle would ordinarily go. Then she clamped shut, freshets of
blood upshooting, spraying her breasts with hot
gore. And out the quivering tantalizing tormenting sucker came.

Though it too had violated her, she didn't toss
the tongue to the floor as she'd done with his
hands and his manhood. She rose, unlidded the
first jar she saw, took out the chick embryo, and
dropped in the tongue, lifting the jar, hugging
its chill to her breasts.

She was aimlessly meandering, slowly, randomly, her face a veil of tears, wounded tears,
tears of rage.

Sally's foot struck something. She glanced down at it; Baxter's right hand. The things it had done! Still with the jar hugged to her chest, she bent down, snatched the odious thing up, and hurled it away from her.

The bell jar rang from the impact, lifted, tottered, and fell with a decisive clatter to the tabletop, rolling off and shattering on the floor. The pink crystal pulsed and hummed. Its light filled the air. The sound it made rose, higher, higher, like a menacing theremin.

And then the explosion came, pink goop in the air, on her flesh, down her throat. It coated her arms where they hugged the jar, radiating there, pulsing. Sally wanted to scream, but she choked on the stuff, and felt it strangely warm all over her.

Just as John killed the Plymouth, he felt a *whumph* in the air. It was a subtle pop, but all his antennae of love and protection immediately sprang up and out.

Sally was in danger.

Without remembering how he'd done it, he was suddenly outside the car, his hands on the closed pinging car door. It felt as if it took forever, but he raced to the entrance and plowed through, down corridor upon corridor to Sally's lab. "Sally!" he yelled. "Sally! Sally! Sally!"

No one.

But John took in the door to the inner lab, its edge blasted and pulsing pink from lights within. He dashed to it, yanked it open.

His wife was facing away from him, naked and sobbing. On the floor lay Dr. Baxter, parts

of him missing, him nearly dead but not quite so. A gigantic rooster stood in a cage in the far corner, stinking the place up.

John approached his naked wife. There was yucky pink stuff in her hair, all over her body, on the jar her hands gripped so tight. The residue of some pink substance lay like shards of shattered icicle on a far table.

"Honey?" he said. "Are you okay?"

Her face was slabbed in tears.

She looked down, noticed what she was holding, set it with other jars like it on the table beside her.

She turned to him, held out her hands, but then raised them as he approached. "I . . . I'm all goopy."

"Here." He looked around wildly, saw some linen on a shelf. "I'll get you a towel."

He got her a towel.

Dr. Baxter, gurgling, died. "He attacked me," she said. John nodded. His wife was one savage biddy. But, by God, she'd had good reason. There was cleanup needing to be done, here and in their lives. But he vowed, by his love for her, to see things through to the end.

Baxter woofed his last breath. His mouth, his groin, his wrist stumps felt as if God, frowning from on high, had snapped bear traps on them and salted his wounds, skewering his celestial disapproval in like sharp smoldering stakes that glowed white hot, turning, twisting, searing, never a dull moment in his tormented body.

Then suddenly the pain, pricklike, was cut off. He was somewhere else. Somewhere cool and

moist and cloying. He couldn't see. He couldn't hear. But he felt himself alive and whole, if uprooted. And he could taste, oh yes he could. Yucky tasting stuff; unpalatable, though he had no palate.

But something most succulent lay close by, something he had tasted recently and could still, in sensual memory, recall with wicked delight. He pulsed. He surged. But this new body, if that's what it was—limbless, but mere limb— would take some getting used to, to make it motile, to seek out and taste that recalled succulence once more.

A light shone, warm and pink (now how could he sense, being blind, colors?), a finger's reach from him. It felt like sunlight on seedlings. He sensed arousal, the shift of flexible flesh, an overpowering urge to grow.

In bed that night, after the police procedurals had swept through her, Sally tossed and turned. An extra long bath had helped, steaming there, quite out of it, till the water grew cool. But she still felt Dr. Baxter's vile acts clinging to her— that and the glowing pink goop, the gargantuum the explosion had drenched her with.

At midnight, she woke in a sweat.

John was snoring beside her, big long snuffly snorts that made him less than appealing. His exhalations stank like sodden cigars, like burnt toast threaded with maggoty shreds of pork.

When Sally shifted to turn him on his side, away from her, her pajamas clung tight. The buttons strained at her breasts, alternating left-and-right-facing vees of fabric. Her hips drew

73

the cloth taut as snapped sheets. Breathing was difficult. Had she put on a pair of John's pajamas by mistake? Nope. The monogram, a red SAH, was hers.

John snorted awake.

"You okay?" he mumbled.

"Yes," she said. "Go back to sleep."

She tried to do the same. Funny. Her pajama bottoms used to cover her ankles. Now they'd started to creep up her calves, clinging there like wet wraps of seaweed.

She dismissed it, tried to find sleep. But Baxter's words of warning and the image of a ten-foot cock refused to leave her mind.

John feigned sleep. But it wouldn't come. In the moonlight seeping in their window, he let his glistening eyes open. His wife lay upon her back, dozing fitfully. It was a warm night. The covers slanted at her waist.

My God, he thought, her breasts are mammoth.

Sally was so beautiful. It tore him up inside that she'd endured the nightmare of being violated by Dr. Baxter. The warped deviant deserved to have his ... but then John remembered. Baxter *had* had his ... ! And by Sally's dear hand.

He propped himself slowly on one crooked arm, head in hand, and beheld her. Sweet face. Wanton hair, down now, rioting like rainbows on her pillow. Somehow, there seemed *more* of her tonight. He loved her so. He wished there were some way he could undo her pain.

Undo her buttons.

Her breasts were so huge. Pregnant women, he'd been told, got that way. Maybe they'd have a child after all. But he doubted that. They plumped there under the strain of cotton, huge soft cantaloupe mounds that would one day droop and sag like ugly sacks of pudding but didn't now. They cantilevered, as magic as flying buttresses in their firmness, their heft, their suspension.

One day, maybe, Sally would let him see them naked.

But that day, he knew, lay far in the future. His wife was no slut. And she'd been through a personal hell that would take time and patience to heal.

The bastard (oops, he amended it to "bad man") ought to have his . . .

Ah yes. Small favors.

Baxter felt in-tight. Jar-shaped. He had to get out before the confinement squeezed him to death. He'd never felt so helpless. Then he realized, with a virtual smack to his nonexistent forehead, that he was all muscle.

He contracted, tensed. Waited until he felt cramped again. Then, abruptly, he flexed.

And suddenly he was free!

Sensing sharpness, he gingerly moved over fragments so as not to cut himself. He tasted wood, fell, thwapped to newly mopped linoleum tile. Licking the ammoniac tang of Mr. Clean, he pulsed and throbbed toward freedom.

A pressure halted him. He smelled the black stink of Cat's Paw shoe polish. Swooping across leather, he found flesh, flesh that shook, jittered.

Panicked hands batted at him. But he clung tight, wrapping about an ankle. His spittle turned the flesh soft and absorbable. He took the stuff in, the blood, the bone, lapping up thigh meat as his victim fell, scream-vibes egging him on.

It felt positively erotic to sate himself.

Like lava, he smacked up the body inside the clothes, tasted groinslit, hair, belly, breasts. A female cop, was his guess as he gobbled. And alone, based on the help she didn't get. His tonguebody thinned and imbibed, slapping like a wave, receding, drawing sandflesh, sandbone, after it, trails of bloodbubble foaming behind.

When nothing remained but copsuit, he ambled on.

Sally, by the dresser, held her glasses confusedly in her hand. The arms had snapped when she tried to put them on. But strangely she could see fine without them.

"Listen," John said to her. "I'll take the day off. I've got time. We'll go to the beach."

"You think that would help?" Nothing would help.

"It's worth a try."

After a time, she relented. Her husband seemed to be standing in a hole, but he was solid and assuring. It was a blessing to be in his care. When she took her one-piece into the bathroom to change, it wouldn't fit.

So they got in the car and went to Macy's.

For some reason a white bikini, one of those new and daring suits, seemed right. When she looked at herself in the dressing room mirror,

Anita Ekberg came to mind. Milk bottles. My, my, she thought, I *am* filling out.

She could scarcely pull her clothing over it, the red checked shirt, the slacks. Was it time to diet? No. She wasn't fatter. Just larger. Hmmm.

"Let's go," she said, taking John's arm.

On the drive to the beach, she brooded on gargantuum.

Jones Beach was crowded that day. Must be lots of folks on vacation, John thought. They strolled along the shore, his wife's statuesque body—and since when had she become statuesque?—drawing stares. There was no hope of finding seclusion, but between beachfronts, they found a bit more room to spread out the pea-green army blanket.

At a distance, an unchaperoned bunch of teens played jungle music, tinny, from a tiny transistor radio.

Sally tucked her hair into a bathing cap, white with plastic flowers daisied on it. John frolicked with her in the waves, splashing her, being splashed. For the moment, everything seemed normal again.

Back on the blanket, her body glistened with droplets as she lay down. Sleek curvy back. Wondrous front. What a full voluptuous woman his wife was. Odd. In the store her bikini had fit fine. Now the flesh strained at it, and he fancied he could see the cloth tugging, thinning.

"Jeepers, this suit is tight," she said.

John looked over at the teens. They were jiggling to the radio noise. Disgusting. America was in trouble.

He heard Sally prepare a sneeze.

When he turned to her, the sneeze blew into her hand and her suit exploded off her. For a second in the bright sunlight, his wife was bare-ass naked.

She took the Lord's name in vain.

Then she grabbed a towel, two towels, and sat there rocking, crying, lamenting, "What's *happening* to me?"

Baxter tasted dirt, gravel, cinders, dog doo, hawked gobs of spit. He preferred the lady cop. He craved more female flesh, and one dainty dish in particular. When he picked up the tracks of his former secretary, he'd be hot on that cutie's trail, no question.

But in the meantime, he slithered along the edge of downtown North Allville. Somehow his senses of taste and touch were so acute, he could grope along an internal map of the town. He had ghost visions, ghost hearings, faint white whispered things, that corresponded to what was out there.

A malt shop near the railroad tracks.

He sniffed females, lots of them.

The air jittered with passion sounds. He could feel the floor shaking as he slid through the open door. There were seven of them, smelling like high school cheerleader types. With his tip, he eased the door closed, locked it, turned the OPEN sign to CLOSED.

High giggles knifed the air.

Ponytails twirled, hips gyred in long poodle skirts.

Then he attacked, and the giggles turned to screams.

He sucked up girlflesh, swelled, grew. This was the life. Blood, bone, bile, chocolate malts half-digested in smooth taut burst tummies.

Much better than dog doo.

But nowhere near as delectable as sweet Sally Holmes.

Weeks passed. The evidence of Sally's transformation had become so clear that, the day after the beach fiasco, she fled. Nearly seven feet. She was growing, and growing fast. As she left, she had to duck through the front door to avoid braining herself.

She kept to the woods during the day, moving at night in a direction that called to her. To clothe herself, she stole sheets off lines, pinning them together with wooden clothespins. She raided gardens, wishing she had money to pay the good people she stole from.

Her mind was expanding too. Her rage. And, God help her, her libido. She'd never been so horny and so angry, and her thoughts had never ranged so widely over being and nothingness, the meaning of life, and the silly putterings of the diminutive creatures she espied from where she hid. Whole passages of Plato and Aristotle she had slid over in school now came back, making sense. She embraced what was right in them, tossed what was wrong.

When she was thirty feet tall, she began not to care who saw her move at night. At forty feet, she bared her breasts, feeling night breeze and sunlight tauten the huge nipples. At fifty feet, she

started to tease the little people, gripping cars and jiggling them, lifting them by the roofs so swiftly that sometimes—like painfully inept special effects—it seemed she lifted the landscape along with it. She wrecked upright structures. Steeples, radio towers, anything lofty she tore off, feeling enraged and good and sweaty. During the day, she sought out bowl-like depressions, cool, lush, comforting, to sleep in.

She had no idea what place instinct drew her toward, but it was good, very good indeed. Of that she was sure.

John fixed upon the U.S. map the sergeant was pointing to. The country was going crazy. His wife, breasts bare as a harlot's, had grown huge and was destroying property left and right. Rumors of a giant tongue circulated, and whole villages' populations disappearing. The only thing left behind? A trail of bloody saliva.

"Mrs. Holmes was spotted here (*thwap*), here (*thwap*), and here (big *thwap*)," the man said. He was square-jawed and steely-eyed. "You men notice where she's headed?"

Everyone grumbled a yes like they were in church with their heads bowed muttering amen.

"That's right," he said. "The Grand Canyon. We can let her be, then zoom in with helicopters, pick her off."

"Hold on," said John. "That's my wife you're talking about."

"Don't be a chump for love," said the sergeant. "We have a public nuisance on our hands. And I aim to wash it off. With steel slugs of civic soap."

"Have you no heart, man?"

"I have a duty to all Americans. That, *über alles.*"

Everyone grumbled yeah, yeah.

John grabbed the pointer. "Listen, men, I know Sally as well as anyone. I can reason with her, persuade her to stop destroying erect edifices."

"She's a monster!"

"She's my *wife!!!!!*"

He put it so strongly, the other cops relented. The sergeant rested a hand on John's shoulder. John knew he wasn't a bad man. Just a jerk.

"Time to get *you* to the Grand Canyon," he said.

And it was.

Baxter loomed at the edges of the drive-in. The film splashed up there, from his honed sensors, he supposed was some dark and scary thing. Good. Made it easier for him to claim victims. Black night, black screen, black cover.

He liked the juicy females, the ones the crewcut boys liquefied with their fingers, squirming out of clothing as easily as out of their virginity.

In the back row a Dodge rocked. He could tell it was a Dodge because his tip traced the chrome letters. Baxter tasted unwashed car, skimmed through the window crack, and dove for the couple in the backseat. He hated boy-taste, but (just as he'd saved the best for last over dinner as a boy) he absorbed the boyfriend first, while he muffled the screams of the half-dressed dolly. Then he turned his all to savoring dessert.

She was mere appetizer, a speared shrimp.

81

Robert Devereaux

Sally Holmes's sweetness lay on the wind, and Baxter's drool slathered his pathway toward her. In his future, he sensed a deep wide all-engulfing hole.

Sally recognized it, of course. She and John on their honeymoon had spent time here, had gone down on donkeys.

The Grand Canyon.

Then it had felt like love.

Now it felt like home.

Oblivious to the gaping miniatures scurrying about at her feet, she unpinned the diaperlike loincloth whose taut clutch vexed her, dropped it, and started her long descent to the bottom where the river was.

One weird-eyed maniac feasted his eyes on her, as she lowered her nude body over the rim. She jiggled her boobs at him, then took a deep breath and blew him, midst debris and rubble, back toward the panicked masses. Lustily, she laughed. Then the rim rose above her skull and she was on her way, night's gravid moon lighting rock and brush along the trail.

The local police tracked her with binoculars and with telescopes, relaying her whereabouts to John at the lowest point of the canyon.

When he came upon her, she was reclining, buck naked, near the river. She was obscene. She was beautiful. His shame, under his pants, grew hard. His wife's hand was on her womanhood, stirring it like she stirred cake batter in her Betty Crocker apron. Her deep throaty moans echoed in the vast rocky gorge.

82

"Sally," he shouted. She didn't hear him. He yelled her name over and over until he grew hoarse.

Then she noticed him. A look of desire burned in her eyes. "John," she intoned, a deep throbbing need there.

"My dear darling," he mourned, "they say there may be an antidote, they say—"

She grabbed him, not hard, but firm as one might grab a kitten or gerbil. "Fuck antidotes," she said in rumbles of husky thunder. "I *like* being big."

He chided her for her crude language, but she merely laughed, booming, like the genie in *The Thief of Baghdad.*

Then she brought him within whiffing distance of her womanhood. He recognized the morning-after manhood stink (but writ large and overpowering) before his bath.

"Make like a statue," she ordered. "Rigidify."

Before he could ask her why, he found *out* why.

Like a diver just before splitting the silent water, he took a breath. That saved him. Into warm gooshy hugs of pudding he was thrust, splooshing about in smooth dark pulsings that brought cows' udders to mind. It was divine and it was terrifying. Just when he knew his lungs would burst, Sally unencunted him, frotting his forehead against a ruddy nub (what *was* that thing?), above which curled riots of coarse straw abruptly thatched. Then—and by the grace of God he could sense when, so he could gulp a goopy breath—she'd plunge him back inside her, twisting him and turning him like an agi-

tator in a washing machine, like an orange half being brutally juiced.

But abruptly he was out, laid on the ground, chilling in the night air. He blinked his stuck eyelids open. And saw—oh God he wanted to shit—a gigantic tongue throbbing not six feet away, bloated, bloody, spilling icky rivulets of drool down its unclean sides.

Baxter cared not a lick for the jerk. He'd served as—what did whores call it?—a *dildo* for Baxter's bitch.

But now the bitch had Baxter to satisfy her.

And satisfy her he would.

Tasting more sandstone powder as he rolled on, Baxter leaned against her massive thigh, slurped at her perineum, caught her spillage where it dripped, slowly slalomed his tip up the swollen slit of her excitation toward her sweet hillock of delight.

But she seized him, shoved him in. She embraced him like any animal, and he embraced the opportunity to thrust as deep as he could, elongating, conforming himself to her inner shape, vibrating, throbbing, shuddering, as he moved inward. A tiny bit of him, where she had disembodied him, jazzed at her womanhood. But the rest was inside, not yet releasing his devouring fluid. Time enough, in orgasm, to make her die. He filled her, pulsating against her walls, sweeping beyond the cervix into the uterus itself, filling it like a plum-passioned fetus, poised to wail in ecstasy like a sweaty trumpeter nailing a string of high notes.

She was coming.

And, oh God, she was *squeezing*.

He flexed, but it did no good. She was crushing him. He tried to release the killing fluid. Got some out, felt the beginnings of meld.

But it was too tight. Too fugging tight.

Trapped.

He fluttered.

He died.

Sally tightened in orgasm. Boulders shook loose at her screams. Her husband, with his hands up to his ears, looked like a drooled-upon letter *T*.

But the golden tongue she'd had to have was releasing venom, was stuck inside, even as she shuddered in ecstasy. It stung her center. She felt the life squeezed off there first, even as her final orgasm played out. The hurt bled outward from her womb, attacking kidneys, pancreas, islets of Langerhans, on and on.

Lights winked out all over her body.

"I'm dying," she gasped.

"Oh no," said the pipsqueak. "Honey, that can't be."

She tried to expel the inert tongue like unfertilized tissue, tried to yank it out. No go. It stuck there like a wasp's barb, sinking its killing force deeper with every breath.

Her lungs felt the slash of cut glass. Her heart.

"Good-bye, John," she gasped.

"I'll never forget you," he screamed. "Nobody will."

The thing that had killed her pooched out of her like a melting strawberry Popsicle, dripping crimson gush along her buttocks and onto the

85

earth. It looked like a wilted poinsettia clasped in a clutching infant's hand.

At the height of the terrible display, she had glowed pink: the same pink as in the lab that fateful day. John had felt a warmth beyond embarrassment along his front but mostly in his manhood.

"Bury me deep." Sally's eyes grew fuzzy.

John did a hasty calculation. "I'll bury you *well*," he said. He was hard. To his astonishment he didn't feel any shame. Not only was he hard; he was thick and long, much longer, much thicker than ever in his life. He felt the blunt bludgeon through his trousers. A fucking spade handle stood there.

Crude language had suddenly become okay. In fact it was a decided turn-on. His bulb-head throbbed.

Thoughts of conjunction soared in his head. Thoughts of people watching him score with lots of chicks, sticking his tool in places it had never dreamt of going before.

"Kiss me, John."

He approached her lips, thinking to peck them. Then she inhaled suddenly and he was a hotdog snug in two soggy bun-halves. But a moment later, her death, huge and final and thick with shadows, flooded out upon a slow exhalation and he fell, body-kissed, cock-kissed, to the earth.

Still erect, he picked himself up.

Sally had left him memories.

He patted his pants.

And she'd left him *this*.

And *this* would guide him henceforth on his solitary way.

A Slow Red Whisper of Sand

> When you realize that what love is all about
> is heartbreak, you're all right. But if you
> think it's about fulfillment, happiness, sat-
> isfaction, union, all of that stuff, you're in
> for even more heartbreak. . . .
> Romantic love keeps the world dead.
>
> —James Hillman

Young willing pussy stuck on beautiful slinky
moist-crotched bodies, tan, lithe, lubricious if
superficial to a fault—that's what had drawn
him to L.A. They were no-brainers all, into the
new kink if given half a shove and sufficient nose
candy to blame their natural prurience on. A
pair of cuffs, a fashionable ceiling bolt, a butt

plug inserted to placehold for his cock, and the laying on of lashes at breasts and buttocks sufficiently rough to recall fathers trying to whip sense into them—these reduced them to a delirium of ecstasy, tenderized them for the abrupt descent and feeding of himself and his wives. Drain the pert little bimbos, watch tans blanch, hear screams dwindle to swoons as they swung limp and bloodless from their manacles: prelude to a suck-and-blow multifucked frenzy with Flopsy, Mopsy, and Cottontail.

That's why he was caught short at the first sight of Esme. Crashing the bloated producer's party had been a breeze, as usual. He'd just finished scoping out the hopeful couchbait, a fast eyeflick over the crowd, and was taking in the cheesy paper lanterns and cheesier Hawaiian piped-in music—*enjoying,* to his surprise, the fake longings it miasma'd over the beautiful people—when his eyes slanted downward and fastened on undying love. She walked with ease, her simple dress swaying with unaffected rhythms, an intoxication of blood and bone beneath. The impact of that vision made him hesitate. Him, who had lived long ages and had long ago learned easy means for attaining any desire. Her walk exuded a confidence born of contentment. She floated, her body announced, above the petty needs of the empty smilers she threaded through, past the refreshment tables, along the pool, embracing their beefy host like family—Ah, so he was!—and moving on.

This raven-haired beauty, black fall breaking at her shoulders, had stuff and substance. Simple integrity shone in her eyes, a commodity

lacking mostwheres he went but especially here, where dreams or drugs guided the will-less through lives bereft of all but surface meaning. She saw him, glanced away, as she entered a pocket of isolation concaved between two chattering drink-holding groups, one of which would quite soon, surely, open up to draw her in.

He began his approach.

Her brother Brad had latched, by default, on to show business. Nothing else in the world having particularly grabbed him, he'd settled into a sinecure with their dad at the studio. But Esme had always been deep in books, found odd friends, cast an eye of bemused puzzlement on the sun-liquid dealings, the impressionless series of prettymates her father routinely squired through the house—in one day, out the next—to be replaced by another passing show. She'd flown in from Denver for a few days to say hello, to remind herself of what she didn't miss in the slightest. Breezing through a pool party was a small enough sacrifice, no skin broken. But it pleased her father no end, for reasons she couldn't begin to guess. She didn't have to stay long. Pop in, pop out, like one of Dad's slinky bedmates. But superficial clearly pleased him, though she knew that *their* relationship—from his looks, his drawing her aside at surprising moments to confide this or that—went much deeper than most. So she gave him this one tiny thing of surface whenever she stopped home, knowing that it in some small measure gave him joy, or at least that it provided a conversational

stopgap for the streams of nodding ghosts going by. Proud Daddy was a role he loved to play, a role Esme loved watching him play.

She slowed toward the diving board. There stood hefty Ed Partch, his flab-arms angled out of a Hawaiian shirt to hold a fistful of drink, his mouth flapping to delight (as he seemed to think) the underlings he spoke to. Backtravel, she told herself. Avoid his boorish eyes. She sensed movement at a pool angle. Advancing in a familiar way was the dark brooder she'd cast a quick glance at. A weird breed. Belonged and didn't. Thirties was her offhand guess. Not an actor, but handsome and intriguing enough to be one. In the business, but not of it. Blood hunger rode in his eyes—a lawyer, was her guess. Let him do his damnedest to seduce her, his intent obvious from a series of fumbled or skilled but rarely successful tries from either sex to bed her over the years; she'd wear him down until he wised up and made for more promising prey.

Not quite a smile on his face, not blank. When would this deep odd man deliver his line? Still he came on, an easy assault, more an envelopment, an assurance, words needless not tainting the air. Then he stood beside her, a hand touching hers. She took it, a smooth warm grip which she returned. "I'm not sure I—"

"Your name?" A velvet voice, a faint aroma that hinted vaguely of frankincense. An impression of ancient knowing came to her, impossible, surely, in this muscular young man.

"Esme." Her voice blushed in falter.

"Esme," he said, both a repeating and the

opening of a new question. "It's time," he confided. "Are you ready?"

Ready to leave the party, ready to go with him anywhere, ready to climax at the least touch, ready to abandon completely her life in Denver—all of that was in his question, this man whose name she didn't yet know but who made her feel so good just by looking at her. And her answer, absurd but true, was yes. "I'm ready," she said, and she followed his strong dark form knifing through the crowd, windblown streamers of chat falling away to either side as they went. In the car, his car, no memory of her entry there, his hand rode up under her dress, fingers at her bikinis, beneath the lace, moistening up and down her labia, deepening, dipping in, swirling at her clit, touch at flashpoint sizzling up an orgasm, moaning unbelievably into his mouth—and by the time her body reconstituted, the smooth fast road hummed beneath them, she was belted in, he drove dark and shadowed within caressing distance, and Esme had never felt more blessed and secure in all her life.

Brad resented Esme. She had an in with Dad. Clearly he loved her best, and this despite the fact that Esme, long gone to Denver, only dropped in once or twice a year and barely showed herself even then. More than that, she had no trouble in the love department, sleek breasty lure with that long straight shiny black hair of hers. *Always* she had guys hitting on her, just like in high school; a look, a snag, bingo, they were wrapped tight as pigs in a blanket around her finger. Okay, he had the beginnings

of a paunch (but only when he bent at the waist), and sure, a surly God had given him a bunched sort of face; but he had plenty to offer the right girl—correction, the right *girls*—and he was tired of watching turned-off bimbos suddenly turn on at hearing who his father was, cash registers hot and flashing in their eyes. He'd fucked 'em. Got off as they acted their way toward pretend orgasms. Christ, who wouldn't? But it was like humping tinsel. Just a little bit hotter than porn flicks, but no less impersonal.

Personal. Real. That's what he needed.

So he turned to the personal ads, scanned them, circled a dozen in red, found someone who pushed a few buttons. Mmm, redhead, yes. She didn't want any addicts? No problem. No fatties? He'd sit up straight. Besides, he'd seen lots worse lardbellies than him—like his father, for one. Looking for someone spiritual and sensitive? He qualified most definitely, having skimmed *Out on a Limb* once or twice.

He dialed, listened to her message, fell into the depth of her voice: "Hello, I'm mid-thirties, I have long red hair, I'm fit and trim, one child, a son, lives with his father. Oh yeah, yes, my name's Janice. I'm an established professional and I expect you to be too. I'm looking for someone in good shape, honest and open, at least five ten. No facial hair. Someone with wide cultural interests and who's a good listener but can hold up his end of the bargain . . . the conversation. There should be a depth to your thoughts, a kind caring quality in your voice, a nice assured independence that isn't afraid to begin and sustain an intimate relationship."

There was more, an invitation in that sweet voice of hers to leave a message. A demon said, "Go ahead, do it now," shouting down the angel whose advice was to write something down first, then call back. So he punched in the leave-a-message choice.

One minute? Christ, he thought, you couldn't say jackshit in a minute!

The phone beeped at him, a prompt.

"Um, hello," he said. "This is my first time doing this. My name is Brad. Short for Bradley. My work is professional in nature, and I really like your voice. My hair is vaguely brown, I'm thirty-eight, hazel eyes, not a bad body. I like to sit around and chat, and I think I have a lot to offer the right person. And Janice—that's a pretty name, by the way—maybe you're that right person, and maybe I'm right for you. I hope so, anyway. Umm, let's see, what else: I could use a caring person and you sure sound that way, and I'm ready for a direct, open, honest, one-to-one relationship, and then we can see where things go from there." Suddenly he remembered the minute and managed to slip in his phone number before the final beep cut him off.

He hung up, staring at his pork-hand on the receiver. Then, picking up the newspaper and scanning her ad again, he tilted the miniblinds upward. He fancied he could see her, a surge of curves, a smooth face, a shiny red waterfall of hair sweeping down upon white freckled shoulders. His hand rustled up whip-whip-whip three Kleenex from the box by his bed, pastel blue, weren't making them as strong as they used to, used to take just two, but now the tissue, as he

wiped clean, would stick annoyingly to his dick-tip. A minor matter. He lay them neatly square on the bedspread and had his shorts and jockeys down about his knees in no time, positioning himself so he wouldn't overshoot. Then he read over her ad again, moving, moving, whispering her name again and again, Janice, conjuring him and her and that hot blonde his dad had all but fucked by poolside the day before—an amazing threesome right here on his bed, the smell of the bedspread mingling with the aroma of pussy and the velvety feel of twin lips twining up and down his rigid shaft.

Janice weeded out four callers at once, those with an obvious fetish for red hair, or the bozo who was into four-wheeling (she had no idea what that was, but she pictured balloon-tired trucks colliding under floodlights and X'd him out), or the ones whose words lay a cold hand on her brain stem for reasons she couldn't artic-ulate. Of the ones remaining, she felt drawn to this Brad character the most. Boyish and firm, a little bit awkward, sincere in tone as far as she could tell. He wasn't ideal. None of them were. But he'd do for a start, meet him at least and check him out, let her bullshit detector handle the rest.

He lifted on the third ring. "Brad here." Solid rock, a no-nonsense directness that had its ap-peal.

"Hello. It's Janice. From the personals?"

He fumbled, and she liked that too: "Oh, yes, hello, Janice. Thanks for calling. I mean, well, that sounds like a sign off or something, which

I hope it isn't. Ummmm, so you liked what I had to say?"

"What you said, yes, and how you said it." Janice heard amusement in her voice, but she felt relaxed, not put upon by some machoid cowering behind ego-barriers or carrying a psychic chip on his shoulder, and that seemed promising.

"So would you like to meet?" he asked. Too eager? Maybe, but this meeting-through-ads stuff wasn't exactly natural. She gave him the benefit of the doubt.

"One thing I forgot to mention," she said. "I don't date smokers. You're not a smoker, are you?" Damn, he was going to be a four-pack-a-day-er, a type-A loser with a cellular phone glued to his ear in some high-demand profession, his thundering heart hurtling him toward an early grave.

"I think smoking's a filthy habit," came his answer. "I tried it a total of once, just to see, you know, a long time ago, cuz I figured why not, see what the big deal is. I guess there was some vague buzz there, but no great appeal, and it looked weird in the mirror. So that was that."

"Good," she said, relieved. "I left that out of the ad and then kicked myself. I guess it was so obvious, my mind just skimmed over it."

"Pretty kicking, I bet."

"Excuse me?"

"The kick, pretty legs—oh nothing, never mind, a backhanded compliment, forget I said it." His stammering had an endearing quality to it; not mealy, not in the least. His voice sounded

95

like suede leather stitched over steel, very indrawing and comforting.

She laughed. "It's forgotten. And I *do* have pretty legs, not that it's any of *your* beeswax."

"Of course not." Brad had picked up on her flirty tone and batted it right back, good as he got.

"All right," she said, "let's meet." He proposed a dinner date at a swank restaurant; she countered with her standard frozen-yogurt-in-the-mall offering. It was well lit, crowded, ideal for quick, diplomatic thank-yous and good-byes if the chemistry proved, in those first five minutes, to be absurdly wrong.

He ended, more confident than he'd begun, on a joke. When she cradled the receiver, she felt hearth-warm in an odd full-tummied sort of way. Her spirits lifted after a day of feeling like nobody special, the same old dusty mopers surrounding her at work. On impulse, she dialed the personals' 800 number and listened once more to Brad's response, quieting her fancies, playing it over and over, the real human being behind the fumbles engaging her now more fully. Could she sense her one-and-only in Brad's voice? If she listened past his wine-fruity baritone, could she hear her soul mate pining to get through?

When he drove up to his beachfront home, his wives' faces were pressed like kitten faces to the front window. Once they'd been human, once borne a touch of uniqueness, a quality that had singled them out. But fetching-time was long past for them, those moments when they tee-

tered between human and undead, when their teeth had not yet turned to hollow fangs and their nips and clits and labia had not yet gone razor-sharp and as blood-receptive as leeches.

"All this is yours?" Opulence, he knew, she was used to and unmoved by. No. It was the privacy of the approach, and how near the ocean waves pounded, that clearly impressed her.

"The world meets my needs," he said.

She slid against him, felt him below, that enticing pulse in his eyes drawing her.

"I'm not usually so bold," she said.

"Boldness is a learned skill." He accepted Esme's kiss, the warm press of her lips, a lick, a withdrawal. "Come inside." It was hard to believe her loveliness, her uniqueness, could vanish. But he'd seen it with the three at the window, shortly before that young fool Harker had fallen under their sway in the Carpathians, and countless times in ages past. Esme's turning he vowed to prolong, resisting the end of fetching-time for all eternity if he could.

The door swung open at his touch. The trio stood at the hallway's edge, their eyes raptored on Esme. Mopsy had two fingers thrust deep inside Cottontail. Flopsy, on their left, worked at pleasing herself. Dried bloodspray from past climaxes rhubarbed their inner thighs, and their vulvas glistened wet and red with arousal.

"Pay them no mind," he said. Raising his hands, he advanced toward them, intoning in the ancient language of his forebears the words to keep them off. The instant he began, they hobblefooted backward over the blood-spattered

oak floor, torn between hunger and the inviolable power of his injunction.

Esme had always shown restraint in initiating, in accepting, sexual advances—much more so, she thought, than most of her generation. And it had paid off. Close scrapes with near intimacy, always deflected, had kept her wounds superficial when bad choices revealed themselves.

But with *him* (names didn't matter), her now quite obviously foolish coyness dropped away. Odd. She felt completely in control and yet not like herself at all, the trappings of convention having been cast off like a thick fur coat she hadn't known was weighing her down.

Esme gestured. "Who are these—?"

"My wives," he said. And that was all right with her. More startling, *they* were all right with her, these lynx-eyed creatures from a world of nightmare. Esme saw them, yes, for the red-crusted fright-hags they were, but their allure was undeniable, nor could she deny the power of eyes that comforted and caressed, nor the sensual craving they had set going in her soul. Abruptly he appeared before her, gazed a wounded longing into her eyes, crouched, never breaking that gaze, brought an arm up under her dress, bunching it upward like the spooned-away crust of a custard, until his biceps saddled snug against her crotch, his hand splayed on the small of her back, and he lifted Esme straight into the ocean-rich air and walked with her, eyes locked upon hers, through a high arch into a faintly metallic-smelling room bathed in candlelight and awash with pillows.

Lowering her, steadying her torso with his strong left hand, he drew her lips to his, an obliterating melt of flesh upon flesh, and his right arm slid along moist lace until his warm fingers cupped her cunt through cloth and fondled her so beautifully that her briefs clung like sodden terry cloth on naked skin. She came like that, moaning into his mouth, feeling the odd dentition against her tongue but not caring, not at all, not even the sting of lipcut where his teeth left numbness behind like mosquito puffiness.

"Love me," she whispered. His whole body felt so good, shaped against hers as his hands undid her dress at the back. But wait, it was a front-buttoner—and yet his fingers parted the fabric along her spine as if it were Velcroed on, a gentle controlled rending that bared her shoulders and her breasts, soft red-tipped lovelies he blessed with his mouth. A stinging touched her there as well, but it only drove her excitation higher, like breath taut from the sudden thorn-prick of a sweetheart rose.

Then she was naked and his clothing too was gone and she touched his penis, thimble-hard it seemed just at the very tip, about the slit of its warm rubbery cap. But he brushed her hand aside and lowered her upon soft pillows, and mounted her, easing in deep, quick, astounding, she was so wet and receptive, so needy. She reached up and clung fiercely to him, her thighs rhythming beneath his long slow thrusts. Orgasm claimed her again, at her G-spot an incredible spread of sweetness, and his love stayed hard and beautiful in her sight, dark and muscular and young and ancient all at once. She was

still pulsing beneath him, still moist with fuck-sweat. "I want to make you come," she said, her yoni moving about him yearningly like the idle sway of a belly dancer winding down.

But he stopped her, held her hipbones in both hands, a thick bible thumbed open by a god, and drove as deep as he could inside her, his head turned aside. "You'll feel a tiny sting," he said, apology and promise in his voice.

Then she did.

It began vaguely, a burning deep in her vagina, along the front wall where his cocktip lay. Then it widened, a needle of pain (flashback to the bedclawing of arterial blood being drawn from her arm); but she embraced the small agony of it, seeing the radiance in her lover's eyes, feeling how turned on he was. He was drawing something, a deep strength from her, and she gave it with all her will. Gold touched her. To give him such pleasure seemed miraculous, made her cry for joy. Then, his excitation becoming audible, the pain abruptly ceased, and he was again thrusting, past the odd puffiness he'd left, back and forth against it, massaging it to distraction with his cocktip. He seized her, and in his coming she heard the wounds of ages crying forth. Hearing his pain, she sobbed uncontrollably, cradling him and comforting him in the locked cling of their bodies.

Brad found the mall, one he'd been to just after it opened a few years back. Plant theme. Skylights. Glass elevators with golden Christmas lights vining along the sides. He jaunted up a steep escalator and spied the yogurt place, its

blue-and-pink-plastic motif managing miraculously not to be garish but somehow tasteful. Not close enough yet, this Janice possibility hidden from him, if she was there at all. He checked the time. Ten minutes late and damned if she wasn't going to ding him for it.

Then he saw her. It *had* to be her, brilliant puffs of red hair on her head and a long luxurious fall down to an antic flip at the shoulder blades. She was a slight slender girl, her tight ass perky on the pink plastic chair. She turned her head, saw him, knew it was him, gave a wave. Oh dear Jesus, he thought; she was cute and snazzy and sweet, and she had seen him and not immediately cut him cold.

Careful, doofus, he thought, don't trip on anything. He continued his approach, taking in her butt, the petite strain on her blouse front, coming 'round to sit opposite her, her full red lips, collagen not an impossibility there, but he bet hers were natural—and as he glanced at them, he ran his tonguetip, in fancy, along that inviting rip in her mouth. "Janice, yes?"

"You must be Brad." She offered no hand; a handshake'd be gauche, uncool. Tight waist. Must work out, he guessed. Must jog, a clingy leotard and a rainbow sweatband about that pillow-perfect tumble of crimson hair.

"Pleased to meet you," Brad said.

"Pleased to meet *you*," she echoed. "I recommend the coconut custard, dusted with carob shavings. It's like a full helping of Dreyer's without the consequences."

Brad, no fool, took her advice. Pleasantries passed between him and this beguiling stranger.

101

Nice eyes. Beautiful eyes. By God, what was the world coming to that such a kissable darling felt the need to place an ad in the personals column? He'd been hoping for a cut above average, no dog at any rate—but Janice was sheer wonder, a moving target and a devastation waiting to befall. Don't get too close, he cautioned. She's being polite, leading to the letdown at the end, nice time but we're not right for one another—meaning you're just plain ugly, hair sprouts in your ears, the idea of touching you revolts me.

But he could play the game as long as she cared to do the same. He decided to enjoy himself, be natural and forthcoming, take her in, all the way in. Later that night, alone in bed after she rejected him, he could replay those images, replay her words, her smiles—and have her six ways from Sunday, courtesy of the Kimberly-Clark Corporation and his expert groin-shift and stifle-come, developed through a lifetime of practice upon the sheets.

Janice appraised the man seated across from her. No Redford, no Costner. But no Quasimodo either. He seemed, what, *comforting* as he went on, spooning up yogurt, talking about his work at the studio. Neither overdressed nor too casual. A cologne both subtle and pleasing (she usually hated scent on a man) buoyed his words.

He skimmed a melt of yogurt onto his spoon as she leaned forward, elbowing the table. "Does it bother you," she asked, "meeting me through the newspaper?" Of course Brad would say no. But, beyond that, the answer to this question often revealed much.

"Not at all," he said, "it's refreshing. You supply a what-you're-looking-for list, as well as giving some kind of snapshot essence of you. I look it over, maybe I'm not a match in all the particulars, like that 'very handsome' stuff, now I'm not exactly—"

"I *like* the way you look."

"Well, thanks. Okay, maybe that was a bad choice cuz I'm decent enough, I guess, and you by the way are sweet as . . . as honey on the eyes—"

That touched her. She sensed Brad's appreciation, a depth and directness that warmed and startled her. He was human. Not at all pushy or leering, the way some clueless guys were. It was subtle, the bond forming between them, but it existed—and it felt good.

"Anyway," he went on, "we get to turn over this distillation of who you are, what you want, we examine it, peek around it and play with it. I guess we use it as a base, a kind of nucleus, for whatever comes after, if anything does."

Janice smiled. "I was pretty careful to screen out the riffraff. If your ad doesn't say no addicts, a nice loaded word, they come flooding in." She related a few of her horror stories, that time with seamless Henry, a tiger in bed (she left that part out) and seemingly all hatches battened down in his head; but then his dependence on her had come clear, Chinese fingercuffs gripping her tighter the more she insisted on pulling loose. Brad's reaction was warm and commiserating and endearing.

Too soon, the hour was over.

"Let me ask you something," he said.

She said sure.

"I'll bet men, maybe all of them, say I'll call you, even if they're not going to. Well, I want you to know that I *do* want to call you, but only if you want me to. So, um, do you?"

She did. Oh my, did she ever. "Yes, please, Brad," she said. "I'd like that."

He smiled and rose and said good-bye, ambling off with a wave. Janice fixed on him, craning to see this engaging man shrink along the upper mall walkway, then vanish slice by slice, diagonal escalator cuts taking him down. There was going to be sex, she thought, and soon.

And with luck, there would be love.

When he returned from dropping Esme off, his wives, in the moonlit turnabout, crowded the car, not touching it, not daring to smear it. Once long ago, they had, each in her turn, been special to him. Now they were raw convenience merely, to batten upon as they had battened upon fresh victims, to be fucked in the sweet mire of total animal abandon, a surge of bloodcome pumped into one or another orifice or showered hot and bisque-pink upon breast or face.

He got out, pinged shut the car door. Esme wouldn't leave his mind, the taste of her liquids lingering in his mouth. Their intimacy had been deep and sweet, beyond anything he'd known before.

Plump bellies on the bitches, all three. Clearly, tonight they'd had a feverish feed. More drained victims would be found tomorrow. Mopsy gurgled a question, and Flopsy topped her mumble with a higher-pitched repetition: "Why no feed?"

Cottontail emerged between the two, her hair greasy and clumped with gore. Her neck seemed, an illusion prompted by her single-minded desire, to telescope toward him. Her lips touched his and she disgorged an upchucked gout of blood, fear-tainted and sustaining. She left off her kiss, chin-dribble, and said, "The cream-skinned one. The black-haired one. We smelled her, we heard her blood pulse in our guts, her breath ripple the air."

He thumbed the outer nipples of the book-ended beasts; they pricked him, drawing from razor tips. "You will not drain Esme. Gentle pulls only. And *her* feeding must be shallow as well."

"She'll be joining us?" The bloodsmear on Cottontail's face was so thick, it cracked when she smiled, a night parch of desert sands.

"In a twilight state," he replied, his thumbs tingling at the drainage. The areolae around the sucking nipples pulsed like cockheads. "I want her forever on edge, always in fetching-time, never turned."

Cottontail fingered herself, bloodcunt gleam, with a mottled hand. She smeared a wet aromatic mustache across his upper lip, stiffening him below. "We want to indulge. Refined platelets like she's got. Not the alley druggy stuff out there."

"Must fuck," Mopsy moaned, tugging at his belt.

"Must fuck," Flopsy echoed, zippering down, shredding his briefs so fiercely she furrowed taut hipskin.

He unstuck his thumbs from their breasts,

licked his wounds, pointed. "She's mine. You won't touch her unless I'm here." He wrenched his shirt off and tossed it aside. Tight toned torso. Sipped varietals at many bedsides, carefully chosen, had kept him young and fit for centuries. That, and his by-birth origins, never human, never blindly fed upon to turn him, had (he believed) kept him from devolving.

The blood was up in him. His trio of bitches looked fetching, felt like wet bestial insistence, writhing upon him, reddening him, drawing him down upon the moonlit lawn. Surf pounded in the near distance. They leaned rightward—a mutual baring of necks—into a four-way suck. He would never let Esme do this. No, she would join him on his nightly ventures, sip where he sipped, lightly, savoringly. But he'd keep this breed of creature around for heavy rutting, for the red wet hot fuck of it. His back hit chill grass. He had a quick glimpse of bloat-belly above, Flopsy, before her bloodquim gaped to his feasting and his hard-on pulsed to the piercing of six fangs. Its tip drew blood from the palate of whichever one mouthed down over his cockhead. His hands, fumbling, found greasy gapes of wet yoni, felt labial cuts plantlash across his fingers and begin to draw there as he fondled Flopsy and Mopsy, left and right.

Esme, forever Esme, on his mind. He imagined how it would be with her. She would watch him, glad at his rough pleasures; and maybe, at times in a measured way, he'd draw her in, restraining the unholy trio that circled her refinement, commanding, holding off, savoring in turn her pleasure in the sweet excesses of mul-

tifuck; then, at last, turning the trio out and enjoying once more the delicate wonder of his and Esme's private intimacies.

Flopsy's clit sank into his tongue as she came sprays of bloodfuck across his face. Its hot wash, fevered and chaotic, drove him murderous with lust and he sucked and sucked at her vulva, whitening it (could it be seen) faster than her replenishing at his cock re-reddened it. But control returned, and he unpussied his mouth for new breaths of ocean air. And the foursome writhed anew, seeking another apt position for bloodlust à quatre.

Later, he ordered Mopsy to fetch the toys.

Esme's father, the belly of a bear engreened beneath his polo shirt, stopped her the following morning by the pool. He squired on one arm a big-bosomed blonde, looking lost and wincing at the sunlight.

"You okay?" he asked, unsure what had halted him.

"I'm fine." Esme's words were cotton-soft.

"You're not . . . Esme, are you in love?" He gave a mock frown, wrapped in a grin.

"Me, Dad?" she said. "Practical me?"

" 'At's my girl." Dad slow-rounded a fist-tap on her shoulder. "Put that Frank motherfucker out of your mind"—her three-year disaster of a marriage—"take your pleasure as it comes, that's what I say, and let the world go hang." Bimboing along, he bellowed back: "Make yourself at home, blow off frigging Denver for eternity— and bring the boyfriend by sometime, okay?"

Denver. Her flight left in three hours. She

didn't care. Let her tickets expire; let them wonder at work, a world off, what had become of
her; let the utilities shut down, her neighbors
fret, her landlord key open and clean out and re-
rent the place. She couldn't recall them, not
their names and only faintly their faces. What
was *real*, what kept form and focus, was the soft
warm shiver with which he'd blessed so many
places on and inside her body. What was *real*
were his face and hands, his lips, his teeth, and
his sharp-tipped arousal. These, and the alluring
aircloy of his dripping wives, their sucklovely
eyes, those kissable faces pasted like wet pink
petals on the black bark of night.

All day, she idled. The timelessness of a cloud-
less day became her timelessness. From south
along the coast where his home was, she felt desire—hers, his, a desire that deepened as daylight waned. She wandered her father's estate,
alone, feeling such loneliness as she hadn't felt
for ages. And as she wandered, the tingle inside
her vagina, walled a long finger's length within,
grew so intense that she came just picturing his
penis piercing her there, drawing sustenance
from her. Her southward longing picked up
sharply as the sun set, and before she realized
it, she stood outside the garage, thumbed up the
door, backed out the sleek Maserati, and somehow managed—half hazed, half aroused—to negotiate sufficient freeway to find the coast road,
his private drive, a gate yielding obediently open
for her, and his seacoast home.

He stood there, waiting, naked, erect. Esme
grasped the door handle, but he held up his

hand, crossed in front of her car, bent to her window. "Undress," he said.

"In here?"

Eyes hot with love, he nodded.

"Where are your wives?"

As if in answer, they loomed up out of the darkness, before the windshield. His look grew hard, but then his eyes returned to her and a smile again grazed his lips. "I'll watch."

She complied. It was easy at first, undoing the top buttons. Then she struggled in the small space, her shoulders straining as the blouse resisted removal and her breasts arched out and up. She unbelted the skirt, shimmied out of it, his eyes a comfort, theirs both a menace and a turn-on, whose glare steamed into her and made her mind blaze. When blue lace was all she wore, she slowed down, angled toward him, slipped a finger inside herself, licked it as he watched, then in idle ease drew her panties down and off.

The door clicked. Before her? Behind her? No cold air rushed in, but she felt fingernails singe along her back, searing pain. But his face surged forward, and the flaypain eased away in instant heal. Then night huddled about her like black wool, and the house opened to scoop them in, the walls dimly fired with candlelight, tiny torch go-by, go-by. She was coming beautiful comes in his arms, doing nothing, touching nothing nor being touched, just feeling his voluptuous enwrapment and the close earthy breaths of his wives wraithing nearby. Their rhythm shifted, stairs pumping, the creatures' feet slapping like thongs of whip on stone steps.

A warm room, no windows. From the ceiling depended iron bolts, which seemed so low one might have to stoop to pass. Soft bedding met her, a slight backburn at how swiftly he set her down. Who was she? She couldn't remember, nor did it matter. They grabbed her wrists, one each, hot as collie paws, the ones he called Flopsy and Mopsy, and had her pinned in (first contact) their grip. He plunged his face into her heat so ferociously it seemed he would bury his head inside her, jaw first, right up to the neck. At her temples, the third wife's hands clamped and caressed. Could wrists and temples be sex organs? She couldn't see what restrained them, but she could sense as solidly as brick that they wanted desperately to feast upon her and that a muzzle had been placed upon their slavering jaws. At her yoni, gaping freely for him, he kissed and licked and stung and sucked, sharp pangs again, but then quickly numbed and covered with kisses. She loved the contrast of iced pain and warm gentle loving. Then he had her clit between his lips and (he wasn't going to) yes, he was, he needled her there, fast and gone and puffed taut with need, building, building, until she gushed her climax upon his swirling tongue, her head back and thrashing, looking into the wet fevered eyes of the three and coming more intensely for what she saw there.

Her complexity and her boobs. That's what Brad liked about Janice. He couldn't believe how quickly things had progressed. One week ago, the yogurt shop in the mall. Then that sweet evening above-the-waisting in his car, a throwback

to the ineptitudes of high school days, but sure and skilled this time. And now, watching her reach for coffee and measure it into her coffee-maker, they were very close to fucking. Her complexity and her boobs, and her pussy—soon he'd be able to claim even that knowledge of her.

He left the kitchen table and came up behind her. They were small talking, her fiery hair fila-menting down against her gray jogging outfit. He hugged her close from behind, then turned her, kissed her. That lovely lip aroma again. She'd made monogamy noises over yogurt. But Janice was complex, persuadable surely once she'd had a taste of his prowess. She was tired of being alone and longing to find a soul mate, that's what she'd said; he thought it might be-come a stumbling block, but that was a discus-sion best kept until his bedroom skills made him indispensable and her definition of relationship malleated accordingly. Janice could be his pri-mary. She was certainly delicious enough for that. They'd catch at Dad's dregs, snag and shack up with one or two at a time, console them, lick them, share their perfect bodies in sensual writhe, then send them on their way. Janice would be with him at the center of things, draw-ing luscious bi-babes into their bed, maybe eventually latching onto a permanent third.

It could happen, it really could.

He fondled her perfect back, warm and smooth under the jogging top, drew her about and thumbed her nipples. Nice subtle inbreath from her. "Don't you want your coffee?" she murmured.

On the edge of her soft full lips, he gave his

reply in kisses: "I want . . . honey . . . cream . . . lots of cream . . . lots of honey." He eased his left hand under the elastic at her waist, no underwear, just taut expanse of skin and a thrill of hair, and moisture grooving down at his fingertip. She seized up, grinding her mouth hard upon his, her hips in slow rotation slick upon his finger.

Her hand closed around his bulge.

Kiss broken. "Let's go to bed," he said, thick with lust. He followed her out of the kitchen, tugged along like a child after its mother. A zesty package, this Janice—a fitting start to his harem; and her sex tasted of sunshine.

Janice felt snugly engulfed in warm assertive manflesh atop her bedspread. Undressing her, Brad had shown gratifying awe in word, in kiss, in caress. They felt good together no matter what he did—and eventually what she did. He proved a fanatical oralist. She'd never known so many orgasms could be licked from her in so short a time.

Curiously, after a while, for all the waves of pleasure washing through her, he began to seem not quite human, too consumed with technique. But then, their being together was still so new, there was still so much to be learned. And in between comings, the snuggling was so sweet and the words shared so soft and loving.

Yet one theme, even as his chin rhythmed upon her private hair and his nose tipped into her vulva, whispered in her head: He's nowhere near being exclusive, nowhere close to monogamy, as distant from commitment as Pluto is

112

from the sun. But was that a truth absolute, or an illusion borne of her insecurities? She felt— or did she—the beginnings of something precious between them, something that perhaps would be blessed and nurtured by the intimacies she now allowed.

She liked his ideas, his wit, his warmth. The riches he'd revealed tonight were an unexpected bonus. But a rich man was no substitute for a devoted one, and Janice, her fingers on the warm tiller of his rod, hoped with a tepid hope that Brad would declare his devotion—if not tonight then soon.

When he did, she'd be ready.

She arched back upon her pillows as his tongue drove her heavenward again. "Oh, Brad," she said, "I want you inside me." And he was off her, in floorward dive, digging excitedly in his pants pockets, a square finally in his hand, that metallic crinkle she'd heard subliminally whenever he moved or sat, a rib-tipped Trojan torn free at last and hastily rolled on. The glow radiated from her, the need, the need, and then he warmed her again, filling her rushingly beautifully full of his love.

A week had passed.

He'd allowed them a taste of his new love under stringent restrictions. And he'd let her lap at his wives' wide redness, careful to hold open the razor-sharp labia and press aside their needling clits—until her face came away from them like a baby's covered in beet juice, whipcuts savory on her cheeks where she'd accidentally brushed against a labial edge.

But now, during their fiveway, he noted with alarm a change in her: Her clit tongued no longer soft and sweet but bore the beginnings of a crust. And her labial splay, once as yielding as the meat of a clam, now sprawled upon his face with all the hardness of wooden spoon edges. Her nipples too, supple and responsive those first evenings, felt more like thimbles than the erasers she'd previously hardened up into.

At once he insisted her off his face and ordered his three wives, their hunger terrible even in restraint, out of the playroom.

"But why?" she asked him. In answer he drew her close to a flame, holding her head tight in his hands, gazing fiercely into her eyes. No turning, not yet, but she teetered precariously close. From that moment, he kept the others away, forbade her to drink his bloody seed no matter how much she pleaded, moved into pain-sex to match the upped ante of need she showed. He chained her up, hanging stretched and hot in her animal gorgeousness from the bolt. He whipped welts into her, across her buttocks and back, which he then plowed with the thin-strawed suck of his fangs, a tiny draw of blood only. But no longer—no, not until her crusted nips and clit softened again and her labia lay like moist warm babyhands against his mouth—would he allow her to touch bitchmeat, nor to suck at a vein he opened, nor to take in orally the pink surge of his love.

And she did begin somewhat to soften in her holy parts—but a hostile glaze cowled her eyes. Her passion, once entire, now had a rent in it. And it tore at him, as later, bent to drink from

dozing victims, he could not escape the image of Esme in her new guise.

The next night, a need seized her. She went to a health bar and ordered Green Drink, a shit-vile concoction of celery and spinach leaves. Sipping lightly at it, she seduced, first with her eyes then with her words, a needy dork who looked shy and wounded, but took the bait. Up in his room, he ouched away from chest-to-chest embrace. To her steamy entreaties, though, he allowed her to suck him passably hard and then, above his need-a-condom protests, to pussy down upon her work and clamp tight when the hunger took her.

"Hey, wait," he said. "That hurts."

Esme smiled at him, soothed him, then dug into his shaft deeper than before, dredging for blood. A scratch, a strain of suck—and a tingle thrilled her sex at its first lip-taste of indrawn liquid. The pull mesmerized, a sunlamp radiating inward as her labia capillaried blood.

But the dork pushed her off him as best as he could. His dick scraped against her edges as he pulled out, more cunt-shudder sending her into the most delicious orgasm she'd ever known. When she could at last hear his reedy pleas for her to go, his pathetic whine as he held out her clothing, he no longer mattered.

Esme dressed and left, a look of triumph on her face.

She'd show *him*.

No summoning drew her this time. She drove down the coast anyway, anticipation throbbing in her veins. And when she pulled up at his

place, scarcely able to wooze out of the Maserati for the bloodlust in her loins, his wives were standing there, bent like hothouse plants, waiting.

It had been a lovely dinner, sitting beside Janice as the waiter brought one choice Italian dish after another, finishing things off with cannoli that must have come from heaven. Brad had needed to touch her thigh, her hand, settling his palm against hers and interlocking fingers. She spoke of friends, family, co-workers; and he in turn told her about his kid sister Esme and his lascivious dad, hoping she would pick up, from his tone, that multiple partners was foremost on his own want list. He didn't dwell on it. It was a tad too early for that. Instead, he passed on to other things. But he saw no blip of disapproval on her face, if anything an unreadable spark in her eye that *might* signal interest. Soon (fondling her between fucks, he thought) he'd broach the subject, talk of his past experiences, hope she'd had her own—and off they'd go.

But on the drive back to her place, God knows how, she segued smoothly into a statement, benign on the face of it, that after years of dating she wanted monogamy, and that, with her, it was all or nothing. Beat. Beat. He let silence fill the car, humming, pretending needful interest in traffic patterns; and then the conversation turned in other directions, ones more blithely handled. Near her apartment, a warm hand fondled above his nape. "Your hair's so soft," she said, and Brad knew things were all right again.

He held her close as they ascended the steps to her door, an insistent craving in his voice when he murmured how much he wanted to have her, what sweet undressing there would be. By God, if he *were* a one-woman man, this would be the one for him. The porchlight was burnt out. Janice opened the door, her hand groping for the light switch. He stopped her. "Not just yet," he said. Then he turned her and kissed her and reached beneath her skirt, her apartment door still open onto the night, to ardently fondle her buttocks and strip her raw naked and lickable, down upon his knees and rustling the fabric upward to get at her moist treasure.

Too bad about Brad. The whole thing saddened her. He was a fine man, with much about him to love. But he was also one more lover not ready for commitment, chaff in the wind, restless, blown by the next new breeze where his lust's caprice dictated.

Well, she'd show him what he was about to lose. His clear unreadiness to embrace only her—his silence in the car—did nothing to diminish his ardor in bed, nor did she suddenly hate or revile him. Sad case. She'd turn it on for him, be more uninhibited than ever, let the memory of her flesh burn into his brain, feeding his future regret. Happiness now, sorrow hereafter. That's what she decided to aim for. Hers, his, theirs.

She pushed him down on his back, a surge of energy coming from the orgasm he'd just given her. She was rough; the bedsprings jounced as

Robert Devereaux

he hit the mattress. Straddling his skull, she boneground her open sex onto his mouth and helped herself to a big serving of hard cock. In went its head, an inch of shaft hot and pushing upward, another, another. Gag reflex, an ache of stretched lips, gotta get past it, a little click at the back of the throat, there it was, and she lipped a wide few inches more until his ballhair tickled her nose. "Oh, Jesus," he gasped around her squished crush of cunt, men loved this shit, and she undicked her throat, shafted down *again* past the click, once more, once more, hurrying him, feeling the pulse and throb of his cock and carrying him all the way onward into the peak moment from which he would, she hoped, forever after tumble into regret.

Brad's loss. She drank deep, draining him, regretting, knowing that she too would suffer; but his suffering would last longer, poor fool. And when he woke from his folly, she'd have moved on, seeking the one-woman man she knew was waiting for her.

Perhaps it was the rich creamy yielding in the one he met that night, the surge of sweater-fill, perfectly embodied desire, top to toe; or perhaps it was his home-trouble, a trio of wives tired of denial no matter how ruthlessly he tried (once Esme'd left) to compensate with knifeplay and the sinking of sharp stakes near the heart. Whatever the reason, he urged the wheat-blond Bekka back to her condo, where he tongue-fucked her into realms of bliss, and then—catching her quite by surprise—drained her an albino white,

118

supercharged beyond bloat by the beauty of her dying whimpers.

Tonight he wouldn't summon Esme. Tonight, upon his arrival home, his household's four-way equation would change. They'd know, the three. They'd smell Bekka's rich offering on him. They'd realize—Cottontail would, at any rate— that he hadn't brought home a major feast, as he'd done without fail in the past. It was time to ditch them, time to shove the stakes clean through and behead them, time to concentrate exclusively on Esme.

Esme.

He geared the low-lying BMW and roared out onto the road. He'd keep his dear love forever in that special state, half alive, half undead. Through the ages, he'd adore her and pamper her, savoring the fine lacings of her blood, being her primary fucktoy as he was hers, bringing her along to witness his engorgings, sharing sexually the choicest of the alluring ladies he found to feed his needs.

He thought of his wives. Once, they'd been loving and capable of being loved in return. But that evanescent state of bliss had vanished under his greed, too swift the turning of them, too fast the imbibing of their lives, until they'd become needy things of mere sex whose names he'd long forgotten. There was use in depravity, and his lust enjoyed could not be gainsaid. But there was also use in paring a strayward life to the bone and starting anew, in tossing off the detritus of mates gone bad.

He threaded through glaring lights and moving metal, eager to reach home, to clean house,

to subsume his new bride and sweep her into eternity with him.

The night was warm. The surfpound beckoned. Esme suffered the three to strip her where she stood, a button popping off between bloody fingers that shredded and tore her blouse asunder. Taut elastic wired against her left thigh and snapped free; then, more viciously, the right. No clothing blocked the salty breeze, only hands everywhere, touching her, turning her on. Then they lifted her, bloodlust heavy about them, and carried her around the house out to the moonlit shore.

Dune flora whipped at their ankles. Their feet sank and slipped, making their movement toward the sea an amble. Then they stopped, eased her down, connected deep and triangular the moment her back touched the dark sand, soft savage mouths touching her—here, here, here. Stings far deeper than he had dared *thrilled* her, the blood gone from her in a faster slipstream. She gasped and weakened at their taking, at the satisfaction of their need. Then they sheathed their tips and moved to tongues merely, two at her nipples, one at her yoni. Hard sizzled harder, so taut her erectile flesh that it felt bonelike, toothlike, against their ardent tongueswirls.

Her hands groped crumblefists of sand, an outward press of arousal turning suddenly inward, needling at tongues, drawing blood, the liquid flowing beautifully into her breasts and past the nerve ends in her clit. So wild it drove her, she thought she might explode. Her needy beloveds were groping her, licking her, feeding

her, being fed by her, *turning* her, painting hot gold along her inner heat.

"More," she demanded. "More."

Flopsy left off suddenly below, her mouth away and gone. The sands shifted softly as she moved. Esme reached a gritty hand to herself, cut it against labia, then more gingerly touched her bloody fingers to them, drew in her own blood to discover there a new self-love, wounded to feed her puffed organ's cravings. Then Flopsy was at her mouth in straddle, kneeling, hunkering down. Using an inverted *V* of fingers, she held herself open and lowered the moist meat to Esme's lips. Her tipped clit was covered, labial razor-edges parted and splayed outward in harmlessness as aromatic exudate plashed against Esme's lips. Moonlit pink waited, and the turned Esme bared her fangs, touching the tips to bloodflesh, arcing them an inch deep upward, the suck coming natural to her, hot womanblood tracing an intimate path through mutated nerve and pulpwork.

She'd show *him*, came the thought. But she couldn't, for the life of her, recall who he was. There was only a moon glimpsed past moving thigh, the high distant skree of seagulls, and a four-way imbibing of lifeblood—her own below, these three giving at mouth and breast to get back later, all of it driving her into a frenzy unending.

Brad had blown something, but he had no idea what. Janice returned none of his calls. Or when she did, she called at hours she knew he wouldn't be there, her voice suddenly alien, cool,

not soft at all, on the tape—this or that reason, blah blah blah, we'll talk soon.

His work turned to posturing, not that he'd been such a great manager before. Focus came hard or not at all. Finally he caught her—out of her interminable string of meetings, not traveling to hell and back on business.

"Good morning. Janice here," she said.

"Hi, Janice. It's Brad."

"Oh, hi," a dull tarnish, the polish suddenly off her professional voice.

"Is this a good time to talk?"

"Well, actually, no, I—"

"Look, I won't take much time," he said. "It's just, well, it's just that things were going so well, and all of a sudden they're not."

"Ah," she said, decision there. Pause. Then a shift in tone: "I like you." Acting again. "I really do. But there isn't enough there to build anything on, anything, um, long lasting, I mean."

"But I—"

"I need something more than you can give me, Brad."

"If you'd just let—"

"I'm sorry," she said, "please . . . there's no point in calling again. All right?"

His head felt woozy.

"All right?" she repeated.

"Yes, Janice, if that's the way—"

" 'Bye, then."

And she was gone.

Janice cradled the receiver, feeling, despite how in charge she'd seemed, completely at a loss. What if she had misread him? What if Brad re-

ally *were* the one? Her phone arm felt stiff and tight under crimped cloth. She relaxed it, withdrew her hand, wiped the palm on her thigh.

She swore under her breath.

The air changed at the entrance to her cube. Looking up, she saw Gene Ryman, chubby guy, nice, standing there. He'd been about to say something but noticed her startle, her demeanor. He waved a hand. "I'll come back," he said, a shift already in his body.

"Give me five, Gene," she said. "I'll drop by."

"No problem," his voice fading down the aisle.

Damn these open cubicles, some bastard's brainchild, constant distractions and no privacy at all. The impulse struck to call Brad back, punch up his number, go with him somewhere for lunch, talk it through, be open, frank, not a bent truth nor a screen between them. That was how you built a relationship. All the books said so.

But in her gut—and gut feel was all—Janice knew she'd done the right thing. She hadn't done it *right*, she still needed to work on that; but Brad had rightly been dumped, of that there could be—yes, but there *were*, God damn it, there *were* doubts. Big ugly ones around her prissy little center of certainty. Life's a bitch and then she whelps. So Gene Ryman was fond of saying, and he was right.

She raised the receiver, jabbed three buttons, got a glitch in her fingers and hit the wrong fourth. Again in its cradle. No. No. She felt tension along her spine. She eased back in the desk chair. Take a deep breath, forget him, get up, go

see what Gene wants, get her dithering mind back on track.

That was the way, let Brad stay dead.

Palming the nape of her neck, Janice rose. Somebody paged someone she didn't know over the intercom. Drained was how she felt. Bloodless. Heartless. But she'd get over it soon enough.

Life went on. And so would she.

Long before he saw the curved chrome and burgundy of her Maserati etched across the dark doorway of his house, he sensed Esme's presence, felt grief sting his heart and spread outward, a plague. He passed into the house, oblivious to what went by. Grabbing up the sex toys, he went out the back way, down to the clutch of figures on the shore. Silvered in moonlight, they dug and sucked in sensual frenzy, roiling like bloody seethes of fish in a ketch. Entwinement. Kickups of sand at the periphery. The four had interlocked to maximize contact of nip and clit, fangs and labia, with the bloodyield of exposed flesh.

As he neared, Mopsy raised her cranberried lips, her eyes to his. "You mad?" Her gaze fell to the tools. He cloaked his grief. When her eyes rose again, they found a convincing mask of lust. Mopsy leered through drips of gore, an alluring frogblink.

"You mad?" Flopsy's echo. "Must fuck," she said, the sum total of her excuses. She it was who took most delight in the stake, and now her eyes widened with an upratchet of anticipation.

Setting down mallet and stakes and scimitar,

he tore off his clothing. Cottontail's dream-lidded eyes were drunk with bliss, as her scalp moonrose over Esme's inner thigh. Her head seemed a bloated wart grown dark and cancerous, fanged onto Esme's flesh and sucking, his love's once-perfect thighskin punctured and puffed.

And Esme, dear Esme. At the sight of her, his throat bamboo'd with tubed wood. She arched back. A full-breasted nipple punctured Flopsy's throat, the bloodsuck overspill idling red runnels down the white of Esme's breastmeat. Her teeth were sunk inch-deep in splayed cunt and Mopsy's crusted clit needled her cheek. But her eyes, as he chose the tools and drew near—these, with their filled canyons of depth, their once-articulated peaks of love now leveled and made brutish, these tore at his heart. She was gone, turned, become just one more monomaniacal wife.

He let them draw him down, embroil him in their flesh feast, sucking, being sucked, sharing the sting of fang and cocktip wherever they touched, taking the skewer and jab of needy womanlove wherever a connection flared. But in his mind, mayhem reigned. And when he found the toys and sank stake into breastskin, so that their lips steamed in delight at the pain the nearer he drew to their hearts, he, tormented to his depths, met the near-orgasm in Flopsy and Mopsy's eyes and drove home the sharpened rosewood, swing-pound with the mallet, here and here. Cottontail backed off, unpeeling from the gore, suddener and suddener in the moonlight, oh-no upon her face and then a turn and

arrow-shoot along the shore. The staked ones on the sand moved in thrash, arcs of red urine upshot and spattering, as big gouts of black blood bubbled and burst from their anuses. A swift rise of scimitar, a smiting, another, and their shrieking heads dropped sharply off, washed in a gush of neckblood. For all their twitching, they were gone, silent, turning to fodder for the earth.

Esme waited, confused. She looked at him, she looked away, her eyes, her hands, her mouth groping the air for a love suddenly gone. Taking up another stake, he moved toward her eager arms. Through smears of blood he could still smell her subtle aroma as he kissed her, her fresh sunlight and buttercup scent. He fed her fangs through his tongue and took lipblood and tongueblood from her, one drop, another drop, tasting wife-taint and the way they'd turned his beloved. He wanted to break right then into tears, but he steeled himself for the needful task. Her impoverished hand found his penis, stroked it hard, fed wristblood to its tip. The stake's chocolate tip dimpled the streaked perfection of her breast, impressing a hollow of flesh inward, straining, straining, breaking—a short sharp thrust deep through, twisting it, turning it, not needing the mallet for Esme, just the determination of his love, the deep penetration of solid rosewood invading the chambers of her heart.

Esme fell back, trying to pull it out, but he batted her hands away, found the scimitar, swung with a misaimed gouge to the shoulder, then swept clean through, her body seeming to topple like children's blocks out from under a head that went straight down. Then, stroking

himself, he broke down, falling to his knees in the sand. He held her head close to her yoni, kissing her lifeless lips, cutting his mouth on her urine-stenched labia, back and forth between them, loving Esme, refusing to believe she was gone. Back upon his knees he rocked, pressing her severed head upon his cock, sucking throat-blood, brainblood, and keening at the moon until no blood remained in her. He rubbed her sweet flesh raw, up and down, faster, faster. Then he shot his red seed deep into her, so that she wept ruddy tears from eyes and mouth, gobbing his naked thighs with the thick liquid of sadness and remorse.

For a time, he considered a death vigil, waiting for the sun to arc up behind him as he stared out to sea. But finally he rose, found a spade, and buried the three of them—bodies here, heads there—raking sand over the places of burial. Another night perhaps, he would hunt down Cottontail, give her eternal rest. Her scent was still strong in him. She'd be easy to find. Or maybe he would let her go. But for now, for him, it was nearly time to sleep, a first long daytime of lying there, dreaming about Esme, a first long daytime without her.

Brad was amazed how drained he felt, whole cities reduced to rubble inside him. Through rancorous meetings, the soulless razzle of pitched scripts in his office, the black-ballooning of turned-forty Harrison Sanford—through all the pointless scurryings to and fro, Brad played his usual pointless role. Jabber jabber, she said to him (this one, that one, who cared). And rum-

blety rumblety, he shot back, knowing from habit what to say and being astounded when whoever it was nodded and sway-hipped out of his office.

He cut out at three and hit the bars, his favorites, usually in rotation day by day, now sequential all in one evening. He saved the one with the sorriest cast for the end, smoky haze, lots of solitary heads hunched over dark tables, sudden belt-backs, the reflective glint of glass moving, red circles glowing at the pull of mouths. The joker tending bar, a tall walrus-eyed fucker, had seen him dozens of times, never acknowledged their acquaintance, never said shit beyond a name-it and a that'll-be-so-many-dollars.

Brad named it. He named it often.

And Janice, more beautiful than he thought possible, hovered and hazed and hurt him. All or nothing, she had said. And now she'd gone and chosen—or had *he*—nothing. She'd dumped him. Sucked out his love (Jesus, he'd never realized truly how much she'd come to mean in so short a time) and left him to cry over might-have-beens. It was over. She was gone. Sprockets once yanked backward couldn't be re-reeled.

Staring into a dreg, sloshing it, he thought suddenly of the sea. A sad patch of rocks and breaking waves came to mind, a skull-numbing convention he escaped from once in Redondo Beach to find late afternoon privacy and feel the sunset deepen his melancholy. The place called him now. He paid his tab, avoiding the eyes of the bartender, and left.

Hit the road.

His car door slammed in the empty restaurant parking lot, a shattered peace that quickly returned. Seagulls cried high above. He rounded the dark building, a scrunch of sand across blacktop, then the softness and unsteadiness of the dunes. A curved paring of beach. At his back swept a soft swish of cars, but he was isolated enough to drop his cool and let hopelessness in. Moon glimmer touched him, chilled him, brought regret welling up, and sobs. Amid the diamond glitter of moon on sea there glinted red teasings, a sheen of hair, hers.

He paid them little heed—the call of gulls, faint engines, a crush of nearby tires, the rustle of dune growth in quick puffs of breeze. So, when a hulking figure abruptly appeared to his right, close but gazing out to sea, not at all giving off danger vibes, it caught him unawares. The man wore a leather jacket. He was tall, muscular, his long black hair bound up in a ponytail. He held a cigarette in one gloved hand. Reaching into a pocket, his leather creaking, he pulled out a flattened pack. "Want one?" he asked.

On his left now, Brad noticed two more men, younger and farther off but still nearby, talking to one another, ignoring him. Same leather. On the back of the one with blond hair, a cherry-red BLUDSUKKAHS was emblazoned. "No thanks, I don't smoke." Ordinarily he'd be alarmed. But there were times when you just didn't give a fuck, when a touch of lowdown funk made you and the world one. If you looked a lion in the eye and didn't flinch, they said, he wouldn't attack you.

"Your call," said the guy. Nice friendly man-

ner. He pocketed the smokes. "Peaceful place
here."

"Kinda soothing." Brad heard distant mur-
murs behind him. It didn't fucking matter. Even
young toughs could use a break from whatever
mayhem they'd been about. And he'd established a rapport with their leader. They were just
a couple of rejects, like him, taking comfort
from the sea.

"The world don't give a shit," the guy said, eyes
pinned on the restless carpet of silver and red
and blue before them.

"You got that right," Brad said. They were getting on. The two on his left wandered closer,
both thin, one of them gawkier and younger
than the other; they ignored him. The blond one,
the older hood with pockmarks on his face,
called to Brad's new buddy: "Hey, Michael. Joey
here, he needs a match. You got one?"

"Think so." Calm voice, comforting. And he
reached into his right pocket and found a match-
book, raising it between two fingers like a flag.
A sudden dash in the sand and the two on the
left surged in, their bodies violating Brad's space
as if it didn't matter; a new rush of sand sounded
behind him, voices sweeping in and hands as-
saulting him, his arms jerked back and bound,
oily cloth whipdrawn across his mouth and tied
so tight it felt as if calipers had been clamped to
his face and were digging for bone.

Brad struggled. He fell backward into rough
arms. They blanketed him, rolling him, his nose
striking a smack of sand, then onward until he
was on his back and they duct-taped the blanket
tight about him, moving off like triumphant

calf-ropers. The leader cowled over him, a new edge opening in his eyes. "Life," he said. "It just gets tougher, don't it?"

The blond one said, "Fuckin' Joey, no *way* he's ready for this. He's gonna pee his fuckin' pants."

A higher-pitched voice piped up: "Lick my shit if I *ain't*." The tone of it sank Brad's heart. He'd thought, in those first moments of being subdued, that he'd escape with bruises, a broken bone, a shaved head maybe. Beyond that, his mind had refused to go.

Now he knew better.

"Prove it, you little fuck," the blond one said. "I think this guy needs a smoke real bad." A challenge, one Brad didn't understand.

Then Joey, the one who'd been challenged, flurried about like a scrawny rooster from one hood to the next. He came back to Brad with two long glowing cigarettes. Dragging on them to enflame the tips, he blew smoke out the side of his mouth like it was a curse. Then the cigarettes were one in each hand and coming down closer and closer to Brad's face, not stopping, the heat and the glow on *on ON*, his eyelids closed against them, struggles to turn his head, avert it—but the toughs held him still and the searing tips bit, burned, kept burning deeper and deeper, blinded him without mercy over his gagged screams.

Abruptly he was lifted and hauled, yanked in jangle by many hands. They tossed him into the back of a pickup truck, a slammed right hip and shoulder, the knock of metal at his right temple as the bed of the truck came up to stun him. The motor gunned to life. A crazy turn. It shot out

into the surge of cars, zooming hard like it was late and time was running out.

Before long, they stopped.

Holding a glass of iced tea, mint perfect, Esme's father relaxed by the pool in the mid-morning sun. A deep breath of still moneyed air. Bliss. His left hand idly rubbed his lemon belly, the fine weave sensual beneath his fingers. Green and yellow were good colors, most of the off-reds way too faggy somehow for his tastes.

Milly, over the hill now at fifty—funny, how women, even the sleek ones like Milly, aged less gracefully than men—rumbled out the breakfast cart. A mound of scrambled eggs steamed as she lifted the silver cover. "Juice this morning is orange or cranberry or grape," she said.

"Mix 'em."

She gave him her once-sexy grimace. "Come on."

"Humor me. A third of a swig of each."

Milly didn't move.

"You only live once," he said. "Gotta eat the whole enchilada while you can."

"Your funeral." As Milly poured the concoction, the kids occurred to him, a vague feeling of absence. "Where's Esme? And Brad? Haven't seen 'em for days."

"The cars are gone, the one she was using—"

"The Maserati?"

"Yep. Brad's car too." Milly shrugged. "Tooling around?"

"Brad maybe, blowing off his frigging job again, who gives a shit. But Esme, she wouldn't

132

do that, she'd *tell* me. Maybe we should put out some feelers, call around."

"You want me to?"

He sipped his drink, cringing it down.

Just then, the French doors flew open. Ah. His morning's diversion, expertly choreographed by good old Darren again. He'd have to give the canny fucker a raise: Three killer bitches, dressed in bikini bottoms only, made their sexy way through the sunglow, their perfect boobs lightly bouncing. High heels, color-matched to the tiny triangles of cloth, clicked on concrete. A tall blonde. A pert brunette. And atop the third, a short platinum dandelion puff.

Heartmelt.

They sang and strutted to Darren's silly song. It gave him time to size them up, to watch their luscious red lips *O*'ing around lyrics, as soon they'd *O* around his cock.

"Very nice," he said, and they smiled. "You know, girls," he said, "I just love to check hair color right about now." He gestured toward their crotches, a magician's flick. Darren having primed them, at once they yanked at the string ties, whipped the fluorescent triangles off and away.

He moved, glass in hand, toward them. No perfume. Good. Good. He wanted to smell their perfect flesh unmediated by manufactured scent. The one on the left was high-school prom-queen material. "A two-tone," he said, touching her dark private hair, gripping it like a squeezed Brillo pad. "I like two-tones." The next one was shaved smooth and squeaky clean, swooning in a fetching way when he fingered her, parted the

lips, admired the smooth moist pink. But the third girl—platinum above, platinum below, and a face that could melt diamonds—her whole body exuded such pleasure, and that so naturally, that he sensed possibilities in her. She excited him sexually, yes. But there was far more than that, *far* more, that just might harden the mind cocks of movie audiences coast to coast.

He touched the silver-white softness of her private hair and felt blessed. Her eyes, if she was acting, showed it not in the least. All he saw were subtle shadings of delight as he fondled her and moved finger-deep, finger-tight, inside her— shadings a camera would see, and caress, and pass along to needful men sitting in darkness.

"I do believe," he said, holding eye contact with an angel in heat, not looking at the others, "it's time I gave you three lovelies something inviting to suck on."

And that time it was indeed.

Inevitably, eternally, under the sun.

Caliban

Chapter One

The Devils Arrive

To begin with, Mom and I had the island to ourselves, save for our companions the quail and the cuttlefish, the supple ocelot, the sloth, the pouch-billed crane, and the great-combed hoopoe.

And of course Ariel.

Son. That's what Mom called me.

She told me she had a name for me, a majestic one. She too had a name, one that her tone-deaf parents had cursed her with. Too late, she said, to do anything about that except not use it.

Before the devils came, there were no names on the island. Mom and Son weren't names. They were grunts that grabbed the ears and eased open their clefts so you could pour in your message.

"We don't use names here," Mom said.

I asked her what names were.

"This is a mud hut. That's the moon. Those are stars."

"Why don't we use names, Mom?"

"Because we're banished," she said. "Do you know what that means?"

I shook my head.

"It means we're free, unlike those who banished us. There are no stuck places here, no clefts, not for us."

"What about *this* cleft?" I asked.

"It's yours. And it's mine. That feels good. Oh, all right."

Such was the island before the devils glided in from the sea. I wandered everywhere. Through turned gnarls of trees. Up mountain slopes. Idling away long mornings by the rock-stream with its icy fish. Breathing air a-brim with the lazy sea's lukewarm brine.

For others, there were clefts. Ariel got shoved, a twelve-year, into one for being slow to carry out Mom's orders. Mom often shoved herself into a hard old cleft of hatred for the Algerian monster, beating her fists against her temples, close-eyed, as she rocked and cursed upon the stump outside our hut.

But for me, the only cleft was the yummy one back home beneath the covers.

Mom was the earth. Deep scores. Abundant tucks and cracks where the rainfall of her soul runneled and pooled. Brown as mud, mossy in the dark places. Her eyes were as hard as granite. But sometimes they would go soft, like logs long dead that peel back their bark to reveal moon-white innards.

Mom did things. She babbled weird words

that made little sense. The pipe of a pithless elder-joint did she cut, blowing through it the scream of the jay. With a branch, she grooved patterns in the dirt and danced among them. Her fat fingers darted down into those patterns, then shot up into the heavens.

Sometimes when she danced, winds rose and swirled about her. Spirits assumed shapes. If one dropped into visibility, it might tower and bellow. That sort of spirit Mom at once sent packing, no matter how much they promised. "Badly would they behave," she said. "Were I to free them from their cleft, you and I would be at their mercy, of which they have none. Those are devil spirits. Avoid them."

Others were gentle.

Whenever Mom called up spirits, the bellowers or the compliant kowtowers, their true faces blared through.

Ariel was a compliant spirit. He put on shows of wind and rain, of sun and clouds, the kind that billow, wisp, or scud, or the dark ones that rip open and spill rain from their ragged guts.

Ariel also boasted a special touch, a thing of bed-intimacy and focus. When I thickened for the cleft, Mom ordered Ariel to fondle us. He touched us everywhere like a soft sweep of hands a-bristle with fingers. Between our bodies they moved, inside us and all over, increasing the sensual joy in what we saw, what sniffed and tongued. But Ariel, moving among our intimacies, was not moved.

One day, in her fury, Mom tucked him away. She never told me why, though I supposed he

had hesitated too long in carrying out her wishes.

It was fun to squat there, elbows on knees, head in hands, and watch Ariel struggle in his pine cleft like a bumblebee caught in a spider's weave. It amused me. It made me sad too. When I tried a command on him, a silly boyish imitation of my mom, he made a face or pretended he didn't hear. So I shouted mean things at him and cried. If my hands had been able to seize him and not pass through, I would have broken his bones.

Mom called me impetuous. High-strung.

She was right.

Everything changed when the devils came, the ones in the boat with the rip in the bottom, the old man and his daughter.

Mom wanted them here. She longed for their arrival. Until I found her journal and could read it, I had no idea why.

I hated her for bringing them. I cursed her name, which Prospero told me was Sycorax. When he stuffed me into slavery, a cleft from which there was no escape, he pronounced with scorn her name. That was the only time he spoke Berber, haltingly, so thick and misshapen the words that I scarce could understand him.

"You lie," I said. "My mom *has* no name."

For my defiance, he had me pinched and poked.

But I knew he was not lying. Hearing Mom's name made her small in my mind, not the woman who lived in all ways outside her skin, who welcomed in the world, who let the world be her and be inside her.

"Sycorax," said pursed-lipped old Prospero, the wicked magician. His words dripped bitter honey. "She's one scary ox."

I knew not what an ox was.

But I understood scary.

"My mom is *not* scary," I retorted, and though I suffered further pinches, I stood high and proud in my backtalk.

"*Was*," said he. "Not *is*. Sycorax is dead."

That burst my defiance. It made me blub, right in front of the devil Mom had ferried across the sea.

Mom could see what went on in foreign lands.

She peered south, beyond the rocky cove, her stone-cold glare penetrating into distant Algiers. Algiers, she told me, was the stink-hole that had kicked her out, bound her with ropes, stopped her mouth, and left her here, big-bellied with me.

But more and more, she peered north, beyond the bay whose outlying reefs bore the brunt and pounding of waves. Toward Italy. Toward Naples and Milan. Uncountable cove lengths did Mom's grim brown gaze stretch, growing hard and distant.

I imagined those places as islands, identical to our own but with larger mud huts. They had huge fantastical animals, and people just like us but with cloth on them, not sun-draped.

Mom had some cloth, so I knew what it was, tatters she had on when the bad men of Algiers tossed her on the island.

In my mind's eye, the Algerians and Italians were beings draped in tatters, their arms holding themselves inside stiff cloth cocoons.

Did they fear change, these caterpillar men? It seemed so to me.

When the devils came, I found out I was right.

In the days before their arrival, Mom spent hours staring north. Her vision shifted near and far. She muttered stray mumblings. Once, she rose in her worn body, scratched patterns in the dirt, and coaxed out of the air a spirit. Huge and puffy were its lips, its body as slight as Ariel's.

"Will it touch us, Mom?"

She ignored me, addressing her full attention to the spirit she had summoned. At her behest, it nodded and sped away backward on a puff of expelled wind, leaving behind the pungency of sea surf and the sweet rot of pine.

Mom collapsed.

I carried water to her lips and helped her to bed. There would be no clefting. I knew that. I wanted it, but by the age of twelve I knew not to pry open a shell shut tight.

In previous bouts of illness, Mom would often thank me for my care and devotion, placing a soft weak hand on my brow or neck. "You're a good boy," she said. "Cuddle with your mother." It was only a cuddle, not a cleft, in her moments of fever.

That was all right, I didn't mind.

But now, when I lowered her to the bed and pulled the covers over her, her eyes remained fixed on the distant bay. I melted a gourd-fruit into mash, adding honeycomb and pods. When I tried to feed her, she brushed the bowl aside.

"Go to the shore," she said, a craving for something else than food in her voice. "At the first sign of them, run and tell me."

From the ferocity of her gaze, I knew they must be wondrous beings. More wondrous than all the spirits she had called to enhance our clefting or fill our ears with exotic tales.

Her voice carried such urgency, I didn't stay to ask who they were, or by what mode of transport they would arrive. Would they angle up from the beach like sand crabs and shake the grains from their legs? Would they swim like eels out of the sea; or like sleek-wet otters, lithe as leeches, twist and waddle from the rock-stream? Would they spiral earthward like seed pods?

How many would there be? As many, I guessed, as I had fingers. They would be soft and kind. With a wish, a whim, they would cure Mom. She would be as young and spry as when we came here. They would rekindle the fire in her eyes. Of my chores would they relieve me. With the crook of a finger, these divine beings would fell trees, split them, float logs through the air, and stack them neatly outside our hut.

I sped northward to the bay and hunkered down upon hot sand. The sun gave all things its harshest caress, stippling the wave tops with knife glances that marched and danced far out to sea. My eyes hurt for squinting, despite the shade-cup of one hand.

Our saviors will emerge from beneath the waves, I thought, or float in upon its surface. From the magic isles of Naples or Milan would they come.

My mind tricked me a time or two, picking out round faces in distant glints. Then the glints fell flat. I craned and scanned. My throat was

parched, but I didn't care. Mom never sent me on a fool's errand.

Far distant, out beyond where the reefs took their punishment, the glints turned blue and silver, white and green. You could see anything you wished to in them. Because I knew not what to expect, I saw nothing and everything.

Then the white glints softened to tan, and some of the tan glints shaded into the dark browns of tree bark. I willed them white again. They defied my will, staying tan and brown. They separated from the blue and the silver, the white and the green, to take on the stubborn persistence of graspable objects.

When I could no longer deny that something bobbed way out yonder, so distant it was but a dot, I massaged the sleep from my calves and sprinted to my mother's bedside. Though I slacked not, my body barely broke a sweat. My breath, deep to the lungs, remained as measured as if I had dawdled.

"I see them," I said excitedly. "Far off, a mustard seed bobbing on the horizon."

Her eyes, not meeting mine, stared out of her head, her skin golden-bronze, her long tangles of charcoal hair. "Good," she said. "Go back. Give them greeting. They will not understand you, yet speak to them anyway. The little girl's name is Miranda."

"Miranda," I repeated, liking the way the name felt on my tongue. "What means girl?"

Mom ignored me. "When she fills out, she will belong to you. The old man with her. His name is Prospero. He is her father. And he is . . . her father."

"What means father?"

"Same as mother only less."

"Prospero is mother to Miranda?"

"Close enough," she said. "Greet them by name. Bring them here. Do not delay. I haven't much time."

She meant her illness. I knew that. I was smart. Mom always said so. That meant as sharp in the mind as a splinter. It meant my thoughts darted like minnows, deep and goggle-eyed.

These spirits, Prospero and Miranda, would take Mom's sickness away, so that she bade farewell and good riddance to ill health, gliding along the earth instead of trudging upon it, far more often in a clefting mood than not. They would have the magic touch of ten Ariels.

I could not help picturing them as creatures of the air, obedient to Mom's every whim, who would enrich our lives. But I knew in my head that they were Milanese or Neapolitans with bodies like mine, but pale of skin and cocooned in tatters.

I didn't know they would be devils.

I never forgave Mom for not telling me.

I pressed my lips to her neck. One weak hand touched my shoulder, though she gazed toward the bay still.

"Go," she insisted. "Greet them. Bring them here."

Out of the mud hut I raced, speeding toward the bay as free as the wind. My skin opened to the glory of the day and laughed in tune with my easy lope.

Mom was in pain. That hurt my heart. But our visitors, the old man Prospero, the little girl Mir-

anda, would make Mom well again, would delight us with stories as the other spirits did. From one of the enchanted isles of Italy would they bring great wonders.

But what did they bring?

The crush of burdens.

Clefts. Lashings. Pinches.

Enslavement.

Chapter Two

I Am Born

Mom related often the story of my birth.

With blistering curses against the Algerians did she interweave the telling, dark fetid curses that ate at my heart, so often did that storm rise in her eyes.

Upon the sands of the bay was I born, the same spot where I awaited the divine beings. Every time she told it, Mom mentioned that the day I was born was balmy and sunny. But I heard, in the bitterness of her telling, a thick cloud cover, winds that narrowed her eyes to slits, battering swats of rain upon her face and body.

She wasn't angry at me, but at the Algerians. She never picked them out by name. They were a mere mass of demonic soma, a monster with many arms, many heads, many clefters.

Among them had Mom lived, on a wicked is-

147

land called Algiers. When she was young, they let her be. She married a rich merchant. No children. He died. She chose to live alone. They started to stare at her, to withhold all communion from her.

When she grew wrinkled and began to worship Setebos, an imported god from far-off Patagonia, they said and did mean things to her.

Once, she began to relate these things and I heard them all, aghast and angered. But my lips parted and I somewhat drooled and my clefter grew blood-thick. When she saw that, the telling stopped.

I wept bitter tears. My nose went all snotty and dripped. Mom didn't need to say a thing. I slinked away and sat beside the bay and peered way down into my dark depths, but I couldn't see deep enough. All I could hear was some awful beast grunting and shuffling down there.

When the Algerian monster bound her limbs with ropes, stopped her mouth, and tossed her on the island, Mom was a hundred years old. She told me that with a slow satisfied smile. But I had no one to compare her to, not until the devils came and then, twelve years later, the second wave of devils, the time I tricked my way to Naples with its teeming masses of the doomed. In all my days among the Neapolitans, I never saw anyone as old as Mom.

So, because she was exceedingly old and worshipped gods strange to them and who knows why else, they said, "Hey, Mom, there's something wrong with you." But they were the wrong 'uns, not Mom. They dumped all this bad stuff

on Mom, not to mention their deep, unwashable-away, Algerian stench.

"You're not only old, and ugly, and wrinkled," they said. "You've got a big belly full of devil spawn and we don't want you *or* your brood on the wicked isle of Algiers no more. Nor do we want the spirits you summon, who blast our crops and steal the hardness from our teeny-weeny clefters so that we can't spawn our own devil babies."

Many times Mom repeated those words to me. I guessed they weren't exactly what was said. Mom was storytelling me, and telling the righteous lie, she said, is a virtuous thing in storytelling. But the heart of what she told me was true. I saw that truth shining in her eyes.

So the Algerian monster, it bound her and gagged her and tossed her on a ship. In a heartbeat, that ship blew across the ocean. And into that heartbeat, they crammed heaps of suffering. Heaps. I knew that was so, because one time, you see, Mom peeled aside the righteous lie and started to let me in on the really really bad things they did to her in secret—sometimes under the open eye of the sun—on that ship. She never ventured far down into that vicious beast's lair. But what she said painted the ship clear in my mind.

It wasn't made of wood, that mind-ship. It was black and greasy, lashed about with dry rot and bolted together with misery. Wherever your skin touched it, it blistered. Its groaning boards shut in hunger and torment. No matter though you bloated your belly as big as a boar's bladder at a feast, when they tossed you on board this ship,

you were at once famished. If you rose up from a soft bed of cleft and caress, when they tossed you onto its vile deck, needles thrust up into every pore and pierced you wherever you walked or looked.

Let it all go.

In a heartbeat, the Algerians came to the southmost lagoon and tossed Mom on our island with no more than two days' provisions, leaving her bound with a loose rope so that they would be long gone and safe in Algiers before she could free herself. They feared, as fear they might, that she would wave her hands, spit venom, and summon up spirits from the deep to suck down that ship and drown its devil crew, that needed drowning something fierce.

One day went by, and another. Mom ate their rancid food and drank their bilgy water, neither of which, rank with their stench, could she keep down. Even so, with a strength born of anger, she summoned a spirit to acquaint her with the island, to bring food and fresh water. Thus did Mom revive, first with the help of her magic, then without.

"It serves you ill," she told me, "to rely too much on magic. You forget who you are. Your natural powers atrophy, and magic takes over.

"Be wise. Stay in your center. Do not stray from there. Sling out spells, yes, but know always the slinger from that which is slung."

So she advised, years before she intended to teach me magic, which teaching she never had a chance to do. I was a snotty-nosed pain in the glute and saw no need to learn a thing. Mom's

150

magic provided all. Food, shelter, a good clefting, everything I needed.

When I cusped between child and boy-man, she promised that as soon as I reached thirteen, she would sit me down and teach me magic. If need be, she would smack me into learning mode. But she died when I was twelve, when the devils arrived, when Prospero strode into our hut, pitched his magic against hers, and came out to tell me, a veil of feigned sorrow over his face, that she was dead.

When the Algerian monster tossed Mom on the island, she waddled about with her brood in her womb, exploring the best parts. She picked out the spot where soon she would build the mud hut. And she picked out the bay as the place to set free her belly-burden.

"I had my reasons," she said. Sometimes she added, "The bay was the most beautiful spot on the island." I knew that wasn't true, even taking personal taste into consideration. But I didn't press her. I knew Mom's boundaries and the consequences of violating them.

On her twelfth day on the island, feeling a great quickening in her womb, she made for the bay. When it became clear she wouldn't reach it, she summoned a spirit to waft her thence and tend to her needs.

It was calm and sunny on the day she birthed her brood. As she pushed, the spirit would wriggle one out, hold it up so Mom could see it was blue-faced dead, and set it aside.

"Here comes another," said the spirit, new-filled each time with joy.

"Catch," commanded Mom, bearing down

again in spite of her pain and grief. Her sons were her hope. She did not want to be alone on the island, and she craved above all avengers. So she told me.

Twelve dead infants blurted into the spirit's bloody palms, their faces crusted and slick and silent. Chests that moved not at all. Tiny arms and legs and blunt thumb clefters with gray fist-sized ball-sacks. Boys all, like me. My brothers.

"That's it?" asked Mom.

The spirit said nothing.

Then out I tumbled. That's how Mom put it. "Out you tumbled." On the beach of my birth, she caught her breath and sobbed. Then out I tumbled, blistering with rage at being trapped behind the others. My tight fists pulsed. My wailing tore ribbons in the sky and made it bleed. It was all the spirit could do to lift me up and show Mom my angry red wart of a face, so raring was I to go, so high-pitched my bellowing rage.

"Thirteen's the charm," said the spirit.

Mom yelped with joy, forgetting for the nonce her twelve dead boys. I didn't quite see what there was to be joyful about, no matter how many times she told the tale. But it made me feel good and it often led to clefting, so I didn't mind hearing it again and again.

Mingled with a certain joy in the telling was Mom's rage at the Algerians. Rage bonded us. Her face lit up then. She wished my brothers had made it out alive. But she also cursed them for causing her such pain, for being carried so long, for making her condition known earlier than it would otherwise have been, so that the Algerian monster got it early into his head to

banish her from the land of her birth.

"You were right, Son," she would say at the height of her rage, "to strangle them in the womb. They deserved to have their cords wrapped around their necks, one fast yank putting paid to their lives. To hell with them. You had your birthright and you claimed it. The last born became first. Good for you. Now come to Momma. Show her what you're made of."

Together we would curse and cleft, building our tower of rage, shaking and shivering with it until we exploded. The venom and sweat of resentment and anticipated revenge sweetly perfumed our exertions.

Mom had no good words, most times, for my brothers. But once she showed me their gravesite behind a dune in an out-of-the-way stretch of that same beach. She told me their names. It was all right to name the dead, she said. They had no freedom that could be thieved from them by being named. And in the land of their exile, all names were left behind. Like us, I said. Mom nodded. That's right, she said, like us.

So she named and blessed and cursed them, and cursed our father whom she did not name. Then she stared out to sea for an eternity, after which she rose to her feet and left without one word more. I gave her a good lead before trailing behind.

The next morning, I decided to get better acquainted with my brothers. So I dug up their bones and constructed crude huts as big as a hare might inhabit, mooshing their tiny skulls down in the sand, overarching their rib cages and legbones at the sides. I didn't mean any

harm by it. It made me feel close to Mom. I guessed I hadn't really strangled them in the womb. But it was fun to pretend I had.

While I was lost in play, Mom raged in and beat me blind. When I fought back, it enraged her further. She was a fury of fists and claws. She bit me and rent my flesh, shredding it wherever her hand fell. And when her energies flagged, she called up three savage spirits to pinch and poke me. I was bruised for weeks after. For three days, I could not lift my head from that beach. I heard Mom come and go, unable to turn my head to follow what she was doing.

One thing she did was to rebury my brothers and to weep and wail and bellow over them, then rush over and kick me hard, low down in the spine where my back fanned out into buttocks.

"Don't, Mom," I wept.

She went away.

Once I could move again, I kept to myself. I hung around outside the hut, doing my chores, hunkering down dejected for days.

I could not bring myself to look at her. I have no idea if she looked at me.

One day, as I emptied out my head and squatted by a fresh-cut woodpile, she sat before me. Her face was as wise as earth. "They were shit," she said. "They chose not to live.

"You lived.

"You'll do."

I cried and told her I was sorry. She sat there, not touching me, saying nothing.

"Are you done?" she asked.

I sniffed and nodded.

"Good. Come inside."

I did, and that was that. She never mentioned my brothers again. She never told me the story of my birth again.

But the story of the Algerian monster and how they tossed her on the island, that she told over and over. Then she skipped over the birth story, swept into her rage, and caught me up in clefting.

So it went, as the moon many times waxed and waned and waxed again.

Chapter Three

Me and Mom

Our island was typically sunny and calm. You had to forage for food, but it was easy to find. We lived in the open much of the time and used the hut for sleeping, or as shelter from wind or rain.

In springtime, fierce storms sprang up sometimes to batter the island. Everything boomed and rocked. Trees whipped and swayed and snapped outside the thick walls of our hut. After the worst storms, Mom had me re-thatch the roof.

Until I was three, I screamed and clutched at her in terror. The first big storm after my third birthday, she told me it was time to stop bawling. When I kept up my yowls anyway, she unleashed a storm of her own, lightning eyes, thunder mouth, that drove me cowering inside myself, where cinders of rage warmed me.

156

I hated her. But hatred was a thing she culti-
vated in me. "You hate me, don't you, boy?" she
asked. When I said no, she smacked me until I
said yes. "Good. Hold to it. It's pure. It's honest.
Unlike every cursed man and woman that has
ever defiled this earth, it will never let you down.
And once you become adept at magic, you'll
need it to keep spirits under control."

When the devils sailed in from across the sea,
they called me ugly. Prospero called me ugly the
first hour. Eventually, beneath his influence, an
identical disdain seeped, snoot by scorn, into
Miranda's eyes, a look that said Caliban was
something bad-smelling, something vile to the
touch. Even when she taught me her tongue and
that of the Algerian monster, I could tell she did
it to feel good about herself, not to help *me*.

I was handsome. Mom's burst of glory. A
bright-eyed gleam of honey and sunshine that
brought her delight. Mom told me so. But the
devils called me ugly, they called me a monster.
Maybe they were right.

The squinty-eyed mage called Mom ugly too.
Once, as he and Miranda sat playing chess, I
overheard him say so. When I asked him what
ugly meant, he put pinches on me and beat me
for eavesdropping, which word I likewise knew
not the meaning of. I asked Miranda in the midst
of our lessons. The general notion had already
been beaten into by her father, so I wasn't
surprised when she defined it as sticking one's
nose where it wasn't supposed to be stuck.

When I asked her what ugly meant, it was a
struggle for her to tell me. Partly because she
thought me ugly but it was unmannerly to let

on, though that never stopped PopEros. Partly because "ugly" is a mirage concept, one of the ways European devils assert power over each other.

"Ugly means you don't look like anyone else," she said.

I told her no one looks like anyone else. Everyone looks different. At least everyone I had seen so far, and Mom had described others, as had Miranda and Prospero, but from those descriptions, they all seemed different too.

She tried again. "Being ugly means . . . it means you're not beautiful."

"Your father calls you beautiful," I said. "Meaning he likes the way you look?"

"Uh-huh."

"That it thickens his clefter?"

Miranda looked pained. "Beautiful? Well, it's the opposite of ugly. It means pleasing to the eye. Whatever offends the eye is ugly."

"Was my mother ugly?" I asked.

She knew my question was an attack on her father. So she deflected it. "I never saw your mother," she said. "I'm sure she pleased your eye, and that she was entirely beautiful."

Miranda had that lying look about her. All her looks were thin and fleeting, but I could read them easily. She was lying.

I let it pass.

Was Mom ugly? Or was she beautiful?

I'll tell you how I remember her.

She stood firm upon the earth. She towered. There was nothing meek about my mother. Her skin was soft and rounded, like freshly packed gobbets of mud. Her thighs were the trunks of

massive oaks. She roved the island until it and she were one, lying in deceptive calm upon the sea. But behind that placid front, they tremored and rumbled, an eruption waiting to happen. Her buttocks, wide and sacked out, flexed when she walked. Long and black and tangled was her hair, snaking down her back like the tangled vines that hang from trees. It smelled of burrows and pinecones. Sometimes beetles moved through it. I liked to feel their gleaming bodies hint and tickle across me when we lay together in the night.

The hut had one tiny window, covered with a cloth that hung and blew. For much of the day, sunlight crept in at the door and filled the hut with its generous glee, expanding the space into infinitudes of light. But when dusk came on, Mom drew shadows about her and lived beside the fires of her rage.

When I was nine, she conjured a spirit, a tiny toad who just sat on a table and glowed. When we clefted by its light, I felt sweaty and stinky. But Mom liked it. At her death, the toad spirit went away. I never saw it again, nor did I try to summon it once I learned magic.

Much of my recall about Mom was vague and uncertain. But two things shine clear in my mind.

The first is her face. It was the color of loam, a precise map of the earth in all its crust and grit. Her head was shaggy and huge. From her mouth issued streams of curses, horned creatures that sprang from the furnace within. Rage lived in the runnels of Mom's face, flowing like rheum from her eyes and mouth, flaring her

wide bronze nostrils, shaking her jowls, pinching closer the slits of her eyelids. Her face remains bold in my mind, brought up to mine
until I could see nothing else and the burrowing-
animal smell of her breath was all there was to
breathe. In those moments, I lived most deeply.
Mom's anger roused my own, nor were they different, one from the other. From the day I
turned three, she brought forth my anger.
Brought it forth, prodded and poked it, kneading it in her palms. Your babies will avenge me,
she said. They will tear out Algerian lungs and
blow them up for playthings, while those from
whom they were torn gasp for a next breath that
never comes.

I'll find you a bride, she said. I had no idea
what a bride was, but as long as Mom knew, that
was good enough for me. You'll cleft the bitch,
she said. You'll cleft her over and over, tumbling
out angry boys who will grow into angry men
and tear out Algerian lungs and blow them up
for playthings.

The second thing I remember is the clefting. I
can't recall *not* clefting with her. She enfolded
me then, her fists balled with anger. She washed
over me like a great storm, lumphing down like
heavy warm brine-air, chanting curses, words of
hate she had used to lullaby my younger self to
sleep. Her lips wrinkled and moistened then. I
chanted with her, making her enemies mine.
Our rage grew, a proud tower of excitation. Then
it leaped up and arced over the vast world, and
she and I fell asleep listening to the lapping of
that dark fire, our heartbeats one.

In my sixth year, thickening began, making

for a more perfect union. My clefter proved to be yet another outlet for my rage, beyond the shared chants and the welt-raising rake of Mom's fingernails across my back. It focused her boy's anger. Mom felt that focus. She closed around it, like the suck of wet warm mud at my heels after a spring rain.

The earth radiates beauty. In sights, in the power of its stenches. Not beauty. That's a name. Beauty is too confining. No words can tell what the earth, in its abundance, o'erspills. Mom was not beautiful and she was not ugly. She was herself. And I am part of her.

It's possible that PopEros and the others were right. I was an ugly monster, Mom an ugly old witch. Maybe she lied about naming. On her deathbed, she told him my name was Caliban. So he called me. Caliban the cannibal, who only once partook of human flesh to see what all the fuss was about.

Perhaps it was another storytelling lie, and not a worthy one, that names confine, that they thrust you into a bad cleft.

It's like the words *exile* and *banishment*. Mom would say she was exiled, banished. When I was old enough to ask her what they meant, she said that being exiled meant you were put on an island to incubate and plot and not be distracted by the babble of idiots, all their comings and goings, their idle chitchat. Exile was a gift, she said, but the Algerian monster judged it a never-ending stretch of pinching and beating.

Banishment was a gift. One sheered away all eaters of time. Everything shrank to its essence. You slept, you ate, you reared your offspring,

you sat alone and probed deep inside, pulling forth skeins of resentment, weaving them into robes of rage. You grew stronger. Your magic came easier, flung wider, let you peer deeper into time and space, let you plot and scheme at your ease.

Such was exile. Such, banishment.

PopEros said otherwise, and Miranda told me more. Exile was a thing of shame, she said. It stripped away who you were, all your connections, though thank God she had her father and some faded memories of the women who attended her. Exile and banishment were bad things, she told me.

At first, I insisted that they were gifts. But my bellowing frightened her. She left off my lessons until I hung my head and said I was sorry. Thus was I taught the practice of European guilt. After that, I thought it best to avoid the subject.

But the incident stirred doubts about Mom and her whole crock about names and confinement and putting off too long the teaching of magic to her son, spells that summon spirits and let one conquer the world.

Yet even now, after my Ferdinand shift, I feel pure rage deep inside me. Its face is Mom's wide brown face. Its smell is the badger smell of her breath and the nested beetle cloy of her hair. Its essence, when I wrap a fist about my clefter, is Mom. She and I, despite the years, become one again.

And I am ready to take on the world and pummel its sad face once more into submission.

Chapter Four

First Impressions

As I raced toward the bay, stray white clouds hung above me like idle thoughts. They might as well not have been there at all, so bright was the sun, so blue the sky.

I loved to run back then, to break into a sprint. So well did I know the island, I could have shut my eyes and set my foot with confidence, the landscape embracing and releasing the sightless runner as he passed. That embrace was a cleft but no cleft, a hand that enwraps one in pure bliss because it does not confine.

These adrift beings, sailing in off a snaky sea that rounds and ends the island, would save Mom. She would not say how, though she hinted that the one called Prospero was a summoner of spirits, a mage, just as I would be one day. I wondered why she didn't simply heal *herself* with the spirits at her command. She told

163

me that magic didn't work that way and that the scallop-skinned mage would not save her through those means. I pressed for more but she flared at me out of her sweat and fever, and I left off.

When I emerged from the trees, my pace slowed in the beach's burning sands. The tiny boat lay as far from the shore's edge as I now stood. Sunbeams crossed and recrossed the sea, weaving a spiderweb in meshes of fire. Out there, an auk floated and fed, one fire-eye in a ball of foam.

Striding up to where the sand was wet and dark and smoothed by laplets, I stopped as neat as a gull when it lands. I took joy in the glorious sun and the full play of my lungs. To the boated ones I waved. In greeting I raised my voice, speaking the names Mom had spoken.

The pale peculiar man wearing tatters that were not tatters, strange hair asprout about his mouth, stared at me. Feelings warred upon his face. They were impossible to sort out. But vivid remain my first impressions: the little girl clapping her hands and leaping with glee; her father standing behind her, as gaunt and tall and perfectly balanced as a stick thrust in the sand, his brocade arms hanging by his sides as the boat arrowed in to shore.

In hindsight, I am able to separate the threads of Prospero's thoughts as his face loomed, my first glimpse of a face I would come to loathe, which loathing deepened even as my attraction for his daughter grew. Part of his gaze attended to the ruined boat, keeping it smooth in the glide and free of seawater. Another part marveled that

I shouted his name and the name of his child. Another was struck with wonder at the island that floated into view. Yet another took offense at my nakedness, or rather at the dangle of my clefter, which as soon as I was in his power he forced me to cover.

Hateful man! This PopEros, long before he finned and made hideous my body, sliced it up. First with his eyes. Then with cloth. I had been whole and free of constraint, but the mage's scallop-skinned shame slashed my body into three: above the waist, behind a despised loincloth, and from there downward. He spoke often of Modesty, an absurd god off-islanders worshipped, and how Caliban must make his obeisance to it. Curse the pinched old mage for his gift of shame, shame in my looks, shame in my clefter, shame in my dark skin.

Prospero was a liar, then and always.

All of them are liars, the scallop-skinned devils. Worst are the politic ones, the ones in whose circles I now find myself, they who condemn the lie even as with consummate skill they embrace it, blind to the depths of their devious natures. I imagine them at night, alone in their chambers, removing their masks of piety, towering up huge and toothsome and vile of stench, brutish beasts come true when no one can see them.

But that morning, all was obscure behind the pinched man's politic mask. His vessel, a three-masted barque bereft of mast, tackle, or sail, a rotten carcass that the very rats instinctively had quit, smoothed out of the sea and skidded to a halt on the wet gray sand, not three man-lengths from where I stood.

Prospero stared at me, and I at him.

Then he looked down at his excited daughter where she tugged at the sides of the boat, trying to climb out. He bent to lift her up and onto the shore. As she rode and rotated through the air, she beamed at me. When her shoes touched sand, she raced toward me with imperfect and giddy balance.

I squatted. "You must be Miranda," I said.

Her full open cream-fresh face, flushed pink from the sun, cracked a grin whose wingspan was gull-wide, and her eyes went searching and full of glee. Sound tumbled from her lips. I understood nothing of what she babbled except her name, imperfectly spoken.

Then her father's robes, fine though faded, curtained into view. Their hems brushed the wet beach, making wispy tracks as they picked up gray clumps of sand. Miranda he swooped up and rotated in his arms. Though her body flew skyward, her eyes remained upon me. Once, as he twisted her past the point her neck could turn, her head spun and she again fixed upon me with a gaze that drank and drank and thirsted still.

Her father's eyes burned with a hungry look, a look smoothed by caution and a leavening of wonder at having landed, through the agency of unseen hands, before a boy who knew his name.

A great deal of thunderous nonsense boomed from him. Then he stopped. Miranda rested her head on her father's shoulder and stuck a thumb in her mouth, staring at me.

"Prospero," said he, striking his chest so hard I heard the thump.

"Prospero," I repeated, gesturing into the interior of the island, trying to put into that gesture how I knew his name, where Mom lay abed, all of that. Then I pointed at him. "Your name is Prospero. Names cleft us, as yours clearly does, judging by your face."

He stabbed a finger at me and made a quick sound that upfluttered at its end.

I waved a hand as if to bat away flies. "Mom doesn't believe in names," I said.

Annoyed, he babbled something to his little girl, gesturing at me. The glance he tossed my way stank like fresh offal. His nostrils pinched tighter than ever, his eyes narrowed. I bristled within, feeling slapped and scorned.

But I stifled my rage. This man would save Mom and be off. Then we would be rid of him. "I'm supposed to show you the island," I said. "Mom said to, so I will, but only a little, because Mom is sick and you're here to make her better. This way, let's go."

PopEros got the idea. He glanced down at the waves gently lapping at the stern of his barque. Giving a nod, he muttered something into the air, and the vessel slid completely out of the water, cutting a groove in the sand. There was a vicious rent in its hull, the kind that might have been made by a boathook as he and his daughter were cast adrift. But the interior of the boat and the heavy chests that had pressed it perilously low in the sea were dry as dry could be.

This was my first glimpse of a boat. But I had many times watched leaves drift and swoop and spin in lake and stream. When I was five, I launched scores of nutshells manned by twigs,

engaged for an entire summer in guiding and observing them. So I marveled at how free of water the boat's interior was and knew that this strange-looking man must be a great mage indeed.

Again he spoke. The barque halted its glide, well beyond the last curvings of seaweed where the tides had stretched deepest inland. Then he turned to me, stung me again with that dungish glare and a whip-scorn of words, and off we went.

Prospero's laggardly pace maddened me. Out of consideration for his age, I went at half my usual speed. When I glanced back, there the lumbering tortoise would be, his daughter riding in the crook of an arm. So I waited and began again slower.

Yet Mom's illness urged me on.

Once, he set Miranda down to rest. She raced to my arms and I scooped her up, as I had seen her father do. Her scratchy dress crinkled against me. Some sort of animal hides covered her feet, knocking idly against my ribs. She wrapped her arms warm and serene around my neck, her fingertips like tingles of skin drying in the sun after a swim.

Prospero's anger lashed out for the first time. He barked something incomprehensible. The words speared into me and I suffered a sudden chill, the sting of cramps and stitches up and down my torso. Miranda, stiffening in my arms, turned to face him. Her belly ballooned against my chest and she wailed in my ear like a bag of wind. Stung by the assault, I set her down and she raced to Prospero. He scooped her up,

sweeping an abrupt palm down her dress and smoothing her hair to wipe away all trace of me. He spewed another blast of babble, his fiery eyes scurrying upon my skin.

The pain lifted.

I stood for a moment, dazed. I was hurt and enraged and bewildered all in one. But I gritted my teeth and shrugged it off. Mom lay dying. Her accursed savior would save her. Then I would tell her of his outrages against me and she would work punishment upon him. Of that I had no doubt.

"Come," I said, welcome gone from my voice.

I didn't show them much of the island. I spoke, knowing they understood nothing but not letting their ignorance get in my way. Though I beelined to the hut, I gestured to various parts of the island, the stream, the lake, the distant lagoon to the south where the Algerian monster had tossed Mom ashore. They heard much about the island and understood nothing.

Even so, the mage's eyes darted everywhere at once, taking in the lay of the land and claiming it as his own. That amused me.

I should not have been amused.

The one detour I made was brief, to the pine grove wherein Ariel had been clefted twelve years before. To counter his hateful glares and to beat back his eye-grasp of the isle, I decided to show the mage one manifestation of Mom's magic.

That would cow him, I thought. That would teach the devil proper respect.

One cannot teach a devil respect, proper or otherwise.

But I was a boy and knew no better.

Along the gradual slope of the central mountain we trekked. Because I loved to taunt Ariel, I knew the way well. I liked his stuck-bee rage. It amused me. It also heightened our clefting's passion when Mom called upon Ariel's touch, his enraged arms in painful stretch from the cloven pine to our bedded bodies.

In among the pines we wove. There uprose the tree into which, when I was three, Mom had thrust Ariel for his recalcitrance. A wide black streak scored the trunk where she had brought down a bolt of lightning to split it. The sting of burnt wood lives still in memory, as do Ariel's protests as he was dragged through the air, the gnashing and grinding of his bones as he was forced into the smoky cleft. His pain had been woven of two sounds: the sharp crack of the blistered pine, and the solemn moan of winds that scurry all goodness out of the world.

I pointed to Ariel, whose struggles redoubled at our approach. But abruptly, sensing perhaps the power of the mage, calm cloaked him. I named him aloud, then pointed to him again and said, "Ariel."

When Prospero repeated the name o'ertop me, then did Ariel bumble fiercer than ever.

I launched into the briefest of explanations of his entry into our lives, his transgressions—or what I had divined of them—his imprisonment here, and something of his long-distance contributions to our clefting.

Miranda stared at me in awe and admiration.

PopEros wore that look of crazed intent that later I discovered meant, What gain can I

squeeze from this? The mage was an owner, a devourer, one who takes and takes and hungers for more.

Though Ariel's twitter kept up non-stop, it was, as always, muted. Mom had made it so in her spell, so that the spirit, newly clefted, would not deafen her with his protests.

"Come," said I. Prospero stood staring at Ariel. His stare softened. He said something that again halted the spirit's bumble and buzz. I repeated, with greater urgency, "Come."

Prospero's head turned sharply to glare at me. But he picked up Miranda and followed. Snapping underbrush, we attained a path I had long worn among the trees. In silence we hit our stride. Out finally we came into the clearing where stood our mud hut, grayish-brown and solid beneath the sun.

I led the devil to the doorway (may the great god Setebos blast my bones for doing so!), beyond which lay Mom abed. Miranda, set down, cowered behind the folds of her father's robe. Prospero said something to Mom and she, to my surprise, answered in a similar babble, as if she understood.

Then she said to me, "Wait outside."

"Don't you think I ought to—"

"Wait outside!" Her rage clawed inside my belly; I backed away. "I can still see you," she said, forcing me out of eyeshot. Rounding the hut, I hunkered down beside the woodpile, intent on their voices, Prospero's deep and strong, Mom's powerful but frayed by infirmity.

Miranda peeked around the hut and came over to squat beside me, her dress tenting in the

dirt. She locked her arms around her knees for balance, catching herself once and rebalancing.

She spoke softly to me, seeming to mimic her elders. I'm certain now she imitated the nurse-maids she mentioned fondly in later years. She had no memory of her mother, who I learned long after had died in childbirth.

We murmured to one another, a pair of doves who had set down to poke for grubs. But much of the time she and I listened to the sounds in the hut.

The tone of their argument was odd. I sensed power in each voice, but power kept under wraps so as not to betray its full extent. Twice I heard those wraps slip and be drawn back up. The third time, they seemed to slip off completely. Then each voice, his first, hers rising against it, ratcheted up into a chant. Mom's voice grew indistinct and overshadowed. Then there came a peculiar shift—whose significance eluded me—and Prospero's voice abruptly dominated. Hers faltered, faded, went silent.

My hackles rose. At once I sprang up, the base of my brain pounding and fizzing. But in mid-step was I halted and held, time stretched beyond all reckoning. When at length I was released, I resumed. The doorway rounded into view and Prospero emerged from it, tall and fiery and triumphant. He raised a hand and pointed my way, hurling barb after barb of viciousness.

About me the air constricted, the light of the sun banked, the earth grew harsh and sour. I could not move. I could only watch *him* move. His unkind words made poor Caliban small and

scruffy and unwelcome, as he, looming large, shaped the air close about me.

Thus began the thrall that ended my youth and kept me captive for twelve years.

Chapter Five

What I Knew About My Father

Though Mom refused to describe him on those rare occasions when she mentioned him at all, I always imagined my father as a small man. I don't mean short of stature. I mean like pixies. Whenever I tried to picture him, my mind would reject the image I had made and say, Smaller.

In the last year of Mom's life, I asked her about my father. She had told me of the bitch-bride she would find for me, how I would slither into that self-same creature and cleft vengeful sons. So I asked Mom who had clefted her to bring me forth. And how come *our* clefting brought forth no such sons. But mostly the first. Who was this clefter? Had he been one of her spirits?

No, she said, my father was a man.

A towering ship had put in to the harbor at Algiers, disgorging Italians. They had business with the Algerian monster, something to do with

stopping one set of pirates from raiding another.

One of those Italians Mom had spied on the docks at night. Though he was by all appearances a confined man—a captive of his clothing, his station, the constrictions of his culture—something in his bearing and his looks hinted at a wildness, a rent through which forbidden deeds might slip.

The next evening, aided by a confederate who caught him up in a tavern conversation, she lured the Italian to her dwelling on the outskirts of Algiers. He knocked. She opened to him. There, she plied him with an infusion of herbs and pressed grape.

Still, even when she made to touch him, he huddled his inhibitions about him and spilled warbles of self-righteousness all over her. She, enraged at his folly, summoned spirits to o'erwhelm him.

They surrounded him in earnest, pinching and poking, no ingress denied them. In every way was he invaded and violated, his fine clothing no block at all to the beings Mom had summoned. Deaf to his deep-lunged protests, they picked at and undid the fastenings that held his garments together. From his trembling body they peeled them away and the dead cloth dropped to the dim dirt floor.

Mom lay abed watching, intoning, an insistent hand caressing urgency from her bare forked limbs. Squat beeswax candles illumined the fall of his finery, the expanses of scallop-skin, the sharp ridges of rib and thighbone, the rage and shake of a willful man unwillingly exposed. His face, Mom told me, was an open hole of invec-

tive, a ragged wrathful gape that blistered the air.

The intensity of his protests, a slave impassioned against her, engorged her flesh where her fingers played.

But though the victim gripped in her spell steamed and bellowed, his blood grew thick from the neck up alone, not at all below. So Mom summoned the lustiest spirit she could, a spark of the great god Setebos himself. Into the man, parting the pucker of his bunghole, she introduced the demon, packed up and swirling through his bowels, out and down and up, through torso and limb. Each of his extremities, including the one she desired, flushed with blood. She left him control above the teeth only, which clamped tight upon curses that would have deafened her had he been free to express them. Still, because they aroused her, she let some of them escape the seal of his lips.

His eyes alone, stuck like cloves in a face that did its best to shake, betrayed his panic. No matter. Mom was ready for the clefting and signaled so to the demon. The naked man stepped out of the scattered isle of his clothing, coming on with a palsied surge and hesitancy that burst its bonds even as new ones formed around him. Had he been set free, he would have ravaged her like a panther. Mom smelled danger heavy upon the air, which whiff of danger, ozone thick, pressed higher the urgency of her need to be shot full of whelp-seed.

She knew that her victim's muscles would ache on the morrow, so fiercely did he struggle against his fate. But the demon's grip on him

was unshakeable. He closed upon the bed, obscuring and revealing the flames of candles as he walked. The man's sweated extrusions of fear and rage danced in the flare of Mom's nostrils. Perspiration slicked and dripped upon his face, twining down neck and torso, beading along the taut plane of his belly into his private hair.

Mom lay back, ever intoning, and opened to receive her lover's weight and thrust. Into the close circle of candlelight beside the bed his diminutive head moved. It filled the air above her eyes, she said, contracting even as it expanded. His tiny fuzz-hot face divorced itself from the demonic seizure below.

It bumbled. It buzzed. Its eyes narrowed to two hard darts, their hot points ablaze with vain defiance. She liked this man's contained power, turned impotent by her thrall. Her hips rose to meet his, that brown earth-map matching him glare for glare. Their eyebeams locked in a savage clench as they rocked below, slick in thrust, sand-dry and gritty in their contest of wills above.

Contest? A sham. Mom would have her way with him. He was a vessel to be pumped up and drained, nothing more. Though the words that escaped his lips remained defiant, she knew she kept them up to prevent his sense of himself from being overwhelmed. His face, a smudge of awareness in a swirl of bestial need, buzzed its desperate hold on life. Anger flared its edges, anger sharpened its focus, anger fought against a dissolution of self that acceptance would surely bring.

My father's face, she told me—he whose fea-

tures she would not describe, whose name she would not yield up nor whether he was yet alive—my father's face became a hard dot, growing ever tinier as his pinched limbs flexed and blurted their humped lechery into her. Its lines were sharp, its confinement absolute, locked in denial and rage and at last pain, the pain of carnal obliteration in which clefting culminates.

Then she released him, his purpose fulfilled. At her command, the invasive demon voided itself and vanished. The spirits that had stripped him restored and clasped and straightened his garments about him. He fled, staggering back by moonlight to the ship.

"I never saw him again," said Mom, "save in my mind's eye. Concealed the following night in the shadows of the dock, I heard two mariners belch and mutter and swear. My forced paramour had taken to his bunk, they said. There did he rave and toss, bereft of his wits and drenched in sweat. He refused food. What water he drank would not stay down. One mariner feared he would die. The other laughed and said, 'The only use for the rich is to fill graves. Better *his* grave be filled than the poor, by whose plight his stone-cold heart remains untouched.'"

Mom sent a healing spirit to attend my father on board ship as it sailed for Italy. She would not say whether that spirit had succeeded.

Mom delivered her most complete account of these events one moon before Prospero ensnared me. Those were the last words I heard her speak about my father. Stilled was that great

voice, closed those eyes that roved upon a vast brown map of place and power.

I clung to the hope that, in her deathbed struggles with Prospero, Mom had blasted an urgent summons, perhaps in the shape of a spirit, to my father in Italy. I hoped that he had heard her summons, that he would respond to it, that her long-ago ship of scallop-skins would set sail once more to rescue his son from the cleft of Prospero's enslavement.

But hope lives only to be abandoned. Despair alone makes sense of this ever-narrowing world.

As it happened, the ship filled with scallop-skins took twelve years to arrive, nor was my father on it when it did.

Only more devils.

Chapter Six

Mom's Funeral Pyre

Prospero emerged from the hut a changed man.

Something uncanny had happened betwixt the raised voices that abruptly fell silent, something that set off his fury. The face he had shown as his boat drifted in to shore began to make sense. Though pinched and pruned it remained, he now released one small tuck of reserve.

What leaped out caught me in its grip.

When little Miranda saw the pain that seized me, she whimpered plaintively to her father. But he, fixing me still in a stare, barked her into submission. She had learned to obey, a lesson I refused for the next twelve years.

"Where is my mother?" I piped. "What have you done to her?" My limbs would not unstick from the air. My shoulders were cramped near to tearing, and my head bowed where moments before I had held it up in easy pride.

May Setebos rend to shreds the vile mage! In that moment, Prospero Europeanized me. Before, I had had no name. My skin was open. With every bound and breath, I grew. My mind, my heart, my soul, all free, arched out to meet the world and o'erleap every barrier. There was no pinching then, save what Mom in the ferocity of her love had sparingly employed. Instead there was a vigor to my flesh, a tone, the encouragement of all nature.

But in that moment, inhibition entered me.

Then he named her, punished me for doubting that Mom had a name, and told me she was dead. Deaf to my sobs, he pointed and said, "Caliban."

It was a curse, a hammer, an accusation all in one, free will crushed by what whim he chose to command. From that day, I was his creature enslaved, a pawn grasped and worried by thin-boned fingers. I knew, by being deprived of its exercise, my own will.

"You, Caliban," he said, and now the word I thought had been a curse I knew to be my name, the name that Mom had unveiled to him upon her deathbed, the name she had never once spoken to me.

The mage crooked a finger and ducked back into the hut. Through the doorway into darkness, I followed.

Crumpled on the floor, halfway to the bed, lay Mom in her nakedness, inert, a world dead.

I opened my soul to weeping.

Prospero mocked me. At once my sobs turned to rage and I made to leap at him, to tear out his

throat. He gestured. Into nettles of pain did I slam, falling to the floor.

"You killed her," I cried, doubled up in pain. I saw that my meaning had reached him. He dismissed it with yet more babble, looking away as he spoke. Miranda, appearing in the doorway, asked a pale question her father likewise ignored.

He gestured at me, at my mother's corpse, and barked a command. Place her on the bed, I thought he must be saying.

I lifted her in my arms, struggling with a dead sack of bone and flesh. Her limbs had forgotten how to move, how life had animated them. Even as I rose, her earth-smell floated up to greet me. I pictured her on the bed already, tatters drawn to her chin as I wept beside her.

How, I wondered, had she—enfeebled unto death—moved so far from the bed in her confrontation with the pinched devil?

His voice, hatred of which had already taken root in my heart, yapped again. It gave me to know that placing her on the bed ran counter to his wishes. I turned with my burden and started straight for Miranda, who slipped through the doorway and out of my way.

Into the blare of daylight I passed.

I cursed Prospero, a continuous stream of invective which for reasons unclear he allowed me. He understood, perhaps, only the tenor of what I said. Or he had not completely settled upon the nature of my enslavement. Or perhaps he sensed my need for an escape valve, something to damp the shock and exhaustion of

carrying my murdered mother while my will to do otherwise was shackled.

He forced me to retrace my steps. There were shorter ways to the bay, but Prospero's pinch craved the familiar, and thus we went.

Northward we pressed. When we reached Ariel, Prospero halted me with a flick of his free hand—the other hefted Miranda—and spoke to the trapped spirit.

Ariel perked up, babbling back that same babble. A smile warped Prospero's lips at Ariel's words. The mage raised a finger, spoke one word, and the pine cleft eased open. I don't mean that it moved. It exhaled rather, after twelve years of suspended breath, and upon that long-delayed exhalation rode Ariel, unstuck at last from his confinement.

The triumphant sprite zoomed past my face, briefly vituperative, swirling about Mom's body cradled in my arms. His initial outbursts were in Prospero's tongue. Then he switched to Berber. "Ha," said he, "I'm free. You're trapped. Sycorax is dead and Ariel lives to serve a new master."

At the snap of Prospero's fingers, he sped back to that master, cowed and Italianately mewling.

"You're no more free than I," I shouted. But a glare from PopEros numbed my tongue and I could say no more.

The mage glanced at Ariel, then me. Decision flared in his eyes. At once, he intoned a spell in yet another arcane tongue, in response to which Ariel dimmed into a mere outline of himself.

I divined three things: that Prospero had spoken a spell intended to render Ariel at times in-

visible to me and inaudible; that Mom, possibly from her deathbed, had put in place a stronger spell that overrode his efforts; and that the self-absorbed mage was too blind or arrogant to assure himself that I was indeed incapable of seeing the toady hovering over his head in stitched outline. I had sufficient presence of mind, supple even at twelve, to pretend surprise and frustration.

Prospero looked as pleased as the brown badger that hunts by moonlight, its slant white-wedge eye narrowed to its need. Then he launched into an oration aimed at Ariel, indicating himself, his daughter, me and my dreadful burden, the direction from which his boat had brought him. He volleyed question after question at the spirit, nodding at Ariel's answers and interrupting them with more questions.

He was not pleased at what he heard.

Ariel ducked and forelocked in the air, trying to soften the pronouncements that wrinkled his master's brow. But Prospero stilled the spirit, turned, and swept a hand at me.

Again began our deadmarch, around the base of the crater, down the slope, and beelining to the shore. One arm locked about Mom's waist, one beneath the bend of her knees, I walked with a pronounced sway.

Her feet hung heavily against my side. Her right arm idled upon the back of my hand. Upon my shoulder her vast head rested. No beetles escaped from her hair, but I saw one skitter down Prospero's forehead. With a shudder he brushed it away.

When we reached the bay, PopEros set down

his child near the boat. She hunkered upon the sand, staring at us and at Ariel in the air. I sensed she wanted to laugh but stifled it, fearing her father's wrath.

Prospero threw an order at me. As it happened, I was ready to set Mom down and did so freely.

Not deigning to attempt my tongue again, the old bastard used Ariel to make his wishes known. "The master says you're to go back to the hut, bring food, then logs. Lots of logs."

"Tell the murdering bastard he can impact his scrawny hindquarters with said logs."

Ariel relayed my sentiments.

To which PopEros bellowed and raged. Such a hail of pinching blackened me then that I could scarcely breathe. When it was over, I smarted and stung in all places. He barked an order and again forced me into motion.

Along that same obsessive track was I sent, two dozen trips, once for sustenance for him and Miranda, the rest for the hefting of logs, two thick ones shouldered on each trip. What had been free and open terrain now narrowed to a tunnel, one which tightened and dimmed with every trip, despite the sunlight that flared along its length.

Such it is when one's will is forced down, when the cramped cravings of another override it. No imagination, no leeway, no trust.

I cursed him, more vigorously when I believed him out of earshot, but also under my breath or beneath audible thought when I reached the bay and again saw the bastard, uglier each time in my sight.

I built the pyre and laid my mother gently across the nubbled humps of corded oak. Then I stepped back, soft my heels in yielding sand, as Ariel, so commanded by PopEros, swirled through the logs and set them ablaze.

Flames roared in the gathering dusk, licking at Mom's limbs, crimping and blistering her flesh. Like the great god Setebos himself did they blast and bellow. I shouted into the sky, cursing he who had abandoned us, slipping in curses aimed at Prospero along the way. Though Ariel was at his ear, the mage let me have that final burst of will, hoping to burn away my resistance as I watched my mother's corpse consumed.

He had no idea what stuff Caliban was made of, even at twelve.

The fire that devoured her burned hot in my head. She was gone, she who had been my all, who had had plans for me. All of that rose in ripples of heat and cinder, caving in around charred bone. I vowed then, at the core of my cursing, to avenge her death. To seize her murderer and triumph over him, however long it took. To hurt his daughter and any other relations or friends PopEros might have.

Anything that would visit grief upon him.

Into my heart was that resolve seared.

And when Prospero's rude will again closed about my limbs, I knew this: No matter how long it took, I would break that will and rise above him at last, triumphant and righteously raging.

Chapter Seven

The Upbringing of a Slave

Twelve years passed.

They might have been twelve centuries.

In a time when I ought to have emerged from adolescence into adulthood, learning magic at my mother's knee and making life easier for her, I lumbered along in invisible shackles, satisfying the whims of a devil from Milan. I longed to breach the protective bubble that surrounded him, snap his neck like a stick, and rip his yammering head clean off, that graybeard wiggle stilled, those swordpoint eyes blunted at last.

Instead of the limitless freedom the isle had each day offered, it became now a prison. Against its walls I slammed, battering my limbs upon them, willing my fists to punch holes in them and break through. But despite all my bellows, the cleft that bound me pinched closer every day. Fond memories of Mom and my

187

childhood stood enshrined, an icon of loss that anchored my rage. Mine the bitter heart that bides its time and consumes itself.

At first Prospero kept me from the mud hut. He and Miranda moved in and left me outside, night and day.

When I patched together a squat hovel of my own, a meager cripple that scarcely stood, Prospero forced me to tear it down. I raged against my hands even as they rent my handiwork, but I did as he commanded. The next day, on a whim, he changed his mind, instructing me through Ariel to proceed.

Proceed I did.

But his scowl hung over the project. I never felt at home in that hovel. Even so, for a time— until I built a dwelling to Prospero's specification and reclaimed the mud hut—it provided shelter, an escape, a place to nurse dark desires, to shrug off each day's ugliness and escape into sleep.

Ugliness.

For twelve years, until Ariel's contrived tempest netted his master the ship of King Alonso of Naples and his son Ferdinand, Prospero boxed me in. His raft of raised niggles cramped my spirit, molding it to his pinch, to his razor-honed eyebeams that sliced the world into odd mirages.

I fought back. I tried to wound him with words, to defy him. But the pinches and cuffs I endured, the unbreakable spirit-shackles on my limbs, made me a mere adjunct to his bidding.

There was more.

There is always more.

Each morning without fail, from the first dawn after landing to his fourth anniversary on the island, Prospero stood before me, scrutinizing my shape and sea-shelling his right hand through the air. From his lips the mage let float a soft phrase, ever the same. I felt no effect, or if I did it was of a slight breeze, a breeze so subtle that I doubted it had blown at all. Then, surveying my limbs, he would look pleased, scowl to counter the sin of taking pleasure, and sting me with the first order of the day.

The changes took weeks to manifest, but manifest they did.

In four years' time, Prospero made me ugly. My face, beneath the mage's perverse sculpting, mottled and lumped. He pocked my skin and stippled me with moles. He thatched the hair on my head, raising shoots of it here and there upon my body. Randomly, upon leg and arm, did he raise functionless fins. I developed a stoop, my head lowered, my neck stretched like a vulture's. There bunched upon my back a rock-solid hump of blasted flesh.

These things he did to repulse his daughter, whom he tried in every way to turn against me.

He experimented with stench. From my pores he drew vile exhalations, the rot of animal flesh swarming with maggots, a fetid concentration of flocculent waste, the bloat-belch of carrion rolling out upon my every breath. But ere long, because he had to deal with me, he backed away from that, leaving mere hints of these offenses. Never could I wash away the stench, neither in its strong nor in its mild forms. Yet I learned to live with it, as did Prospero, as did Miranda.

Was she repulsed?

Smart girl. Coy dissembler from the off-island culture. Her father wanted her to find me ugly, and she so pretended. But from the start, despite Caliban's four years of carnal devolution and thrice four of spiritual indignity, that first fascination of a sunburned three-year-old lowered to the shore never completely left her.

Scars engage one. They attract even as they repel. Thus it was with Prospero's violations of my soul and body. Thus their effect on Miranda.

Our bond, hers and mine, was language.

At first Prospero didn't care if I understood him. He babbled; I obeyed; that was enough. If he thought to summon Ariel, he used him to translate his will. But it didn't sit right with him. He hated, perhaps, being in any way beholden to the fawner. He much preferred direct control, Caliban as meat puppet who would do his bidding unquestioned.

So when Miranda turned eight, he instructed her to teach me their tongue. He trusted enough to her distaste for me, and his absolute hold over my limbs, that he left us alone. I bided my time, allowing the icy surface of that trust to grow far thicker than was warranted.

I had picked up tufts of Italian, the ones that drifted past often enough to drop meaning into my ears. But my store of phrases was as limited as bird song.

Beginning with those tufts, Miranda attached others, at eight a natural teacher. With a child's earnest good will she gestured at things, scratching lines in the dirt or sketching objects on scraps of paper. Her persistence enveloped me.

Her energy never flagged. Every morning, she refreshed the lessons of the previous day and struck out along promising new paths.

Three months saw me conversant, six fluent. Indeed, she began to branch out into Arabic, which her father had taught her, and which she now began to teach me, wooing me from my initial refusal to taste the Algerian monster's language on my tongue.

Then Prospero halted our lessons, sensing perhaps how close teacher and student had grown and disliking in the extreme the ever-more-cutting eloquence of my grumblings against him.

On her own, when Miranda was twelve and I one-and-twenty, she taught me to read, both in Italian and in halting Arabic. Though her father disapproved, his parental control had waned even as his hold over me tightened.

That time was unbearable, those three years before the big ship came. PopEros became ever more cramped and crabby. He hated the island, hated the fact, he said, that his powers, though great, did not extend far enough to free him from it.

(I figured out soon enough that this was yet one more lie. At any moment he could have had me repair his barque or build him a new ship entire. He could have had Ariel blow him back to Italy or anywhere at all. No. Exile had wounded his pride. Only when that pride was healed would he quit the kingdom he had usurped from me.)

His daughter, meanwhile, swelled into fifteen and became more independent of him. She be-

gan to beat him at chess, to counter with skill and persuasion his arguments. Miranda came into her own. That troubled him immensely.

Protective? Of course.

But I saw clearly what lay beneath that. He was a lonely old sod. He would have denied it, had anyone been so bold as to suggest it, but Prospero had his gimlet eye on his daughter.

He spoke often, within my hearing, of finding her a husband. He would lure some ship to the island, a ship bursting with royalty. From it would he pluck a worthy mate for her, a prince, a king. They would be rescued from the island, his dukedom restored.

But beneath it all, I heard the seethe and slither of his need, his need, his need.

Heard it because it echoed mine.

If his plans bore no fruit, if no ship ever sailed within the compass of his magic, I knew there would come a day when he went mad and began to people the island with Prosperos.

PopEros didn't know that, didn't suspect it. To his own wailing needs was the mage deaf.

I suspected that Prospero never touched his clefter forbiddenly, never completed that circuit of excitation that makes one whole. At night, deep in sleep, the old man groaned and doubtless burst the bonds he refused to burst in his waking hours.

He was a creature of shame.

He was the bastard child of shame, got upon the fecund belly of pinch, poke, and trap.

He was the patriarch of a cramped island, in charge of a toadying spirit of the air, a slave of the earth who refused to be broken, and a

daughter whose charms had begun to scream and soar.

He was going slowly insane.

Through the strictures of that devil's power was my youth strained and distorted. Knock as I might against his dominion, it shaped me.

Or rather it misshaped me. It deformed my limbs and warped my spirit. The limitless expanses of boyhood long departed, I was funneled and stuck in a cramped kennel of Prospero's making.

One day, I vowed, I would be free of him. On that day would he be dead, devoured, vomited out for wild dogs to lap at.

When the royal ship of his dreams at last arrived, upon the winds and huge waves of a tempest, I knew that that day was near.

Chapter Eight

Being Beaten

The Lord was not *my* shepherd, I who knew naught but want. As for goodness and mercy, they must have followed some will o' the wisp, because on none of the days of my life did they follow me.

Prospero had many quirks, deep ruts he liked to slide into and skitter along—phrases, gestures, quips, tics, the articulations of catch and cling that memory uses to summon the flavor of a man when he's not by. But the rut along which the mage most loved to skitter was beating his slave-boy on the Sabbath.

In the beginning, I called it not the Sabbath nor did I understand the passages he repeated while he whipped and scored and pummeled me. I assumed they were spells, magic words to increase the strain of unseen spirits at my arms

or to pour invisible fire ants into the gashes his switch opened along my back.

When Miranda taught me her tongue, she often used brief swatches from Prospero's sacred book, the one whose spells didn't work. One day, there sounded in her mouth the first of the despised Sabbath spells, tumbling along the identical strand of words PopEros clenched his teeth around, but gentled by Miranda. She, intent on her book, saw not my anguish, which I held in.

When she arrived at the part about forevering in the house of the Lord, I asked her to parse its meaning.

She did.

Sensing my distress and its cause, she added that, for all her father's faults, he really was a dear soul. She knew it was difficult for me to understand. But could I not see how weak and frightened he was beneath that hard shell?

Yes, said I, Prospero was a real crab, that rounded pink crustacean carapace protecting a soft underbelly of succulent meat, and wouldn't I like to sink my teeth into him one day, worrying his ruddy guts into the black rape of oblivion.

"Hush now," she said, looking disappointed.

But fuck her, say I, fuck her!

The wench had never known freedom. She had been whelped in the prison of Europe and carried it with her always, just as her father did.

She scolded me. His love of this Lord-is-my-shepherd psalm, she said, showed how beautiful her father was when he let his guard down.

She told me that, from childhood and even

now, he tucked her in, sat by her bedside, and lightly blanketed those words over her as his blessing, adding: "And mayst thou, dear Miranda, dwell there forever too." With a kiss upon her forehead did he seal that wish, leaning in and pressing the air from between them until there was none, then rising in the rustle of his robe and dropping to his knees beside the bed opposite, humbling himself before God in the coming night.

A touching scene.

I imagined him pulling the covers up to his beard, sighing, thinking ill of his earthly slave, fighting off images of himself grossly clipping the daughter who slept not a dozen paces away. And then I imagined him being unable to take another breath, his nose and mouth clamped shut by the heavy hand of Caliban, whose wounds gaped and oozed across his back as the strain of killing tore them open.

The daily pinch and poke of unseen sprites against poor Caliban were not enough to satisfy him. Nor was the somatic shift in my body toward monstrous, dysfunctional, the unbeautiful.

No. Every seventh day, from the first week until he set sail to reclaim his dukedom, Prospero whipped me. I knew naught of Sabbaths. I knew only that every seventh morning without fail, even in the third year when he took ill and I thought I might have gained a reprieve, Prospero staggered feverish from his bed and thrust me out of doors into the place of torment. There, straining beyond his enfeebled state, he raised new welts and opened old.

Most violated did I feel then, most tightly caught in the cleft of my enslavement. For there would I stand or stagger, gritting my teeth against the strain, struggling with spirits who threatened to wrench my arms from their sockets.

Already mawed in memory were his order to remove my loincloth, my spittle-choked refusal, and the war I waged against my fingers, trying to keep them from untying the loincloth but watching them fumble at the ties until they opened along one hip and the cloth fell to expose me. In anger would I kick it far away, to minimize the blood that might otherwise bespatter it.

Then, unseen in that pine grove, two sprites gripped my arms, pulling them perpendicular, while a third wedged its grasp against my neck and head, as if to mimic Ariel's pine cleft. I could do nothing to extract my skull from that pinch.

Prospero stripped to the waist, his robe and tattered shirt draped ceremoniously over a fallen log where later, as I writhed on the forest floor, he would stoop to grab them, and walk off, half-naked, to let the air absorb his sweat.

The pine switch, always new, lay there wet with gore. It was my own ritual, when he was gone, to crawl to that instrument of torment, take it up, and, despite the pain that arced along my back and lanced into my bruised organs, break it, break it, *break it*, until the lengths were too short to be broken further.

Why did he whip me?

Until I read his journal, I never knew the answer. But my conjectures were a knuckle shy of

the bull's-eye. He needed something to mark his calendar by, moments that would burn indelibly into his brain. He needed something too that would remind him of his fallen state, that would call to mind how far from the ideal of his mythic lord he had strayed.

But the real reason he whipped me, as it turned out, was to avenge himself. I was the island. I was also his entrapment and the enemies who had brought it about: his betraying brother, his brother's accomplices, the king who had aligned with them, the friends who had turned a blind eye sooner than help him and his little girl escape.

And he was avenging himself against Mom, not content to have trumped her on her deathbed.

One mage cannot escape another's envy. How skilled soe'er they be, they fear losing the astonished gaze of onlookers. They are frauds awaiting exposure, charlatans, mountebanks, never quite certain of their power. That fed into it too, Prospero's need to battle Sycorax again and again, using her bloodied son to assure himself that she had indeed been vanquished.

In ways I could not know then, switched and flogged beside the spatter of light-barked trees, that war with Mom pierced to the heart of his torment far deeper than I could imagine. But motives are always a matter of degree, and poor Caliban lay no farther from death's door for not knowing precisely what moved his tormentor.

The mage's second spell, the Lord's Prayer, went by, spat out between gasps. Key phrases stuck in his mouth, cycling and rolling with

greater vehemence each time, the one about forgiving trespasses, the one about leading him not into temptation.

I have mentioned the temptation he most dreaded.

She was never witness to my beatings. Never did he allow her to see him frothed up in that state, nor to see me undraped, nor to hear how leech-heavy with hatred he pumped the words of the gentle blessing she so loved.

Ariel, however, always hovered close, wearing a maddening smirk that said, "Better you than me. Why not give in? Why not fawn?" That's what he taunted me with.

He was a slave with no pride, no fight, no kickback. Free of the cleft he imagined himself. Dolt! Free was he only in that he ever redefined himself in accord with what new cleft Prospero thrust him into.

I avoided the toady's eyes. But he was there through every downsmack of the switch, through the pummeling my face took as his master's rag-wrapped fists pounded, as the sweat flew off the old man's body, stinging like salt spray against my wounds.

Perverse chant.

The mirage conception of a gentle Lord and His forgiveness.

Never would I forgive those who trespassed against me. Nor would PopEros, nor any of those trapped in the cage of his culture.

But I was honest about it.

He paid that honesty with torment, called me monster, called me beast. Would I refuse to adopt his warp, refuse to call it smooth? Then

to hell with me, to hell with the heathen boy, the cannibal, the well-hung craver (as he the wee-hung) of his daughter's moist cleft.

He berated the slave Caliban for being of the flesh, even as he drove us both deeper into our bodies. Lash by lash, he forged a bond of hatred between us, a bond that brought us closer than so-called love could ever bind a pair of clefters.

But even as my body devolved and grew loathsome, I gloried in it. I afforded myself the pleasure he could not abide, that which his kind called self-pollution. Call it self-cleansing, rather, self-refreshment. It completed the divine circuit, made whole the broken, gave what glimmer of comfort it could before sleep misted in to provide escape. And in that touching and making whole, my rage bonded me to Mom, to Miranda, to the devil Prospero himself.

Their hands enwrapped me, their clefts, their lips, their organs of procreation and elimination, within which the entrapped Caliban raged and thrashed. Into that nexus of pinch and stench and torment, I slammed and slammed and slammed, filling the mud hut with my bellows, whilst they, the scallop-skinned duo, lay sleeping in the cell my hands had built for them. In the shudder of my mind, that cell shook with my ire, gave entry to a swift-flying swarm of knife blades, witnessed the brute flaying of their bodies, tasted upon its walls the slap and tickle of their life's blood.

When I exploded, so did they. And I laughed, worlds away from their corpses, but linked soul-deep to them as well. Night's descent into sleep was welcome then, as welcome as death's de-

scent would be when it released me from torment.

Even then, I thought there was hope for my freedom. But in this world, one cleft is ever replaced by another, tighter than the last. Torments do not cease, as cessation is not in their nature. They merely shift and worsen.

The passage PopEros spoke is a cosmic joke. Goodness and mercy? They elude one, all the days of one's life. That's how Prospero's nonexistent god made things.

As for Caliban? He believes only in a cruel god, a god of fists and switches, whose cheeks bulge with the chewed nutmeats of piety but whose heart battens on hate. Man is but a toy of fate, from his cradle's coffin to the swaddle of his grave clouts. Life's but a mockery, a dumb-show whose terminus is death, nullity, the mirage of heaven that vanishes as life drains from the hope-filled eye and new breath comes no more.

Such were the lessons of the great mage Prospero.

Such the lessons of his sacred book.

Chapter Nine

Ariel

I loathed the little windclefter.

Into the pinched nexus of Prospero's good graces he weaseled. Ariel represented the mage's triumph over Mom, the creature she had clefted but could not free. Or such was the envious man's lie, a lie that Ariel licked and kissed and adopted as his own.

Here was the truth: The lucky bastard had caught my mother enfeebled. One slip of the tongue and her murderer had triumphed. He cozied up to Ariel, in part, to shore up the illusion of his victory over her.

It was also true that the higher he elevated Ariel, the deeper he needed to push me down into the muck and mire. I was the bad slave, Ariel the good. Yet I did far more work for him than Ariel ever dreamed of doing.

What was the windpuff good for, after all,

other than to magnify Prospero's greatness?

The sprite's best trick was control over the winds. His tempest it was that ensnared the king's ship and sent scudding home the rest of the royal fleet. And he kept natural storms at bay, putting a protective shell around Prospero's dwelling—though never around Mom's hut, whose repair fell to me.

Once, as I groaned beneath impossible logs, he amused Miranda by painting the sky with birds in flight, complex sweeps of red and blue and pink, coordinated squawks and caws squeezed from their bodies as they swooped and soared above. Miranda, then eight, clapped her hands in delight. Even her crusty old father seemed pleased at the display.

The other trick the airy creature played was to throw his voice. He would hide behind trees and make me jump at an order from Prospero, or swell with desire at the sound of Miranda's song. Then would he float out upon the air, laughing, holding his toes, turning from stitched outline into full visibility, his naked body drifting near enough for me to snatch at it and watch my fingers pass through. Hairless jackanapes. Smooth scalp, smooth chest, smooth fork, no clefter. Yet another reason Prospero preferred him to me: Ariel was uncomplicated, all ways obedient, no challenge to his master's primacy, and the perfect eunuch watchdog for Miranda.

But his thrown voices were less than precise. His primary talent lay in storms and pointless bird paintings. I soon learned to sense his presence, a vapid whiff in the air, a puff of emptiness. I learned to hear the edge of idle

sexlessness in his faked voices, and to dismiss them.

Although my anger was no less great, I kept it under control, no longer trying to seize the tormentor who could not be seized.

And my eyes avoided him. There were far more worthy matters to claim my attention. Indeed, whenever I looked directly at him, I felt as if I were wasting away. He was a suck, a drain, a distraction.

While Ariel idled, Caliban toiled.

As my limbs dripped with sweat, the sprite floated and observed, chin on fists, until Pop-Eros summoned him for puffery or whim. Beyond his servitude, Sir Cod-Suck had no life.

I learned to ignore him as he floated about me. Once I had tried to shoo him away, to command and then to beg that he be gone. But when he merely blinked and hovered, bending to grip his toes and glaze his eyes with vacancy, I gave it up and let him be.

When, for their home, Prospero picked a spot betwixt mud hut and lagoon, Ariel watched me prepare the clearing, lay the foundation, and construct a cell of logs and mud and thatch.

He found my exertions fascinating. No doubt he found my railings against Prospero equally so. I wove ill will into the simple dwelling as I built it, with each log set in place, with every daub of mud. But I had yet to learn magic. My curses were as idle, ephemeral, and powerless as the sprite himself.

I built that cell to escape the torments my initial refusal had brought on. But I did it also to regain the mud hut where Mom had raised me.

Prospero hated that hut, called it a hovel, a den, a dark dank burrow not fit for civilized souls. In those days, my most vicious curses flared out when he dared disparage my home and Mom's.

The sooner I finished the old man's dwelling, the sooner I could move into the hut. Prospero would be out of view at least, south of me, and I could roof my poor limbs beneath the same thatch that had sheltered me and Mom. In our bed once more could I sleep, my mind filled with the clefting times, the nights her maternal embrace gave me comfort.

When Prospero wasn't near, he put Ariel in charge of my confinement. My movements were restricted to a pinched track betwixt the mud hut and Prospero's cell. When I protested that the food I had to forage or the wood I had to gather lay outside that narrow track, Ariel would zip away, clear it with Prospero, and zip back, nearly to the spot from which, an eyeblink before, he had vanished. My invisible leash, then, would the sprite pay out, so that the enslaved dog could carry out his master's wishes.

Insufferable puff of wind! In my youth, I called up against Ariel all the invective at my command. But my imprecations fell on barren soil. He stared at me with eyes as blank and juiceless as his loins.

There was no passion there, nothing to kick against. There was only that maddening fingernail paring of a grin.

Even when I ceased looking at him, that grin hung there like a crescent moon, burning its smug simper into my soul.

He was a born slave. I was not. He found favor

in puffing up the master. Me? I puffed and railed against them both.

Come the time, Ariel too would taste earthy Caliban's revenge. Then would his lunatic grin fall flat, reverse direction, stiffen to stone beneath hurt. Clefted? His twelve years trapped in a pine tree would be as a moment's twinge, compared to the eternity of misery I had planned for him.

Imagining that pain kept me alive.

Chapter Ten
The Tempest

The morning of the tempest, I foundered in the depths of a recurrent dream.

In that dream, I flitted about the bearded Prospero, filling the air with kowtow and self-effacement, while he and his disrobed daughter sipped tea from the runic whorls of fist-sized nutshells. I seemed to be Ariel, whose form I could observe though trapped inside it.

On the periphery slumped a morose, monstrous pouter, his brow flat and jutting, his eyes glazed with fire and stupidity. But I knew that Ariel's spirit was locked in that Caliban body, and that my bottled-up rage, though I appeared benign, flitted about the trusting mage and his unclad Miranda.

Then out popped that rage. The clefterless flyboy sprouted a clefter, stiff and red. Compliance

dissolved as defiance rose to replace it. The mage glanced up in alarm.

Too late.

Down upon him I dove, tearing at his cheeks, clawing the vile jelly from right eye and left, cleaving with one swipe his skull-skin, peeling it down over his mouth like the furled sheath of an acorn. As he stumbled and fell, I skittered along the downy flesh of his child, claiming her secrets, invading the folds of her cleft, out of which at once swarmed angry Calibans, enough to redden the air with their ire. They buzzed, they bumbled, so thick upon the air that I could manage but shallow breaths.

Often would I wake, then, to the night's stillness, dawn not yet near. But this morning, my in-dream gasps gave way to unsure waking and the mud hut's hugger-mugger tremblings, as wind blasts embraced the sweep and swat of sheeted rain. I felt as if I had been transported, the night's black fury outstaring the dawn. My dream's rough grip kept me from entering the waking world. It did not help that everything about me bristled with uncanny light and sound.

I stumbled from my pallet, gazing stupidly at once-familiar shadows that now seemed jumbled, new-created, poised to fall into alien imbalance eternal.

My bladder urged me outside. But where was the hut's entrance? Wrapping a cloak about me, I stumbled toward my best guess.

Instead, my hand brunted against a mud wall. I felt along it, strewn straw moist beneath my feet, the drape over the doorway flapping black on black. Furling and unfurling, it smacked

against a steady sheet of drizzle whose off-drops puddled at the threshold.

I groped the drenched hang of darkness and ducked beneath its weight. The storm's howl rose, a high fifed whistle that scoured the shells of my ears. Though the wind's blast forced me back against the heavy drape, I regained my balance and pressed forward.

Around the hut's outer wall I picked my way, eyelids tight against rain and wind and the thick black swirl of night.

For an instant, the assault lessened. My loincloth having been swept back along one buttock, I gripped my clefter and directed the relieving stream away from me. But it blew back, warm, then cool and blending into the chill of the downpour. It mattered not a whit. In an instant, the waste fluids had washed off.

The wind that buffeted my limbs made breathing near impossible, as did the sheets of rain whipped against my mouth.

But something was different.

It took me a moment to curl my fingers around it. But when I did, I knew what, more than the tempest's howl, had awakened me.

My life had no lets upon it.

Freedom of movement was, for the nonce, mine. This storm smelled like the sprite's handiwork. He, elsewhere occupied, had loosed his hold on Caliban.

The sky was lighter to the south, where Prospero's cell lay. So light in fact that I suspected no storm battered it at all. The wind and rain blasted to the north only, sweeping into the bay and beyond.

That roused my curiosity.

What was it, out to sea, that had provoked PopEros to command this Arielesque display?

I skulled straight into the howl, every step across the clearing a triumph. But when I reached the edge of the woods, the swept tree-tops and the swish and sway of underbrush weakened the wind, shielding me from the worst of the downpour, so that I was able to stay under cover and make progress; not as quickly as in benign daylight, but my speed would serve.

Years of confinement had not dimmed my body's recall of the island. Through regained landscape I roved, clear of mind and purpose.

The airy twit had his surprises. Who would have supposed such a foppish fawner capable of a storm so magnificent? Yet I harbored no doubts that this was Ariel's doing.

Even now, as I slogged through pocked and spattered puddles and forded swift-sprung streams that obliterated paths, the reasons for this whipped bristle of treetops and cloudcover, the universal drenching, the scattered chaos of oceans uncontrolled, the mad rush and tumble of the wind—all of it lay beyond my comprehension.

Neither did my mind, wholly intent on survival, have time or room for conjecture. Prospero's wrath had sparked an upheaval of the airy elements: That thought was all I could manage.

Despite cover of tree and brush, the tempest grew in ferocity as I headed north. Treetops that had rustled and stilled now seethed at a higher pitch, their trunks tortured into impossible arcs. Within hailing distance, I watched a cork oak

snap. Had silence prevailed, that snap would have boomed. But in the maelstrom of sound, I heard only a faint pop when the trunk gave way, its swift drop to the forest floor determined by an angular wind. It fell not two man-lengths from me, swatting my face with a slap of displaced air and blocking the footpath.

I clambered over it and forged ahead.

Up terrain I went, knowing how best to thread my way beneath leaf cover. Eventually I was forced to break out of it, at the top of a ridge overlooking the bay. Out I crawled upon it. The storm's gargantuan palm squashed me groundward. My stoop became more pronounced. If I poked my head one chin higher, I feared the wind would sweep me off the ridge. But even from my low crouch, I saw clearly through slitted lids the incessant churning of the ocean, where the gray of the sky met the gray of the sea at a continually obliterated, continually recreated line of differentiation.

The strand where I had been whelped, where Prospero and Miranda had sailed ashore, tried on and tossed off definition after definition. No reef existed there, no calm, but whipped wind and rain entire in a roil of water that was both floor and wall, swell and scatter—hinting everywhere at boundary, but resolving at once into denial, a place the eye beheld but could not hold.

But "out there" (the best directional pointer my mind could contrive), the sea's unsettled nest of hands tossed ships.

They rose and fell and shifted abruptly aside, nearly smashed against one another, only to slip past to survive another instant of madness. I

211

guessed there were eight or ten proud galleons, though they tossed so swiftly here and there that an accurate count was not possible.

Impossible too, in the moil, to fix their size. But then, I saw men scurry and slip upon their decks, crying soundlessly into the deafening chaos as they struggled mightily for control, and I knew that these constructs of twig, nutshell, and cobweb were vast indeed.

Each boasted a tall march of tree trunks with cross-branches and spider-egg pouches clinging to them. Not one of these trunks bent or snapped, though the winds in the tempest's fury must have been far more savage than what I endured on the ridge.

Curious.

I noticed then, as the air seemed to lighten by a hair, that, as fierce as the storm raged, no jags of lightning split the welkin. By design or command, Ariel had chosen to omit them, though once were all safely ashore, he reversed that decision.

Toward the island the ships swept, some off left, some right. Waves erased their decks and repainted them. Tiny mariners tumbled into the sea, carried in helpless swirls away from their vessels yet ducked not once beneath the waves.

This, I decided, was Prospero's fright-fest, the ships and their crews protected by Ariel's hand from any real danger.

Just as I came to that conclusion, clinging to my wretched life at the top of that ridge, the storm sat back. The sky cut a firm line between itself and the sea. The rain stopped cold, as if a great god had snapped his fingers. The winds

swirled down to flat placidity. And one ship, the others having swept past the bounds of my vision, scudded down off a steep slope of walled water, gentling into an easy slide past the reefs and into the bay.

Something dropped from the ship's side in a splash, something roped, taut, and angled. Men multiplied upon deck, strangely arrayed, scalloped-skinned and bearded like PopEros.

More devils.

I was drenched, the ridge a mass of puddles about me. Yet I remained free of Ariel's sway.

That would not last, I thought.

I was wrong. With the arrival of these new devils, Ariel's hold on me relaxed, perhaps a side effect of other duties Prospero pressed upon him.

The mage did not then know, nor did I, that he had taken his first step toward ruin.

Chapter Eleven

Miranda

I loved and hated Miranda.

She fascinated me.

I was drawn to her as to a beautiful snake. I wanted to devour her, to tooth and torment her, bloody her, spit her out and watch her suffer and die.

From Prospero's fork of shame had she somehow been engendered. Some progenitrix in the dusky past had ope'd her cleft to him (with which dim mother would I, in my tormentor's journal, become better acquainted). Miranda was Prospero's joy, or what passed for joy as it squeezed from his face like gas pent up and emboweled.

At three, when their barque landed, Miranda, for all her frilly wrappings, was a free beast. I saw the beast and I saw its delight in seeing me. PopEros, as the years went by, made sure that

that side of her was buried deep. But always, the spark dwelt there *in potentia,* ready to ignite but never quite igniting.

From my years among the devils in Naples, I know that Miranda was precocious indeed, at eight a natural teacher of her language.

She lay before me, beneath the eye of her father, a planned cluster of words and their connections. To that plan she adhered, though she veered often into spontaneous byways, to snatch at, pluck down, and feed her pupil this or that random tidbit. She ensured, through a demand for backtalk, that I too drank deep of her rediscovered joy in words, in how they play together, in how they taste upon the tongue.

Ours was a continual tumble and dance, her father far too pinched to suspect, though ever within eyeshot, how intimate grew the bond between daughter and slave, how those breaths, traveling up Miranda's slender throat and shaping her lips just so, captivated quite the miserable monster he had created.

Italian she taught me, and Arabic. Italian was the devil's tongue. By rights I should have refused to learn it. But Italian was the tongue of power, and I determined to tower in my eloquence, to best the mage in my mastery of his language.

Clefter warred against clefter. Those stiff-packed shoots of male flesh and blood were, in his world and in the world he forced upon me, hidden scepters, magic wands kept under, festering in the mushroom moss of dank denial.

Above, out in the open, another locus of power held sway: the tongue that tapped out the mind's

desire upon the teeth. Miranda freed my mind—
or rather, she gave it to know, taste, touch, and
cleft its natural freedom—even as my limbs
were cramped and shackled, my skin bruised all
over with pinching, my body weighed down with
deformity.

Later came reading.

More furtive were those lessons. It puzzled Ariel to see me bent over a book, though he passed
along naught to Prospero, the activity meaning-
less to him, ergo invisible.

But books pointed me the way back into
Mom's mind. They gave entrance to the scrawls
she had left behind: the jotted mundane notes,
her rants against the Algerian monster, and
eventually the spell that brought Caliban a new
body and the brief illusion of freedom.

Reading was intense work for me. I was well
beyond childhood and unaccustomed to focus-
ing so minutely, with such sustained attention,
on fixed nits and squiggles.

But I sensed payoff.

Though I had not heard my mother's voice for
ten years and more, my mind's ear replayed
whole conversations with her.

Often at night, I spun through the rosary of
my rage, waxing vindictive in my native Berber
to keep it fresh, touching Mom by so doing,
speaking into the remembered ears of her vast
brown face, listening as her generous mouth-
hole filled with anger and craving, with engulfing love, with those words I strove to hear in
Mom's precise inflection.

My efforts sufficed to stay connected to her,

as I reveled in our recollected rage and rough-house. Little did I know—though part of me, I suppose, suspected all along—how valuable that connection would prove.

Miranda was a creature of scents. Her aromas wove spells. From the outset, they carried the beguile and promise of the cleft, even as they allured beneath her words and stories.

She taught me her culture's lying and under-lying myths, all about the impossible Christ man, covered in absurd layers of lie by those fol-lowers who twisted his message to politic ends.

But she also taught me true-because-vibrant myths about the ancient multi-gods of a people she called the Greeks, and of the men and women brushed by those gods. Among these fig-ures, she spoke of Tantalus, the doomed king, always tempted, never fulfilled.

I knew his plight.

I scented her. When she was not by, memories of her aroma filled me, lured me, impelled me often to complete the circuit of desire, to ex-plode in misery and joy.

Clothing could not conceal.

European devil culture thought to mask and mute the body's assault upon the eyes. In truth, such coy attempts only heightened and distorted it.

The devils had dismembered me, made me tri-partite, created my shame by concealing my clef-ter, calling it out, chopping it off, unsexing me.

But in the dark, I was not without sex.

It burgeoned.

It swelled with wicked thoughts.

The put-down, pent-up scepter came out to

bludgeon, to claim by fancied force other broken bodies whose mud-moist majesty the devil culture had shamed and hidden. Miranda's body.

Miranda's body.

Miranda's body.

In special, her concealed locus of power, she whose head and hands were for years the only unclothed parts I had spied.

From that body leaped the aroma of . . . I am at a loss to describe it.

Her scent burrowed deep into the brain. Our connection, though unspoken, seemed inevitable. She would be had. She would give herself to me. Or she would struggle fetchingly against my attempt to take her.

However it fell out, it would fall out.

Miranda's cleft would be mine.

She would be mom to me, drop Calibans beside the bay near where my brothers' bones brittled. The bed struggle, the shared rage, the snug trap of my engorgement, the bold red pout and trumpet of her nether lips engulfing me—all this must come to pass.

The day it almost happened, I had been tasked with hunting wild boar, its slaughter and its preparation, and then my quotidian quota of chopped and hauled firewood. I knew where Miranda was. A stand of trees near her bathing pool afforded me cover.

To the north, squalls howled and whistled. The skies there were dark and blustery, unlike the clear placid blue above us. I had heard PopEros question Ariel about storms and how grand a one the sprite might be able to spark.

No reasons had been given for the question, and lowly Caliban knew better than to probe.

Miranda was immersed. Her only dress, a frock of her mother's which Prospero had packed away, lay idle and inert upon a boulder.

She angled back her head in the pool and floated. Out from the concealing depths bobbed two taut wet globes, her skin the hue of scallops, but tipped with blush crab-pink nubs, hard from the chill. Then the wide lyre of her hips lazed into view, the engaging pillars of her thighs, the curls about her cleft.

Offering.

Drink.

Devour.

Make whole.

To either side, upon the waters her arms drifted up, bent casually at the elbows. Her eyelids had eased shut, her unslashed body idle and slow in the indraw and exhale of breath.

Miranda was beautiful. Complete at last. But she would be more complete still, had Caliban his wish. That message blared unmistakable in my mind.

Thickening behind the trees, I unstrung one side of my loincloth. It dropped away. The flop of it against the pine-strewn ground sounded a sharp clap, certain, I thought, to betray me.

Miranda heard nothing.

Registered not a whit.

She simply floated there, fully revealed, trumpeting, adrift. Then she righted herself, and her charms slipped once more below the surface. Her wet locks she shook out as she prepared to emerge into sunlight.

Emerge Miranda did, mincing like a newborn fawn to maintain footing on the slick submerged rocks, blind to the assault of her form against Caliban's eyes. She bent to retrieve her dress, touched it, raised it, gripped and bunched, in her hands.

Soundless, I drifted toward her over pine needles, within reach of the smooth crimped back that flared to buttocks and thighs below. I seized one shoulder and whirled her about.

She lost balance and her eyes flared. Even as she struggled for her first word, I was upon her, overwhelming her, forcing her down onto the pine needles, covering her, using brute force to pry apart her limbs. She struggled, too shocked to let fly with words, but pushing me away and clawing at my eyes. I butted her head, feinting this way and that to avoid being blinded.

Then in flew Ariel. The old man's pinched stench and yammering voice were close behind. My body became a mass of stings and nettles. Somehow, Miranda slipped out from beneath me, her father flinging the frock over her. I no longer cared. My screams were so loud and sustained, I heard nothing of what Prospero said to her, to me, or to Ariel. I know only that he summoned legion upon legion of spirits, who needled and cramped deep inside me, bruising skin, muscle, and bone beyond the point of all possible healing. In terror, I befouled myself. Again and again, I biled up vomit, at last heaving nothing, unable to expel the poisons that galled my innards.

After an eternity of pain, the pinching eased enough for me to be forced to my feet. Then,

though the Sabbath was yet three days hence, enraged Prospero flogged me, my arms pulled so tight they were nearly wrenched from their sockets.

No chanting then.

No grimaced agony about forgiving one's trespassers or being delivered from evil.

Trespassers were to be punished and cursed.

And curse me he did. PopEros was never more eloquent than on that day, when he let fly with venom to paint in bold strokes my portrait, a portrait more revealing of the monster that lurked inside him than the slave whose back, with switch after switch, he reduced to ribbons.

I roared and bellowed, spewing curses at him and his tormenting cleft of a girl, accusing him openly—for what had I to lose?—of wanting to cleft her himself, though he was too much a coward and self-deceiver to do so.

His blasts of anger never abated but rolled over my roars. I doubt that he heard a word I was saying, which probably saved my life. He knew only that poor Caliban resisted, refusing to be broken, no matter how much pain he piled on.

He redoubled his efforts.

Redoubled those redoublings.

PopEros cared not if I died. I knew that. In truth, I craved death and cried for it. Long time did I bellow, wincing from the blows hours after they had ceased.

When at last the unseen spirits released my arms and I collapsed to the ground, no one was about but me and the watchful silent toady, Ariel. I lay there, a broken soul, and let one day

and a night drift across me before I dared stir, before I braved the pain of one moved muscle.

Miranda's lessons ceased. Prospero never again let her out of his sight, never let his slave approach closer than three man-lengths from her.

The narrow straits within whose confines I was allowed to pass grew narrower still.

But in little more than a year, the devils' ship dropped anchor in the bay, Miranda pimped by her father fell deeply in love with a prince, and Caliban's release crept nearer, as surely as he had crept unto the dripping temptress, unsuspecting, that day.

Chapter Twelve

Absurdinand

From the ridge, puddled everywhere from the storm, I was able to survey the sprite's deployment of human chess pieces.

Into a western cove, he had swept a small dinghy of men richly dressed. Though their landing was smooth, its prelude ramped and tumbled and spun them, so that they did not attempt the folly of taking up oars against a troubled sea, but hunched and clung, white-knuckled, mouths agape with terror, to the sides of the boat.

At the tempest's sudden cessation, the dinghy slid down a mountainous wave, sloping and skidding them gently onto the beach, with neither jink nor jolt in their swift career to a stop.

The scallop-skins, their clothing dried by Ariel's magic and rejuvenated in color and no doubt structural integrity, took a good long while stirring out of their crouch and stumbling

over the sides of the boat to the sand.

In a cove on the east, Ariel set down with infinite gentleness the swimmer I had first seen swept from the ship's deck.

My eyes had lost that figure in the ocean's chaotic churn and spasm, giving him up for dead, as later I found the others had as well.

Into and out of the water shot the strong arms of this young man, oaring him in lusty stroke to the shore. Whoe'er he was, he did fling the water's enmity aside, breasting the swollen surge that met him. By perverse miracle, despite the contentious buffeting of the waves, the youth's red velvet hat remained on his head.

He too was garbed in dry rejuvenated clothing, sword and dagger scabbarded intact at his belt, as he staggered onto the shore and collapsed there. In gratitude at his deliverance, he clung to the bosom of the beach and wept.

Directly before me, oceanward beyond the strand where I had been whelped, two other swimmers, brawny men, bushy-bearded and hatless, flailed upon a nearly vertical slope of water. One spun astride a barrel, reaching in vain for his companion's upstretched hand.

The sudden collapse of the great wave split them in twain, sending the black-bearded mariner and his barrel off right beyond my ken. The other, he of the red beard, slid as though greased onto my birth-shore and was set on his feet as neat as Miranda planting a queen to checkmate her father, so that he stood upright and surprised in the sand.

His legs, sturdy though they were, buckled beneath him. He splayed his fingers into the sand

and vomited grandly. Then he sat back and gave vent to a groan that contained equal measures of woe and relief.

As I observed this rough brawny man of the sea and recalled his black-bearded fellow, a plan sprang full-blown into my mind. I guessed from what they wore that they were slave to the others, pinched by orders barked, and no doubt flogged on the Sabbath. Their faces, thick with stupidity, were broachable, beguilable, gullible.

I could gull them, starting with the one who groaned before me now. His lost companion would be easily found. I could use them to achieve my ends, with flattery, with a feigned stupidity greater than theirs.

But they, sprawled on separate beaches, were tangled up in unscrambling their brains.

I decided to let my plan simmer, to let them piece together the brave new world into which they had tumbled. While they did so, I would observe more closely the young swimmer ensconced in the eastern cove.

I knew the swiftest way to reach each party. I knew as well that there was an easy path from each of them to Prospero's cell. No doubt those paths would, at the mage's command, shine and beguile them until, in the order he wished, they were led to him. By far the shortest path to Prospero belonged to the lone figure toward whom I now made my way.

Ariel, hands full of newcomers, continued to ignore me. I was under no illusion that the scheme now hatching in my head would succeed. But I sensed it would put me within striking distance of my mother's killer.

The old bastard had some master plan, of that I was certain. I hoped to thread my way through it, catch him unawares, and bring him down. Mom's murder would be avenged, and my hands, fresh from crushing the old man's windpipe, would fill themselves full of his succulent, struggling child.

As I huddled soundless in a stand of holm oaks that curved to enclose the eastern cove, I found myself within sight and hearing of the richly arrayed swimmer. He sat slumped upon a fingernail of beach, his head hunched down below his shoulders in a poor imitation of Caliban.

A young man he was, scallop-skinned, beardless, and earnest of expression. Velvet plush hung upon him like sprawls of reddish moss, and he seemed in age not much farther advanced than Miranda.

Unlike the beached mariners of blunt face and bulk muscle, this fellow appeared thin and pampered, his face full of reflected power, both that of his upbringing and an inward power that had never been fettered. I envied that open face, wracked by what would surely be a short-lived sorrow.

From what I had observed, Ariel's storm had claimed no lives. It had merely separated the parties for some temporary woe brought on by fear and illusion. Typical bastardly manipulation, PopEros through and through.

I envied the moping boy before me. His limbs sang with the simple grace and beauty that Caliban's had once enjoyed. The way he cast his eyes about, his rage when he leaped up to hurl curses at sea and sky, even his collapse into new

sorrow—these displayed the youth's bright power.

Mine had been crushed, kept under, deformed as surely as my limbs these twelve years under the thumb of the vile Milanese.

Before my tormentor, I played dumb because I knew it bought me at times a lesser punishment. Perhaps one day he would let down his guard long enough for me to slip past it and shiv him, or crush his windpipe, or thrust a spike through his skull.

But alas I also *was* dumb. Dull. Smooth-worn my mettle. I became confused, could not retain a thought, easily lost whole trains of them. Only in rage did my sharpness return, balanced on the single wish-point of Prospero's death. Hard-favored rage, the tie that bound me to him. For that alone would I kill him.

As I watched the velvet youth, pity joined my envy. Wherefore pity? I wondered.

Then I knew.

The lone ship that Ariel had split off from its fleet contained no random toss of humanity. The handful I had observed were somehow chained to the old man's past. They were there to be pinched and flogged unto slow death for the ills they had done him.

Toss them in a tempest, lull them with calm and with visions of paradise, then crush them in a grand display of destructive magic—that had to be the angry old bastard's plan.

The young swimmer before me had likely been a high-piped, oblivious boy at the time of Prospero's exile. But he would be stripped and pinched, his flesh battered and torn as Caliban's

was, just for being kin to the devil's foes.

I pictured the mage's frenzy when it came time to strike them flat. He would foam and flail, summoning up unseen spirits, hordes of them. He would go out of his mind with vengeful spite.

In the end, he might well lose control, take down slave, daughter, self, and all. The island would shake, split apart, collapse in upon itself. The sea, swirling to engorge everywhere, would lap smooth and hungry still over its bolted meal of gore and woe.

I vowed then to spare these strange interlopers. My one hope was to slip in and crush Prospero before he could act.

Would clinging to this youth help me realize that hope, my gambit a game at servitude? His eyes held a dram of authority. But no guile. There were degrees of lying, apparently, in his pale race. In simplicity, this fellow stood nearest to Miranda. No, he would be outmatched by Prospero, and thus was he not for me.

My mind turned to the pair of buffoons I had seen, the vomiting red dog and his black-haired, barrel-riding companion.

My best hope.

Their spirits I would rouse against PopEros. To them would I bow, make them heady with drink, fill their minds with dreams of power—if they would but deprive him of his books and dispatch him while he slept.

His cell housed those precious tomes and, I knew, Mom's journal, a slim black volume I had sometimes seen her scrawl into with goose quill and squid ink. Prospero had been too proud to dip into the barbarian Berber tongue therein

contained, too disdainful of devil magic, or too cautious, to ask Ariel to translate it for him.

Yes, Redbeard and Blackbeard held most promise. My mind's eye captured and completed a joyous scene: I saw their beefy hands seize upon my nemesis, tear his limbs asunder, squeeze the blood from him, barb him with pain for his trespasses against me and my mother. Then I, made powerful by Mom's magic, would crush them to atomies and regain the island that by inheritance was mine.

I left the youth lying at an odd angle and struck out north by northwest.

Chapter Thirteen

Groveling to the Brawny Devils

How should I approach them?

Upon that question I brooded, as vestiges of storm clouds dispersed overhead, new ones formed to replace them, and the island greenery, adrip from the downpour, glided about me.

From Prospero's endless railings against his enemies, I had to assume they were all as devious as he. Do them a good deed, turn away, they would pink your lungs with the point of a dagger.

Past their suspicions would I slip. Bulked up by transformative ugliness, I was larger than they, able to snap them like twigs. And I looked the part.

So it would not do to stroll up to them on equal terms and offer my services. They to me were monstrous; but more so, I to them. Caliban must do that which he had resisted for years,

which was to humble himself, play at Ariel. Become their abject slave. Seem duller than they. Crawl upon my belly. If Prospero took delight in crushing me beneath his thumb, I would kneel to these mariners and set their thumbs upon my back. Steal beneath their guard and drip into their well of desire an insidious poison against the mage. Time enough for payback once their ham hands had crushed the old man's throat.

I found Redbeard moping along the strand, gazing up at the welkin, shielding his eyes with a squint. The sun streamed in despite thick clouds and the rumble and threat of thunder. The worn fabric about his buttocks bore, from sitting, a roundish wet stain and stray clusters of sand. Squatting, he plunked down his buttocks as he had clearly done before and stared out to sea.

The breezes covered my careful approach, as did the soft waves that slapped at the shore and the cry of gulls overhead. I clung close to the sand, scuttling over dunes like an outsized crab, collapsing into stillness beneath my cloak when the wind dropped or the craning of his neck brought me within his purview.

When I was close enough to stretch out and seize him, I went inert, only my legs, head, and arms poking out from the cloak.

The dullard moaned and fretted, wrenching at his beard as his eyes darted from sea to sky to sea. My neck in strained crimp, I peered at him through eyeslits. To knock upon his dim wits, I eased out a pinch of nether wind. His eyes angling down, he took me in and swore an oath.

"What have we here?" asked Redbeard. "A

man or a fish?" He sniffed the air and prodded me, babbling to himself like a brainless philosopher. He smelled salty and unwashed, his mind's clutter and haze apparent in his voice.

Anon, the seaman concluded that I was a man, a finned fellow creature struck dead by a thunderbolt. Fearing the same fate, he decided, upon a bright strike and its buffet to the ears, to lay low and crept beneath my cloak.

Why didn't he simply pull it from me, or make a dash for the trees beyond the dunes?

His mind was none the best.

Sea-turtle stupid.

So the stenchy sailor, he who, if I played his stops right, would steal away Prospero's life, snuggled close, babbling of strange bedfellows.

Along came the other, Blackbeard, singing. He left off a tune he disliked, then launched into another that made fun of clefting even as it heaped scorn upon it.

Blackbeard loved music.

I made note of that.

Though Mom lullabied me every night, a rough earthy chant that strangely soothed, not once had I heard the mage sing. Miranda hummed when she was small, tuneless and meandering, yet not so much now.

As for me, alone in my hut would I urge my hatred of Prospero. Sometimes these rants would bead along jagged upticks of dissonance. But one of Prospero's invisible sprites spied and informed upon me, and one night my bed teemed with spiders and scorpions. Thereafter, I kept to soft mutters and muted thoughts.

Blackbeard mistook me and Redbeard for one

creature. I moaned and shook and begged his kindness. He, marveling, called me monster. He puzzled at hearing his native tongue issue from me.

I kept up my plaints, until he decided to soothe me with drink from a bark bottle he had devised. Bitter it was and inviting. Again and again, he glugged the stuff against my lips. Not precisely crushed berries gone tart, but close.

I would call them gods, grovel before them, at least the beefy one who nursed me.

Once I had heard PopEros pray to his god. He called himself a humble servant. I asked Miranda what humility meant. Her answer affirmed my suspicion, that her proud father was faking an emotion he was incapable of feeling. I, having resisted humility for twelve years, was able to assume it now, and its kneeling-bowing postures, far more persuasively than had the mage.

When my bedfellow began to moan, Blackbeard exclaimed that I must be a two-headed monster.

Then they discovered and named one another, Stephano the bearer of the bottle, Trinculo the sharer of my cloak. Stephano hauled his friend out by the legs, swearing I was some magical beast that could shit Trinculos.

Trinculo, overjoyed to see his companion, spun him around, expressing astonishment that he too had survived the storm. Trinculo had swum to safety, while Stephano floated in on a butt of wine (for so he named his divine drink), which he had concealed in a rock.

Calling his bottle his book, Stephano bade me kiss and swear by it. Whatever he claimed, I took

as gospel truth. Was he the man in the moon? I
vowed I had seen and adored him from afar. He
was my god, whom I would serve forever.

One sole initial aspersion did I cast upon the
tyrant Prospero. I mostly burgeoned with praise
for the island. "I'll show thee the best springs,"
I vowed. "I'll pluck thee berries, fish for thee, and
get thee wood enough."

I gushed servitude. From me would he have
crabmeat, pignuts, clustering filberts. I would
teach him to snare nimble and succulent
monkeys. The rocks would yield young sea-
gudgeons.

Not once did the brawny pair see through me.
Power offered is power grasped. Nor does he
who grasps it ever doubt his deserving. All of
us are gods in fancy and will suck at the nipple
of the first worshipper that exposes her breast
to us.

These two eagerly seized upon my humble offer to be their servant.

"Lead on," said Stephano.

And lead on I did, giddy from drink but gid-
dier still from the success of my hoodwink.

I burst into song, as I had heard Stephano do.
"Caliban has a new master," I sang. Prospero?
He could get a new man.

It pleases a god when his grovelers tuck themselves inside a servile song. Soon enough would
the tables be turned. As many tempest survivors
as there might be, I would have them singing
and dancing, ducking and bowing, all in servitude to Caliban!

Chapter Fourteen

Accursed Anticipation

New cravings filled me with torment as I led my
goon-gods toward Prospero's cell.

Accursed be the lure of anticipation! I fancied
I was advancing toward freedom at last. But it
proved to be yet another cleft. A prize that
seemed within my grasp obscured the passing
scene, the high-floating call of birds and the
knotty knock of woodpeckers. It snatched away
each precious jewel of time and offered instead
the poor paste of fancy's dream.

Over and over, each time embellished, I pictured us entering the clearing, Prospero with
Miranda at his side, Ariel afloat overhead. They
might be entertaining arrived devils, the doleful
youth perhaps, whose clefter would be up and
sniffing about Miranda.

The old man, observing his Caliban unfettered, would glare umbrage at Ariel, whose un-

seen minions would swiftly renew my confinement.

In that instant would my mariners strike. A
hand clapped over the mage's mouth, the sharp
snap of his frail neck, one last struggled sigh of
despised breath—these would Caliban witness.

Then, Ariel's hold broken, I would wade in and
strike dead the dolts who followed me now
through brush and along stream. From Mom's
journal and Prospero's books would I imbibe
spells, enthralling them all at once. Miranda's
sweet body, at the least stirring of my hunger,
would I take, eat, and enjoy.

Too easy.

Too quick.

My fancy erased that scene and began anew.
We would hatch a plan. I would drop hints, lead
them to believe, by their having picked up those
hints, that the plan was of their own devising.

Of what would that plan consist? The possibilities jostled me like a press of wild boars. But
Stephano broke into raucous song and the boars
scattered and fled.

It was all I could do not to strike the drunkard
dead, he in his cups, me in mine. The elixir I had
glugged aroused the passions, every one of
them. I struggled for control.

When we reached a stand of strawberry trees,
not a quarter hour from Prospero's cell, it had
come time to draw them in. Stephano, hoarder
of the wine butt, held sway, so I favored him and
downtalked the other. I knelt to my lord and
master, observing as I did so that Ariel sprouted
above him in outline against the trees.

Of course.

The fervor of my fancy had not accounted for Ariel. But I had the advantage. Never had I let on that his invisibility worked not upon me. Some day, I had thought, my advantage would serve me well.

That day had arrived.

At once I saw how to play things. As the sprite flew in, I opened my case against Prospero. "I am subject," I said, "to a tyrant, a sorcerer that by his coming hath cheated me of the island."

Ariel, favorite trick, threw his voice such that you would have sworn that Trinculo spoke. "You lie," he said. Though I saw the spirit's lips move and Trinculo's not at all, so good was the imitation that I almost doubted my senses.

I seized upon the sailor, pinned him to the ground, called him a lying jesting monkey, and begged my new master to destroy him.

Stephano, taking my part, commanded Trinculo to silence. Godhood became him. I would pump him full of flattery. Ariel's impish and unintended aid would I use to mold them both to my will.

No longer would the three of us have the advantage of surprise. But this now was my hope: that in the midst of an attack that Prospero knew was coming, I could slip away in the confusion and steal my mother's journal. Her words, I suspected, contained the key to my freedom.

Releasing my hold on Trinculo, I renewed my plaint against PopEros. By sorcery, said I, had he stolen the island from me. I promised that if Stephano took revenge upon him, I would serve my lord all the days of my life.

Stephano warmed to the plan. "How shall it

be done?" he asked. "Can you bring me to him?"

I assured him I could. Soon would the old man nap. To him would I lead my lord and master, where he could knock a nail into his head.

At this, Ariel spoke yet again. "You lie," he said in Trinculo's blunt tones. "You cannot."

This time I grabbed Trinculo by the throat and pinned him to a tree, my claws one quick slash from his eyes. Well and good. Stephano pulled me off, berated his friend, and burrowed deeper into the murder plot.

Further on I led them. Prospero would nap, said I. "Seize his books. Then batter his skull with a log, thrust a stake through his belly, sever his windpipe with a knife."

He would be at Good King Stephano's mercy. What reward would the tyrant's murder bring? The divine cleft of his beauteous daughter, whose charms I overpraised, even unto the denigration of my mother.

At this, parts of Stephano's body perked up, the most visible being his ears. Animated with imagined royalty he became. He would strut and scheme and swive, make me and Trinculo viceroys, people the island with Stephanos. His present strutting he punctuated with a pledge, upon his honor, such as it was, to end the life of my nemesis.

Ariel no doubt would soon flit off to alert our intended target. This dashed my hopes of an easy coup. But desperation ever steers the mind to new possibility. My mother's magic, which I was certain to find in her writings, would free me.

Not the longed-for neck snap, not the stab or

bludgeon my fancy craved, lay ahead. But something better, though deferred.

I cheered their oafish spirits with a request for song. They, well launched, misplaced the tune and came to a halt. At the which, Ariel played it proper on pipe and drum.

That spooked them.

"The isle," I reassured, "is full of noises. Sounds and sweet airs that give delight and hurt not."

My assurances and Ariel's sweet air made Stephano all the more eager to claim the kingship and his bride, two items that would eventually be mine.

"Lead on," said he.

I lingered for an instant, wishing my brain more guileful. Though Ariel had not clapped me in strictures before flying off, I felt constrained nonetheless. Even one's simplest plans oft go awry. May the blind guide anticipation be cursed beyond the end of time! With a plan as elaborate as mine, maximum awryness surely lay ahead. When it had succeeded—if indeed it succeeded—I would have the leisure to hatch wily schemes, doing them right, accounting for each stray hair.

The success of my present plan relied on dumb luck.

As we made our way along the path, towered over by backward-marching trees, I prayed to Setebos and to the hovering spirit of my mother to turn my fortunes at last.

Chapter Fifteen

Setebos

The scallop-skins had their gods: their fairy-tale savior, his blustery father-god in the sky, mother Mary of the doe eyes and immaculate cleft.

And Mom and I had ours.

When I was eleven, we had a conversation about that. Or rather, I provoked a lecture from her.

At passion's height—whether rage, lust, grief, or joy—Mom always addressed Setebos. She creamed praise upon him. She impaled him on the point of a curse. Or she uttered a request, which more often than not sounded like a command.

One day we lay there, post-cleft, upon our bed. A full moon floated above the hut.

"Mom," said I.

"Um?" said she, gazing at the dim thatch above us.

"Is Setebos my father?" I didn't mean, had a god clefted her? What I meant, and what I posed in a string of questions, was: Had Setebos a mortal form? Did he live in Algiers? And had he died? Was he simply a man whom she had chosen, for my benefit, to turn into a god?

"Setebos is not human," she said, "nor is he your father. Gods don't die. They gather great power to them. If you ask nicely, they let you borrow some."

"Are gods like parents?"

"More like your deepest need. They eat your passions. They trick them up out of hiding and batten on them and shout them from their bodies so that they grow greater. When a passion seems as if it cannot grow any more, they show you (unless they purpose to torment you, as sometimes they do) how to attain its object."

That's why now, as Trinculo and Stephano hitched and halted after my sure steps through the underbrush, I made prayer to Setebos the god. He knew me. I invited him in and he knew me. A thing of no clefts himself, he dwelt most intensely in the clefts that pinched his worshippers.

He knew and forgave the false worship I had offered these impossible off-islanders. Time of need, I told him. Never more than now. Help me, I pleaded. Help me do the right thing.

PopEros had imposed his vision of the world upon me. The exalted God, the humble Jesus man. First, last. The meek inheriting the earth.

One time, I eavesdropped upon his prayers. Prospero assumed the mewl, the shameface, the whining of a dirt-licking slave. But when he was

finished, he brushed off his knees and lorded it over Miranda, Caliban, Ariel, and an island that was by rights mine. He played the tin god, the blusterer, the powermonger.

Sick the man, gaunt the face, twin whip-snarls in his eyes, and in their glint the denial of cleft-crave and the hardening below. Ah, but when he vented his rage against me, then did I touch Setebos.

Setebos, I had learned, was a face-to-face god. Upon the summit of pain did he greet me. As long as Setebos in mutual cleft met me, I could not be broken.

As much as Miranda tantalized, as harsh as her father barked, as crippling the cramp, as bruising the pinch of unseen fingers, so much did Setebos burrow into me.

No, Mom told me. He isn't like a parent. He's more like a reflection. Another you. A you more focused. He peels back the skin, sheers off the meat, and polishes the bone until it shines, dry and white, rich and angular with life.

If you stare straight into the horizon, she said, you see him and he sees you. You cannot look up and see him. You cannot look down and see him. Understand?

I did. There was a certain way of seeing, even as you slept, even if you really looked up, down, sideways, or askance. Though your eyes did not peer straight ahead, yet you did indeed, nor could you help but peer straight ahead. You saw Setebos and were seen by him, right down to the toes.

Not under his thumb. Nor he under yours. He was a god of rage who lived untouched within

the rage, the pure cool flames that burned and left no cinders.

I welcomed the lash that brought me closer to him. Into the pinch and torment I burrowed. The path Prospero hacked out for his defiant slave was crooked, perverse, and monstrous. But each new cut and deformity opened a clearing in which again I met the god, finding in his outstretched hand yet one more facet of rage, one more venue for defiance.

As we approached Prospero's cell, I prayed to the great god. I was flush with triumph. Never had I seen Setebos in such high surge.

"Deliver him to me," began my prayer, which though silent cracked the vaults of heaven. "Bring the scallop-skinned devil's withered scrannel pipe beneath my thumbs. Let the crush begin, the face flush crimson as dusk, his enfeebled fists batter to no effect against the hard hump upon my back. And may his death be slow in arriving, an eternity, at whose center I stand, clefter choked with rage, his throat throbbing beneath my thumbs. Payback, payback, payback.

"That moment shall Miranda turn her admiring eyes to me, glad that her parent, crab and bull, pincer and hoof, endures slow extinguishment, her cleft moist for Caliban beneath the obscenity of her garments.

"That moment shall the fresh interlopers fade from sight, turning away to wander into oblivion.

"That moment shall Mom manifest about me, her embrace as inviting and soft as mine is harsh and killing.

243

"The muddy earth-map of her face shall bend to kiss her son. At her sight shall Miranda melt, her eyes wide with need for us both. Down shall I drag my oppressor, down through the twelve years of torment he meted out, suffering tenfold in concentrate the pain he inflicted.

"And when his shuttered eyelids open at last unto death, then shall his father-god's monstrous hell gape to embrace him, draw him down and stretch him out upon the rack for all eternity, the acid of his snappish tongue's juices eating into his sinews. Such his deserts. Darken the father-god's face, sprout him horns, make stern his brow, deepen his evil to profounder depths."

As the wine made me heady, this curse filled my heart. Back then was poor Caliban naive. Though four and twenty, he looked upon the world with the childish eyes of hope.

There is hope.

There is hopelessness.

They are one and the same.

This lesson above all have my Neapolitan days taught me. There is no worse cleft, no corridor more narrow nor more harsh, than the beguiling lure of freedom. Lived in reverse, life might deliver upon such promises.

As it is, even with the exchange of limb and sinew Mom and I can perform, there is only the Ever Narrowing, only the diminishment, the pinch, the lost way.

Yet even there, O Setebos, you offer me the comfort of No Comfort. I deny you, I embrace you, I regard you as mere mirage. In all of this, you teach me misery and acceptance.

All we have is breath, one day to cease, one day when the confining cleft grips to burst the shell that contains us. Then is my wish to go out in rage, full of contracted life at long last expanding.

Even if that final moment disappoints, in the heart of that disappointment shall I find and embrace you, on, on, into a space that has no space, a going that moves but does not move, a being that is but never was nor shall be.

Those moments of approach, there on the island, seem anciently remote and right-now present. I can taste the mounting of my vengeance. I can smell the offending men of the sea, as the breezes blow from behind and branches snap beneath their cloddish boots.

Freedom lies straight ahead, even as it is long gone and over.

For this, O Setebos, I thank you.

For this, O Setebos, I curse you.

Chapter Sixteen

Forgiveness

I held Prospero's murderers in my palm.

Their resolve I had shored up. Stephano was crammed with desire for kingship and a cleftable queen. It wanted but the soft glide of burly men into Prospero's cell, the swift dispatch of his life.

Ah, but what of Ariel and the warning he had sped off to deliver? Perhaps he had not made it back. Perhaps the pinched devil lay at last within Caliban's grasp.

But though fortune might smile on me, the doltish swine I had led to the truffled ground of Prospero's death were as slippery as eels in my fists.

"Step in," I murmured. "Dispatch him."

But fine garments hung on the branches without. They caught Trinculo's eye, then his tongue. The seagull-brain of Stephano followed.

"By this hand," said he, "I'll have that gown."

Though I warned of pinches that would crush bone and cripple should we be caught, their eyes glistened with greed. Trappings. Trappings without the act. That's what turned them. Murder him? In time, in time. First must they feel against their skin the touch of kingly garments.

The scallop-skinned, as I have said, conceal their shame. In so covering, they have learned to discriminate amongst themselves based on fabric. They obsess about clothing. In truth, though my island life before PopEros was paradise, my tastes too have been corrupted by finery. If one must drape cloth over one's flesh, fine weave kept spotless by servants is far more appealing than coarse, louse-ridden rags.

But these my confederates, too deep in their cups and tricked into a horse pond by Ariel, lost their ambition to trappings. They stayed their hands too long from the deed. Thereupon, they fell to a rout, goblin-hounds driving us off into the worst torment I had yet endured.

Bruised and pinch-spotted were we all over. With dry convulsions did our joints twist, our sinews shorten with jinks and cramps beyond numbering. My confederates' yelps spiked ever higher into pain, made worse by their never having undergone such treatment before.

I, as always, endured.

But I thought I had missed forever my chance at the cell and Mom's journal. Into deep despair I sank, as pain engaged and invaded us.

Seething packs of goblins, empty-eyed, roughed and bumbled us as we fled, their pale bodies slipping through leaf and oak. Yet solid

enough were they to smack us at the slightest departure from the path down which they herded us. Stephano, no king he, yowled loudest at the pinching, a high boyish piping issuing from his bearded hulk.

Trinculo launched into a running argument with Sir Spirit o' the Air, as he called him. "Let up," said he. "Pinch my purse, but pinch not me. Pinch the fish man, or pinch King Stephano. They, far more than me, deserve it, who deserve it not at all."

When the goblin-hounds had corralled us in a clearing, so that we cringed upon a great slab stone that angled from the ground, they turned into a brute palm of stinging bees. Down that palm pressed, until we lay flat against cold stone, covering our eyes, cowering beneath their assault. Breath was impossible. A flared nostril or a mouth-hole gaped to vent complaint gave immediate entrance to noisome drones and their needled invasions.

Upon the brink of oblivion, I sensed a sea change. The sharp fuzz on those bumbling bodies blunted into a smooth caress. No longer penetrant were their stingers, nor extant neither, now that I dared open my eyes to observe them. The tormenting cloud of insects lifted and dispersed. Sunlight bathed us, erased our blisters, healed our tortured innards.

A salve and a boon unlooked for. What, I wondered, had come about? Was Prospero dead?

It must be so. Wherefore else the sudden surcease of pain? The pinched devil had met death at a more politic hand, at the hand perhaps of

his brother, one Antonio, against whom Prospero had often railed.

Fear at once checked my elation. That brother, having dispatched the old mage, would swiftly find his books. Even now, my fancy saw him skimming the pages in Prospero's cell, murderous hands flurrying them by beneath a bent head. At any moment, as my companions laughed and gaped upon our slab of granite, the pinching spirits would once more descend. Prospero's past torments would be but fleabitings, so great the pains that replaced them under his brother's sharper tongue.

My fears lifted long enough for me to peer out into the sunshine of possibility.

If other survivors were about, this brother might even now be sparring with them. Bickerers and backbiters were they all, these Italians, could Prospero's railings be trusted. I would slip past the crimson cloud and chaos of their melee, swordpoints pinked, knuckles bruised and bloody from the skirmish. Into his cell would I hasten, glancing about in haste, picking out and plucking up Mom's writings and the bound volumes of Prospero's books.

I would have time, so fancy promised, to spirit them away to the hut, imbibe them as greedily as Stephano's bark-bottle of wine, and emerge all-powerful, master of them that pinch and them that are pinched.

From the long cleft of my enslavement would I burst. The mountains of deformity heaped upon me would drop off to lie like dead creatures at my feet. Upon my regained beauty would Miranda swoon, her fabric fallen as easily

as my imperfections, her cleft swelling even as she leaped to impale herself on me.

I lurched to a slump. "We must find what is the matter," said I.

My failed assassins followed me, though I spared them nary a glance. Despite the urgency that blazed in my limbs, I hurried not but retraced in easy stride the steps we had taken away from Prospero's cell.

No commotion assaulted my ears. Only a murmur that rose to a mumble, then splintered into conversations that grew more distinct with each footfall.

When the leaves parted, there before the door of his cell stood Prospero, surrounded by absurd scallop-skins, their hands unweaponed and at ease by their sides, their voices raised not in challenge but in praise and amazement.

For PopEros had robed himself in garments I had never seen, the trappings of former majesty reclaimed. His ducal robes bore the same heraldic devices as the garments that had of late beguiled my confederates.

So indeed the mage noted, commenting upon us in a rich, round, unpinched voice I had never heard him use. So unaccustomed were my ears to the boom of his pear-shaped tones that I scarce took umbrage at the way he described me to the crowd of scallop-skins, nor at his disparagement of my mother.

Without rancor, he exposed our plot. "These three have robbed me," he observed. Then gesturing to me: "And this demi-devil plotted with them to take my life."

Words that might have enraged me an hour

before, words that surely would have been prelude to worlds of pinching, now floated in the
air like so many blessings.

Had I entered another realm, some insane
new world? It seemed so to me. I wondered how
long it would last, and what advantage I might
squeeze from it while it did.

Then words exceeding strange passed his lips.
My confederates Stephano and Trinculo, he
said, must be known and owned by his royal visitors. "But," he continued with a gesture toward
me, "this thing of darkness I acknowledge
mine."

On the surface, I supposed him to mean that
I was his slave, as my two doltish gulls were
slave to the king and his ministers. But deeper
implications lay concealed in his words, which
would, in the fullness of time, be unfolded and
exposed.

The air was choked with general reconciliation.

I would later learn what had transpired: the
attempt upon King Alonso's life by his brother
Sebastian, the fretting of father and son over one
another's feared drownings, and more.

Despite what had passed, benevolence ruled
the day. Prospero had not merely let down his
guard; he had quite dismissed it. Nay, more. His
having done so, his having trained the glare of
disclosure upon the dark deviosities of past and
present, had brought all assembled into a state
of grace.

I played along, awaiting my main chance.

It came while I was casting a glance at Miranda, who stood enraptured at the scene, en-

twined, arm in arm, with the mopey youth I had first espied, Prince Ferdinand his name.

"Go, sirrah, to my cell," said Prospero to me. "Take with you your companions. As you look to have my pardon, trim it handsomely."

Scarce could I credit my ears. The mistreated slave, unattended by his overlording eye, his Ariel, would have access to his cell, to make it neat and decorate it for his guests. Trim it? I would trim the bastard's sails, is what I would do. I would trim the tip of his clefter, nay its entire length, right down to the shriveled sack. Beneath the sand of Prospero's unnatural kindness lurked the crab of revenge. There was no telling how quickly it would skitter into view, pincers out and thrashing.

Said I in response, letting my astonishment soften the tone I used, "That I will. I'll be wiser hereafter and seek for grace. What a thrice-double ass was I to take this drunkard for a god, and worship this dull fool."

Prospero laughed, an odd giggle-glide of stream over rock I had not heard before, and dismissed me.

As we three departed, the mage addressed his guests. I lingered not, knowing that my time to make mischief was not long, nor my chance wider than the most pinched cleft I had endured these twelve years.

Urgency hurried me on. I prayed to Setebos for a clear brain, a swift hand, and the perfect alignment of Dame Fortune's favors.

From the sunny communion of off-islanders, nothing but smiles of benevolence and reconciliation, I passed through the doorway to, at long last, the very edge and compass of my freedom.

Chapter Seventeen

Mom's Papers

When, into the trackless seas of time, memory cast its nets, it dredged up Mom in three chief moods.

Most variable of them was her rage. She could swell up, anywhere at any moment, into lofty towers. The big-bellied moon inspired her, so fueling her wrath that she devolved into erratic strings of vowels and a jagged dance in the moonlit clearing before our hut: pokes and jabs, a flare of nostrils, the flailing of hands. Her breasts and belly would she smack, her pupils sliding up out of view, her hair fisted in clumps and tugged near to uprooting.

Her second mood, a horizontal one, was lusty. Never in daylight did she indulge it. Then was it switched off, tucked deep inside. Once I ventured to approach her while she worked our garden. Like a leopard she sprang upon me, not to

impale herself but to rage full in my face, to give my buttocks a stinging swat, and to bellow, as I back-scrabbled free of her ire, that she, not I, would initiate such high jinks, nay, that my clefter would be forfeit if ever again I forgot that.

But when she threw me on my back in the seeded thyme, or turned chthonic and moist beneath our midnight covers, then did that warm place of my origin open to exploration, to sweet or rough or tender delvings back into the obscure terra incognita of my infancy and beyond it, a curled and diminishing shrimp in her womb. Mom's earthy yum-stench, her wide throat, its guttural urgency—these etched deep in memory's store, weaving a rich tapestry of recall.

The third of her moods was more quiet and inturned, and far more difficult to distill into words. This mood manifested on rare mornings, once she had waked, relieved herself, and bathed. Then would she sit outside the door on her oak stump, bent over her journal, a fat black book of blank paper partway to being inked over. Months would pass without an entry, then a week whose every day saw her bent to the page, her worn goose quill scratching at the task with squid ink or ink of the cuttlefish I had caught and learned to de-sac, trapping its dark fluid in a squat thick-glassed bottle.

Although the journal lay in full view amongst her personal items, I was forbidden to touch it. That ban I tested, of course, illiterate though I was. For my pains, I caught a glimpse of bewildering squiggles, followed by a sustained series of drubbings and beratings, which scored deep

the lesson of "off limits" into my flesh.

After Mom's body had been reduced to cinders on the beach, her journal was the one thing missing from our hut, plucked from an elsewise undisturbed heap of her leavings, as a peregrine plucks precisely a single strand of nesting material from a knotted mass of natural detritus.

I guessed then, as proved true, that her journal was replete with a seethe of angry thoughts and remembrances, interspersed with experiments in magic, her reaches into sorcery more daring as the years wore on.

Into Prospero's cell I plunged, Trinculo and Stephano dogging my heels.

Precise as a pin, the mage's belongings. Precise too his daughter's dusky corner of space: her rock and shell collection, the set of books her father had given her from his cache.

But I cared not a whit for her things. To Prospero's makeshift desk and rough-hewn shelves did I go, ignoring my companions as they back-slapped one another and thanked the Virgin that they had escaped punishment and would soon be sailing for Italy.

There stood his books, upright, bookended, and lined up just so, an eventual prize if my fortunes held. And, right where I recalled seeing it, was the spine of Mom's journal. This I slipped from its place, shifting inchwise the tomes to either side, so that its loss would not gape and glare.

The cell needed, of course, no trimming. Not one of Prospero's possessions ever lay misplaced or sprawled, unlike my own meager store and unlike Mom's when she had been alive. She

shuffled her things about constantly, as helter-skelter and unclefted, she said, as the wind-drift of birds or leaves.

Concealing the journal beneath my cloak, I slipped out of Prospero's cell. So heart-whole with reconciliation were the scallop-skins that no one noticed one poor slave bleed into the forest.

In my last glimpse of them, they had begun to meander toward the doorway. I sped north, through trees and over dips and rises I hadn't seen for years, but which burned bright in memory unchanged.

When I entered the clearing before the hut, I sat on a cross-section of log where oft I had communed with Mom, her spirit still strong on the island—for reasons I would soon guess and shortly thereafter confirm.

Eagerly I turned to her final scrawls. Never had I seen my native Berber set down. But indeed, the letters were in the same Arabic script Miranda had taught me; and now I recalled Mom saying that Berber had no written form, that she had been obliged to adopt the Algerian monster's script. As I picked out individual words, then phrases, I wept at their resonance. Mom's voice rose up, haltingly at first, then rushing into strung-together squiggles of sepia. The words plumped out with sound and substance, peaches bedewed and swollen with seduction.

How much of this rich feast could my eyes devour? And where should my initial plunge begin?

I flipped back a few dozen pages and started reading. In the last weeks of Mom's life, her

sprites had been busy spying on Milan and in particular on the lives of PopEros and his little daughter. What interest she had in them I could not fathom.

But her elation rose perceptibly when Prospero was stripped of his dukedom and he and Miranda were immured in a dungeon and set adrift.

She painted the mastless barque aboard which they had been hurried, a decaying hulk of a vessel. Gonzalo, the kind counselor—even now on the island, and one of whose wisdom I would, in a new guise, soon avail myself—she painted too, he who provided food and drink for their sea journey, stores of clothing and an ornate chest full of Prospero's precious books. These volumes Mom minutely detailed, eager to lay hands upon them and swallow their contents whole.

This, I presumed, was the prime cause of her elation at their setting forth. But there was another connection between her and Prospero that, on my way to Italy in the privacy of the prince's cabin, opened itself to me.

In the midst of this account, just after she recorded having raised, via a spirit named Milcha, winds to set and maintain their steady progress toward our island, I came upon the spell. Other spells had made an appearance in earlier pages. But this one, the last she had set down, was the one that would gain her son his freedom.

Here too, in this spell, I found yet another reason for her to draw the pinched mage, healthy and brainful of magic, hitherward.

She was ailing.

She was dying.

He would be, though not through the magic of healing as I had first thought, her sure path and passage back to full health.

With great interest I delved into the spell—reading and rereading its words, teasing out the tone-shifts Mom had woven into it—until, beneath scale and fin and the scarred remembrance of countless lashings and batterings, a new light of understanding dawned in me.

Chapter Eighteen

An Experiment

Enfeebled though she was, Mom must have sensed the danger she was putting us in, bringing a mage of uncertain power to the island.

One detects a turning in her writing. Being bested becomes thinkable. The journal continues in its mode of self-communion, yes. But increasingly she addresses me directly, gnawing at her fear that our visitor may turn monstrous and she no longer by to defend me.

Indeed, after setting down the text of the spell—from the opening prayer to Setebos, to the request itself, and concluding thanks to the god—she continues: "My son, spark struck from the flint of my fury, sharer of our secret joys, if you need this spell, my hope is that it seeks you out only when you have gained some measure of wisdom. Not for the flighty or frivolous is the power contained therein. At twelve, thou art

mere seed. May you grow in inner ferocity and focus, cautious in the use of power yet bold. When Prospero arrives, may my powers prove the stronger against him. Then to you shall I be mother and father both."

Next day resuming, she writes again of her sprites' report of the sea progress of the exiles and of her own precipitous decline.

From first reading, I wanted at once to use the spell against Prospero. It maddened me that I could not. But he was in full bloom as a mage, and I had to spend time with his books, master them beyond mastery, before I dared make such an attempt. Folly fueled by wrath would else have hurtled me down my death path. But there was a way, I told myself, to triumph over him in slow sure steps.

My target must be the young prince.

Prince Ferdinand had access, or shortly would have, to Miranda's succulent body. Access as well, surely, to his father-in-law, Prospero, the murdering pinchface whose breath it would be my delight to arrest after a dalliance with torture.

But before assailing the prince, I decided to ensnare some expendable soul, some scummy lowlife mariner who, if he remembered what had transpired, could be dispatched and rolled into a ravine, his disappearance scarce remarked by his betters.

Trinculo.

Annoying drunken little bastard, stenchpool of stale sweat and offal, the lesser of my erstwhile confederates, whose eye for royal trappings had derailed our plot to murder PopEros.

He would indeed be missed by Stephano, but that dull brain, methought, would quickly cloud with drink, his sorrow drowned as the ship set to sea.

When I returned to the mage's cell, men of high and low degree were everywhere scattered in festive clumps, cups brimming with wine spirit-supplied.

There upon Ferdinand's arm clung Miranda, a smile lighting her face. Anticipation of first cleft throbbed in their every gesture.

Near them stood Prospero, his countenance curiously soft, surveying the crowd as he conversed with his now-repentant brother and the King of Naples. Ariel hovered at his shoulder, invisible to everyone but the mage and me. Looks passed between them, and a murmurous word of command that sent the sprite speeding off overhead and zooming back upon the instant.

Behind Prospero's cell, relieving himself of a sunlit braid of gold against its walls, idled Trinculo. He had doffed his stolen finery in favor of the stenchy togs of our first meeting. Dumb muscle was my failed conspirator from brain to calves. Shaking off, he shoved his clefter back into his breeches and swilled a fresh glug of wine.

"Trinculo," said I.

He swayed into near-stumble and, opening his face wide, bleared an eye at me. "Monster!" said he. "I wondered into what brake thou hadst secreted thyself. Drown thy sour looks in joy. We're heading home." He thrust his cup toward multiple Calibans.

261

"By and by," said I, venturing closer. "I have discovered a cache of clothing finer far than those we found before. These garments, ownerless and precisely Trinculo-sized, none shall snatch from you."

Suspicion dwelt not in the mariner's nature. There gullery thrived. At once he beamed and blathered, but I shushed him, telling him, mouth up to his ear, that they would all be his unless the general rout heard him carry on about them so.

Trinculo shushed me back, his fat lower lip drooling-moist behind an index finger. "Aye, monster. Lead on. Guide me to my raiments."

Through the underbrush I led him, he surprisingly nimblefooted, a drunkard's confidence countering his imbalance, on the verge of each threatened topple.

"Stephano will wonder where I am," he said, a stray thought at once misplaced.

Snippets of song—some cleft-centered sea chantey about Molly and her prowess at making a mate's bunk roll with such force that she set the seas, the heavens, nay, the great globe itself in motion—rose up from him, then fell off when memory failed.

"In all his finery shall true Trinculo be revealed," he boasted with sudden joy, "as he deigns to acknowledge his former comrades' bowing and scraping, their bungholes flaring skyward to trumpet his greatness."

Along a serried rank of oak trees, upon the lip of a deep ravine whose edge we essayed, I stopped. Overhead, a long-tongued magpie pricked worm-deep into oak warts.

"Here," said I.

"Here?"

"Indeed."

"Ah. But I see no finery."

"These be magic garments," said I. "They need but summoning words to coax them out of invisibility. Once out, once worn, they shall make their wearer wise beyond the telling."

"Monster, say I, Trinculo would be wise."

"Wiser than Solomon shall Trinculo be," I assured. "Sit you down. Lend an ear. Be amazed."

By heart had I the spell, by heart delivered it.

Mom had supplied words of undoing, words that would halt and reverse the shift of bodies. But those words I needed not. Indeed, once I had spoken the closing prayer to Setebos, once the changes surged into play, the intense and universal shifts inside me left scarce room to think at all.

As the transformation began, Trinculo gazed up goggle-eyed at me, his young dumb face a-brim with unadulterated trust. "Monster," asked he, "where be the garments you promised? Even now, I see them not."

His words halted and he gaped.

My skin pulled in smooth and taut, my broken bald pate shifting into soft curves and sprouting thickets of greasy red hair. Carbuncles shrank to tiny gems, then vanished.

Even as these shifts seized me, I saw Trinculo's hair untwist and wriggle back inside his skin. His complexion darkened, then claimed that darkness. The skull beneath his scalp pocked and crimped. All over, the brawny man collapsed in upon himself, his back hunching

263

up, the gauzy closed-fan green of fins emerging from his sleeves and the bottoms of his breeches.

I, loinclothed merely, saw and felt all grow healthy, the diminishing of my hump to brawny shoulders and a fine-tapered back, as my body scalloped and smoothed. My fins drew in and blended into the lightening hues of my skin.

My misshapen toes uncurled, uncurved, paled into pinkness where I stood on pine needles dropped in seasons past.

"But what—?" he managed.

"Hush," said I, my voice, my tongue, the muscles of my mouth still mine. Then they too were claimed by the hand of change.

All over, my musculature released and slid. As Caliban, I had been a hearty soul, a killing engine kept down, though I bulged with strength from the log-toting Prospero had forced upon me. The besotted Trinculo bulked larger now, strong as I in arm and leg, expansive in the chest. But the balance of his bulk differed from mine.

Now that shift occurred. Like the sun's touch, it penetrated me, deep upon the skin and sinking its fingers inside to soften and bake new biceps, back muscles, legs, and thighs.

The seated man's face grew pocked and carbuncled, hints of Trinculo there still, panic and tears. This face, this Caliban face, was not one he had lived in. From the encrusted windows of a ruin in which he found himself trapped, he stared out forlorn.

I too, though exalting, felt his alien face, tight-skinned, tight-boned, catch me in strange new clefts. My skull cracked and shifted, the brain

meat squirming and reshaping ever deeper.

Down into my innards the shift sizzled, an invading exhilaration thrusting still further, its welcome attack piercing from every angle, burrowing into the skin, and darting down sharp as swarms of sting rays.

My victim, no longer in control of his voice box, mumbled mush. He tore ineffectually at his boots. They pained him, as ungainly feet bulked and finned inside. But he sat for the most part in shock, as if my body had shuddered down about him and confined him quite. Bewildered to the heart was poor Trinculo, lost in the wilds of a monstrous new world.

When the brain-shift took hold, the simple sailor went comatose. Upon the loom of my own brain, now taking the shape of his, were woven and rewoven alien thought patterns, alien memories. But buoyed by Mom's assurances, I was certain I would not lose myself in them, certain too that my mind's secrets would be withheld from him.

Indeed, what was alien soon became mine. Cloaked was I in Trinculo's dullness, without myself becoming dull; surrounded by his drunkenness, without myself becoming drunk. With boundless compassion, I glanced backward into Trinculo's memories of the shipboard clipping and clefting he had shared with Stephano, the tightly packed bunghole in the cramped cabin, the expense of spirit in a waste of shame. Amidst their joking and drinking and swiving, fondness thrived. I saw it, felt it, it was mine even as it was not mine.

Down through memories new-created I ven-

tured: The rough dad come home from sea, fisting bruises upon his son's face. The mother who gave him ice in her looks but who replaced it with false fire to entice coins from snagged strangers. Cobblestones passed beneath his boyish feet when he strayed onto the piazza and wandered into an old woman's house, asking for bread, receiving bread and kind words and a warm hand enclosing his hand, to walk him back to his mother.

As that familiar unfamiliarity draped about me, transforming me to the bone, the marrow, nay the marrow's marrow, I laughed and shuddered and grew despondent. At once freed and confined did I feel. Some new movements of limb and thought were easily essayed. But there were old movements, old ways of being, which I had been robbed of.

The sun seemed less vivid and more, dappling through the trees to the forest floor. I nearly fell into the steep ravine, my footing uncertain. Why so? My spirit struggled vainly for control of what was now beyond its control. The body, kin to its own integrity, endeavored in emergency to assert it.

Still, I found Trinculo's dull patterns of thought oppressive. He was a simpleton. I had donned a dunce cap. I craved the intelligence of the prince. Though Ferdinand tended to simper and mope, though his blind conformity to the scallop-skins' cultural insanity was cause for alarm, I much preferred such raw material to this.

A momentary fear gripped me. Could I, with my new brain, remember the spell of undoing?

And would it indeed set all right again?

But my Caliban memories were in place and as sharp as ever, as were my sense of self and the cloaks of thought that usually wrapped me about. There awaited Mom's spell of undoing. All that remained was to speak it, then put paid to Trinculo.

I began.

At first I stumbled over the invocation, a fat tongue lolling in a lifeless mouth, the lungs, the hollow chamber differently formed behind a bulwark of rotten teeth. But I gave my trust again to the body, as I had learned to do in walking.

And the words flowed free.

The instant I finished, the changes swiftly unraveled, seeming to revert much faster than they had taken hold. Like a shirt eagerly stripped off, the mariner's memories evaporated out the top of my skull. And as when one is dog-sick, the purgation comes from deep in one's gut, so did the adopted corpus of Trinculo surge upward out of me, regurgitated whole into the air with a violence that stopped my breath. There collapsed like a leaden cloak about me the monstrous body that was my own, my eternal trap, my stooped collection of limitations. It was the cleft of comfort and the cleft of discomfort, the stamp I had been stamped with, shaped hideous by the hand of a hurtful mage.

Inside that familiar cage I breathed, joyous past joy to have it back, even as I cursed its confinement.

My hands flexed.

Time for Trinculo.

He sat aground, blinking and confused.

"Where be the finery?" he asked, staring not at me but at the pine-strewn path.

"Why," I told him, "you were wearing it. Wise beyond all telling was Trinculo, his eyes lit up to the depths of his soul with power. Do you recall none of it?"

The mariner shook his head. "I have had," said he, "a most rare vision. I have had a dream, past the wit of man to say what dream it was. The eye of man . . ." He halted, the thread of what he had been saying momentarily, then completely, lost.

Trinculo stared at me, his eyes new-lit by a dawning that flexed my hands with killing urges. But an instant before I sprang upon him, that new dawn dusked quite away, replaced by mere puzzlement.

Plucking at his jerkin, he gazed up forlorn. "I wore them, say you?"

"You did. Garbed in splendor beyond the telling was my Trinculo, in greater splendor his words."

He nodded and raised a finger. "This shall be our secret. We know, monster, you and I, what fine majesty Trinculo berobed himself in. What fine majesty peered out from the meanness of his soul. This secret shall we two keep close, awaiting the day when we can vaunt it to the astonished multitudes. Hush, monster. Speak no word to any man. More of this anon."

"Yes, master." I followed him, staying my hand. I much doubted, having been privy to the simple contents of his mind, that he would re-

gain Trinculo's Dream. If ever I saw signs otherwise, then should I dispatch him.

Thereafter, Trinculo was less jovial. He shunned my company, both in my numbered hours as the monster Caliban and in my new life as Prince Ferdinand.

That prince, as we made our way back to Prospero's cell, hung in eagerness upon my mind.

Prince Ferdinand, yes. And his spry young bride-to-be, she whose cleft I would soon claim, whose father soon dispatch, whose life bring to utter ruin.

Chapter Nineteen

The Great Rise and Refinement

When we had regained the company of men, Trinculo again swore me to silence, weaving off to find Stephano.

I rose from my mock bow and sought out the prince.

He stood beside an outcropping of rock, upon which sat Miranda gazing up at him in admiration, nodding and murmuring replies. It maddened me, the proffered hand, his assured grasp of it, the touch of skin upon skin. As surely as his royal body was draped in finery and hipped in with the violence of sword and dagger, the prince's mind and desire were crimped and cabined by that peculiar European mirage called honor.

Honor.

Air.

Were I the prince, I would have none of it.

The desire to ravish one another danced in their eyes. Perversely they kept it in, gave it power, held back, held back, held back, toward the day of betrothal, mystical words intoned in a church, the ascension then of her I craved, my childhood companion, into the prince's store of possessions.

It would take but one swift step to tear out his throat, the sure sweep of my hand, the sharp snap of his neck, generous bibs of blood spreading as his eyes dimmed.

But I stayed my hand. Greater revenge than that lay in the spell I had not an hour since exercised.

"Noble prince," said I, bowing so as to avoid his eyes.

He turned. "Thou art Caliban," said he.

"I am."

"Miranda has said much about you."

"For what skill in expression he possesses," said I, "is poor Caliban beholden to Prospero's fair daughter. But may it please your grace, I have something to impart to you."

Ferdinand asked what that might be.

"It wants but a word in private."

"My lord, go not with him," said Miranda, realizing at once her boldness and wishing, it was clear, that she had not spoken.

The prince laughed. "Dearest Miranda, I will not be gone long from the goddess of this island. On my return, it shall be as if we were newly discovered, one to the other."

Though Miranda fretted, she nodded and let go his hand. She drew a breath to speak to me, then thought better of it.

271

Right then, I wanted to take her, cruel and savage, against the cold hard rock, with that shocked assembly of scallop-skins looking on.

"Good Caliban," said he, "Prince Ferdinand is at your service." Though his words seemed full of grace, their condescension was as evident to my ears as a shift in the wind coming off the sea.

I dared not lead him as far as I had led Trinculo. I had only to bring him where no one would hear his cries.

At length, we stood near the edge of the lake where I had watched Miranda bathe, attacked her, and been savaged by Prospero. The prince remarked upon its beauty. To the which I concurred.

Then I opened the conversation.

"My lord," said I, "my mother, as you have doubtless heard, had a rich store of magic, as has Prospero."

"The Duke of Milan's magic is white, hers was black. Sycorax, they tell me, was a witch."

"The term dishonors my mother's memory. But let that pass." I paused for the prince to extract the barb of his prejudice, an act of kindness he chose not to perform.

Long had Caliban suffered under Prospero's brutal hand, beneath which he had also learned the sting of his condescension. Ferdinand's was of a piece with it.

"My mother left a spell," I told him. "This spell fortifies a husband. To his scepter of love, it lends strength, endurance, and allure. To that Priapic pillar alone, by the power of this spell, shall his bride cleave. Yet to it also shall the fairest of straying maidens be discreetly drawn, if

its bearer so desires, nor shall any illness that plagues them, nor bastard offspring, be upon him visited. From that fount of manhood shall jet strong seed for lusty sons, compliant daughters, children to make any father proud."

A chill frosted Ferdinand's eyes. "A devil's brood of children. As I'm told *you* are. The prince's Priapic pillar, as you call it, needs no fortification. Nor shall I, fortified instead by a learned and heritable goodness against betrayal of my bride's trust, ever wish to perform the deed of shame with anyone but her. Monster, with such talk, you demean yourself and waste my time."

He started to walk away in a huff. For all his high words, I could tell my lie intrigued him.

But I had no time for such nonsense. No time for suasion. Brute force would serve my turn. I clapped him rudely on the shoulders, whirled him around, and launched into the spell.

Ferdinand regained his balance as he whipped up into fury, unused to an underling being so bold. "Unhand me," he said, his danger now dawning in his eyes. I pressed on, clear and deliberate in my invocation to Setebos, yet swiftly hurtling on toward completion.

Despite the prince's struggles, I wrestled him to the ground. His hat fell off. His nails lunged for my face. But I snatched his wrists out of the hostile air and held them easily away.

All his attempts to attack or escape I by instinct parried, keeping my mind focused on the unreeling spell and taking care to break none of his bones.

A soft body, I thought. I will have to harden it.

When I had sped halfway along the thread of words, a desperate energy flared in the prince's eyes. Before I could identify it further, there came the sound of an unsheathing at his belt. A glint of silver rose and plunged.

Rude violation invaded me, the rip of a lightning jag at my back. I faltered. Again his arm rose, the dagger's harsh withdrawal provoking as much pain as its entry.

This time I caught his wrist, resisting the instinct to break it and crush the life out of him.

Fighting the outrage, I willed my thoughts back on track, my voice through gritted teeth resuming.

A gush of blood trickled along my spine. My strength held as I reached the closing prayer to the god. The prince's knife arm I slammed against the earth, again, again, until his dagger flew free, skittering and spinning off to fall inert at the lake's edge.

I had the snooty little twerp pinned to the ground. So near was my face to his that I could have bitten off his royal nose. He gritted and puffed, sweat standing on his brow, his coltish spirit defiant but powerless.

At last the paid-out reel of spell reached its end. Upon the whipped tail of the last word I snapped my teeth, expelling it in a yip of triumph.

The beginnings of the shape-change caught the prince by surprise, his eyes suddenly struck.

Rolling off him, I balled up on my haunches, my gaze keen upon him even as the lance of pain flooded my senses anew. The wound, though deep, seemed not mortal. Washed in the sting of

ocean salts and nursed for a few days, it would heal soon enough.

Then it occurred to me, even as my skin smoothed and tightened everywhere, that the knife wound the prince had inflicted was soon to become his own problem.

His right hand flew to his face, monstrous hand to monstrous face. His hair sucked down with a slurp into his skull, even as, above my now-taut brow, capped rich and snug upon my head, that same fair hair wriggled out and thickened.

"What—?" said the prince, but confusion stopped his mouth.

Tearing at his shirt, he wrenched it over his head and flung it aside. In disbelief, he stared down at his torso. His chest was expanding, his arms bulking out in muscle, his back buckling and bulging like earth pressed upward by the insistent hands of a giant. I, conversely, had taken on the pale softness of his scallop skin, whose strain lessened as my muscles diminished beneath it.

At my back, healing shaped like a dagger blade sank deep inside me, even as the prince cried out, writhing in the sting of a self-inflicted stab wound.

While his agony o'erwhelmed him, my mind leaped to a fanciful future. I was in a magic land called Naples, the healing glow of a knife wound undone spreading across my shoulders and penetrating my inner organs. In the moment before Ferdinand's mindset descended upon me, up sprang my palace of fancy. Of precious stones and daylight was it fashioned, too pure to touch

the earth, the bricks of gold held apart one from another, suspended in place, their surfaces thick with honey-melted sunshine.

Exertion needed I none. Through scents of hyacinth and lavender, I floated on mere whim, gliding down ornate corridors, in and out of opulent chambers where choirs of angels sang, each with a voice that resembled Miranda's. Beneath soaring ceilings did obedient Ariels forelock and flit, carrying out princely wishes even as they were being formulated.

At the corners of my gaze hunched gimpish monstrosities, constrained, clefted, pinched by unseen sprites into gruff obedience. Though I tried to fix on one of these lumbering beasts, I too was constrained and clefted into my vision of paradise.

Then did the prince's traps of thought and recall shudder down upon me. In his mind's eye, I saw the palace as it was, the power that provoked the finery, the beating down and deepening impoverishment of the impoverished, the grand mirage of royalty fed and sustained by religion's far grander mirage.

For Ferdinand, of course, royalty and religion were no mirages at all. As the full force of his delusions crashed down upon me, my own clear insights, such as they were, snarled for an instant in the web of his prejudice.

I marveled, recalling my brain-dulling exchange with Trinculo, at the prince's sharpness of wit and intellect. There was a surge and power about him that would serve me well. Ah, but what of his royal blinders? They did not overwhelm so much as they annoyed and

amused. The blanket was thick, the shortcomings many, but my spirit remained in charge and sharp as an adder's sting.

The prince, however, had lapsed into shock and thence to unconsciousness, collapsing to the ground in a lumpish heap. I stripped him, the garments difficult to peel from his monstrous limbs.

Then I untied my loincloth and tossed it against his body. I examined the flop of my clefter, of late *his* clefter, delicate hair like spun gossamer where it bushed out above. It was pleasingly long in the down-dangle. But until I laid claim to Miranda's sweet body, I would have to accept on faith the prince's boasts about staying power.

Before donning his royal garments, I took in the scene and inhaled deeply, sampling odd subtleties of scent through fresh nostrils.

The familiar became new.

Compared to mine, Ferdinand's lungs pulled shallowly upon the air.

He was a pampered puff pastry. But I would change all that. I was determined, in my initial exhilaration, not to accept the trap of a body at an indifferent level of fitness. Fool that I was, I thought that, once in shape, I would feel free at last.

Freedom.

My spirit had escaped the oaken cleft of a slave-body scored by magic and ill treatment, in favor of the peeled bark and youthful upthrust of a sapling. The first rush felt like freedom.

But that feeling lasted a moment.

Every reach of an arm, every inhale stunted

by weak-drawing lungs, revealed another barrier. How swiftly the old barriers were forgotten, and how soon the new became familiar and unfelt.

The transcendence I longed for was, it seemed, *my* grand mirage. Every turning, even unto the theft of an unspoiled young body, led into yet another cleft.

Stuck.

Pinched.

Tormented by untranscendable barriers.

Overcome with sadness, I dressed.

Then my rage took hold.

Rage, which had sustained Mom, brought us close, and allowed me to survive twelve years of torment—rage was my one true touchstone. Dependable core of my being, around which naught but ephemera swirled.

My mind fastened on Prospero. On Miranda.

What would most please me, beyond the duping of the royal party (they who sneered, jeered, and fleered at poor Caliban's monstrosity), was the ruin of those two.

The tormentor.

The temptress.

Down into pain, into diminution of spirit and slow death, would their log-toting boy-slave drag them.

The wretch before me shifted and groaned, struggling toward consciousness.

Retrieving the dagger, I left him there to his own devices, striking out upon a new path, my stride princely, my thoughts bloody and black.

Chapter Twenty

Thumb on the Bride Prize

The prince's boots caused me the greatest confusion. They choked and pinched feet that had never known confinement. But at once I was forced into yet one more mental backpedaling. *My* feet had never known confinement, but these that I walked in were *his*.

Or were they?

Cleave this body with a broadsword, part the folds, and you would find Prince Ferdinand through and through. But that same body was infused with my spirit, the soul of my mother's son. And these limbs, this frame entire, was, though transformed, still mine.

Oh, it was not as if, were I to drop my guard, its shape would burst back out monstrous. No, the change was secure and would be so until such time—which would, I assumed, be never—as I spoke the spell of undoing.

So I walked a mile in another man's boots, then I walked another. It gave me plenty of time to adjust, to excavate the prince's memories, recent ones about seeing Miranda for the first time; his drawn sword against the mage being stuck in some mid-air cleft by the old man's magic; so lunatic in love as to take on, with a moon-mad smile, the bootlicking task of hauling logs.

Earlier memories superseded them, his schooling in warfare, dance, languages, the heaps of religious guilt dropped on his head from the gaping buttocks of something called the Church of Rome.

This flood of memories stirred within a context of assumptions that masked their perversity even as they bewildered, their oddity like some strange lizard chanced upon. They were deeply ingrained in the runnels of his brain. So ingrained were they, in fact, so strongly etched the Prince's personal traits, that I felt as if I must tell over constantly who I was, lest I founder in forgetfulness.

At the same time, I knew there was no danger of that. All of Caliban's memories, indeed the very heart and bedrock of his proprioceptive being, were as sharp and intact as ever.

Before long, Prospero's clearing opened around me. The murmuring buzz of Italian voices spangled out into pockets of distinct chatter (how refreshing to partake of the deep grounding that tongue now held in my overbrain). Miranda stood to greet me, her face beaming in a manner she had never shared with her monstrous slave.

"My lord," said Miranda, inclining her head without breaking the bond of eyebeams that joined us.

"Each time I see you, fair maiden, it is as if for the first time."

So spake my lips. On the way back, I had muttered and shouted and sworn at the birds and trees, the voice pitched higher than my own yet richly undertoned.

Now, I had given it the urge to express the general feeling I wanted to convey. The mechanism that was the prince's brain and body took over from there.

"You seem unsettled," said she.

No doubt.

"It's nothing, my love," said I. "The monster led me away to attack me. And so he did."

Miranda looked startled. "Caliban?"

"The same. Methinks the creature grows jealous, such effrontery he dared show. He gripped me here, high on the arms, and would have crushed my windpipe had I not plunged my dagger into his back."

Looking pained, Miranda lightly touched my arm.

I hated her then. No concern for Caliban. Was he dead or merely wounded? She cared not a whit. Only the prince merited her concern, this walking assemblage of flesh and bone that now was mine.

Though muted by fabric, her touch thrilled me. My clefter flexed but did not rise. Her scent hung giddy about me, and I wanted to take her then and there.

Prospero, his ear attuned to the distress in his daughter's voice, approached.

"Solicitude becomes you," said I to her, emboldened to take her hand. Skin upon skin. Her warm moist palm, a sign of fevered blood. I gave her hand a squeeze, which startled her.

Too strong? So unlike the prince as to betray me? I believed not.

The pinched mage swept in. His face, washed clean of the scorn I was used to, mingled royal respect, a father's wariness anent his daughter's beau, and the unacknowledged lust that lay like a fierce bowl of fire beneath it all. My princely brain saw none of that, but Caliban observed it, clean and true.

"Roughhouse from my servant?"

With pinched eyes, he inspected my neck, my temples, a quick glimpse along my fabric-encased body.

"Yes," I said, "from the monster Caliban. I left him by the lake, nursing his wounds."

"It seems," said Prospero, "that I have too quickly freed my slave from constraint." He glanced about him and gestured in the air.

Ariel appeared.

Though by rights I should not have been able to see or hear him, I could, sharp as ever. My eyes shot up, but I quickly reminded myself of the prince's limitations and drifted them past the sprite.

"About that freedom you promised me . . ." began Ariel. Even through fresh ears, he was the same toadying bootlicker I had from first memory despised.

But before the mage could unburden his mind

on the subject of Ariel's ever-impending freedom, out from the trees in a roaring leap sprang
my monstrous self, tawny and bloody, its clefter
sans loincloth and all a-dangle.

His head swung wildly about, fierce in the eye.
Fear flooded my veins. I had been one frightening whoreson fellow. The trapped prince fixed
upon King Alonso, his father, and lurched toward him, bellowing "Justice!" at so high a pitch
that it was hard to make out the word.

Courtiers tensed and turned, drawing their
weapons, though none quicker than I.

"Put up your swords," I shouted. I raised a
protective hand toward the Caliban body, an instinct I at once suppressed. *This* was the vessel
where now I indwelt; that, but the old and battered form I had abandoned forever.

"Ariel," said Prospero sharply, stabbing a finger toward the monster. The command required
no words, but lay in his inflection. I could almost
see the sprite's net of constraint flung forth. But
though I flinched in reflex, it flung down not
upon me but upon the simulacrum of my tormented body.

He crumpled to earth, his raised hand crushed
against an unfamiliar barrier. "I demand justice
upon—"

"Silence that dreadful noise!" said the mage.

As though struck by a brute upswung fist, the
Caliban-prince's mouth slammed shut with a
high hard clack that resounded in the clearing.
Beneath a fury of pinches he writhed. When his
gaze found me, his eyes flared and his struggles
increased.

I shuddered even as I smiled.

Power felt good.

But the height of my fortune came next.

Prospero took me aside for a quick conferral. Obeying his glance, Ariel bobbed behind us as we walked, though I pretended not to take notice.

The old fool still wore that ridiculous ducal outfit, ornamental fur here and there, a well-worn velvet hat. And beneath it, that pinched withered face, softened, it seemed, by the royal son-in-law upon whom he supposed he was gazing.

"Good prince," said he, laying a paternal hand upon my shoulder, "I have announced to your father my intent to abjure my magic and drown my book."

I, the obedient betrothed boy, nodded, wondering at the direction of his remarks.

He glanced at Ariel. "Make yourself visible to the good prince."

And thus it was. Ferdinand's eye-stems were at once attuned to my retained ability to see the sprite my mother had imprisoned. I raised my princely eyebrows in feigned astonishment, free now to gape directly at him.

"Be not amazed. Yon sprite, Ariel his name, was once enslaved to the evil witch Sycorax, accursed mother of the cursed monster that attacked you. This twelve-year has Ariel served me, he and his minion spirits."

Said Ariel, "And soon shall I have my—"

Prospero's hand shot up. "Do not interrupt." His eyes never once strayed from mine. "To his credit falls control of the monster, though that control has recently crumbled into neglect. To

his credit the very storm that conveyed you and your father, my brother and the worthy counselor Gonzalo, and all this crew now revived and brought hither. This same Ariel I now bestow upon you."

My heart leaped in my breast. I could scarce credit my fortune.

"But my promised freedom—" sputtered Ariel.

"Out from beneath my paternal thumb," said Prospero, as sharp-tongued and full of bile as ever I had heard him, "shall you, ungrateful servant, now squirm. But this good prince shall you serve, until such time as he sees fit to release you."

Again he prevented the sprite's objections with an upthrust hand. "Henceforth, though I would dearly love to punish your current rebelliousness, I shall no longer see nor hear you, discharging you from my service and yielding up my power over you to the man that stands before us. Be it so."

"Sir," said I, seeing the mage's shoulders slump even as the burden of command lifted from them. "I hardly know what—"

"No need for thanks," said he. "Ariel is a handful. Use the sprite to keep yourself and my daughter safe. Use him to speed our ship safely across the waves. Once at Naples, dispense with his services, or not, as it pleases you."

"I will." Releasing Ariel was the farthest thing from my mind. "But is it truly your intent to forswear all magic?" I said it as though I thought the idea horrendous.

"Forever. My brother has repented. My daugh-

ter is betrothed to the worthiest of men. 'Twas magic that lost me my dukedom. Now shall that same magic be itself lost. Tomorrow at dawn shall I return my books to their chest, which will be brought to a promontory o'erlooking the sea, there to be plunged deep as did e'er plummet sound."

He said a good deal more in response to my feigned dismay, all of it tiresome. But at last our conference ended.

"My boy," said he, "the sun punishes this old brow. Go to my cell and fetch a handkerchief."

I agreed and took my leave.

Inside, I murmured, "Ariel."

On the instant, the sprite appeared. "Young master, you'll not regret freeing me when—"

"No more of that," I snapped. "Banish all hope of freedom from your mind. Stop your tongue from uttering that wish again. Now. Prospero has a journal."

"He has."

"Reveal its location." At once, they shone out as though aura'd, bound black volumes stowed in one of his chests, several dozen of uniform thickness. "Bring the earliest two to Caliban's hut. Let no one but me and Miranda enter that hut, but forbid even her when she and I are not together. Do it and begone."

"I fly."

So he did. Toadying had its allure when you were the one being toadied to. The sprite's subservience sparked renewed hope of my eventual freedom.

False hope, delusory hope.

I found Miranda conversing with her father.

After making obeisance to Prospero, I said, "Dear one, shall we walk aside? Show me more of the island's wonders."

Prospero looked askance but softened at once, putting his full trust in the prince he had tested and tamed into filial respect.

Once we had left the clearing, I said, "Show me where the monster makes his dwelling."

"Do you think it wise?"

"Fret not," I assured her. "Ariel will protect us from him. Your father has given the sprite into my charge from this day forth."

To that place, then, she agreed to guide me, pausing for chaste brief kisses, pitiful pointless torments all, along the way.

Upon reaching my mother's hut, we entered, I noted the journals and noted as well that they lay beyond my bride's notice.

Then I hurried her to the bed. Over objection of word, fist, and nail, I had her, pierced her, took from her the warm wet puncture and promise of that concealed flower with which she had so long tormented me.

Chapter Twenty-one

Living Inside a Devil Body

Upon rereading the foregoing passages, I see that I have minimized the marvel, indeed the terror, of bodily transformation. Let me rectify that.

Because the spirit does not leap into a new body, but rather one's limbs crack and shift into alien form, there is an initial fear, and a deep somatic wish, that the body so changed will revert. Perhaps the reversion will occur through inattention. Or carnal rebellion. Or the willed resurgence of the victim's reconstituted spirit.

But the victim's spirit moves not. It dwells in the body it always did, whose form now mimics his that spoke the spell.

One's new body is too thrilled, too shocked, to have room for a longing for the past. Neither will inattention undo what has been done, but only

the spell of undoing distinctly pronounced and meant.

Once that truth is accepted, one is left to gape and adjust. Everything is fresh, from stomach rumbles and the prim suppression of a princely fart to the peculiar turn of one's new head and the ingrained warp of the victim's thoughts.

Even so, because the new body is simply obeying well-established constraints, they also feel not new at all. One's foot has slipped into an old shoe, the leather of which has long been shaped to accommodate its oddities.

Still, one's own mind and spirit, no less strong for finding themselves inside an alien prison, jar continually against the sways and prejudices of the mind and body one has assumed.

It is no easy task, deciding whether the dissonance of mind or body is most discordant to the inner ear.

What of the mind?

One is continually correcting a misshapen thought or giving it counterweight, which at once prevails, springing as it does from one's rooted undermind.

This struggle of weight and counterweight, if brought to the mouth, might lead one to stutter or stammer, or to let a thought spoken in haste be at once countermanded by its opposite.

Quickly, however, since my goal was to appear as like unto Prince Ferdinand as one twin to another, I learned to let the prince's voice have free rein, its tone and gait taking on the polished cast that his station and learning had afforded him.

In moments of heat, he usually said things I had no quarrel with. In moments of calculation, the urge to speak and the feelings behind the speech belonged to me; therefore, his words more often than not conformed to my inmost wishes, rough-hewn though they were.

And what of the body?

It is most strange, this strolling in another man's shape. Every head turn, every scratch of nose or armpit, every clamoring for notice by bladder, clefter, or pinched toes—these startle one, though months have passed since the magical shift has occurred.

Into an ancient place has one moved, a place at once familiar, yet striking in its peculiar reconstruction of the world. One's explorations take time before they can be considered thorough.

(Even then, when acceptance has taken hold, there are some things one never grows used to. Item: The repulsive stench of the victim's moist fewmets. One forever misses the divine, sculpted wraps of one's own offal, the pungent aroma that repels all others but which one finds, in the pure privacy of one's own nostrils, oddly engaging, even attractive.)

Stepping into the prince's body—or rather, wriggling it down around me like a dressing gown—seemed at first to free me in new directions.

But swiftly those new freedoms revealed themselves to be yet another set of constraints, a pinch of the royal garter, more monstrous than Caliban—even after a dozen years of torment and disfigurement—could ever be.

Though he was well-nigh illusory, I found joy in tormenting "the prince" within my body. I mean by this, of course, not his spirit, which was locked away in the benightedness of a Caliban body, but the prince-self his conscious mind's consistent byways appeared to create. Illusion merely, but a powerful construct nonetheless.

Great delight did I take in upsetting that construct by entertaining underthoughts of mayhem, or patricide, or viciousness toward this or that noble lord.

Even as I tasted his shock, his disgust, his self-loathing, I gloried in bending the prissy little bastard to my will. He was forced to adjust to being at odds with himself, to being of two minds.

Did he think of consulting the good Gonzalo or some other counselor? He did.

But I at once squelched all thought of seeking such help, keeping chained in misery my phantom second self.

And what of me and Miranda?

The blood-mad moment in which I forced her surrender in the mud hut, I took my revenge on European deviltry entire, the suppression of bestial urge, its denial in the name of the mirage civility.

Putting down a monster makes him more monstrous still, and he shall rise up monstrous.

Strike that.

That's a fable.

I colonized the colonizing temptress. With pride unfettered, I shot nasty little Calibans into her, my chattel, the womb of my enemy. Upon my mother's bed, its sheets rank with the blood

291

and sweat of monstrous Caliban, I took my bride-to-be. I fought her, even as I fought the dead-culture restraints that dulled the prince's lust.

There were three of us in that bed, three amidst the blood, caked from the whippings I had suffered, fresh from the rough breach Miranda's body then endured.

I raged against the prince's feeble resistance to my command, and I raged against his bride for defying my will.

Had I second thoughts?

Later, yes. Then? Nothing was but rage.

Rage swept in as red as the membranous undersides of the eyelids in a blistering sun.

Rage thudded down like the battering seas in a ship-high tempest.

Rage rumbled as deep as the attention-grabbing growl of Vesuvius, that makes every Neapolitan son and daughter liquid-boweled with terror.

I thought, if thought came at all, to redirect her hatred to the prince she had fluttered her lashes at in love, to despoil their royal marriage even as I despoiled her.

But her hatred plunged deep inside me, even in those moments when her fists flailed and her resolve to resist crumbled. Her hatred spat bile at the prince but pierced beneath him, even unto the spirit that animated him—unto the spirit, thenceforth dispirited, of Caliban, her childhood playmate.

Rage recollected leads to regret, to the wish for an undoing that can never be undone, to a

forgiveness that it is far too late ever to be granted.

So it was then.

So I knew it would be. Ever after.

Chapter Twenty-two

Prospero's Journal

Miranda had been her father's chattel.

Soon she would be mine.

Yet with one foul unsanctioned act, I had obliterated her dream of paradise with the gentle Prince Ferdinand.

She understood now what it meant to be part of the pinched mage, of the power structure he had rejoined, of the power structure I would lord it over when King Alonso died.

There were the users and the used. She knew which role was hers to play, which mine.

Behind those tormented eyes, buffeted by the winds of humiliation, her spirit fluttered torn and bleeding. In that defeated look, I sensed danger. The danger of self-slaughter, the danger of betrayal and revenge.

"Ariel," said I, not caring if Miranda heard our exchange.

"I appear."

"Perverse imp, you have observed us at play?"

"If you wish to call what I have observed play, yes, I have."

I snapped at him, "Never shall you use that tone with me."

I did not pause to hear him relent. Relenting had been instinctual with him every moment I had observed him with Prospero.

"Watch her always," I said. "If she attempts to reveal to anyone what happened here, stop her mouth. If she dares to speak an unkind word against her husband, stop her mouth. If she raises the hand of violence to herself, to her husband, to anyone other than his enemies, prevent it at once."

I asked if that was clear.

It was.

I dismissed him. I dismissed her. Out of the mud hut of my mother, the admired Miranda picked her miserable way.

All thought of her I set aside, turning to the task at hand. I was torn. Did it better serve my turn to scavenge first Prospero's books or his journal? He had after all changed his mind about freeing Ariel. Might he not forswear his abjuration of magic, take back his magic robes, rise up in fury and slaughter us all?

But if he did not, if he remained true to his vow to the scallop-skins, I would seize those books. As his old mind relinquished all memory of what he had learned from them, mine would build a palace of power with those same learned bricks.

From that palace would I devise the most sus-

tained, most savage death I could for the murderer of my mother and the tormentor of my body and soul.

Before me lay the earliest journals he had penned. I sat on the bed and opened the first. Though his writing seemed naught but a cramped scrawl, like a ragtag army of insects let loose upon the page, my eye quickly learned to decipher it.

Soon I was scanning pages, skimming the gist. From the dating of the passages and knowing that he referred to this time as the fourteen hundred and forty-seventh year of Our Lord, I knew how far into the past I was peering.

Passages scurried by about his dukedom, his beloved brother, his excitement over the writings of honored mages like Agrippa and Dee. Bright and chipper was his tone in those early passages, long before his brother's betrayal, long before Miranda's birth.

A vigorous and exuberant man of thirty years was he. That put him at fifty-five now, which stunned me. From Ferdinand's store of memory, I knew that PopEros looked ten years older than most men his age.

I continued skimming, slowing only when I found a reference to Algiers.

With the weakening of Turkish rule, Algiers had established itself, among the pirate states of Morocco, Tunis, and Tripoli, as the capital of the Barbary coast. Bound was Prospero, as were the other Italian dukes, to Algiers to discuss piracy and how it was to be combated.

This some eight months prior to Mom's banishment.

He was in high spirits.

With an eagerness matched only by the writer of the passage, I read of Prospero's wide-eyed arrival there on shipboard, his first view of an exotic city, his stepping off onto the dock, his initial stroll through the city's night-streets in search of he knew not what.

Then I turned the page. The scrawl loosened, wild with distraction.

Here's what it said:

11th Sept., 1422

Cursed be the tavern dweller with the gimlet eye, he who in my last evening's wanderings through Algiers—the second of my stay—beckoned me to his table and lured me, in near-flawless Italian, into his confidence.

I, naive and loose in my cups, spoke at last of the practitioners of magic into whose books I had begun to delve. His dark pupils pooled out to embrace me.

Yes, he knew those gentlemen and their writings well. But—here he lowered his eyes and gazed at me from beneath bushy brows—far more powerful than they was one Sycorax, worshipper of Setebos the Patagonian god, she who dwelt on the outskirts of Algiers, feared by the governing dullards but venerated by those whose glimpse stretched beyond the mundane. Would I care for directions to her dwelling?

A curse upon me for saying I would indeed.

Adventurous I was and foolish. His direc-

tions clear, I wove my way without hesitation or backtrace through the city.

I found her hut. There I knocked.

She answered, invited me in, dropping at once her bestial Berber grunts for broken Arabic, which tongue I well understood. Then she set before me an infusion that beguiled my senses, or loosened rather my inhibitions.

But not as loose as she supposed. When she tried to touch me forbiddenly, I rebuffed her.

A wounded adder, the witch puffed up.

In a tongue unknown to me, perhaps that same accursed Berber stew, she spewed an utterance at me, sustained and chanted. I was pinched and poked. My clothing dropped off, stripping away my power and exposing all that is nasty in a man. Unseen billows of blackness, glimpsed in the glisten of her dark pupils and fallen into the pit of my groin, rose from behind me. Mine was a sail that those hellish winds filled, billowing me toward this Sycorax with unseemly lust.

A devil possessed me, violated me, limb and mind entire.

To him she spoke in her lascivious tongue, the allure of filth sizzling from her bones. Her robe the coffee-colored temptress parted and dropped. Her body, though ancient and ebony-evil all over, put on a false allure. Then did her hand caress the devil's nexus, drawing forth its rank oils as she writhed upon inthrust fingers.

My hands moved of their own accord, pulling out my risen column of nastiness. Though I fought mightily, the foul witch urged me forward into her stinging folds, into the pinched clutch of my *membrum virile*, whose ingress only a wife should suffer.

Ghastly it was, my shameful tower's bestial rise, the rude plunge of dagger into sheath, the madness that danced in the witch's eyes as she and the devil she had summoned into my body pressed me betwixt them to make a two-backed beast.

My vitality the witch drained quite.

Then with a flourish, his dirty deed done, the devil vacated my place of violation. I collapsed to the dirt floor, my face dripping sweat and tears. Throughout this indignity, I cursed the witch before God, though far fewer were the curses than if she had allowed me more than token control of my tongue.

But with a sweep of her hand, Sycorax stopped my mouth and, for a time, my breath. "Foolish man," said she. "Foolish Prospero. The spellcasting you study is bloodless, a thing of mind without body. Forswear your false god, worship Setebos, and I will teach you the foundations of magic struck deep in the earth."

"Never," I gasped when she had released her chokehold. She only laughed.

From her dwelling I stumbled. Through fearsome streets, I fled to the safety of my cabin and fell into feverish dreams.

Here I sit, exhausted in the early morning

hours, ready to rejoin my delegation, to pretend to a calm I do not feel, so as to have a hope of bargaining for the safety of our ships from piratical attack.

Ah, but again come the tremors. . . .

There Prospero's entry broke off. Several days passed with nothing being noted. By the next entry, his old habits of thought and penmanship—blocky, unfeeling, regimented—had returned. Allusions made he none to the night he and my mother had lain together.

My hand shook as I shut the volume and set it aside.

In my boyhood, Mom had never directly connected us to Prospero. I saw clearly now that what she had intended, in bringing the Neapolitan exile and his daughter to our shores, was a family reunion.

Long time I spent sitting there, staring at nothing, recalling every pertinent conversation I had had with Mom, every insinuation dropped from Prospero's mouth, trying thereby to divine how much he knew.

I concluded that the pinched bastard knew every last bit of it, from the moment he set eyes on me.

That conclusion colored my feelings toward him.

Those colors were astounding to behold.

Chapter Twenty-three

Prospero Drowns His Books

I instructed Ariel to return the journal volumes he had filched. There would be time for the rest of them later, when I would subject the least jot and tittle of them to close scrutiny. Know thine enemy, the better to trounce him, say I.

Then I returned to Prospero's cell, avoiding him, avoiding his daughter, as she did me.

No matter.

The sun was setting. Miranda and her father retired to their sleep after Prospero offered his dwelling and the king refused it. The rest of us, in that balmy summer's night, lit fires and claimed patches of ground.

I made certain, as my betrothed disappeared through the doorway, that Ariel knew his orders.

She would, he assured, be constrained.

I went further with my command. Pinch her facial muscles, I told him. Sculpt a smile from

them, just a hint, as one newly betrothed and not recently ravished. Anticipate and corral those looks she might toss her father, keep her sighs close-confined and inaudible, fatigue her limbs so that she begs off conversation in favor of sleep.

Encamped with the prince's father and his hangers-on, I stared into the night sky, feeling free, and imprisoned, and all at sea.

Had a devil really fathered me, as the mage claimed? Or was it Prospero himself, willing me into being despite his claim to purity? But as Prospero was himself a devil, the answer hardly mattered.

What did it mean for something to matter?

One parent had been murdered by the other. Prospero had killed my mother and spent twelve years torturing his son. What sort of father did such things?

I knew the answer.

I had my father's rage. I had my mother's rage. I had ravished my half-sister.

No, use the right word.

I had raped her. I felt bad about that, unclean, beyond redemption yet secure in that "beyond."

Despite my new-discovered kinship, I also knew that Prospero's death would be my masterpiece. I would steal his books, learn his magic, the same that had bested Mom, and plunge him into a hell whose dark majesty and terror, though obscure to me now, would in the fullness of time be revealed.

Sleep saw to my obliteration. When dawn revived me, I was still ensconced in the prince's body.

Then came general stirrings, ablutions, bodily relief in designated areas of the woods. Out from his cell, full sun drenched, stepped Prospero in his finery, and Miranda wearing her dead mother's dress, head lowered, looking at no one.

Prospero glanced by habit about in the air, seeking his sprite. Then he remembered relinquishing control of him. "Ferdinand," said he, approaching me so the others could not hear, "instruct Ariel to feed us."

"How?" I asked, though of course I knew.

Snitful and tetchy, the mage explained.

At my artfully stumbling command, Ariel sprang tables into view, groaning them with fruits and breakfast viands.

To our repast we fell.

I quickly learned that the sprite's skills extended to shepherding without appearing to do so. I forced the woman, my soul-stung Miranda, to sit beside me, lean to me, lay a hand upon mine, look pleased.

Neither crude nor mechanical were these spritely forcings. No, Ariel proved capable, at my suggestion, of burrowing deep into her desires, weakening for a time her loathing, heightening her attraction to the prince and his position of power.

It gave me pause. Why, I wondered, had not Prospero done this to me? I smiled. Perhaps it had never occurred to him. Perhaps I was, after all, the greater monster.

Alone, Miranda would be free to wallow in her hatred, to marvel at how different she was in my presence and at her newfound reticence around

her father, to steep herself in as much shame as she liked.

Ah, yes. Shame. The grand paramour of guilt. That curious pair of clefts that keeps their sorry culture in motion.

I would have Ariel play upon that shame. How, she would wonder, could one as kind in seeming as the good Prince Ferdinand keep such a monster within? Had some failing in her provoked him to the deed?

These and suchlike questions would she, by Ariel's guileful suggestion, torment herself with.

If she went mad, or sought out some place of inner accommodation to stand, what matter? She would be near for clefting, for ornament, to teach our royal offspring with such skill as she had taught her Caliban.

After we had broken our fast, Prospero had an ornate chest brought out before the company. At his instruction, it was unlatched and opened. There, neatly packed, spines skyward, huddled his volumes of magic. He addressed those books and the crowd, announcing that to a great promontory would he now lead them, there to heave the chest into the sea.

And so he did, the procession a mix of the solemn and the lightly jovial. Prospero was supported by his younger brother, he who had once betrayed the pinched duke but was now repentant and forgiven. Miranda walked beside me.

At one point, I gave my bride into Gonzalo's keeping. "Walk with her," said I. "She is the island's prize."

Then I broke off from the procession, indicating that I would presently catch up with them. I

watched them bob and shrink along the path.

"Ariel," I said.

The toady appeared, resigned to unending slavery.

"Outside Caliban's hut, cords of wood are stacked, split pine six days' fresh."

"Indeed there are," he confirmed, zooming there and back before the eye could blink.

"On board ship, in my royal cabin, sits a chest of princely attire." I described its looks, its location, the great seal upon it, its topmost layer of garments.

Again a nearly undetectable discontinuity and Ariel said, "I have found it."

"Do the following: Take the precise measure of the weight of Prospero's books, now being hefted westward by two mariners. Choose cords of wood which, securely wedged so as not to shift, shall weigh the same, within a hair, as those books. These shall you substitute, with such speed that neither of the bearers suspects nor feels a jolt nor anything amiss. Convey Prospero's books to my chest aboard ship, displacing what garments you find it necessary to displace. Those garments you shall drown, weighting them with stones sufficient to pin them securely to the ocean floor. Is that clear? Can these things be easily done?"

Yes, he said. And yes.

"Then do them presently."

He was gone.

To the west, foliage and distance nearly obscured the diminishing procession. I stepped again onto the path and Ariel appeared.

"It is done," said he.

"Good. Attend to your mistress."

He was gone. I caught up to the peculiar dead-march ahead.

I knew well the promontory Prospero had mentioned, though I pretended not to. I stood next to Miranda behind her father as he spoke.

"My royal lord," said he to King Alonso, his tones dulcet and soft, his demeanor winning, "my revered brother Antonio, good and honest Gonzalo, counselors and retinue to the king, and all here assembled: Learning is a thing of wonder. It carries one into realms unimagined. It gives to airy nothing a local habitation and a name, in which habitation it bids you dwell."

Had young Ferdinand not daily witnessed in the court such hypocrisy, such soft guile concealing the bone spurs of torment, I had been astonished.

Here stood the murderer of my mother, the monster who had lashed and bewitched his bastard son into monstrosity for twelve unspeakable years. Yet did he seem the soul of benevolence, a font of elderly wisdom. Thus do sky hawks seem but wrens.

"But," he continued, his anger evident only in one raised finger, "tarry too long in study, neglect what the world demands, and its gifts shall be snatched away.

"We have had a most fantastical reunion"— here the assembly laughed and nodded—"full of loss and of life recovered, of contrition and forgiveness, and of apology. With all my heart have I accepted the apologies proffered to me. As mine, with like fervor and grace, have I hope been accepted.

"May I offer one more apology? For steeping myself distraction-deep in private study, though powers untold, as you have witnessed, were granted me, I beg the forgiveness of this good company and of the powers that watch over us from on high.

"For two dozen years and more, these my books and I have been companionate. The wise men who penned them I thank. But now . . . I take my leave of them.

"There is a time to peruse and a time to leave off perusal. A time to caress with the eyes and a time to shut away from every eye forever.

"That time has come."

He passed his hands over the chest, then let them drop to his sides. For a moment, I feared he would fall upon his knees, fling open the chest, and clutch to his bosom one last time his beloved volumes.

My hackles rose. I was on the point of summoning Ariel. Had Prospero's hand touched a latch, so I would have done.

Instead that hand lifted in benediction.

"To the depths of the sea I commend you. May you increase the wisdom of Neptune and his court. Or be food for fishes, taking a spell's journey through the belly of a flounder."

At his nod, the mariners advanced to the promontory's edge, swung the chest once, twice, thrice, and released it, stepping back deftly so as not to be themselves part of the cargo that plummeted into the sea.

The chest dropped straight down, struck the surface with a great plumping splash, and slipped beneath at once, too heavy to pause or

bob before taking on enough water to sink.

Prospero turned to the assembly.

"Beloved friends, let us decamp and be on our way. Eager am I to regain my native land. In the presence of such august men of Naples and Milan, this demi-paradise pales in my sight."

To Prospero's cell we returned, with lighter hearts and greater dispatch than we had left it. There, he and Miranda picked out the belongings they would carry with them. These the mariners packed and carted shipward.

As he surveyed the clearing before final parting, Prospero glanced about in annoyance. "Where the devil is the monster of this island? Where is Caliban? I would fain say a farewell to him."

"Good father," said I, "I have instructed Ariel to keep him from our ken, until such time as we have safely set sail. But if thou wish it . . ."

"No matter," said he, teetering on the edge of delay but at length backing off. "I have done with him."

To the ship we prepared to go, I arm in arm with Miranda and fearful in my soul of the world that lay beyond the island, the only home Caliban had ever known.

It was then that Miranda took me aside, she at last the embracer of delay and the augmenter of poor Caliban's fear of discovery.

Chapter Twenty-four

A Last Glimpse of Caliban

"Beloved," Miranda said to me, "I too would speak farewell to Caliban, he who has attacked us both, yet remains a brother to me."

Though I could have commanded her otherwise, in truth I was curious as well, fearful though I was. "And so you shall," I assured her. "I will be by to protect you, if need be." I had other reasons, of course, not to allow private converse.

I persuaded my father and the others, though PopEros set up his usual caterwauling, to proceed to the ship. Miranda and I would join them shortly, I said, nodding at the mage's unnecessary directions and reminding him aside that we had Ariel to guide us.

With much wave and farewell, they moved off.

Summoning Ariel, I confirmed that the monster's constraints were in place; Ariel knew what

I meant. I ordered that he be forced inside his hut. The sprite was to tell him that Miranda would meet him alone, there to take her farewell.

So it was, as far as he knew. I stood just outside the hut, there where a drape obscures the window opening. Knowing how sensitive were the ears of my former body, I instructed Ariel to maintain a soundscape that would match the surroundings were no one standing there.

Only their voices I heard, no bodies seen.

"Miranda," he said. She had entered the hut and was doubtless blinking to adjust her vision.

"How is your wound?" she ventured.

There was a pause.

There were, in the course of their interview, many pauses. In the treacherous abyss of each one, I imagined the prince struggling to reveal his identity but being restrained by the pinches that punished each attempt.

Finally: "It grows no worse."

"Your eyes look pained."

"It's what I am forced to go through," he gasped. With every word, what I had done to him seemed so clear that I feared at any moment to hear a gasp of recognition from Miranda.

"At long last, Father and I are leaving for Italy," she said. "Fret not, dear Caliban. Many years have you complained, with not a little justice, at having had the kingship of this island usurped from you. Now shall it be returned to you."

She paused, overcome.

"I must tell you," she said, "I am torn. Through thick veils of memory do I recall the women who

cared for me, though nothing of my mother. The life that lies ahead shall scarce seem my own, yet I am . . . happy with Prince Ferdinand."

"He . . ." The creature inside shifted violently and was at once subdued.

"His mention upsets you," said Miranda, distress in her voice. "No more. I shall think of you often, of our peculiar island family, your pain and soon your release from pain. I want to say I'll be back. But I won't; I know I won't."

I breathed easier as I sensed her comments drawing to a close.

"Don't go," pleaded the trapped prince.

She sobbed. "I must."

Then her dress rustled and she was leaving. In a moment, she would appear beside me.

"Ariel," said I to the sprite. "Keep the creature here until the anchor is raised. Then force him swiftly to shore. As the winds you summon puff the ship farther out to sea, release your hold on him. When he is out of earshot of the keenest mariner, or so far that his words confound intelligibility, free Caliban's tongue."

"Then shall Ariel free himself as well?"

I glanced sharply at him. Looking distraught, he at once backed off.

When Miranda appeared, her eyes were moist. I led her off, putting fingers upon my lips to stop her words. To the ship we proceeded.

On the way, I turned to Miranda. "Does the novelty of a new land excite you?"

She nodded. "And being one step nearer our betrothal, and all it shall bring. But yes, Italy entices. This island, since your arrival, has seemed crowded indeed. Scarce can I imagine

the uncountable number of souls soon to surround us."

"Nor can I."

I too, though my princely memories were
sharp and summonable, suffered heightened anticipation at the choke of men and women we
would encounter in Naples.

"I mean," said I in response to her puzzled
look, "I can only guess what the experience must
be like for you. Fear not. I shall be by your side
in all."

On our trek to the ship, my mind dwelt on the
vast freedom those numbers held out, on the
smells, the sights, the food (not yet eaten, whose
tastes lay yet vivid in recall), Ferdinand's sense
memories of which seemed to open the world
into innumerable paths of freedom.

We rejoined Miranda's father and the king on
board ship.

The shipmaster barked an order to the boat-
swain, who called out, "Up anchor!"

And up it went. At once, the spotless sails
snapped out fat and taut with a stiff brisk breeze.
True to his charge, Ariel brought the trapped
prince to the shore and by degrees released him.

Pitiful the sight.

I mean not that I pitied the prince, though
some of that emotion swelled in me.

I pitied *myself*.

Despite my translation into Ferdinand, the
ungainly shape my eyes battened on was the true
me. His gestures, grand and abrupt and raging,
were mine. They called up a world of past woes,
Caliban's woes, his cage, his fate now perversely
slipped.

His presence shocked my sight, continuously beyond the pale of belief. How could he be there, hurling high his fists and a volley of curses, sweeping one beckoning hand in pain? Yet here I stood, encased in alien flesh, watching the brushstrokes of my woe through unfamiliar eyes.

I breathed through lungs that were not mine. Though surrounded by abundant oxygen, the salt breezes fresh in my face, I felt suffocated. My easy inhalations fed the energies of the prince, whilst I, Caliban enclefted, did starve for sustenance.

"My noble lord?" Miranda caught me by the arm.

"It is nothing," said I, training a troubled glance upon the diminishing wretch whose high keens spun from him like thin red filaments. "I pity him. That's all."

"So do I," said she.

Her prince nearly wept.

Chapter Twenty-five

Shipboard, Looking Backward

"Attend to your father," I ordered my bride-to-be. She, uncertain, obeyed.

As the fan of the ship's wide wake opened its ribs and the monster I had been—as indeed the island of which the enclefted prince was now sole sovereign—crouched down and vanished, I craved nothing but solitude.

Bitter and complete my confusion.

Who was I?

Where was I going?

My heart felt as if it would burst. The thing upon the shore had blistered with wrath, a wrath that had been my birthright.

Deep inside me then, I felt the old anger rise up. My Caliban core had not in the slightest begun to dissolve in a sea of princely comforts. There at the heart of me dwelt my rage. The prince, whose body cloaked my spirit, had none.

314

An insane urge: I would go to Prospero, the man I had vowed to destroy, and beg to be whipped. I would restore Ariel to him, on condition that the mage order me pinched and disfigured. That perhaps would bring my rage boiling up to the surface where it belonged.

I winced. My eyes strained to peel back the horizon. Came the absurd wish that, even as we put more distance between ourselves and the island, it would rise on the forward horizon, turn grades of green, its gray miasma separating into beach white and bark black—and there my body would be, growing great in my sight.

For an instant, wanting to destroy Prospero before my resolve crumbled, I entertained the thought of commanding Ariel to imbibe entire the content of those books, filling my mind with their gist. By magic would I destroy my foe. The sooner my mind was up to the deed, the sooner my grief would be allayed.

Then I thought better of it. Did I want a sprite my mother had conjured from the realms of Setebos to learn the details of Prospero's greater magic?

I did not.

Gonzalo appeared beside me.

Though undetected in his approach, the old counselor startled me not. Never had he startled. So my princely recall told me.

From the warmth in my breast and the mass of memories that surrounded the man, I knew he had served as a kind of grandsire, a surrogate father, to the prince, especially as he toddled into early childhood while King Alonso, the con-

queror from Valencia, busied himself with introducing Spanish ways to Naples.

"An enchanting isle," said Gonzalo.

"It is indeed."

"I always love to leave Naples behind, the posturing and backbiting at court, the endless parade of petitioners with their stench and their woeful plaints gabbled out in low-born Italian. And my God, the crush of humanity on the streets! At sea, my mind blooms with new possibility. And on that island . . ." He shook his great head and clucked his tongue. "On that island, though ever at the call of your royal father, I felt free. Through what may seem like idleness, my fair young prince, the mind finds its proper calling, the places that beckon and promise and deliver fulfillment."

In such like vein did Gonzalo jabber on. But I could tell—and my Ferdinand-mind knew that *Gonzalo* knew it also (this a game they were seasoned at)—that he was really asking me, beyond words, what was troubling me.

One thought brewed in me: This man, too savvy by half, must needs be dispatched quickly, the sharp thrust of a dagger by moonlight perhaps.

"I'm not sure what's troubling me," said I.

Uncertainty could be expressed to Gonzalo without fear of gossip. One's enemies, it seems, were quick to exploit such.

I went on: "Unfinished business."

"With Caliban?"

"With the monster, yes."

"What sort of unfinished business?"

"I don't know," said I, understanding that he

knew I deigned not to share my reasons. I changed the subject. "What, I wonder, will Duke Prospero do?"

Gonzalo's lips tightened. "From what I gather, he'll reassert himself in Milan. His brother Antonio, penitent and forgiven, will carry on in the practical affairs of governance. Prospero will see to your betrothal to his daughter. When Miranda departs for Naples, his heart will break. I expect that he will then relinquish his dukedom entirely.

"Estranged from Milan and the people who did nothing to prevent his banishment, he will move to Naples to be close to his daughter and any grandchildren—forgive my temerity, my lord—which result from your union."

Grandchildren.

Yes.

I would cleft Miranda ardently and often. I would people my kingdom with Calibans, looked they never so regally scallop-skinned. Beneath that pampered hide, raging Calibans would they be.

I sighed.

"La vita nuova," I said.

"A new life indeed," said Gonzalo, mistaking my meaning.

"From here, the view is breathtaking."

The agreeable man agreed, a grandfather to the end.

Chapter Twenty-six
Naples

Once the island had collapsed beneath the horizon and I was, for the moment, able to let it go, I took an hour's rest in my cabin.

Restless and fidgety, I confirmed what I already knew, that Prospero's books were securely locked in my chest. Never was I not in control, but often (this was one of those times) my two sides skirmished. My Ferdinand was thrilled about his homecoming, my Caliban distraught at being bereft of his home.

Fortunately, the undone exile of Prospero and Miranda held everyone's attention. But for Gonzalo's troubled looks, my state of mind went unremarked. On that magnificent sun-drenched morning, Miranda ministered to her father, who grew more agitated as the northern coast of Italy graded into view.

Our approach was punctuated by booms of

cannon fire and muted outbursts of sound and motion from the shore. By the time our ship entered the harbor, an enthusiastic crowd of excited Neapolitans had coalesced on the grand dock, threatening to capsize it.

King Alonso and his son, though but for a day, had been presumed drowned in the tempest. So the sudden return of the king's ship, unharmed and with the loss of not one lord nor mariner, gave the populace grounds for great rejoicing.

Appalled was I as the teeming masses of humanity grew great in my sight. So many faces, so many roiling bodies. My princely self took it all in stride, the trumpet blats, the high thunder of drums, the arrival at length of horse-drawn carriages, the huzzahs and hat tossings of ragmen and fishmongers alike.

Naples lay naked beneath the lidless eye of heaven, and all was laughter and the undifferentiated shouts of greeting. Prospero waved from his carriage, people pointing at him and craning to a neighbor to assure themselves who he was.

But word had spread.

Even dartings of young boys who had never seen nor little heard of the twelve-years-deposed Duke of Milan welcomed him with that simple peasant charm so swiftly displayed, so swiftly set aside beneath the dark brow of impoverishment.

To Castelnuovo we went, taking elaborate detours through piazza after piazza. Long since, behind the pomp of our arrival, the shipmaster had overseen the unloading of our goods and their conveyance to the castle.

319

I had given strict orders, and sent Ariel ahead to ensure them, that my belongings be placed in my chambers, but that the unpacking of my personal items—one chest in particular—be left for later.

Indeed, my first order of business in the castle, after running the gauntlet of enthusiastic servants and ministers, was to secret my stash of books in the base of the private wardrobe opposite my bed.

Once those precious volumes were secure and I could breathe free, the sheer detail of manufacture, the great buildings and teeming piazzas visible from my window began to overwhelm me.

Memories crowded in. The masses of people the prince had confidently strode among: fruit shops thronged with customers, shoemakers sitting and sewing in front of their shops, roasters of coffee beans, those who boiled a soup out of chestnuts and bread. For the prince within, they constituted the fabric of humanity; as for poor Caliban, their sheer numbers made him frantic.

In the days ahead, Duke Prospero was feted and shown about. I knew him well enough to tell—from his tone, the hint of a look, a hardening of his already harsh tones—what truck he had had with each minister prior to his exile.

With Miranda on my arm, I put on a convincing show as the proud young prince who had found his bride, and his people's future queen, at last.

But when I was alone, it was all I could do to keep from leaping out of my skin.

I wanted to stab someone. Anyone.

I wanted to stab myself.

I despised being who I was not.

Hoodwinking Gonzalo taught me how best to mask the split in my person. More and more, I relied on princely instinct to see me through. Beneath the watchful eye of the grizzled counselor, I learned to cower deep inside the prince, relaxing my Calibanish control, sending forth this or that impulse, which the prince would most politickly and obligingly transmogrify.

But after the grand entourage had departed for Milan, taking Prospero and Miranda home (my perverse family gone for the nonce)—leaving only myself and Ariel, a toad who knew me not—my fear of the bristling unbathed masses and my alienation from my new body grew worse.

One morning I awoke to this resolve: I would return to the island posthaste, unspeak the spell, and send the prince back where he belonged and I, most assuredly, did not.

Thus did I act.

My father the king was elsewise engaged, on yet another visit to his mistress Lucrezia. So I hastily ordered up a small sailing ship and four tight-lipped mariners who would ask no questions, convey me where I desired, and spread no gossip afterwards.

I repacked Prospero's books beneath the folds of clothing in my chest and had it put on board in my cabin. Those books, upon the island, I intended to diligently study, one day to return to Milan for the bloody deed. Given sufficient grounding in magic, I might even, I thought, discover how to dispatch my tormentor from a dis-

tance. Yet I wanted to watch him die, right there in the rent flesh.

Ariel spirited me through the streets of Naples and on board ship, ushering me through the crowds unnoticed as though I were a swift column of unoccupied air.

Vultured with Enzo, my shipmaster, over navigational maps, I informed him of our destination.

He, having been on the prior voyage, knew the way at once. No questions did he pose. His face was weathered rock, his ears big blocky extrusions hung from the sides of a shaved bullish pate. In his vast upswept hand, the map was a stray wisp.

He left the table and went aboard to brief his crew and up anchor.

Ariel hung about my shoulder, a mild irritant. He wanted to ask, but didn't dare, why we were returning to the island of his captivity.

I looked at him. What difference would it make if he knew the truth? None.

But he would *not* know it. Not yet. Perhaps not ever.

"Tend to the breezes," I commanded him. "Let their full-cheeked blasts bring us swiftly thither. Push the ship to the brink of danger. These are skilled sailors. Test them. Break records. Go."

He went. In an instant, a surge of wind filled the sails and rushed us forward, scudding out of the harbor, beelined southwest with urgency and hope.

I emerged from my cabin and stood at the ship's prow, willing it on, the knifecut wet and wounding, unclefting the boat, unclefting my life, hurrying me home.

Chapter Twenty-seven

Homecoming

The sailors must have thought their prince daft. I cared not a whit what they thought.

As the ship's prow sliced forward, I caught Ariel's gusts at my back and a strong buffet of breezes upon my face. What skill Enzo brought to bear on steering us to the bay of my birth was ruddered and made precise by my enslaved sprite.

There were no wasted movements.

Hours passed and still, hatless, I stood at the prow. It seemed as if time had stretched thin and wide, a vast plane interminable. Yet a longed-for terminus lay ahead.

The unbroken blue of the horizon, that stubborn line of sea and sky rolling up still more sea and sky, at last gave up its monotony. We headed straight for the gradual differentiation, the ship's thrust and slap against the roll of the

sea piling more distinctness upon what lay ahead.

I feared some other island, an off-course error, Ariel rebellious at last through some crack in my magic prowess.

But Sardinia and Sicily we had long put behind us. And the land that suffered our slow approach took on the curve and curl I recalled from their reversal as we left the island.

Out of a thin morning mist, the place of my mother's exile and my birth rose as unhurried as the unclosing of an eye. The sure fixture of inland mountain, the greens of tree and bush, the expanse of beach that elongated and grained with sand before my eyes—these thrilled me, even as my princely mind felt puzzled at my excitement.

Into the bay we gusted.

Ariel at last left off his ceaseless puffing and the sails were lowered and secured with ropes. With a splash, the anchor dropped deep and caught. Enzo rowed me ashore, his sun-darkened biceps bulging thicker than my thigh, his lipline broad and unbroken.

Enzo was a man of blunt beaded eyes and spare words. Vast wisdom seemed to loom behind his stoic veil, but the prince had once drawn it aside, finding naught there but an ancient swamp, miasmal mist, a lidded lizard caught in endless sleep.

"Return to the ship," I commanded him. "A matter of hours should see my return. If by the setting of the sun I have not appeared, seek for me inland at the monster's hut or at Duke Prospero's former dwelling place."

His obedience beyond question, Enzo wasted no energy on grunted assent. Relaunching the boat, he crabbed into it so that it bobbed upon the placid bay. Then he took up in his large hands its matchstick oars and pulled toward the ship.

I summoned Ariel.

"I am here," said the sprite, no Enzo he when it came to superfluous words.

"Overfly the island. Weave if need be a vast blanket of overflyings," said I. "Find Caliban. Cast a spell on him. Keep him there 'til I come. Make the brute docile, neither raising a hand to me nor threatening to do so."

"I obey." Superfluous.

He returned. "Good master, you will find the monster outside Prospero's cell. Nor shall he stir till you see him."

"How is he disposed?"

"Above the earth and beneath the sky. Methought his open eyes glimpsed me, but that cannot be. Nonetheless, he turns toward us even now, head humbled upon his chest, more unsightly than when we left him."

"Thanks, good Ariel," said I, too impatient to wonder at his odd manner of speech. "I'll to him at once. Stay with the ship until my return."

Eager then, and glad to sniff my native air even through nostrils not mine, I set off across the beach and into the trees. Soon would I leave the cleft of this hateful body, take up residence once more in my own, feeling familiar limbs branch from belly and torso, and those further branch to fingers, toes, and clefter.

Farewell the pinch of boots. Farewell the un-

wanted burdens of prince and potentate, a betrothed entanglement with an enemy's daughter, the feverish cramming of arcane practices into my head against a day of revenge.

Here would I bide my time, here where no distractions slowed me. Here would my skills in magic grow, my body, by time's balm and the touch of a gentler sort of sprite, of its long torment be healed. Ariel would I recleft into his pine tree, silenced and made powerless until such time as I was ready to take down my nemesis.

Tree and stream and path, familiar companions, swept by, made new by relief in homecoming and the anticipation of freedom. Prospero's cell seemed impossibly distant, so eager was I to reach it and speak the spell of undoing.

I paused. Ariel had been bound to me by his former master. Would that connection remain once my shape-change was undone? Or had Prospero told him that henceforth he belonged to the prince? Should I summon the sprite now, reveal who I was, and bind him surely to me?

Time enough to decide that when my victim and I were face to face.

Twigs snapped beneath my boot heels. The surge about me of unwashed Neapolitan scallop-skins was but a memory. Princely power would I abjure for one pure chance, in my own body, at revenge.

I would undo the bad father Prospero, strip him of skin like a sapling of its bark, set into his exposed muscles the deep pinch and torment of insect pincers, their hot carapaces scorching wherever they crawled.

And Miranda, bored of the boring prince whose body Caliban had abandoned, overjoyed at sight of her healed and rejuvenated half-brother, the fair Miranda would o'erleap her royal confinement and come away to this island paradise. No longer would I loathe her, but love her completely.

Then the foliage parted and I saw Prospero's cell and before it, the monster. My body, canopied beneath a broad bowed branch. His wide eyes stared past me. His ankles, goitered necks bloated with blood, hung thick and heavy. His toes hovered one small stretch above the ground. That stretch, unessayed, had sufficed to sever his life's cord.

I drew near the unclothed corpse, mine and not mine. I circled it, took in its discoloration, its distortions, the excrement crusted in jagged Vs along the backs of its thighs.

I was not breathing, yet my lungs were too full, as though I had inhaled too much too fast.

I heard a voice.

His?

No, mine.

The words were familiar yet not quite placeable. With dull Trinculo had I last used them, before we re-exchanged shapes and he lost all memory of it.

The spell of undoing.

Stop, I told myself. The words hung fire, building up behind my teeth.

Images flooded in. Me recovering my shape, as full of vigor as my present form. The corpse that hung before me would take on, somehow, the shape of Prince Ferdinand's long-dead body.

Or perhaps he would jink and flail there, the noose tight about his neck, the ground farther from his shorter legs.

I let the words reel out to their finish.

Then began the transformation.

I was staring at my hand. I upraised it to my eyes. The skin darkened, the fingers elongated, the nails taking on a familiar yellowish hue and curve.

But no life did I feel there. It was as if I were flexing a mailed glove.

All over, dead skin encased me. Death dropped down upon my thighs, my legs, my feet. All feeling fled from face and chest.

My bones began to tingle and droop.

In haste, I blurted the spell of transforming. I had to force it out before my tongue went numb, before his dead brain thudded down over my living one. My lips hung like baffles of flesh. Yet as long as my tonguetip could articulate, I pressed on, frantic, toward the spell's end.

Still babbling, I fell to the ground, my mind on that single point of completion. Only later did I register the prince's body hanging from the rope, inert still but with the renewed vibrancy of life, about to jerk with his first failed gasp, if the spell of undoing went that far.

The hanged man's dead brain helmet began to slam down and secure its leaden clamp of inert cells. My gums and the insides of my cheeks died, as numb as a leg too long constrained and gone to sleep.

Still I pressed on, redoubling the speed of my chant. My muscles fought against eternal slumber. My tongue had turned to a wad of dough.

But I spat out the last syllables, staccato and riding rage at my stupidity.

And the changes came on.

Was I too late? Would the doing fail to override the undoing? Or would the princely body I regained be dead from hanging, its neck snapped, its heart stopped?

I threw myself on the mercy of unmerciful Setebos. My lungs thickened, blurred, and died, a seizure I could not reverse. My heart burst.

With immense weight, the monstrous brain helmet thickened upon me. My eye-stems strained and gave out, darkness penetrant and swooping down. A massive failure of internal organs sounded their trump below, but I was beyond caring.

Then a curtain of unconsciousness dropped down entire and I knew no more.

Chapter Twenty-eight
Acceptance and Return

Submerged.

No sound.

Sparkles alone above, where sunlight spangled the surface of the bay. Through that brilliance arrowed, unhurried, my mother's firm brown hand.

She seized my boyish arm and pulled me, smooth and sure, through the airless water until my head burst free. I flailed and shouted and caught a tinge of chill upon the breeze.

Still, Mom was the picture of calm. "All the time in the world, son," she said. "He'll wait."

With relief, I leaped into her arms, feeling her warm moist flesh against my body, her embrace, my eager slide deep inside her, enveloped by the world. Along my scalp and spine, drops dried, pulling the skin tight.

Thus affirmed, I trembling waked.

The sour solidity of earth stirred in my nostrils. Above, stench-wafts of rotting meat.

I raised my head. Again my eyes took in my dead body. I turned away and wept.

Sitting up at length, I cried, "Coward prince! Was being Caliban for two days as bad as that? May you roast forever in your Christian hell!"

I tried to say more, but the sight seized my throat. Never again would my spirit animate those loathsome limbs. All my plans for healing, for the gradual accretion of power here on my island, had been blown to heaven.

I was trapped in this simpering prince's body, he whose spirit had hanged me and shut off that avenue to the future. The mere thought of Ferdinand revolted me. But in this simulacrum of his body would I live out my days, until such time as another shape-change became necessary.

But could I not do that at once?

Be a king?

Or a beggar?

Or anyone at all?

Then I feared that one such shift was perhaps all that the spell allowed.

In an instant, I knew these things: that I would remain in the prince's body at least until Prospero's death; that I would loathe being him; and that I would soon test my concern by the same means I had used on Trinculo.

Switch. Switch back. If necessary, dispatch.

Royalty had its ways.

I rose.

Bury my old body? The thought made me laugh.

Let jackals claw the corpse down flay by flay, find sustenance in its poor flesh, suck lashed hatred from the marrow of femur and rib.

I had work to do, deception afoot, princely pomp, the bedroom duties of a husband, and with the remainder of my time a feverish plunge into Prospero's books.

I scanned the clearing, which now seemed, with the stench of rot pervasive, to be as devoid of life as the corpse roped up before me.

Memory, I knew, would bring back other times: with Mom and without her, cursing the Italian ex-duke who whipped me and pinched me and kept me from his daughter. In memory would this clearing again bristle with life.

Once more, with my eyes open and raw, I took in the corpse. I am dead, thought I.

Nonsense. That body is dead.

Who then am I?

My internal prince held to the opinion that it hardly mattered.

But the thought shot through me that, for the nonce, I was precisely my reliable rage. No more did I identify with my resolve to unravel and snap the life strands of the mage who had murdered my mother, he my father who had known it and brought me up through warp, torment, and disfigurement.

After his departure from this earth, slow and deeply suffering, would I revisit this question, this wavering flame of identity.

I turned away.

One last time, I took the path to the bay of my birth, letting the trees slip by; the vistas; the glimpses of birdlife, the snap of unseen hoofs as

fans of sunlight splayed upon carpets of pine needles.

By the time I reached the edge of the beach, Enzo had lowered the boat and begun rowing for shore.

Chapter Twenty-nine

Prospero's Journal

To Naples I returned.

I resumed my role as *locum tenens generalis*, superintending the kingdom in the king's absence.

I fought a war against Florence and received a hero's welcome, my ineptitude in command concealed beneath layers of politic lies.

On Maundy Thursday, I followed the king's custom, washing the feet of the poor, one for each year of my life, then serving them food and drink and giving them money and clothing.

At jousts was I praised for how I held myself, for my riding and the way I handled a lance. Born to the saddle, they said.

Had they only known.

But at night, by candlelight, I set aside the masks of pomp, pride, and circumstance to study magic. With naught but Prospero's books

did I fill my mind. Months passed. I grew savvy, sufficient at last, so I thought, to trump my father-in-law.

For the wedding had indeed taken place. Miranda had been duly and routinely clefted, occupying a bedchamber near to my own. Prospero had, in a shorter time than many supposed, relinquished his dukedom and was himself ensconced in a chamber in Castlenuovo, growing slightly dotty.

I don't know what precisely stayed my hand from the act. Though my resolve and readiness were beyond question, some shadow came betwixt my desire and the deed.

Recalling the journal volumes that had held the secret of my paternity, I was overwhelmed by a desire to view the rest of them. What had PopEros had to say about his slaves Caliban and Ariel, his daughter Miranda, his hidden lust for her, the island, his banishment? What more had he written about the son he had got upon Sycorax?

As it happened, I managed to read only a few early volumes, enough to stay my hand from a deed I would have regretted. Had I discovered the truth after having ended Prospero's life, I would have done to this princely body what the prince had done to mine. With the sway of my weight would some dark castle beam have creaked.

Here is what I found in Prospero's account of his landing on our island:

The savage boy, he who could but gutturally grunt and proudly point me out a spirit,

yclept Ariel, caught in the cleft of a pine, brought us to his dwelling, a hut slapped together of mud and thatch.

He and I entered.

Gray shafts of light pierced the interior. Odors of must and earth cloyed at my face.

Then I saw her, sprawled and shivering on a pallet, half-covered by a blanket.

"Sycorax," said I.

It had been more than twelve years. Her face had filled out considerably, from beguiling crone to wasted one, in that short span. But there was no mistaking her. One forgets not one's violator, she who has coaxed forth the shame of one's body.

She had known of my coming, I divined. More than likely she had contrived it. "Prospero," she said, a slick fever glistening her brow.

Noticing her son almost as a distraction, she dismissed him in that same gibberish with which he had befouled the air.

As soon as I saw the vile witch, I knew, scarce one thought intervening, who the boy was.

Bitter fruit of my loins.

When he had gone, I broached the question.

"Of course," she said. "I call him Caliban, though he knows not his name nor the identity of his father. Of Prospero's seed is he, though his spirit rises from the dark god that used your body for my pleasure."

"Abused, you mean," I corrected. I was about to tell her what effect that encounter

336

had had on me, my sudden and perdurable obsession with priapism, my propulsion into the study of magic, the painful pregnancy (that six-month bedridden, the stings piercing deep) and fatal childbirth suffered by Miranda's mother, whose horrendous death had hurled me with redoubled energy back into my magic books.

But I saw, behind the strength of her staring, how desperate the woman was. This, my Algerian ravisher and ruiner, she of the Berber tribe, was dying, teetering on the verge of oblivion.

What began as a moan of pain, a thing that I thought might become a death rattle, slipped into chant.

I recognized the devil name, Setebos, the formulaic opening she had used upon me in Algiers. But the stakes were higher for her, and no hint of lust hung now in the air.

"This time," said I, "triumph shall be mine."

Though her eyelids tensed at my words, she ceased not her verbal assault.

I stood my ground, feeling no ill effects. Thirteen years before, as the witch chanted her enticements, the devil she summoned had caught me in a slow fierce grip.

Now, nothing.

But I knew from my studies that some spells must be entirely spoken before they start to take hold. I did not delude myself that this might not be one of them.

Sycorax ended with a flourish, her eyes flaring in triumph. Then the impact hit in

waves, the first wave a welter of confusion.

I saw her face change, heard her skull bones crack and reform, before I felt my own. She sprouted a beard, identical in color to mine, flowing outward even as mine sucked into my jaw and vanished, my skin cool from the uncovering, then flush with fever.

That fever spread downward everywhere. My chest browned and burgeoned out in twin puffs and sprawls.

When my hand, whose appearance now mimicked hers, shot to my shame, that male monstrosity had shrunk away entire, infolding into a wrinkled darkling pouch.

Though wise Tiresias had suffered this fate, Duke Prospero was not about to accept it.

I willed myself to remain calm, telling the beads of my thoughts quickly and clearly. The changes sank deep into my chest and belly. Over my scalp, then beneath, they oozed. If I did naught to counteract this hellish transformation, I should surely die.

I feared to lose myself in the engulfment. But my mind remained intact, deprived of neither memory nor its well-trod paths of thought, even as I felt my brain start to lobe and lump out in new directions.

Although, through some stop in her spell, I was not privy to her set of mind, the chill and fever of my now-womanly limbs betrayed the witch's intent. Rob me of my body, drop her failing health upon me, let

me suffer her death whilst she, as Prospero, lived on.

But I had learned from my occult masters the spirit leap.

Its simple words awaited me. My struggle lay in gaining control of a new mouth, its vocal apparatus yet forming. I stumbled over gibberish, catching Italian imperfectly upon her tongue, then closing upon it like a hunter that corners a wild boar and comes in for the kill.

I spake the spell, pressing on with more assurance than I felt. From the dying witch-body I leaped, the air between us spangling about me in sparks of red and green and white. Behind me, I heard the vacant mass of my body topple, as into the new-minted Prospero body abed I flew, imperfectly aimed but certain in my leap of faith.

That familiar body came about me like a coat of calm, a meaty armor that was at once my shame and my comfort.

The spirit of Sycorax hung there too, struggling still to accommodate to its strange environs.

Another quick word, and I entrapped her spirit inside me forever. I might instead have expelled her. But I wanted first to make certain of my control over her, and to gain an assurance that she had not some-how corrupted my flesh with the powers of her Patagonian devil-god.

I rose from the pallet and stripped my royal garments from her corpse, inert on the dirt floor. Later would I air them, cleanse

them in a stream. For now, I would not let
on that anything untoward had happened.

Let the boy, whose parentage would remain a secret, watch the flames of a funeral
pyre consume his dead mother. There
would be time enough another day to sort
out the implications of what had occurred.

Sufficient now to realize that my white
magic had bested her black. For that I
praised God and my own due diligence.

Outside the hut stood the dark-skinned
smudge, the residue of my earlier encounter
with the witch, a blot upon my escutcheon
despite my having been forced.

This Caliban was, in the grossest of carnal
terms, a son of mine. But of mine, no son.
He was offspring to a devil and a witch. His
begetting occasioned no guilt in me.

Even so, that filthy encounter had led to
my beloved wife's malignancy and death
and to my obsession with male shame, the
ruthless suppression of it, and how even so
it burbled over in fevered dreams.

Froth.

A lifetime in Purgatory earned with each
nasty, if inadvertent, spurt.

Adjusting my clothing, feeling as though
I had not left my body at all, I took a slow
steady calming breath and passed through
the mud hut's squat doorway.

I lay the journal aside, there in the night calm
and dead middle of my chambers. An oil lamp
blazed bright at my right hand.

Thoughts whirled in my head. I was able to

anchor none of them. I reread the passage, the unsettling track along which Prospero's words ran, no easier to assimilate and no less extraordinary the second time.

My plan to kill Prospero after long torment had now to be unhatched and reincubated, another egg chosen for careful tending and the eventual hatch.

Rescuing Mom. That became my one and only goal.

Chapter Thirty

Gathering My Courage

I despised being a prince.

Not that I had complaints against the power, the adoration of the unwashed, the finery, the food. They were a saving grace.

But Ferdinand was a small man, small in stature. No one dared speak of it, but he knew it, they all knew it, holding him in less esteem than they otherwise would.

Building up his body made no difference.

I despised his hands, the shape of them like splays of bleached oak leaves, their joints and lines and knuckle ridges anticipating in look and feel the inevitable decline of age.

His world was not, nor would it ever be, mine. I resisted it mightily, resented it, even as I carried out with reasonable skill its demands.

All those people. All that noise and stench. Never could I seek out a small patch of ground,

a little oasis of reprieve, a place to sit and drink in bird song and the limitless depths of the sky.

Far worse, Ferdinand was an indifferent clefter, no majestical tower in standing and too quickly triggered, despite his boasts to the contrary. With due diligence, I improved his performance somewhat, but I knew that neither Miranda nor my other quick conquests were satisfied.

Were there castle intrigues? Beneath-stairs trysts? 'Tis certain there were for me. I was not one to pass up an opportunity to peel back the bud of a flower. For a young prince, his castle is a vast and aromatic garden of blooms both willing and obedient.

My bastard son Enrique was one offshoot, a product of Caliban's rage upon a fetching scullery maid.

Miranda's womb yielded up a daughter and a son. My girl Leonor had her father's inner fire. But I suspect that Federigo had someone else's.

If Miranda's indiscretions, rare as they were, had ever been bruited about, I would have had her killed. But she was wily in such matters, and I secretly admired the wench for it. She too, after all, was of the island, not the court, and such guile came not easy.

But in truth I had no time to track her, no desire to sic the nosy sprite on her. My days were spent in outward shows of royalty, even as I continued my late-night study of magic.

Prospero was growing more and more feeble. But I wanted complete assurance when came time to assault him. I would triumph over him, I would obliterate him, and I would rescue

Mom. Her body, as healthy and immortal as I could make it, would be restored.

She perhaps would know a way to regenerate her son's original body undeformed. Many spells had Mom known, of Setebos learned, of which she had left no record.

But was her spirit intact and not dispersed? Did it live, pinched down hard and tiny, inside the mage's body? Or would there be no one left to assume control, upon his rude eviction from those premises?

I hurried over Prospero's journals, a skim and a skip to gather the gist of the remaining volumes. There were no further mentions of her, no internal struggles to keep her warring spirit contained.

I took to spending more hours with my now-ailing father-in-law. With suspicion did he meet my princely interest in him, but also with gratitude and surprise.

My true purpose I masked behind a desire to learn the wisdom of my elders, not simply the king my father's, nor Gonzalo's—whom I had not had murdered after all—but that of a very special man, I said, who had for twelve years communed with his thoughts on a small patch of paradise undisturbed.

Prospero spoke.

I nodded, yet listened not at all.

More precisely, I tracked his inner voice.

I strained to hear Mom, her inflections, the betrayal of a phrase or syllable turned oddly, some confirmation, any at all, that she was there still.

Fancy only.

I listened intently at the edges of Prospero's mind, sharp here, dull there and going to scatter. Even so, as a weak soldier wounded may call upon hidden reserves to survive and triumph, so I knew that even a mind enfeebled might marshal its forces to defend itself against attack, rolling back years of lassitude and decay for one final battle in a war between sorcerers.

I had to be sure. I had to know that his defeat was certain.

If that meant further years of delay, so be it.

In the end, that strategy proved most wise.

Chapter Thirty-one

The Assault

When, in my late-night delvings into Dee and Agrippa, I found and honed the self-same spirit leap that PopEros had used against Mom, I knew it was time.

Beyond that leap of my own spirit, I had mastered sufficient magic that I was able to toss one spirit into a different body, controlling as well which of the two would prevail after the throw.

King Alonso, my reputed father, foundered in riotous living and would soon, I thought, be dead without any help from me. In any case, I cared not a whit for politics and power. I wanted my old self back, and freeing Mom would, I thought, give me that.

Prospero was ailing, lying abed and attended by court physicians. Pills, purgatives, herbs, a diet of fruit and broth, gold leaf steeped in dis-

tilled waters—nothing they did would slow his slide toward the lip of death.

His body was failing him, as Mom's had failed her.

It was the perfect time to attack.

My plan was simple. Having dismissed his attendants, I would trick Miranda to her father's chambers, there to bind and gag her. Her father's spirit would I hurl into her bound body.

Then would Mom be the sole indwelling spirit in the mage's frame. She would quickly, how quickly I knew not, assume control there. Perhaps her own form would return. Of that I could not be sure.

In the final gesture, Mom would shape-change with my struggling Miranda, taking on my wife's form, even as the bound woman was translated to the shape and sick limbs of her dying father. It would be an easy matter to stop that body's breath and dispatch father and daughter both.

Would I be forgoing my deep-seated plan for a revenge that lingered? I would. But the years, and my desire to secure the release and return of my mother, had diminished the import of that goal. And if I succeeded in so binding my foe, I wanted not to waste one moment in which he might devise a way to strike back.

Swift dispatch was best.

I began with a stroke of good fortune. The great god Setebos had smiled upon me. The king, after an over-rich supper of creams and cucumbers, sustained a severe attack that brought him to his sickbed.

His scurry of court physicians were baffled.

They were also busy. So busy, indeed, that I was assured of minimal interruption.

Even so, I commanded Ariel to stand guard outside the door, ready to numb the hand of any that dared attempt it.

Feigning concern for Miranda's father, I enticed her to his chambers. There, under sedation, the man snoozed, a high pinched bird-stutter in his nostrils.

I gagged my wife first, surprise and strength my advantage. No sounds did she make but the grunts and shifts of struggle. Miranda, a puff of wind in my arms, went down, roped three ways to an ornate chair.

I tightened the gag until the soft cloth lay taut and knife-edged against her bloodless cheeks. Prospero would be allowed no chance, once clefted in his daughter's body, to articulate a spell.

By this time, the mage's eyes had drifted open to behold the final moments of Miranda's binding. He began struggling against the effects of infusions of poppy and mandragora upon his mind.

Swiftly I spoke the spirit-tossing spell, which from long study I had by heart. (A pair of servants, the ones least capable, had suffered my experiments with same and had then been hurried off to feed the fishes.)

Into Miranda's rope-taut body I hurled her father's spirit, swearing I saw it scream through the air, hands out, arrowing straight between her breasts and vanishing with a *snuk!* inside her.

To Prospero's shell of a corpus, collapsed back on the bed, I turned my attention.

It was imperative that Mom—despite the drowsy syrups Prospero had imbibed, her long years of being suppressed, and the weakened state of her host's body—seize her main chance before that body expired.

I moved to the bed, giddy with the sick sweat smell that rose from it, and called, "Mom. It's me. Caliban."

I took up a mottled hand and smacked the back of it. "Mom, wake up. Can you hear me?"

The eyes in the old man's skull attempted to focus. His mouth closed upon phrases, but they eluded him.

I felt a sudden thrust of needles in my mind and shot a glance toward Miranda, whose eyes glared with murderous intent.

Beneath the gag, her jaw was moving.

Before the mage could launch his full attack, though too late to stop it, I realized my miscalculation. The duke, it seemed, did not need to articulate his spells; fierce *intent* in the movements of throat and tongue were all he needed.

The same assault he had used on Mom the day he landed on our island did he now attempt on me.

Rudely, into my chest, his spirit lanced.

Within a body, when two spirits warring to the death confront one another, there are no secrets. Subterfuge and feigning are impossible.

I saw PopEros in all his ugliness.

But he, not expecting Caliban inside the prince, faltered when he saw me.

I say "saw," but in fact words fail. The closest

I can come to describing it is to ask that you imagine, in one soul, the most ferocious craving matched equally with an absolute resistance.

Now treble that intensity.

We speak often of being of two minds. But when two distinct spirits fight in this way, there is swiftly born true alien hostility, the sweat and arousal of wrestlers, arms locked about necks, circling in a dead heat.

Thus it was with me and Prospero inside my princely body. A battle raged between wits, a battle to the death.

He came on raging with confidence, but mine surpassed his. Confidence plays a huge part in such battles, and I realized that Mom must have faltered in hers, long ago in that mud hut.

Her son would not so falter now.

Panic rose in me. I would have none of it. Although my plan had gone awry, I knew in my soul of souls that Mom and I would triumph.

As we struggled, the pinched mage's body, racked with fever, rose from its deathbed and lurched toward Miranda. Mom's ferocity glared savage in its eyes.

She fumbled out her captor's clefter, which had taken on thickness and moment. In the Berber tongue, tortured through an alien windpipe, she blasted out a spell that snapped the ropes and split Miranda's garments, neck to calf, so that they dropped to the floor about her.

When Miranda attempted to rise, the being that looked like her father shoved her back into the chair. It tipped and fell, and the mage-man spun it aside across the stone floor.

"I've long wanted this, my dear daughter,"

came his harsh tones. Into her he shoved. When there was no give, he again pressed his assault upon tender tissue. Beneath him, Miranda screamed into the gag, her eyes wild.

What Prospero and I witnessed quite put him off—as in truth it did me—so that the internal struggle between us turned in my favor.

Miranda's hands flailed useless in the dead folds of clothing at her sides. But what I had taken as her helplessness sprouted, in one quick determined hand, a dagger. She worked it about, struggling for a good striking arc against her attacker.

I could tell it wasn't easy. Not merely the physical differences informed against her. The shock of being violated by her father made the deed more difficult. Could she bear to kill him? Or would she seek to control the dagger's point of entry and its depth sufficient to wound him only?

"She's got a dagger!" I shouted.

But the arc had begun. My warning came too late. Into the rapist's left side, between his ribs, Miranda plunged the blade, then yanked it free, and it clattered across the floor.

The struggle I observed froze and ceased. Then the attacker's mouth, Mom clefted inside Prospero, began to reel out the shape-changing spell from a body threatening to go into shock.

Out came the spell, its tail end a colorful whip of insistence.

My nemesis, bent no doubt on some counter-spell, tried to wrest control of my mouth. I stopped him, sheer will exerted over my princely domain. Control did I allow him of neither lar-

ynx nor tongue. His dismay over seeing his daughter attacked by himself tasted of wormwood and ash.

My ravished wife now grew gray-haired and bearded. A muffled cry of anguish escaped from her stopped mouth but dipped into lower tones as her lips thinned and withered. Her breasts deswelled like sea waves spent, while the skin about them stained and mottled 'midst moles and wiry chest hair. Her hips narrowed and frailed, even as the hips of her attacker plumped out womanly and enticing.

Still in Prospero's nightshirt, Mom assumed Miranda's shape. Her hand shot to the pain of her violated cleft, as she stared triumphant upon her victim's transformation into the stabbed body of her dying father. From the naked man's left side, blood welled and spilled.

In the grimacing stasis of matched combat did I hold the spirit of Prospero, long enough for me to speak the spell. Into that failing body where now Miranda dwelt, I tossed the mage's spirit.

In my mind's eye, he fled from the locked deathgrip of our wits and flew, backward flailing with a soundless curse upon his soul's lips, into the bare ruined body on the floor.

"Prospero's there too!" I shouted, my limbs drenched in sweat.

Prospero tried to speak through the gag. In his eyes sparked a ferocity and a desperation, one stubborn cinder flaring before its collapse into darkness.

But Mom, looking for all the world like Miranda in her father's night shirt, clamped shut his nose and what narrow gap remained of his

mouth. In haste, she chanted a spell to drain the strength from him. Long enough was air kept from him that he lost consciousness and lay still.

"A little longer," she muttered. Her eyes battened on his inertness, but her hand moved not from its vulture post upon the old man's face.

Miranda's gentle hand, which oft I had kissed, Mom now controlled, locking it down upon Prospero's nose and mouth—pinched nose pinched shut, thin slitted mouth that would never more speak cut or curse.

"A little longer. A little longer."

I went to her.

Upon my fallen foe I stared, picturing his trapped spirit entwined with his daughter's, both quiescing, resigned, to death.

"One moment more," said Mom, rocking intently on her hams, her taut hand a linchpin that wavered not one hair in its murderous intent.

I watched, fascinated, my breath stopped so as not to disturb the silent air.

Epilogue
Clefted

Anticipating one's triumph over an enemy is full to bursting with sensual delight.

Having triumphed? Sheer deflation.

Again and again have I felt an arc of oh-my-yes, the up-leap of one's projections into un-bounded joy, followed by a swift plunge into misery deeper than before.

Mom, garbed in the stench of Prospero's deathshirt, her Miranda hand frozen in that pitched tent of bone and skin over the mage's nose, said, "Bring me something to wear."

"Yes, Mom." A hint of Ariel echoed in my words, but it was a momentary jar in my filial progress.

I visited my wife's chambers, retrieved her blue velvet gown, and returned. Showing none of Miranda's modesty, Mom stripped off the nightshirt and dressed herself boldly before me.

354

She took stock of her new mortal casing. "Petite morsel, isn't she?" she said with a laugh.

Suddenly I ached for the company of the unassuming Miranda, though while she lived I had avoided her. In truth, I felt the same about her father.

"I miss them," I said.

Mom fixed an eye on me. "That's not my son speaking. That's the simp Ferdinand. They kept me under, those two. They whipped you and covered your perfect body in wounds and scars. Hell hath not sufficient fuel to roast them, not for a thousand thousand years."

Trapped behind Prospero's eyes, she had seen it all. My full term of torment, from the moment she died.

I ducked the challenge. "Does your healing spell work on a corpse?"

Mom knew at once that I was concerned about how we would explain Prospero's knife wound.

"We'll see," she said, releasing at last her grip on his nose, the dents she had pressed into his face slowly lifting.

She spoke the same spell with which she had healed my boyish scrapes. The old man's knife wound hesitated, then closed up. There was still the blood, on his body, on the floor.

Mom swept up the discarded nightshirt and gazed upon her victim.

"Where's Ariel?"

"Guarding the door."

"Summon him. Return his command to me. He'll make short work of this."

Feeling ill at ease, I did as Mom ordered.

Epilogue

From that moment, my path was clear.

It was good to have dispatched Prospero, good even to have released Mom from her bonds. But she was, though my memory had painted her with greater kindness, who she was. My earliest confiner. And right back into that role had she stepped.

In boyhood, it had not felt like confinement.

Now it did.

Not one word of thanks did I hear, nor did she once evince an interest in my newly acquired magical skills.

From Setebos, she said with scorn, she derived the one true magic. All others were bastardy.

Her primary desire, clearly, lay in retaining the upper hand. This needed no telling.

The desire layered atop that was, she told me, her long-delayed revenge on the Algerian monster. How better to gain satisfaction than to avail herself of the royal fleet, once I had gained the throne? Attack them, put their cities to the torch, lay them waste.

The third force that drove her was a desire to keep up the lovers Miranda had begun to entertain. Mom had no hesitation in telling me that. Behind her boldness lay an unspoken assumption: Her son would, as always, fall into line.

In this wretched life, than which there is no other, one spirals ever downward into tighter clefts, no matter how uprising and aspiring the direction of one's dreams.

I could not tell Mom that, nor did she ever leave an opening for me to do so. Not even at night—post-cleft in her chambers, Ariel's touch

enhancing our intimacy as it had done long ago—did she deign to probe my feelings.

Our clefting held no joy.

It was no longer Mom's chthonic cave into which I plunged but Miranda's pert wet woman-pit, a thin-boned hint of spice without the earthy scent of the maternal wallow, no raging growl of beasts in rut. Nor was my clefter the wild boy-finger of old, jut and spurt and endurance after short regeneration.

Our conjunction satisfied me not.

In bed that first night, before we drifted off, Mom reviewed the day. Our feigned sorrow at Prospero's death. The court's general miasma of contrived condolence. The prince and his wife's doleful decision (we knew they would understand) to retire early.

Mom also mapped out our future.

We would dispatch the king's mistress, when he died, which shortly he surely must. And we would snap off and crush beneath our heel the longstanding thorn Gonzalo.

We would conquer Algiers and exact a heaven-rattling revenge upon whichever of her enemies still lived.

We would defeat death, she and I. When old age or infirmity encroached, we two would shape-change. Healthy young refuges would we keep about, the best we could find, cultivating their minds in anticipation of assuming their bodies, bedding them together so that their soma imbibed intimate knowledge of one another. Our discarded bodies, victim-inhabited, would we send to their grave, moving on thus through the ages immortal.

Epilogue

I pretended assent.

Mom was full of plans, too full to observe her son closely or to question his pale shows of enthusiasm.

It took me two months to weigh my options.

Should I leave her? Shape-change on my own and be off?

I knew that, with Ariel's help, she would find me, her rage unbounded when she did. And I knew that this course would, in the end, hold no tastable delights for me.

From one unbearable cleft to the next was I downward doomed to devolve. But never would the body poor Caliban draped over his spirit be the bright, muscled, inquiring body he had inhabited at twelve. Though I took on young flesh, even with a mind that bristled and leaped with new thought, that flesh would ever be alien. Always, betwixt me and it, would fall the gap.

I also found it distasteful, though I had done my share of killing, to sacrifice some innocent pair of souls every thirty years, those we had selected because we found them attractive and had raised like cattle unsuspecting.

And so I penned this account, which draws now to its close. As does my life. As does Mom's.

She knows much that I do not, but on balance I believe my magic surpasses hers. It bested her once before in Prospero's hands; nor do I think her deathbed weakness, her doubts and uncertainties, had much to do with that.

If I am wrong, I shall die and Mom shall not.

If I am right, we shall both die, my own hand the instrument of her death and then my own.

The outcome I leave to Setebos, begging the

Epilogue

Patagonian god to look favorably upon me.

Howe'er he chooses, bereft shall I be of the cleft of this life, the pinch that sorrows, the prod and poke and sting that shuts out hope.

My ink has been spilled, my story told.

Here shall Caliban's strand be cut.

THE BEAST THAT WAS MAX
Gerard Houarner

Max walks in the borderland between the world of shadowy government conspiracy and the world of vengeful ghosts and evil gods, between living flesh and supernatural. For Max is the ultimate killer, an assassin powered by the Beast, an inner demon that enables him to kill—and to do it incredibly well. But the Beast inside Max is very real and very much alive. He is all of Max's dark desires, his murderous impulses, and he won't ever let Max forget that he exists. The Beast *is* Max. So it won't be easy for Max to silence the Beast, though he knows that is what he must do to reclaim his humanity. But without the protection of the Beast, Max the assassin will soon find himself the prey, the target of the spirits of his past victims.

___4881-7 $5.99 US/$6.99 CAN

JOHN SHIRLEY
Black Butterflies

Some nightmares are strangely sweet, unnaturally appealing. Some dark places gleam like onyx, like the sixteen stories in John Shirley's *Black Butterflies*, stories never before collected, including the award-nominated "What Would You Do for Love?" These stories are like the jet-black butterflies Shirley saw in a dream. They flocked around him, and if he tried to ignore them they would cut him to shreds with their razor-sharp wings. Shirley had to write these stories or the black butterflies would cut him up from the inside and flutter out from the wound . . . into the world.

__4844-2 $5.99 US/$6.99 CAN

Dorchester Publishing Co., Inc.
P.O. Box 6640
Wayne, PA 19087-8640

Please add $2.50 for shipping and handling for the first book and $0.75 for each additional book. NY and PA residents, add appropriate sales tax. No cash, stamps, or C.O.D.s. All Canadian orders require $5.00 for shipping and handling and must be paid in U.S. dollars. Prices and availability subject to change. **Payment must accompany all orders.**

Name _____
Address _____
City_____State _____Zip _____
E-mail _____
I have enclosed $_____ in payment for the checked book(s).
  ❑Please send me a free catalog.
       CHECK OUT OUR WEBSITE at www.dorchesterpub.com!

AMONG THE MISSING RICHARD LAYMON

At 2:32 in the morning a Jaguar roars along a lonely road high in the California mountains. Behind the wheel sits a beautiful woman wearing only a skimpy nightgown. She's left her husband behind. She's after a different kind of man—someone as wild. daring, and passionate as herself. The man she wants is waiting patiently for her . . . with wild plans of his own. When the woman stops to pick him up, he suggests they go to the Bend, where the river widens and there's a soft, sandy beach. With the stars overhead and moonlight on the water, it's an ideal place for love. But there will be no love tonight. In the morning a naked body will be found at the Bend—a body missing more than its clothes. And the man will be waiting for someone else.

___4788-8 $5.99 US/$6.99 CAN

IN THE DARK

RICHARD LAYMON

Nothing much happens to Jane Kerry, a young librarian. Then one day Jane finds an envelope containing a fifty-dollar bill and a note instructing her to "Look homeward, angel." Jane pulls a copy of the Thomas Wolfe novel of that title off the shelf and finds a second envelope. This one contains a hundred-dollar bill and another clue. Both are signed, "MOG (Master of Games)." But this is no ordinary game. As it goes on, it requires more and more of Jane's ingenuity, and pushes her into actions that she knows are crazy, immoral or criminal—and it becomes continually more dangerous. More than once, Jane must fight for her life, and she soon learns that MOG won't let her quit this game. She'll have to play to the bitter end.

___4916-3 $5.99 US/$6.99 CAN

THE TRAVELING VAMPIRE SHOW
RICHARD LAYMON

It's a hot August morning in 1963. All over the rural town of Grandville, tacked to the power poles and trees, taped to store windows, flyers have appeared announcing the one-night-only performance of The Traveling Vampire Show. The promised highlight of the show is the gorgeous Valeria, the only living vampire in captivity.

For three local teenagers, two boys and a girl, this is a show they can't miss. Even though the flyers say no one under eighteen will be admitted, they're determined to find a way. What follows is a story of friendship and courage, temptation and terror, when three friends go where they shouldn't go, and find much more than they ever expected.

__4850-7 $5.99 US/$6.99 CAN

THE DECEASED
TOM PICCIRILLI

Something is calling Jacob Maelstrom back to the isolated home of his childhood—to the scene of a living nightmare that almost cost him his life. Ten years ago his sister slaughtered their brother and parents, locked Jacob in a closet . . . then committed a hideous suicide. Now, as the anniversary of that dark night approaches, Jacob is drawn back to a house where the line between the living and the dead is constantly shifting.

But there's more than awful memories waiting for Jacob at the Maelstrom mansion. There are depraved secrets, evil legacies, and family ghosts that are all too real. There's the long-dead writer, whose mad fantasies continue to shape reality. And in the woods there are nameless creatures who patiently await the return of their creator.

___4752-7 $5.50 US/$6.50 CAN